Hiking the Mountain State

The Trails of West Virginia

Allen de Hart

APPALACHIAN MOUNTAIN CLUB
Boston, Massachusetts

HIKING THE MOUNTAIN STATE:
The Trails of West Virginia
by Allen de Hart
Copyright © 1986

Editorial direction: Aubrey Botsford
Production: Renée Le Verrier
Book and cover design: Joyce Weston
Composition: Camden Type 'n Graphics, Camden, ME
Cover photograph: New River Gorge, Grandview
                    State Park/Gerald Ratliff

ISBN: 910146-57-8

5 4

To the volunteers who design, construct, and maintain the hiking trails of West Virginia.

West Virginia's state animal, the black bear/Photo by Nancy Eisner,
Elkins Inter-Mountain

Foreword

West Virginia, every acre of its area, lies within the Appalachian Mountain system. Hills are everywhere; all the horizons are broken. Residents know, and visitors quickly learn, that any land-bound journey involves climbs and descents.

In the state's eastern portion, these hills tend to arrange themselves in a northeast–southwest orientation, with deep, narrow valleys separating the ridges. West of the Allegheny Backbone there is no patterned arrangement of the hills; they are scattered as nature has carved them.

Tucked away among the hills and valleys are gems of scenery, natural gardens, cool trout streams, precipitous rock outcrops, filmy waterfalls, geological treasures. Many of them cannot be approached by any existing highway or even on a primitive trail; they must be visited afoot, or not at all. And here the hiker comes into his own.

Allen de Hart has met the hiker's need with a splendid new book, *Hiking the Mountain State*. In essence, the book is a conducted nature tour of the state's topography, flora, fauna, geology, and history, all expertly presented by a true *aficionado* of the outdoors. De Hart has hiked over 1700 miles of trails throughout West Virginia. He presents them with maps; detailed information as to campgrounds, sources of needed supplies, nearby attractions; and mileage charts. West Virginia has not before had so complete a catalogue of its attractions and how to see them.

Areas of special interest are given fuller attention; wild tracts such as Otter Creek, Cranberry Back Country, and Dolly Sods are treated in detail. So are such mountain bogs as Canaan Valley and Cranberry Glades, sheltering as they do remnant biota of the Ice Age. De Hart does not attempt to rate the attractions for the reader; he simply suggests things of special interest. If you wish to see magnificent virgin hemlocks, he tells you where to go. If you are looking for hawks in passage on autumnal migration, he directs you to the promising rock overlooks. Should your interest center on alpine climbs, he conducts you to the right cliffs and explains their degrees of difficulty.

Allen de Hart does not write as an outsider visiting the Mountain State. He has the happy faculty of becoming native to those areas of which he writes. This is a rare gift; West Virginians will appreciate it.

With a copy of *Hiking the Mountain State* in hand, a lot of hikers — residents and visitors — are going to enjoy our mountain outdoors with new insights and new understanding. They will know and enjoy West Virginia as they have not previously done. Above all, they are going to help all of us in protecting and preserving the fine things with which we have been blessed.

Maurice Brooks ("Dr. Appalachia")
Professor Emeritus
West Virginia University
Morgantown, West Virginia

Acknowledgments

This book has been made possible with the assistance of numerous federal, state, and local government personnel, private research assistants, and hiking friends. One of these friends is Dale Bowman, a long-time hiking companion and whitewater enthusiast. For a number of years he lived in Charleston and worked as a research assistant for the Department of Commerce. He and his wife and three children have been a part of this book from the start.

Joe Tekel, recreation and information specialist for the Monongahela National Forest headquarters in Elkins, has provided constant support with statistical, historic, and current trail information. Other assistance from the MNF came from John Hazel, ranger, Jim Grafton, assistant ranger, and Mike Ledden, forester, of the Cheat District; Robert Bodine, ranger, Gail Lantz, assistant ranger, and George Hersel, CMVC director, of the Gauley District; Kathy Travers, ranger, and foresters Tamara Malone and Sue Duffy of the Greenbrier District; Dale Dunshie, ranger, Bruce Frizzel, assistant ranger, and foresters Jim Markley and Beachy Hammonds in the Marlinton District; Jerry Bremer, ranger, in the Potomac District; and Donald Martin, ranger, James Miller, assistant ranger, and Edgar Hall, recreation technician, in the White Sulphur District. Assistance in the Lee District of the George Washington National Forest was provided by forester Ann Zimmerman; George Blomstrom, ranger, in the Dry River District; and in the Jefferson National Forest, George Martin, ranger of the Blacksburg District.

Among those in state government whose help was essential are Ken Sullivan, editor, Department of Culture and History; Bob Mathis, district administrator of the Division of Parks and Recreation; Art Shomo, information specialist of the Wildlife Resources Division; Robert Titus, director of planning, and Frank Eder, head of mapping section, planning division, Department of Highways; and two other personnel who gave special help in the last days of manuscript deadlines — Nancy Buckingham and Jeff Harpold, information representatives in the Division of Tourism and Marketing, Department of Commerce.

Craig Ackerman, superintendent of Greenbrier State Forest, was of exceptional help in researching the Greenbrier River Trail; Linda Rader, assistant curator of the West Virginia University Herbarium, contributed greatly by identifying plants; and Arnold Schultz, MNF wildlife biologist, assisted with animal studies.

Sharing in the four years of field work was a dedicated team of hikers and backpackers. They hiked with me in all seasons, in perfect weather and in storms, and assisted in logistics. I am grateful to Andrea Alter, Tim Averette, Robert Ballance, Pat Barnes, Mike Batts, Michael Beaman, Stuart Boyd, Jimmy Boyette, Cliff Brummitt, Richard Byrd, Ray Carpenter, Charley Carlson, Gary Cliett, John Cohn, Vance Collom, Don Cox, Paula Crenshaw, David Critz, Don Davis, Loree Davis, Richard Davis, Kirk Dickerson, Tony Droppleman, Alvin Edwards, Brooke Faircloth, Jeff Fleming, Steve Harris, Stephanie Hickey, Dick Hunt, Mark Ivey, Jeff Jeffreys, Sheri Lanier, Leslie Marchant, Reuben Massey, Daren Matthews, John Matthews, Steve Miller, Scott Morris, Wade Potter, David Salling, Scott Sanders, Edward Seagroves, Joe Smith, Gary Stainback, Gwen Struzik, Mark Suelflohn, Eric Tang, Greg Taylor, David Torain, Ryan Watts, Wayne Williams, Travis Winn, and Doug Wood.

I am also deeply indebted to Dr. Maurice Brooks, professor emeritus of wildlife management at West Virginia University, for sharing his support and knowledge. His legendary contributions to those of us who love the outdoors are unequaled. "Dr. Appalachia" was my inspiration.

Ox-eye Daisy/Photo by Robert Ballance

Contents

Introduction

"Hiking is my means of transportation both away from and into myself to think clearly and to give pleasure to living."
— DOUG WOOD

West Virginia, the mountain state of 24,282 square miles, is approximately 75 percent forest (11.6 million acres). On thousands of rugged wild mountain ridges, steep hills, and cloistered hollows grow what N. Bayard Green called "one of nature's greatest miracles," the magnificent stands of cherry, oak, hickory, beech, birch, maple, spruce, hemlock, and pine. Although these forest lands are 90 percent privately owned, there are three national forests, which together cover a total of 969,014 acres; nine state forests, with 79,364 acres; 41 public hunting and fishing areas, with 247,505 acres managed by the state; and 71,440 acres of preserved forest in the state's 34 parks. Aesthetically inviting and commercially valuable, the state's woodlands annually provide more than 414 million board ft of timber, 42 million of which are cut in the Monongahela National Forest (MNF). It is in these woodlands that I have been hiking for 50 years, and I have found a priceless heritage. This is where Maurice Brooks experienced "nature as it was intended to be" and Peter Josimovich found a "natural flavor of life and values." "A culture is no better than its woods," wrote W. H. Auden in *Bucolics*.

Timber harvesting has long been the concern of citizens'

groups that advocate wildlife protection and careful management of natural resources. This concern was demonstrated
nationwide in 1984, when the U.S. Forest Service (USFS) proposed a 50-year long-range plan to increase timbering, mining,
and road construction by approximately 70 percent. Estimates
were that reforestation and natural succession were perpetuat-
ing one third more trees than were being harvested.

In West Virginia, the MNF, in compliance with the USFS
directive, distributed its Draft Plan and Environmental Impact
Statement (EIS) for public review on December 7, 1984.
Within a year, more than 17,000 citizens, as well as several
conservation organizations, expressed overwhelming opposi-
tion to the draft plan. The major public concerns were that the
MNF was "a special place" and that it should retain its natural
character, conditions, and remoteness; that excessive roads
and timbering in the deciduous forests would greatly decrease
the bear and wild turkey populations; that expanded mining
would further damage the environment; and that tax dollars
should not be used in the national forests to benefit private
timber and mining companies.

In the spring of 1986 the MNF revised its plan to what "the
public had defined," and again submitted the plan for public
review before implementation. The new plan designated additional "special place areas," dispersed recreation, stabilized
timbering at the current level, and protection of wildlife. It
provided public involvement in coal mining decisions and, to
increase remoteness, confined motorized traffic to about 25
percent of the MNF. The new plan is being implemented following an Integrated Resource Management format, and a
new monitoring system will assure the effectiveness of the plan.
"People are our most important resource," said Larry Henson,
regional forester. "We must trust the integrity of our associates
and respect their feelings and become leaders in conservation
and land stewardship." Ralph Mumme, MNF supervisor,
agrees with Henson and has said that "we must protect the
unique environment of the national forest."

Recent surveys indicate that West Virginians wish to keep
the mountains and hills green with trees, a goal of great signifi-

cance if examined in terms of global forest conditions. For example, in the summer of 1985, *CBS News* reported that the world's forests were disappearing at an average rate of 50 acres each minute; that is 3000 acres an hour, 504,000 acres a week, or 26,208,000 acres each year — more than twice the total acreage of all West Virginia forests.

Although the mountain state has a valuable and expendable resource in timber, its major natural resource is minerals. It leads the nation in annually exporting 44 million tons of coal from a total mining of 126 million tons. It has been estimated that coal lies under 65 percent of the state and that it will last for another 400 years. Petroleum and natural gas are found in 33 of the 55 counties. Other prominent minerals are limestone, sandstone, sand, clays, and salt. Hikers will see considerable evidence of coal mining, oil and gas drilling, salt and stone quarries, timber harvesting, and a few pristine places unchanged since the days of the American Indians and early explorers.

The first known white explorer to stand on the Blue Ridge Mountains and look over the Shenandoah Valley toward the Alleghenies was John Lederer, who reported in his *Journal* (1669–70) that among the plants, geology, and animals he saw "lions and peacocks." With less imagination, but with more hiking stamina, Thomas Batts and Robert Fallam, professional explorers searching for the "waters on the other side of the mountains . . . and discovery of the South Sea," went as far as the east boundary of current Monroe County in 1671. In 1763, James Needham and Gabriel Arthur were successful, after a first attempt was repulsed by the Occaneechees Indians, in reaching the Kanawha and Cumberland valleys. In *Elderberry Flood*, Louise McNeill, a West Virginia poet laureate, describes the explorer's forest from the Shenandoah to the Ohio River as "15,000,000 acres, span-on-span of leafy distance/Like a hunter's dream." Trans-Allegheny exploration began in earnest after 1710 when Virginia's governor-explorer Alexander Spotswood organized expeditions westward. Members of his party were called "Knights of the Golden Horseshoe."

Indian tribes that claimed areas that became West Virginia

were the Shawnees, Tuscaroras, Cherokees, Delawares, and Mingos, but their infrequent settlements (because they mainly hunted and fished in the area) had disappeared before the major English settlements. After the Indian battle of 1774, when Gen. Andrew Lewis repelled Chief Cornstalk and his warriors, Indian power claims ceased on the frontier. Hunting, fishing, and trade routes the Indians had followed became access routes across the mountains for migration of white settlers. Among the routes was the famous *Seneca Trail* (also called *Shawnee Trail*) with a network of connecting trails along the rivers. From the South Branch of the Potomac it followed the North Fork to Seneca Rock, where it branched east into the Shenandoah, and west to cross the Cheat Mountains and Shaver's Fork to Elkins. Here it turned north to Parsons and on to Oakland, Maryland. The southern trailway from Elkins was to Mingo Flats in Randolph County. Again, it divided; the western route followed the *Little Kanawha Trail*, which went west to join the *Scioto-Monongahela Trail* into Ohio. The southern route of the *Seneca Trail* followed a route similar to US-219 to Marlinton, Lewisburg, and on to Bluefield. Other Indian trails were the *Warrior Path* in the present eastern panhandle and the *Buffalo Trail* (also called *Kanawha Trail*), which followed the Kanawha River along what later became US-60 from Ohio to White Sulphur Springs.

Except for early settlers clearing land for pastures and crops, the forest changed little until the turn of the twentieth century, when the original timber was devastated by logging companies. Ralph Widner, in his *Forests and Forestry in the United States*, said that by 1920 the "cream of the virgin forest crop has been taken with only scattered tracts remaining." The peak year had been reached in 1909 when a record 1.473 billion board feet were cut. In *Tumult on the Mountains*, Roy B. Clarkson described trees in the primeval forest that "grew to six or seven feet in diameter." Fortunately, a group of enormous trees remain in the 118-acre Cathedral State Park in Preston County. The state's largest hemlock (21.6 ft in circumference) is here.

The state's trail system includes 1774 miles on 520 named foot trails (of which 970 miles are in the national forests); 452

miles of skiable cross-country trails (79 miles of which are specifically designated for cross-country skiing); and 138 miles of bicycle trails. For many years the hills and valleys on which these trails wind, wave, and curve have been admired by tourists, hunters, fishermen, naturalists, poets, and composers. For example, one of the state's late poet laureates, Roy Lee Harmon, wrote that "the hillman, though he's young or old/ Enjoys life's finest frills/When springtime puts her magic touch/On West Virginia hills" in *Roses in December (Poems of a Mountaineer)*. And Louise McNeill wrote in *Elderberry Flood* that she loved "West Virginia's worn-out hills" and that all the "hills that convex us" would be larger than the state of Texas if they were rolled out. "But roll the hills! I wouldn't try!/Or send the mountains sprawling!/Some even say they hold the sky/And keep the moons from falling." Other poets have written about the hills in William Plumley's anthology of *Poems from the Hills*. The first song to be adopted as an official state song was Col. Julian G. Hearne Jr.'s "West Virginia, My Home Sweet Home," "where mountains and hills and valleys too . . . all have charm." Another official song is "The West Virginia Hills," written by the Rev. David King in 1879 and set to music by Henry E. Engle in 1885. "How majestic and how grand,/with their summits bathed in glory . . . How I love these West Virginia hills."

All these hills are part of the geographic features of a state whose average altitude of 1500 ft is higher than any state east of the Mississippi River. The state lies wholly in the Appalachian region, a large land province that extends from southeast Canada to central Alabama. As a result, the state is often described as the "land of ten thousand valleys." It is also called the "Panhandle State" because of its irregular arms extending east and north. The easternmost tip, at Harper's Ferry, has the same longitude as Rochester, New York. The western boundary is as far west as Port Huron, Michigan, and the north panhandle extends farther north than Pittsburgh. On the southern border it is 60 miles below Richmond. It is 237 miles from the north to the south of the state and 265 miles from east to west. The Allegheny Plateau has 6500 square miles and the Allegheny Highlands have approximately 6000 square miles. The prominence of these scenic areas led to suggestions by delegates at the state's first constitutional convention in 1861 to name the seceding part of Virginia "Allegheny." Other Indian names such as Kanawha and Potomac were suggested, but on June 20, 1863, western Virginia became West Virginia, the thirty-fifth state. On the reverse side of the great seal the new government chose a latin logo, *Montani semper liberi* ("mountaineers are always free").

How to Use This Book

The purpose of this book is to describe the foot trails clearly enough for you to locate the trailheads and follow the trails with reasonable security of direction. It is recommended that you read the information about the trails before you leave home. This will enable you to plan your supplies, road directions and conditions, and campsites. The book has been designed to enable you to carry it with you in a pack or jacket pocket. All the trails described are grouped in five parts: National Forests; National Parks and Corps of Engineers; State Parks and Forests; County and Municipalities; and College, Private, or Special Trails. Each chapter and section has an introduction to acquaint you with the area and to provide information on access, address, and support services.

Ten national forest districts are covered. Each district has been assigned trail numbers by the USFS. I have used these throughout the book because many of the forest service trailheads and intersections have them for guidance. The Cheat Ranger District of the Monongahela National Forest has numbers 100–199; Gauley, 200–299; Greenbrier, 300–399; Marlinton, 400–499; Potomac 500–599; and White Sulphur 600–699. (One exception to the numbered sequence is that the *North-South Trail* #688 is in the Gauley District and another North-South Trail #688 is on Shavers Mtn in the Greenbrier District. The latter is now also #701, the *Allegheny Trail*.) The *Allegheny Trail* is #701 because it traverses more than one district. The George Washington National Forest numbers in West Virginia are 1001 to 1050. There are no group numbers on the partial trails in West Virginia for the Jefferson National Forest, except #71 for the *Virginias Nature Trail* in the Blacksburg District.

The first trail in the book is the *Plantation Trail* #101. Under it are listed connecting trails. When grouped in this manner all trail lengths are in parentheses with an open total length. An effort has been made to follow a numerical sequence from low to high numbers rather than an alphabetical sequence of trail names. In some groups, however, the trail numbers are not in sequence.

You will see numerous trails described singly, such as *Tablerock Overlook Trail* #113, because it does not connect with other trails. Some trails, usually two or three, such as *Mountainside Trail* #114 and *Bennett Rock Trail* #112, may be listed under one heading because the main trail does not have a group of appendages or because it is difficult to make satisfactory loops. They do, however, connect at some point. In connecting trail groups the main or primary trail description is interrupted by material in parentheses to describe the spur or connecting trail. The objective in this arrangement is to give you options on how far you wish to hike before backtracking, making a loop, or following only the main trail. If the latter, the sections in parentheses can be ignored, but the information will always be there if you change your mind. In the Gauley District, the *North–South Trail* #688 has nine directly connecting trails. A tenth trail, *District Line Trail* #248, is added within parentheses because it is an important connector between two trails. The parentheses around the name of the connecting trail also mean it has been covered before or will be covered down the list in more detail. You will notice this same arrangement again with the *Pocahontas Trail* #263. The Index is alphabetically arranged with page numbers, but only the national forest trails will have both a USFS number and a page number.

Although I have copious notes on each trail, I have used brevity in trail descriptions for two reasons: book space and to leave some options for your feelings of discovery. Because you will likely be on the trail at a different season from the time I was there, you will experience a different show of plant and animal life. Where I found rare or endangered plants and animals I have omitted describing their exact location.

Roads to the trailheads are described according to the Department of Highways road names, signs, and numbers. An *I* is an interstate, *US* signifies major federal roads, *WV* is used for state primary roads with square signs, usually paved, and *CO* indicates county roads, which are usually not paved and have circular signs. The CO roads are significant because they are the chief access to the trailheads. Each CO is described by its official name and number (though the local citizens may call it by another name). You will find exceptions. For example, in Monroe County, CO-15 is named Limestone Hills Rd on the state list, but the state sign at the Waitesville Rd junction is Gap Mills Rd. County road name and number may change at the county line. It is wise to expect a remote and isolated road to be rough, eroded, or rutted and difficult for passenger vehicles. Another county road is the Delta road, with a triangular sign, designated *D;* it is usually short and receives minimum maintenance. An example is Workman Rd (D-19) at Stony Bottom in Pocahontas County. The forest road *(FR)* may also be difficult for passenger vehicles, or it may be locked, or lacking in snow removal. Nevertheless, the condition of some forest roads is superior to that of the adjoining CO roads.

Abbreviations

An effort has been made to save space in this book by using abbreviations wherever possible. Most of these are part of everyday usage; specialized ones follow:

AT	Appalachian National Scenic Trail
ATC	Appalachian Trail Conference
ATV	all-terrain vehicle
CO-	county road
ct	combined trails or groups of trails
D-	"Delta" road
DNR	West Virginia Department of Natural Resources
elev	elevation

FR-	USFS forest-development or protection road
GWNF	George Washington National Forest
I-	Interstate highway
jct	junction
JNF	Jefferson National Forest
L, R	left, right
mi	mile(s)
MNF	Monongahela National Forest
PATC	Potomac Appalachian Trail Club
PHFA	Public Hunting and Fishing Area
RR	railroad
rt	round trip or backtrack
SR-	secondary road
US-	United States highway
USFS	United States Forest Service
USGS	United States Geological Survey (map)
USGS-FS	USGS map showing USFS boundaries
WV-	West Virginia primary highway
WVHC	West Virginia Highlands Conservancy
WVSTA	West Virginia Scenic Trails Association
4WD	four-wheel-drive vehicle

Maps

The first map you should have is a West Virginia official highway map. They are available at service stations, chambers of commerce, and free from the West Virginia Department of Highways, Public Information Division, Charleston, WV 25305, tel: 304-348-0103. Other sources are the state travel councils, listed in the introduction to *State Parklands and Historic Sites* (Chapter 6), or the Office of Economic and Community Development, Capitol Bldg, Charleston, WV 25305, tel: 800-624-9110. A more detailed map of each county is available at county courthouses, local chambers of commerce, and from the Department of Highways for a nominal cost. Descriptions, directions, and trail map designs in this book are based on the state highway and county maps to simplify the process of finding the trailheads. Some county and U.S. Geological Survey

(USGS) maps do not show all the national forest roads. An update, with additional access points, is given in "Maps," which follows the Index. The trail narrative should be sufficient without use of the USGS topographic maps. In addition to these basic maps, there are special multicolored contour maps of the Monongahela National Forest for a small cost. Write or call USFS/Monogahela National Forest, PO Box 1548, Elkins, WV 26241, tel: 304-636-1800. Addresses and telephone numbers are listed for other forests and parks in the chapters where they are described. The most detailed maps are the USGS maps. They are on the scale of 1:24,000 (1 inch = 2000 ft), 7.5-minute series. Where I have referred to USGS-FS it means the regular USGS map is modified for the USDA Forest Service and shows only the forest areas in green. It is preferred over the standard map if you plan to be in the national forest. Some of the USGS maps are vintage and you will find their trail lines in question. If a local blueprint company does not have your desired map, write to Branch of Distribution, US Geological Survey, Box 25286 Federal Center, Denver, CO 80225. Because you must pay in advance, write for free information, West Virginia Index Map, and order form. A list of stores in West Virginia that stock USGS maps is in the index. State parks and forests also have maps of their areas. Write to them at the addresses given in Chapters 6, 7, and 8.

Markers, Signs, Numbers, and Blazes

For directional purposes trails usually have a trailhead lettered sign or a number, or both. This also applies to intersections. Blazes, usually painted on trees, are along the trails at irregular intervals. Some trails have neither a blaze nor a sign. Because of this, I have described the trails with more emphasis on other factors such as trees, streams, bridges, or mileage in the event the markers are missing. Signs may be wood or metal. Wood is usually routed and painted, but some signs (now in the wilderness areas) may be only routed, as in Cranberry Wilderness. Others are only painted. Some signs are bolted on posts or trees, as on *Shavers Mtn Trail (Allegheny Trail)*. Some may be metal on high metal posts as in the Otter Creek Wilderness. One state park has a sign that shows a 3-mile error. A MNF trail sign was 2.2 miles off. Although these and many others have been reported, it does not mean the signs have been corrected. Where there is a discrepancy between the sign mileage and this book, depend on the book because many trails, particularly in the national and state forests, have not been measured. The forest service claims to have rounded off the trail mileage to the nearest half mile or quarter mile.

MNF blazes are always blue. The *AT* blaze is always white; side trails are blue. The *Allegheny Trail* is always yellow, and multiple colors exist in the George Washington National Forest and in state parks and forests. All USFS blazes are supposed to be a 2" × 6" vertical rectangle. Some have an unnecessary 2" × 2" square above the blaze (a nationwide procedure), but the most recent trails have only the 2" × 6" rectangle and in many cases only splotches of blue paint much larger than 2" × 6". A few trails have other designs, such as circles in Cacapon State Park, where as many as four different colors on a tree indicate trail overlap. Some trails have the diamond-shaped metal or plastic or painted marker for cross-country skiing. If you find a trail sign in error, please report it to the ranger or superintendent rather than trying to redesign it yourself.

Trail Types, Length, and Difficulty

Most trail types are called *primary* or *main* because they are maintained, blazed, or marked. The opposite is true of *primitive* trails. An abandoned trail may or may not be blazed or passable; it is not maintained. A *side* or *spur* trail is usually shorter than the main trail and may serve only as an access route to a water source or point of interest. A *multiple-use* trail is authorized for people, horses, and wheels. A *jeep* trail may be used by hikers, horses, ORVs, and ATVs, or it may be posted for foot travel only. A *gated* trail may be a foot trail for pedestrians during a protective season for wildlife but open to both hikers and vehicles at other times. A *wilderness* trail is for foot traffic only. An unnamed *hunter's* trail or *fisherman's* trail may be easy to hike, though it is not maintained by the park or forest service. Other hunter's access roads have trail names, for example those at Lewis Wetzel or Sleepy Creek Public Hunting and Fishing Areas. A number of *ski* trails and trail-roads are easy and accessible for cross-country skiing. The major ones are mentioned this book. I have described trails as *scenic* if they have impressive views of the natural environment in or out of the forest, *recreational* if used mainly for exercise, *historic* if emphasizing a heritage area, and *nature* if they are interpretive. *Special use* trails are for special populations such as the visually handicapped.

The length of the trails has been measured by a Model 400 Rolatape measuring wheel. Although it measures each foot, I have rounded the trail length off to the nearest 0.1 mi. Where you have to backtrack, I have described the distance and used an *rt* for return trail or round-trip. A *ct* may appear after the total mileage to mean combined trails. Miles are used without kilometers because none of the state's trails are marked or signed with kilometers.

Each trail is listed as *easy, moderate,* or *strenuous,* and it is based on the ratings for average hikers, not athletes or the very old and very young. *Easy* means that if you are in good health you can hike the trail without fatigue or exertion. *Moderate* means that there may be some exertion involved and you will probably need to rest occasionally. When climbing steep areas or traversing rough and long trails, I have classified them as *strenuous* — greater exertion and more frequent rest stops. Of course, the size and weight of a pack can make a difference in any classification.

Animal and Plant Life

Wildlife is abundant almost everywhere and particularly in the national forests. The state animal is the black bear *(Euarctos americanus)* and the state bird is the cardinal *(Cardinalis cardinalis).* I have mentioned some of the species I saw on the trails, and your chances of seeing wildlife are good. For the best observation, know the animals' watering and feeding places, leave the dog at home, and walk softly in the woods. You may be closer to them than you think. For example, Robert Ballance and I were on the *High Water Trail* in Dolly Sods one early summer morning. We saw a barred owl *(Strix varia)* about 50 ft away. We stopped, stood motionless, and the owl flew to within 10 ft of us, frequently turned his head, was unafraid and curiously watched us. In some state parks, such as Canaan Valley, deer *(Odocoileus virginianus)* and woodchucks *(Marmota monax)* graze by the dozen, generally ignoring the public. On the *Meadow Mtn Trail* an amiable striped skunk *(Mephitis mephitis)* glanced at our feet and fortunately continued his dig for grubs. At the junction of *County Line Trail* and *District Line Trail* in Cranberry Wilderness a bear sat chewing on a signpost. He stared at me but continued to chew on the post. Some recommended books about the area's wildlife are *West Virginia Birds* and *Mammals of West Virginia,* both by George Hall, and *A Field Guide to Reptiles and Amphibians of Eastern and Central North America,* by Roger Conant, of the Peterson Field Guide Series.

The state's 45 public hunting and fishing areas, described in Chapter 8, have hundreds of wildlife food plots. "They are the best places to see game and nongame wildlife," said Art Shomo of the Wildlife Resources Division. If you are hunting or fishing, a license can be secured at most of the rural general stores. Alternatively, contact the Wildlife Resources Division of the Department of Natural Resources, 1800 Washington St E, Charleston, WV 25305, tel: 304-348-2771. Addresses and telephone numbers for the nearest DNR officers are: District I, 1304 Goose Run Rd, Fairmont, WV 26554, tel: 304-366-5880; District II, PO Box 1930, Romney, WV 26757, tel: 304-822-3551; District III, PO Box 38, French Creek, WV 26218, tel: 304-924-6211; District IV, Gen Delivery, MacArthur, WV 25873, tel: 304-255-5106; District V, McClintic Wildlife Sta, Pt. Pleasant, WV 25550, tel: 304-675-4380; District VI, 6321 Emerson Ave, Parkersburg, WV 26101, tel: 304-485-5521. The telephone number of the Elkins Operations Center is 304-636-1767. Be sure to ask for *West Virginia Hunting and Trapping Regulations* and *West Virginia Fishing Regulations.* Also ask for *West Virginia Fishing Guide, West Virginia Impoundment Fishing Guide,* and *West Virginia Stream Map.* Fishing is a popular sport in the state. In the MNF alone there are 576 miles of trout streams, where state and federal hatcheries stock more than 500,000 catchable-size trout annually. Izaak Walton summed up the sport in *The Compleat Angler* when he said "God never did make a more calm, quiet, innocent recreation than angling."

If you are a vascular plant enthusiast, the estimated 2200 species in the state await your study. I have mentioned some of them in this book, but this list is minuscule in comparison to what I saw. Within the MNF at least 1500 plants have been catalogued. The state tree is the sugar maple *(Acer saccharum)* and the state flower is the pink-white great laurel *(Rhododendron maximum).* Your bible for plant study is *Flora of West Virginia,* by P. D. Strausbaugh and Earl L. Core. It is available in a combined volume or in four separate volumes. Other books are the *Audubon Society Field Guide to North American Wildflowers* (Eastern Region), by W. A. Niering and Nancy C. Olmstead; *Ferns,* by Norma J. Venable, of the Center for Extension and Continuing Education at West Virginia University; *Spring Wild Flowers of West Virginia,* by Earl L. Core; *Dictionary of Useful Plants,* by Nelson Coon; *A Field Guide to Edible Wild Plants of Eastern and Central North America,* by Lee Peterson; and *Mushrooms of North America,* by O. K. Miller. A number of brochures are distributed by the West Virginia Department of Agriculture, State Capitol Bldg, Charleston, WV 25305, tel: 304-348-2201. Among them are *West Virginia Mid-Summer Wild Flowers, Common Mosses of West Virginia, Rare and Endangered Plant Species of West Virginia, Edible Wild Plants,* and *Poisonous Plants.* Additional information may be secured from the Division of Forestry, West Virginia University, Morgantown, WV 26506, tel: 304-293-4411. The harvesting of some plants such as ramp, ginseng, wild fruits, berries, and nuts is allowed by the national forests. For information contact the headquarters of the MNF, PO Box 1548, Elkins, WV 26241, tel: 304-636-1800; of the GWNF, Federal Bldg (PO Box 233), Harrisonburg, VA 22801, tel: 703-433-2491; and of the Jefferson National Forest,

210 Franklin Rd SW, Roanoke, VA 24001, tel: 703-982-6270.

Health and Safety

It is recommended by forest and park officials that you hike with one or more companions to reduce the danger of hypothermia, poisonous snake bite, injury from a fall, being lost, or becoming sick. Accidents happen to the most cautious hikers, and even minor mishaps can ruin an otherwise exciting and pleasant journey. Carry pure drinking water on all trails, and use water officially designated safe by the forest or park. My listing of springs and clear streams in this book does not mean the water has been tested. I have been drinking from Judy Springs for years because it appears to be as pure as the nearby forest service pump. I have never been sick after using either source. Properly boiling the water remains one of the best ways to be sure, or use Globaline or Potable-Aqua purifiers. Be sure someone in your party has a good first aid kit and snake-bite kit. Two poisonous snakes, the timber rattler and the copperhead, exist in the state. The largest rattler I have seen in the state was on a trail in Coopers Rock State Forest. The best precaution against snake bite is to watch where you place your feet and where you use your hands around rocks and logs. Hypothermia — the number one cause of death for outdoor recreationists — is caused by the lowering of body heat. It can be fatal even in the summertime. Sweaty and wet clothes lose about 90 percent of their dry insulating value and wind chill increases the danger. The best lines of defense are to stay dry; get out of the wind, rain, or snow to avoid exhaustion; and know the symptoms and treatment. The symptoms are uncontrollable shivering; vague, incoherent speech; frequent stumbling; and drowsiness. The victim may be unaware of all of these. Treatment for a mildly impaired victim is to place him or her in a dry place, in dry clothes, and in a warm sleeping bag and give warm drinks; if the victim is semiconscious, try to keep the victim awake, and provide person-to-person skin contact in a warm sleeping bag.

Lightning is another danger in the outdoors. Some precautions in an electrical storm are: stay off sharp, prominent peaks; avoid standing under a cliff or in the entrance of a cave; avoid vertical cracks or crevices in the rocks, and avoid standing under prominent trees or other tall objects. Sit or lie down and insulate yourself from the ground if possible. Exposure can also be dangerous; a 2-inch snow in Bartow may be an 18-inch snow on Spruce Knob. You should be prepared for sudden changes in the weather in all seasons. Flash floods and snowstorms can maroon you and your vehicle. In remote areas some hikers take a small radio in their backpacks for weather reports. Mean Fahrenheit temperature in the state in winter is 36°, spring 55°, summer 74°, and fall 57°. The number of clear days averages 110, partly cloudy 105, and cloudy 150. Snow may be more than 15 to 20 percent of the precipitation in Randolph County and less than 5 percent in Mingo County. The average snowfall is over 70 inches in Preston, Tucker, Pendleton, and Grant counties, with Pickens in Randolph County having the highest seasonal average: 127 inches. The Canaan Valley area has recorded below-freezing temperatures in all months of the year; the same for Spruce Knob. Some of the counties with the greatest rainfall are Grant, Harrison, Upshur, Gilmer, Taylor, Marion, Lewis, and Randolph. Fall is the driest season. On the trails, it is a good idea to carry warm clothes, rain gear, notepaper and pencil, waterproof matches, a compass, map, first aid kit, and a dependable flashlight with extra batteries and a bulb. If you get lost off the trail use the universal distress signal of three of anything — shouts, whistles, light flashes. One of the best books on this subject is *Wilderness Survival*, by Bernard Shanks. There is a saying that states to be safe in the woods you should "Use your head first and if things go wrong remember to keep it."

Support Facilities

When camping is not allowed on the trails, I have mentioned the nearest campground, public or commercial. If full service is indicated it means there are spaces for tents, RVs, and trailers that use electricity, water, and probably sewage lines. Such camps also have hot showers, public phones, and possibly a store or restaurant. Free brochures from the Travel Division, Department of Commerce, tel: 800-CALL WVA. Among the brochures are *West Virginia Camping Directory*, *West Virginia Lodging Directory*, and *West Virginia Park and Forest Lodging Rates and Reservations*, and *West Virginia State Parks and Forests*. A comprehensive directory is Woodalls *Campground Directory* (Eastern Edition), available at most bookstores. A free brochure, *Recreation Areas and Schedules*, is available from the MNF, tel: 304-636-1800. In the Appendix I have listed support organizations, the addresses of stores that have camping and allied outdoor sports supplies, and addresses for mountain climbing, spelunking, whitewater sports, and skiing. Other trail guides are the *Hiking Guide to MNF*, edited by Bruce Sundquist, PO Box 506, Fairmont, WV 26554; *Hiking Guide to the Allegheny Trail*, by Fred Bird and Doug Wood, WVSTA, Inc., PO Box 4042, Charleston, WV 25304, tel: 304-727-8463; and *The Big Blue Trail Guide*, by Elizabeth Johnston, PATC, 1718 N St NW, Washington, DC 20036, tel: 202-638-5306; *Guidebook to Hiking the Kanawha Trace*, by Charles L. Dundas and John A. Gibson, Tri-State Area Council, BSA, 733 Seventh Ave, Huntington, WV 25701, tel: 304-523-3408.

Planning the Trip

Unless you are an experienced hiker, I recommend that you acquire a guidebook on backpacking and camping. An example is *Walking Softly in the Wilderness*, a Sierra Club guide by John Hart. Its main focus is on supplies and gearing up, preparing for the trip, trail travel, managing camp, family hiking, and how to deal with problems. Your trail-shop personnel will have other guidebooks and the most current information on equipment quality and specific outfitting needs (see "Resources" in the Appendix).

Many of the trails are isolated and nearby stores may be seasonal or they may close early in the evening; it is wise to make yourself as self-sufficient as possible. If there are questions about road conditions and weather, call the rangers, superintendents, or managers at the numbers listed in each section or chapter. After you have chosen your trails and equipment, do not forget to service your vehicle with plenty of gasoline, a guaranteed battery, spare tire and jack, a jumper cable, tool box, and distress kit. Park only at designated places, remove all your valuables from sight, and lock your vehicle. Other standard suggestions for all of us are to take a highway map and compass, let someone know where we are going, have a leader in our group, do not cut any live trees or shrubs, carry out what we carry in, take warm clothing and rain gear, use a propane stove for food preparation, boil or test our drinking water, bury human waste properly, carry a first aid kit, respect the rights and privacy of others, help preserve the plants and animals, and do not feed the bears.

Walking in Wild, Wonderful West Virginia

Part of my childhood was spent in Raleigh County, between Coal City and Lillybrook. It was there I learned to walk, and my mother has said that the first time I was allowed to walk on the lawn I headed for the woods. When I was five, my older brother, Moir, took me on an exciting hiking trip in Virginia. The woods of the world have since been a physical and emotional source of health for me. Dr. Paul D. White has stated that "walking is as natural as breathing." To Margot Doss, "walking is a way of living." But many walkers do not think of themselves as hikers. How does it start? George Rosier of the West Virginia Scenic Trails Association described it this way:

Being a hiker comes from having gone for a walk with someone, probably older than yourself, when you were quite young. It was a happy experience and is a happy memory. Then, when you are old enough, you go walking alone. Soon you realize that if you carry a sandwich you will not have to come back quite so soon. Before you know it you have your pockets so full of sandwiches and identification books for flowers and birds and trees that there is almost no room for a camera! So you decide to buy your first day-pack. Then you realize that if you had a larger pack and a sleeping bag you could stay out even longer. Eventually someone asks, very innocently, "How long have you been a hiker?" and you realize that you are.

From the stroller to the explorer, there is a long trail or a short trail for everyone. The six longest trails are the *Allegheny Trail* (150 mi, of which 124 are in the MNF); *Greenbrier River Trail* (75.2 mi); *Big Blue Trail* (144 mi, of which 65.9 mi are in West Virginia); *Kanawha Trace* (31.7 mi); *Wyatt Trail* (30 mi); and the *North Fork Mountain Trail* (23.8 mi). The two shortest trails are the 85 yd *Garden Trail of the Five Senses* and the 100 yd *Gentle Trail*, both the results of local citizens providing trails for special populations. The longest asphalt trail (2.8 mi) is the *Wigginton Arboretum Trail*. The highest trail is the 0.5-mi *Whispering Spruce Trail* (4861 ft in elev), and the lowest is the 1-mi *Virginius Island Trail* (255 ft in elev). The trail with the greatest increase in elevation (a climb of 2380 ft) is the 5.1 mi *Flatrock Run Trail*.

It has taken many years for me to hike and study all the trails of West Virginia, 520 of which are described in the following pages. (I hiked another 103 that were abandoned or private.) I have my favorite trails. You will too, with your choice of superlatives; there are some trails whose welcome is so magnetic that you will return again and again. Welcome to the wild, wonderful walking trails of West Virginia — trails of natural history, mystery, incomparable beauty, and challenge.

PART ONE

National Forest Trails

Lake Sherwood from the Meadow Mtn Trail/Photo by David Salling

1.

Monongahela National Forest

Hiking is to see Nature as it was intended to be.
— MAURICE BROOKS

The 849,783-acre Monongahela National Forest (MNF) received its name from the Monongahela River, whose headwaters drain the northwestern area of the forest. The Indian word *Monongahela* means "river of sliding banks." The first land acquired in the state by the U.S. government for national forest purposes was the 7200-acre Arnold Tract in Tucker County. This took place on November 26, 1915. Half of the original tract, 3640 acres, was set aside in 1934 to form the Fernow Experimental Forest, in memory of Bernhard E. Fernow, a pioneer in forestry research. The other half is the NW tip of the Otter Creek Wilderness. Both areas are in the Cheat Ranger District.

Following the Arnold Tract the acquisition of land expanded into the Alleghenies to encompass parts of Grant, Greenbrier, Nicholas, Pendleton, Pocahontas, Preston, Randolph (the state's largest county), Tucker, and Webster counties. The magnificence of the forest is accentuated by its natural landmarks, some of which are lofty mountain summits such as Spruce Knob (4863 ft), the state's highest mountain, and Bald Knob (4842 ft), the second highest; the four wildernesses — Otter Creek, Dolly Sods, Laurel Fork, and Cranberry — with 77,965 acres preserved forever; the natural botanical wonder of Cranberry Glades; and Seneca Rocks, a towering natural sculpture of Tuscarora sandstone.

Within the splendor of the MNF are 1208 mi of forest roads (often more scenic than the major highways); nearly 850 mi of hiking trails (including 124 mi of the *Allegheny Trail*); 21 developed campgrounds; 567 mi of stocked trout and bass streams for anglers; and abundant wildlife for hunters. In the past year the game animal harvest included 101 black bear, of an estimated population of 500; approximately 797 turkey, of an estimated 4200; and 9788 deer, of an estimated 55,000. The forest has 72 species of fish, 374 vertebrate wildlife species and 1500 species of plants. There are three pioneer zones — Seneca Creek, with 11,000 acres; Hopeville Gorge, with 4500 acres; and Smoke Hole, with 5800 acres — chiefly under MNF administration for semiprimitive, nonmotorized recreational environments.

Under the Multiple Use–Sustained Yield Act of 1960, the USFS has equal responsibilities for the appropriate use of basic resources such as wood, water, wildlife, historic values, and recreation. In 1985 approximately 42 million board ft of saw timber were harvested, and plans are to increase this fourfold by the year 2030. Recently, the MNF distributed $885,052 to 10 counties and to the Department of Highways from receipts generated by timber sales, mineral leases, grazing permits, land use permits, and recreation user fees. By Congressional order, about 30 percent of this fund can be used only for schools and roads. Other funding to counties comes from the "payment-in-lieu of taxes" (PILT) program established by Congress in 1976. These funds, in the amount of $500,000, may be used by county commissioners for governmental purposes.

Perhaps less emphasized are other renewable resources provided by the MNF. There are approximately 54 grazing allotments for sheep and cattle in 7300 acres, and assigned areas for firewood harvesting. The public may harvest berries (strawberries, blackberries, elderberries, blueberries, and service berries); nuts (walnuts, butternuts, and filberts); grapes; mushrooms; ramps and wild onions; and herbs for folk medicine at no charge.

In a recent survey the MNF headquarters office in Elkins reported that over one million people use the MNF annually. Their activities in order of preference were camping, motoring, hunting, fishing, hiking and walking, picnicking, swimming, and "viewing outstanding scenery."

There are nominal user fees at most of the recreational areas, and a license is required for hunting or fishing. Last year $150,956 was collected from hunting and fishing stamp money from all three of the state's national forests. The revenue is used to improve game and fish habitat, and for trout stocking.

Hikers will immediately notice that many trails in the MNF are in need of maintenance. Rangers have stated that reduction in funds and limited staff are the reasons. For a period in the late 1970s the Youth Conservation Corps (YCC), the Young Adults Conservation Corps (YACC), and the Student Conservation Program (SCP) assisted in trail maintenance, but with federal cuts the YACC was eliminated, the YCC severely reduced (to a total of only 26 workers in 1985), and only two student slots remained in the SCP. The budget allowance for the Senior Citizen's Program was for 71 full-time employees. Their work is mainly at recreation areas. Because of the reductions in paid staff, the MNF is increasing its dependence on volunteers. An example of volunteerism is the work by the West Virginia Scenic Trail Association on the *Allegheny Trail*, and the "adoption" of trails for maintenance and of footbridges for rebuilding after the 1985 floods by the West Virginia Sierra Club.

• INFORMATION: Contact the district offices (listed at the beginning of each section) or the main office. The MNF main office is on Sycamore Street near the main entrance to Davis-Elkins College. Its address is PO Box 1548, Elkins, WV 26241, tel: 304-636-1800. The MNF publishes a newsletter titled *Monongahela National Forest;* it is recommended that hikers ask to be placed on the mailing list.

▶ SECTION 1: CHEAT RANGER DISTRICT

There are 126,890 acres in the Cheat Ranger District. The largest and most central acreage is in Tucker County, and the most southern section is in Randolph County. In the northeast corner small tracts are in Preston County, with one tract adjoining Garrett County, Maryland. The district is the most northern of the six districts and is also the oldest. Its major section on the E boundary is between Blackwater Falls State Park and Canaan Valley State Park W of WV-32. On the S side the boundary is N of US-33 from Wymer to the Stuart Recreation Area. The W side is more irregular, with a boundary along Cheat Mtn, Laurel Mtn, and Limestone Mtn. River drainage is N, with major flows from Shavers Fork and Dry Fork converging at Parsons to form the Cheat.

The district has over 150 mi of hiking trails; the four longest are the *Allegheny Trail* (26 mi, see Chapter 11), the *Otter Creek Trail* (10.9 mi), the *Shavers Mountain Trail* (10 mi), and the *Plantation Trail* (8.4 mi). The 186 mi of forest roads also provide some excellent trail connections, hiking circuits, easier treadway, and scenic routes. The 20,000-acre Otter Creek Wilderness is the district's major hiking attraction. Adjoining it to the NW is the 3640-acre Fernow Experimental Forest. Although it does not have a trail system, its Zero Trail and roads provide exceptional chances to bird-watch, learn from a forest laboratory, and picnic. Camping is not allowed. Guided tours are provided. For more information contact Information Services, Timber and Watershed Laboratory, Nursery Bottom, Parsons, WV 26287, tel: 304-478-2000. Other major hiking areas are the Canaan Mtn Spruce Plantation Area and the Horseshoe Run Recreation Area.

The district ranger reports that all the trails receive light maintenance every 1–3 yrs, and heavy maintenance (brushing, widening, and tread improvement) as funding is available. Some trails receive attention once every 10 yrs. Trail usage is rare on some of the most remote trails. The majority of the trails are hiked occasionally, and hunters frequent many of the trails during the hunting seasons. Vandals and bears have destroyed some of the trail signs.

Wildlife in the district includes 51 species of mammals such as deer, bear, wildcat, red and grey squirrel, raccoon, beaver, muskrat, and chipmunk. There are 31 species of amphibians and 21 species of reptiles. Among the reptiles are the copperhead and the timber rattler. An endangered mammal, the Indiana bat *(Myotis sodalis)* and a less endangered species, the Virginia big-eared bat *(Plecotus townsendii virginianus)* are protected in the Shavers Lick area. For anglers there are a number of streams stocked with rainbow, golden rainbow, and speckled trout. More than 130 species of nesting birds may be found in the district. Flora is widely varied (a remarkable 1100 species) because of the deep shady valleys, bogs, open fields, and high mountains with their northern evergreens and hardwoods.

There are three recreational areas with campgrounds: Bear Haven near the S entrance of Otter Creek Wilderness Area; Stuart, E of Elkins; and Horseshoe, S of Lead Mine. Two of three recreation areas used only for picnicking have observation towers: Olson Lookout on FR-717, off US-219 between Parsons and Thomas; and Bickle Knob on FR-91, near Stuart Recreation Area, off US-33. The other picnic area is at Alpena Gap on US-33 near Alpena.

• ADDRESS AND ACCESS: District Ranger, Cheat Ranger District, PO Box 368, Parsons, WV 26287, tel: 304-478-3251. In downtown Parsons go E on US-219/WV-72 across the Dry Fork bridge and turn R at the sign.

• MAPS: Numbers 1–5

▶ CANAAN MOUNTAIN AREA
(Tucker County)

Canaan Mtn is a high E–W plateau, ranging from 3000 ft to 4000 ft in elev, between Blackwater Falls State Park and the Blackwater River on the N, to Mozark Mtn and Canaan Valley

State Park on the S. The Canaan Loop Rd (FS-13) connects WV-32 on the E to Blackwater State Park on the W. Its passage from the Blackwater Falls State Park for 6.6 mi may be impassable for passenger cars. High water on Lindy Run may also prevent fording. Passage is easy for passenger cars from WV-32 for 9.3 mi on a gravel road to a gravel parking area. It is another 0.5 mi on a rocky and less passable road to the crest of the mountain and the W terminus of the *Plantation Trail*. The improved gravel section of the road was made possible by the Amoco Production Co. of Texas, when it spent approximately $750,000 on the road in its unsuccessful $2 million search for oil. Formerly called the *Davis Trail*, the *Allegheny Trail* runs N–S, as does the Columbia Gas Co. pipeline. The most prominent trail in the area, the *Plantation Trail*, runs E–W. Because the area is rocky and frequently wet, tent sites are scarce; there are two shelters.

Before 1885, Canaan Mtn had a red spruce forest of unbelievable grandeur; then the West Virginia Central Railroad and the lumber companies arrived. Two major companies were the West Virginia Pulp and Paper Co. (Wesvaco) in 1892, and the Babcock Lumber and Boom Co. in 1907. The town of Davis (named after railroad and coal entrepreneur and US senator [1871-83] Henry Gassaway Davis) suddenly became a boom town of over 3000 inhabitants. Most of them worked at the sawmills, pulp mills, tanneries, and on the timber railroads. For 38 yrs Davis was an example of the timber feast that depleted the state's virgin hardwood and conifer forests. One company in Davis manufactured over 1.5 billion board ft of spruce, hemlock, and hardwoods. After 1920, however, the population fell sharply.

Nearly 200 mi of timber railroads were like tentacles out of Davis to Canaan Mtn, Canaan Valley, Cabin Mtn, and Dobbin Ridge. With the competitive challenge of the timber industry came also the railroads and the competition to run the best trains. Safety records were usually good, but a single curve was the nemesis of a speeding train at least once. On February 5, 1924, as described in Homer Fansler's *History of Tucker County* (1962), Fred Viering of the Babcock Lumber and Boom Co.

went on an inspection trip over Cabin Mtn (E of Canaan Mtn). In order to be back in Davis at the time he had promised his wife, he told his fireman, George Kline, to speed up the train. Kline said it was not safe, but Viering said, "I'll eat my supper with the old woman in Davis tonight or eat it with the devil in hell." Kline and two workers safely jumped from the speeding train before it left the track, overturned, and killed Viering in a Blackwater swamp.

• ACCESS: Northwest entrance is on FR-13 at the end of the paved road near the ski warming hut in Blackwater Falls State Park. The E entrance is on WV-32, 3.1 mi S of Davis at Canaan Heights at the Wilderness Rd sign on FR-13.

• SUPPORT FACILITIES: The nearest campground is Blackwater Falls State Park in Davis (see Chapter 6). Davis also has restaurants, a grocery store, motel, hardware store, service station, and bank.

Plantation Trail (8.4 mi; USFS #101)

• CONNECTING TRAILS:
  Fire Trail #3 (0.8 mi; USFS #104)
  Allegheny Trail (Davis Trail) (5.2 mi; USFS #701)
  Fire Trail #6 (1.1 mi; USFS #108)
  Lindy Run Trail (2.8 mi; USFS #109)
  Railroad Grade Trail (3.1 mi; USFS #110)

• TOTAL LENGTH: 21.4 mi

• DIFFICULTY: moderate

• FEATURES: red spruce plantation, forest history

• TRAILHEADS AND DETAILS: The *Plantation Trail* is named for a 2462-acre plantation of red spruce *(Picea rubens)* in Canaan Mtn Spruce Plantation. It is the result of work accomplished by the Civil Conservation Corps (CCC) in the 1930s to reforest one of the best spruce forests that had ever existed. In addition, the CCC planted a few stands of Norway spruce *(Picea abies)* and red pine *(Pinus resinosa)*. They also built fire lanes and a number of cement dams called "water points" or "pump chances" for watering the seedlings and for foot-trail firefighters. The connecting trails to the *Plantation Trail* may be used for loops between the trail and Canaan Loop Rd.

The E (3580 ft) trailhead is 2 mi S on WV-32 from the Blackwater River bridge in Davis. Park beside the road. Enter a young forest of maple, birch, and spruce. White snakeroot (*Eupatorium rugosum*) borders the trail in the summertime. Descend to and cross Devil's Run at 0.5 mi. Ascend gradually in rocky areas with spruce, mountain laurel, hemlock, and rhododendron. Ferns are prevalent. Reach the jct, L, with *Fire Trail #3* at 1.1 mi.

(*Fire Trail #3* ascends through the spruce plantation, generally straight but rocky with dense undergrowth and dense stands of spruce. Sections of treadway are usually wet, with carpets of ferns and mosses. The S trailhead is on FR-13, 1.4 mi from WV-32.)

Continue on the *Plantation Trail*, cross a drain with a small dam built by the CCC, and reach the Columbia Gas Co. pipeline at 1.8 mi. Reach another small dam at 2.3 mi at Engine Run. At 2.7 mi reach the jct with the *Allegheny Trail* (formerly *Davis Trail*, USFS #107, was on this route). A six-person Adirondack shelter is here (constructed by the Youth Conservation Corps in 1981) and a dependable spring is nearby, W, on the *Plantation Trail*.

(The *Allegheny Trail* crosses here, 1.6 mi from its N beginning at the horse stables in the Blackwater Falls State Park, and 1.2 mi S to the Canaan Loop Rd [2.7 mi W from WV-32]. It follows W on the Canaan Loop Rd for another 1.2 mi before it turns L and S toward its entry into the Canaan Valley State Park at 5.2 mi. The blaze is yellow, but a diamond blue marker indicates the trail is also a cross-country ski trail for the first 6.3 mi. See Chapter 11.)

The *Plantation Trail* continues ahead on a level contour with a number of drains from the L. Sections of the trail are rocky. Yellow blazes are seen for the former or alternate route of the *Allegheny Trail*. At 3.8 mi jct L with the *Fire Trail #6*. This is the W end of the Canaan Mtn Red Spruce Plantation. The trail continues under this name, and so do numerous stands of spruce.

(*Fire Trail #6* goes 1.1 mi S to Canaan Loop Rd, 4.2 mi W from WV-32. Pass through rhododendron, yellow birch, spruce, mountain ash, and mountain laurel. Hay-scented fern and club moss are part of the ground cover. At 0.7 mi cross a fire lane and follow a wide trail that has been damaged by 4WD vehicles until the USFS recently installed a "tank trap," a rock barrier, at the Canaan Loop Rd entrance near the north fork of Red Run.)

Ahead on the *Plantation Trail,* cross a small drain, Shays Run, with a miniature cement dam at 4.3 mi. Ascend a rocky area into a hardwood stand and level off in spruce at 4.6 mi. (Yellow blazes on the trail are from the former route of the *Allegheny Trail*.) At 5.1 mi reach a crossing with the *Lindy Run Trail.*

(It is 1.5 mi N on the *Lindy Run Trail* to Canaan Loop Rd. From there to Blackwater Falls State Park it is 1.2 mi. Going S on the trail it is 1.3 mi to Canaan Loop Rd, 4.5 mi W from WV-32. The N section descends gradually on the R side of Lindy Run and crosses the stream at 0.8 mi. The most frequent species of trees are hemlock, maple, cherry, and yellow birch. Rhododendron arbors are common. On the S section ascend slightly on a wide but rough treadway. Thick patches of sphagnum, ferns, and mountain laurel occur on a level area at 0.9 mi. Descend gently through a wet area and reach Canaan Loop Rd at 1.3 mi.)

Continue W on the *Plantation Trail* and immediately cross Lindy Run. Follow the trail on a level contour through an increase of hardwoods and a decrease of conifers. Reach the N–S jct with the *Railroad Grade Trail* in a flat area at 6.3 mi.

(On the N side of the *Plantation Trail,* the *Railroad Grade Trail* descends gently for 1.4 mi to the Canaan Loop Rd, 2.6 mi S of Blackwater Falls State Park. There are obvious signs of the old RR grade along the way. On the S side the RR grade trail also descends gently, but is in a more deciduous forest. At 0.6 mi reach a stream crossing and a six-person Adirondack shelter with a picnic table and grill. This exceptionally attractive area is in a cove once spanned by a 0.1-mi RR trestle. At 1.4 mi cross a small drain and continue descent. Reach the Canaan Loop Rd at 1.7 mi, 6.5 mi W from WV-32.)

The *Plantation Trail* crosses the *Railroad Grade Trail* obliquely, SW. Trail signs here are frequently chewed up by the bears. Follow a level, mossy, and occasionally wet treadway. A hardwood forest is more dominant, and there are thickets of mountain laurel, usually blooming in late June. Pass through a boggy area at 8 mi and reach the Canaan Loop Rd at 8.4 mi (3312 ft), only 268-ft elev difference from the beginning. Here is the W terminus, 6.6 mi R to the Blackwater Falls State Park and 9.8 mi L to WV-32. Within 65 yds to the L on the road is the trailhead of *Tablerock Overlook Trail,* and 1.2 mi to the R on the road is the trailhead for the *Mountainside Trail. (USGS-FS Maps:* Blackwater Falls, Mozark Mtn)

(Nearby, there are three fire trails that do not connect with other trails in this area and whose main purpose is for fire access. *Fire Trail #1* [0.4 mi; USFS #102] has termini 0.4 mi W on the Canaan Loop Rd from its jct with WV-32 and 0.4 mi N on WV-32. *Fire Trail #2* [0.4 mi; USFS #103] has termini 0.8 mi W on the Canaan Loop Rd from its jct with WV-32 and 1 mi N on WV-32. *Flag Run Trail* [1 mi; USFS #106] has termini 1.9 mi W on Canaan Loop Rd from its jct with WV-32 and 1.7 mi S on WV-32. The latter trail was relocated in 1984 and is now entirely on National Forest land.)

Tablerock Overlook Trail (1.1. mi; USFS #113)

- LENGTH: 2.2. mi, rt

- DIFFICULTY: easy

- FEATURE: Tablerock Overlook

- TRAILHEAD AND DETAILS: From WV-32, drive W on Canaan Loop Rd for 9.8 mi to the trailhead on the L (65 yds before you reach the W end of the *Plantation Trail*). Ascend slightly and follow a rocky tread in a basic hardwood forest. Pass through a damp area arbored by rhododendron at 0.9 mi for the final 0.2 mi. From the magnificent overlook you can see the Red Run

Valley and Mozark Mtn range SE and Shavers Mtn and the Otter Creek Wilderness SW. The naturally sculptured rocks have indentations and fissures. Wintergreen and huckleberry hold tight to each other. Backtrack. (*USGS-FS Map:* Mozark Mtn)

Mountainside Trail (4.1 mi; USFS #114); *Bennett Rock Trail* (0.7 mi; USFS #112)

- LENGTH: 9.6 mi, rt

- DIFFICULTY: moderate to strenuous

- FEATURE: wildlife

- TRAILHEADS AND DETAILS: This is a longer trail than 4.1 mi because you will have to backtrack or hike out to Canaan Loop Rd for 2.5 mi on FR-244-A and FR-244, both of which are gated. With a vehicle shuttle on the Canaan Loop Rd, 3.1 mi E from the trailhead, your hiking mileage will be 6.6 mi. To reach the trailhead from WV-32, drive 11 mi on Canaan Loop Rd to *Mountainside Trail*, L. (It is 5.4 mi on the Canaan Loop Rd N to Blackwater Falls State Park on a rugged road frequently unsuitable for passenger cars.) Begin on an old road that soon becomes an old RR grade. Cross a small stream, Laurel Run, at 0.4 mi. Cross it again four times and leave the stream area L at 0.7 mi. Descend gradually through a hardwood forest of yellow birch, cherry, and maple. Vistas of the Dry River Valley are best when the leaves are off the trees. Pass L of an old logging road at 1.7 mi. At 2.8 mi reach a jct with *Bennett Rock Trail*.

(The *Bennett Rock Trail*, R, descends on an exceptionally steep grade, dropping over 1000 ft in elev in 0.7 mi to WV-72, 2.3 mi S of the Blackwater River bridge in Hendricks. Entrance here is R of large boulders in forest of hemlock, rhododendron, maple, and beech. The trail has been listed by the USFS as abandoned for the past few years, but it will soon be blazed and reinstated.)

On the *Mountainside Trail* curve around the Canaan Mtn arm at 3.1 mi and reach the end of the trail at 4.1 mi and the beginning of FR-244-A. Backtrack or continue ahead to the Canaan Loop Rd as described above. (*USGS-FS Map:* Mozark Mtn)

Pointy Knob Trail (USFS #139)

* LENGTH: 4.2 mi

* DIFFICULTY: moderate

* FEATURE: plant life

* TRAILHEADS AND DETAILS: The E terminus is 4.1 mi from WV-32 on the Canaan Loop Rd and the W terminus is 1.9 mi farther on the Canaan Loop Rd. At the E terminus begin on a jeep road through a meadow, enter a forest of red spruce, cross a small drain at 0.1 mi, and turn L off the jeep road. Ascend gradually on a ridge with rocky treadway and through dense areas of mountain laurel, rhododendron, and conifers. Sections of the trail are overgrown, but the district office has promised to maintain them in the future. At 2.2 mi reach White Raven Rocks. (An overgrown, faint blue-blazed spur trail goes S toward *Pointy Knob Trail* to private property.) Turn NW and begin descent to the headwaters of the south fork of Red Run. Rock hop the stream a number of times and follow a section of an old RR grade with beds of ferns and running cedar, and a canopy of birch and hemlock. At 4.2 mi cross both the S and N forks at the confluence of Red Run and up an embankment of Canaan Loop Rd. A hike R to the point of origin is 6.2 mi for a loop. (*USGS-FS Maps:* Blackwater Falls, Mozark Mtn)

▶ BACKBONE MOUNTAIN AREA
(Tucker County)

Although there is no campground at the Olson Recreation Area (3736 ft) on Backbone Mountain, there are picnic tables, grills, vault toilets, and a hand water pump. The 130-step Olson Lookout Tower provides spectacular views of the entire Cheat District. This magnificent scenery is on any hiker's "must" list. Views W are of the Cheat and Dry Fork basins and the Laurel Mtn range. North is the extension of Backbone Mtn into Maryland. To the E are Canaan Mtn and Cabin Mtn, and to the S, McGowan Mtn and the Otter Creek Wilderness Area. The tower was dedicated in 1963 to Ernest B. Olson for his 28 yrs of service in forest fire control.

Canyon Rim Trail (3 mi; USFS #117); Fansler Trail (1 mi; USFS #118)

- LENGTH: 5 mi, ct, rt

- DIFFICULTY: easy

- FEATURES: scenic, wildlife

- TRAILHEADS AND DETAILS: The E terminus is at the scenic area of Big Run on the Canyon Rim Rd (FS-18), 0.2 mi E of the W terminus of the *Boundary Trail* and 1.9 mi SE of US-219. The W terminus is 0.1 mi N of the Olson Lookout Tower. Trail elev range is from 3100 ft to 3600 ft. If hiking from the E terminus, park at the side road on Canyon Rim Rd. Descend into a hemlock grove to rock hop the cascading Big Run. Ascend, cross a small fork of Big Run, and follow an old RR grade. A decorative border of rocks is a reminder of the CCC's trail work. Pass through rhododendron, spruce, hemlock, mountain laurel, maple, birch, and red pine. The treadway is mossy, grassy, and wet in the springtime. Cinnamon and hay-scented ferns, and club moss are prominent. A number of natural vistas of the Blackwater Canyon follow at 0.5 mi, 0.9 mi, 1 mi, 1.2 mi, and 1.4 mi. Cross a small drain at 0.5 mi where deer are likely to be seen. At 1.7 mi pass jct L of abandoned *Flat Rock Trail*. Curve R and slightly ascend, level off and reach the W terminus at 3 mi on the Olson Lookout Tower Rd (FR-717). To the L it is 0.1 mi to the Olson Recreation Area. To the R it is 1.6 mi on the road to a jct with Canyon Rim Rd (FR-18) and another 0.3 mi to US-219.

The *Fansler Trail* begins on the S side of the picnic area by entering a wall of naturally sculptured rocks and follows the blue blazes. The trail is arbored with hemlock, oak, spruce, and maple. Mountain laurel and rhododendron form a border in sections, and club moss and ferns form part of the ground cover. Follow an even grade on the Blackbone Mtn ridge for 0.7 mi before descending to a dead-end at FR-717 at 1 mi. Backtrack. (*USGS-FS Map:* Mozark Mtn)

Boundary Trail *(USFS #116)*

- LENGTH: 3.5 mi

- DIFFICULTY: easy

- FEATURE: old strip mines

- TRAILHEADS AND DETAILS: In the town of Thomas turn off WV-32 (near the post office) on Douglas Rd (CO-27) and drive 2.4 mi to the MNF boundary line. Here the road becomes graveled Canyon Rim Rd (FR-18) and also the route of the *Allegheny Trail.* On the R of the road is the E terminus of the *Boundary Trail.* (The red blazes are MNF boundary marks.) Ascend and descend gradually in a hardwood forest to a strip mine area at 1.3 mi. Cross Finley Run at 1.4 mi. Scotch pines are along the boundary. Climb a strip mine headwall in a spruce stand and descend first to cross Tub Run Rd and then Tub Run at 2.2 mi. Enter another strip mine area and reforestation area of red pine. Sections of the trail through here are overgrown and difficult to follow. At 3 mi enter a boggy section, go through rhododendron and yellow birch, and reach the W terminus on Canyon Rim Rd at 3.5 mi. To the R it is 1.7 mi to US-219, 6.3 mi W of Thomas. To the L it is 0.2 mi to the jct with the *Canyon Rim Trail.* Also to the L an 8.7 mi loop can be made by following the scenic Canyon Rim Rd (FR-18) for 5.2 mi to the point of origin. (*USGS-FS Map:* Mozark Mtn)

Limerock Trail (USFS #142)

* LENGTH: 4 mi

* DIFFICULTY: moderate

* FEATURES: remote, scenic, RR history

* TRAILHEADS AND DETAILS: The NE trailhead is on Canyon Rim Rd (FR-18), 0.2 mi W of the Tub Run crossing and 5.6 mi from WV-32 in Thomas on the Douglas Rd (CO-27). At a narrow parking area descend between a cherry and birch tree on an unmarked, unblazed path through spruce and hemlock. In less than 0.1 mi turn R to follow an old RR grade. (On the 1968 Mozark quad map this entrance is listed as trail #144. Trail #143 is in the wrong place; it should be trail #142.) This sylvan route through the gorge is rich in RR history. Where once you would have heard logging or, more recently, the Western Maryland RR trains on the wall of Blackwater Canyon, you now hear only the sound of Blackwater River and the cascading tributaries. At 0.7 mi go R of the old RR grade fork, and at 1.3 mi reach the E end of a vanished RR trestle that spanned the thundering Big Run. Rock hop Big Run, whose waters can be impassable in wet seasons. At 1.4 mi rejoin the RR grade. Black cohosh, ferns, and mosses thrive in this damp shady area. At 2.2 mi leave the Big Run Canyon and return to the N wall of the Blackwater River. Reach a jct with the abandoned *Flat Rock Trail* at 3.7 mi. Rock hop Flat Rock Run and leave the old RR grade to the Western Maryland RR at 4 mi. Turn R on the abandoned Western Maryland RR and hike out 2.1 mile to the town of Hendricks on WV-72. A switchbox, signal light, and the beginning of double tracks are at 1.4 mi. Ironweed, soapwort, Joe Pye weed, jewelweed, and virgin's bower are thick on this scenic route by the Blackwater River. (*USGS-FS Maps:* Mozark Mtn, Parsons)

▶ PHEASANT MOUNTAIN AREA
(Tucker County)

Pheasant Mountain Trail *(3.3 mi; USFS #120)*

- CONNECTING TRAILS:
  Shingletree Trail (4.5 mi; USFS #121)
  Clover Trail (2 mi; USFS #124)
  Ridge Trail (0.8 mi; USFS #122)
  Mail Route Trail (1.7 mi; USFS #123)

- TOTAL LENGTH: 12.3 mi

- DIFFICULTY: moderate

- FEATURES: wildlife, RR history

- TRAILHEADS AND DETAILS: In the town of Parsons at the jct of WV-72 and US-219, drive N for 0.4 mi on WV-72 to Mt Zion Rd (CO-17) and turn L. After 1.7 mi reach the ridge crest and park on R. The *Pheasant Mtn Trail* ascends L and curves S of the ridge through hardwoods of black birch, hickory, oak, maple, and sassafras. Trail bikes and ATVs use the entire trail; except for some erosion the treadway is smooth. At 1.1 mi reach the jct with *Shingletree Trail*.

(The *Shingletree Trail* crosses here with 3.1 mi L to US-219 and 3.6 mi SW of Parsons, and 1.4 mi R to Clover Run Rd [CO-21] and 3.7 mi W of Parsons. If hiking the L section, follow the old RR grade for 0.6 mi to a saddle between two ridges. Former RR trestles were at 0.8 mi and 1.4 mi. At 1.5 mi leave the old RR grade from Sugarcamp Run drainage and turn S on an old wagon road. At 1.7 mi ignore the old trail on the R that shows on the Parsons topo map as *Shingletree Trail*. Instead continue ahead, pass the abandoned *Hawk's Run Trail* on the L and take the R trail. Follow around a knoll, weave in and out of coves, some with small drainage, and descend through long sections of rhododendron. At 3 mi cross Shingletree Run and follow old woods road arbored with wild roses and elderberry out to US-219 in the community of Moore. If taking the R [N] section of the *Shingletree Trail*, begin on an old

RR grade but after 0.1 mi leave the grade and bear L. The first of four switchbacks begins at 0.9 mi; exit under a stand of white pine and hemlock by a branch at Clover Run Rd at 1.4 mi.)

Continue ahead on the *Pheasant Mtn Trail*. At 1.7 mi is a small wet-weather waterhole. Bear and deer tracks have been seen here and elsewhere along the ridge. At 3 mi is jct R with *Clover Trail*.

(The *Clover Trail* is exceptionally historic for its example of logging RR switchbacks. Until 1930, it was on the RR grade that lumbermen hauled timber from the Clover Run Valley over Pheasant Mtn [for 500 ft in elev] and down to Moore for the D.D. Brown Lumber Company. The train would pull up to one switchback and back up the other until reaching the top. Descend on five RR switchbacks for 0.7 mi. Pass the site of an old RR grade trestle at 0.9 mi and another at 1.2 mi. Spicebush and striped green maple are part of the understory in a hardwood forest. At 1.6 mi leave the old RR grade for a narrow foot trail, curve L around the ridge, and descend on two switchbacks to a small stream and parking area. A number of deer trails cross this trail. From the exit it is 4.3 mi E on the Clover Run Rd and Mt Zion Rd to Parsons.)

Ahead on the *Pheasant Mtn Trail* reach a jct L with the *Ridge Trail* at 3.1 mi. The area has mainly oak, maple, dogwood, beech, and black birch.

(The *Ridge Trail* descends, as the name implies, on a ridge for 0.7 mi to private property on US-219. Follow a switchback to an old logging road by a bank of trillium and meadow rue. Go through the hollow to an exit at an A-frame home on private property. [The owners welcome hikers passing here, but please do not block the driveway.] It is 5.7 mi E on US-219 to Parsons.)

After the next 0.2 mi the *Pheasant Mtn Trail* ends at 3.3 mi, but it is joined by the *Mail Route Trail*, R. A backtrack can be made or an exit taken from the *Mail Route Trail*.

(The *Mail Route Trail*, part of an early route for mail carriers, descends gradually on an old wagon road, crosses two spur ridges, and descends to Mail Route Hollow at 0.9 mi. Follow down the hollow of hardwoods, mountain laurel, sycamore, and tag alder to a crossing of Clover Run that can be rock hopped in normal weather. Parking is available 50 yds to the L on Clover Run Rd. It is 5.3 mi R [E] on Clover Run Rd and Mt Zion Rd to Parsons.) (*USGS-FS Maps:* Montrose, Parsons)

▶ OTTER CREEK WILDERNESS AREA
(Randolph and Tucker Counties)

The Otter Creek Wilderness is a 20,000-acre oval-shaped forest of Allegheny hardwoods, red spruce, hemlock, and rhododendron thickets. Ferns, wildflowers, and mosses cover its floor. There are rock outcrops on the canyon walls and plateaus on the ridge tops. In its center flows cascading Otter Creek, fed by tributaries whose headwaters are high in Shavers Mtn and Green Mtn on the E rim and McGowan Mtn on the W and N. Elevation ranges from 1829 ft to 3811 ft.

The wilderness is a haven for wildlife. There are 19 species of amphibians, which include the Cheat Mountain salamander and gray tree frog. Among the 12 species of reptiles are the Northern redbelly snake and two poisonous snakes — the copperhead and timber rattler. At least 42 species of mammals have been identified; the most frequently seen are bear, deer, squirrels, raccoons, woodchucks, rabbits, fox, and chipmunks. Mink and beaver are in the creeks, but the river otter (*Lutra canadensis*), for which the creek was named by the early settlers, is conspicuously missing. Blue crayfish are frequently seen along damp trails. Nesting birds number 76 species, which include six species of owls and the black-billed cuckoo, grouse, and wild turkey. Neither the hummingbird nor the mockingbird live here.

Hunting, fishing, hiking, and camping are allowed but the use of all motorized vehicles or equipment is prohibited. Although permits are no longer required, it is requested by the USFS that you register at the access points. The maximum number allowed per party is ten. Pack out all refuse and treat or boil all drinking water. For hunting and fishing it is necessary to check the special regulations for the Otter Creek area.

In keeping with the wilderness character the area is primitive, wild, and rugged. Safety is an essential consideration because the weather can change suddenly; flash floods and snowstorms are particular hazards.

• ACCESS: From the S at the jct of US-33 and FR-91 at Alpena Gap drive N on Stuart Memorial Drive (FR-91) 1.3 mi and FR-303 for 0.6 mi to a parking area. From the N on US-219 and WV-72 in downtown Parsons follow the sign for Fernow Experimental Forest for 5.6 mi to Big Springs Gap.

• SUPPORT FACILITIES: Bear Haven Recreation Area has seven camping units, picnic area, hand pump water, and vault toilets (no hookups). Access is 2.8 mi on Stuart Memorial Drive (FR-91) from US-33 in Alpena Gap. Open April 1–Nov 30. Stuart Recreation Area has 27 camping units, 51 picnic units, spigot water, and vault toilets, but no hookups. Open May 18–Sept 9. Access is from Alpena Gap 2.6 mi W on US-33, R on Old US-33 (CO-33/8) for 3.7 mi, and R on CO-6 for 0.4 mi. A commercial campground, Alpine Shores, is 2 mi W on US-33 from Alpena Gap. It has full service, recreational facilities, restaurant, and hot showers. It is open April 15–Nov 15 (tel: 304-636-4311). Shopping malls, banks, motels, service stations, and restaurants are in Elkins, 10 mi W on US-33 from Alpena Gap.

Otter Creek Trail *(10.9 mi; USFS #131)*

• CONNECTING TRAILS:
  Hedrick Camp Trail (1 mi; USFS #165)
  Yellow Creek Trail (1.3 mi; USFS #135)
  Mylius Trail (2.4 mi; USFS #128)
  Moore Run Trail (4.1 mi; USFS #138)
  Possession Camp Trail (3.2 mi; USFS #158)
  Green Mtn Trail (4 mi; USFS #130)
  Big Springs Gap Trail (0.9 mi; USFS #151)

• TOTAL LENGTH: 27.8 mi

• DIFFICULTY: easy to strenuous

• FEATURES: nature study, scenic, history, isolated

• TRAILHEADS AND DETAILS: The *Otter Creek Trail* parallels Otter Creek, fords it three times for 10.9 mi from its main trailhead at Condon Run in the S to its N terminus at Coal Run. Steadily descending for 1170 ft in elev, its treadway is on sections of logging railroad grades that were abandoned early in the century. Its natural beauty through a wilderness forest of mixed hardwoods and conifers is unsurpassed in the Cheat District. Always audible and usually in sight, the creek sometimes roars as it cascades over large boulders and sometimes it ripples at pools where polished stones rest from nature's tumbling box. A popular trail, it is the trunk line for seven immediate and six other connecting trails.

(From the parking area the first connecting trail, R, is the *Hedrick Camp Trail*. It goes 0.1 mi through a hemlock and rhododendron grove to Otter Creek where flash floods have washed out the footbridge. Wade across and ascend SE on an abandoned woods road with a gentle contour level on the N side of the stream. Reach the site of the vanished Hedrick logging camp and jct with *Shavers Mtn Trail* at 1 mi.)

From the parking area cross the footbridge over Condon Run, follow a graveled road for 0.2 mi to a registration sign on the *Otter Creek Trail*. Continue straight on an old RR grade (the road to the R descends to the Otter Creek Fishing Water Improvement Station where limestone is ground to neutralize the stream acid). Drainage on the L frequently makes a wet treadway under yellow birch and hemlock. Dense rhododendron is an understory. At 1 mi rock hop Yellow Creek (excellent campsites here), and at 1.1 mi jct with *Yellow Creek Trail*, L. Here may be seen an example of the high metal posts and signs used to prevent damage similar to that caused by bears to wooden signs.

(The *Yellow Creek Trail* follows an old RR grade W, parallel with Yellow Creek, under hemlock and yellow birch. At 0.7 mi is a jct, R, with *McGowan Mtn Trail*. Rock hop Yellow Creek at 0.8 mi and at 1.2 mi reach a saddle and a small open area in the ridge where a sign indicates the wilderness boundary. Here the

3-mi *Baker Sods Trail* forks L and leads to the 4-mi *Little Black Fork Trail* and the 1.6-mi *Middle Point Trail*. The *Yellow Creek Trail* proceeds ahead for 0.1 mi to its W terminus with McGowan Mtn Rd [FR-34]. The McGowan Mtn Rd entrance at 6.8 mi in Fernow Experimental Forest is gated to vehicle traffic April 15 to August 15.)

Continue on the *Otter Creek Trail* through a heavy stand of hemlock and red spruce. At 2.2 mi is an excellent grassy campsite area, R. On the L at 2.9 mi is a spring and on the R is a jct with *Mylius Trail*.

(The 2.4 mi *Mylius Trail* crosses Otter Creek, ascends for 0.7 mi to a saddle on Shavers Mtn, crosses *Shavers Mtn Trail*, and descends 835 ft in elev for 1.7 mi to the Kuntzville Rd [FR-162] and Galdwin Rd [CO-12]. See *Shavers Mtn Trail* below.)

On the *Otter Creek Trail* at 3.6 mi cross Otter Creek either by wading or rock hopping. A sign here warns of the danger of flash flooding and high water in the streambed. At 4 mi intersect with *Moore Run Trail*, L, and *Possession Camp Trail*, R. The *Otter Creek Trail* continues ahead.

(The *Moore Run Trail* immediately crosses Otter Creek to the R of Devils Gulch — a forbidding, impenetrable rhododendron coppice where water splashes from a maw of darkness. Follow the old RR grade around the E slope of the mountain in a gradual ascent through a spendid forest of cherry and maple. Rhododendron is common; ferns and wood shamrocks cover the treadway. Grouse are often seen. At 1.2 mi cross a small stream; pass an old RR timber loading dock, L, at 1.7 mi. At 2.1 mi rock hop Moore Run in an area of boulders, rhododendron, and hemlock. Ascend steeply to the S and N forks to another RR grade, but turn off the grade at 2.4 mi to skirt the wide glade. Reach a jct with *Turkey Run Trail*, R, at 2.7 mi. [See *Turkey Run Trail* below.] Cross a small tributary at 3.1 mi and enter a soggy open area where thick sphagnum can hide a watery path on the old RR grade. At 3.5 mi reach the end of the bog and pass through a rhododendron thicket to a jct with the *McGowan Mtn Trail*, L at 4 mi. [See *McGowan Mtn Trail* below.] Continue for 0.1 mi to a jct with the McGowan Mtn Rd [FR-324]. From here it is 3.9 mi L on the road to the W terminus of *Yellow Creek Trail* and 2.9 mi R to Fernow Loop Rd [FR-701] in Fernow Experimental Forest.)

(From the jct with the *Otter Creek Trail* and the *Moore Run Trail*, the *Possession Camp Trail* ascends on an old RR grade through a hardwood forest with an understory of rhododendron. At 0.5 mi turn E to cross a stream in a deep cove. Continue on the W slope of the mountain and curve E again at 1 mi to parallel the S Fork of Possession Camp Run before crossing the stream in another cove. Remains of a stone RR bridge are at 2.1 mi. Birch, beech, maple, and scattered hemlock and spruce tower over rhododendron thickets. Pass through a section of large boulders at 2.6 mi and reach a jct with the *Green Mountain Trail* at 3.2 mi.)

To continue on the *Otter Creek Trail* at the *Moore Run Trail* and the *Possession Camp Trail* jct, go downstream to the six-person Adirondack shelter at the site of an old logging camp at 4.1 mi. From here veer L and wade or rock hop Otter Creek at 4.2 mi. At 4.4 mi pass a scenic area called Pothole Falls, the highest falls in the river, where powerful whitewater has churned pebbles to carve shafts in the rocks. Forest cover is birch, hemlock, rhododendron, and witch hazel. Rock hop or wade the mouth of Moore Run at 5.5 mi. Pass near Otter Creek at 5.7 mi and move temporarily away from it; rejoin it at 6.2 mi. Wade across Otter Creek again at 7.1 mi and reach the site of an old logging camp called Camp Two at 7.3 mi. Beyond the camp 0.1 mi on the R is jct with the *Green Mtn Trail*.

(The *Green Mtn Trail* follows an old timber road SE on an exceptionally steep climb for the first 1.2 mi [over 1000 ft in elev] to the top of Green Mtn. It joins an old RR grade in a forest of maple and yellow birch and curves E at 1.6 mi. At 2 mi reach a jct with another RR grade and turn sharply S. Pass through rhododendron thickets and under yellow birch and cherry. Reach an old logging campsite, Possession Camp, and a jct with *Possession Camp Trail* at 2.7 mi. From here ascend gently E to the ridge crest and turn SE on an easy contour level of 3600-ft elev. Ferns and moss cover the treadway. Follow S of an open glade and jct with *Shavers Mtn Trail* at 4 mi. See description of *Shavers Mtn Trail* below.)

Continue on the *Otter Creek Trail* and cross a drain immediately beyond the jct with the *Green Mtn Trail*. At 7.8 mi reach a rock overhang called Camping Rock, R. The canyon becomes narrow here but widens after 8.3 mi. Hardwoods, hemlock, and rhododendron are mixed. Ferns and black cohosh are frequent. Reach a jct with *Big Springs Gap Trail*, L, at 8.6 mi.

(The 0.9 mi *Big Springs Gap Trail* is the district's preferred N access route to Otter Creek. This access avoids the use of private property near the mouth of Otter Creek and problems of fording Dry Fork. To hike *Big Springs Gap Trail*, ford the creek, L, and ascend the river bank to a camping area. Follow an old rocky wagon road up a gulch on whose mountainside remain apple trees from a pioneer's vanished homesite. A wet summer can change the hollow into a rain forest; the Big Springs water disappears under your feet to underground channels, tall cinnamon ferns drape the trailside, and large, curling grapevines hang nearby. At the trailhead is the boundary of the Fernow Experimental Forest, a parking area, and a registration stand. From here it is 5.6 mi on the Fernow Loop Rd [FR-701] to US-219/WV-72 in Parsons. Also at the trailhead is a convenient alternate loop back to Otter Creek. If taking this route, go L on the road, ascend to a gated road jct on the L at 0.5 mi to the N terminus of the 5 mi *Turkey Run Trail*. The *Turkey Run Trail* joins the *Moore Run Trail* for another 2.8 mi back to the *Otter Creek Trail*.)

The *Otter Creek Trail* now begins a curve E around the toe of Green Mtn. There are four wildlife meadows where deer are frequently seen at 8.9 mi, 9.2 mi, 10.5 mi, and 10.7 mi. Heart-leaved skullcap *(Scutellaria ovata)* grows in the rich, damp soil. Reach the N end of the trail at the forest boundary and Coal Run at 10.9 mi. Backtrack. Ahead is private property for 0.5 mi to Dry Fork. (*USGS-FS Maps:* Bowden, Parsons, Harmon, Mozark Mtn)

Shavers Mountain Trail (USFS #129)

- LENGTH: 10 mi

- DIFFICULTY: strenuous

- FEATURES: wildlife, scenic

- TRAILHEADS AND DETAILS: At the jct of US-33 in Alpena Gap (3022 ft) and FR-91 park at the picnic area L, and enter the trail across the road near the picnic shelter. Ascend on three steep switchbacks through a hardwood forest to a curve W around a knob. At 0.9 mi and 1.3 mi skirt L of the forest boundary line and USGS bearing trees. Rattlesnakes have been seen on the trail. Reach the Otter Creek Wilderness boundary at 1.8 mi. Begin descent on an old logging road, make a number of turns, and reach the headwaters of Otter Creek at 2.4 mi. There is a rhododendron copse near the stream area. At 3 mi reach jct, L, with Hedrick Camp Trail.

(The 1 mi Hedrick Camp Trail follows the Otter Creek on a gentle contour line for 0.9 mi before fording the stream. The footbridge has been washed out. Follow the trail through a hemlock grove to the Condon Run parking area and entrance to the Otter Creek Trail described above.)

Continue ahead on the Shavers Mtn Trail and climb to the mountain ridge on four switchbacks in a rocky, and sometimes wet, area. On the crest, pass L of a fence and private property at 4.7 mi. Deer and red squirrel are often seen here. At 5 mi begin a series of undulations on the ridge crest for 1 mi. Hardwoods predominate with striped green maple common to the understory. Occasionally there are thick stands of hemlock, red spruce, and rhododendron. At 6.8 mi on Rough Ridge is a vista of Middle Mtn. Begin descent on switchbacks to forest boundary sign at 6.7 mi. Reach jct with Mylius Trail at 7.3 mi.

(The Mylius Trail crosses here in a gap. To the L it descends 0.7 mi to the Otter Creek Trail. The trail goes through three small fields and a hemlock stand to reach Otter Creek. Rock hop or wade the creek, pass a good camping area in red pine on the L near the river bank, and connect with the Otter Creek Trail. The R section of Mylius Trail drops 835 ft in elev from

Shavers Mtn to Glady Fork. The descent is on a well-graded footpath for 0.6 mi, then joins an old open logging road. Cherry, poplar, maple, and oak dominate. Fern and wildflowers are prevalent. Pass through three wildlife food plots and reach Quarry Rd [FR-228] at 1.2 mi and the registration box at Kuntzville Rd [FR-162] at 1.7 mi. It is 0.1 mi R to Galdwin Rd [CO-12] and a parking area. Right on Galdwin Rd it is 4.7 mi to US-33 at the Alpine Springs Lodge. Right on US-33 it is 1 mi to Alpena Gap picnic area and the *Shavers Mtn Trail* point of origin.)

Continue ahead on the *Shavers Mtn Trail;* ascend steeply for 0.4 mi to the ridge top in a hardwood forest. At 8.5 mi enter a section of rhododendron, hemlock, and virgin red spruce. At 9.4 mi reach a 150-yd spur trail E to a six-person Adirondack shelter at the rim of the ridge. Vistas are outstanding with views of the Middle Mtn range across the first valley — Glady Fork — and SE to Briarpatch Mtn (4430 ft) and part of Spruce Knob (4861 ft). Thunderstruck Rock is visible, NE, on Mt. Porte Crayon (4770 ft). Springs are nearby for a water supply. Descend and reach the end of *Shavers Mtn Trail* at a jct with *Green Mtn Trail* L at 10 mi. Backtrack or make a loop.

(The 4-mi *Green Mtn Trail* proceeds NW on an easy descending grade S of the swamp and headwaters of Shavers Lick Run. At 1.3 mi jct with *Possession Camp Trail,* L, that leads 3.3 mi to the *Otter Creek Trail.* Ahead, the *Green Mtn Trail* slightly descends on an old RR grade through a mixed forest and dense fern beds. At 2.8 mi begin a 1.2-mi, steep descent on an old skid road to an old logging camp, Camp Two, and the end of *Green Mtn Trail.* Here is a jct with the *Otter Creek Trail* that goes S for 7.4 mi. A N exit is 1.2 mi farther downstream to a jct with *Big Springs Gap Trail,* L, and 0.9 mi up to Big Springs Gap and the Fernow Loop Rd [see *Big Springs Gap Trail* above]). (*USGS-FS Maps:* Bowden, Harman, Mozark Mtn, Parsons)

McGowan Mtn Trail (USFS #136)

- LENGTH: 3.5 mi

- DIFFICULTY: moderate

- FEATURES: red spruce forest, wildlife

- TRAILHEADS AND DETAILS: Access from the S is by *Otter Creek Trail* 1.1 mi and *Yellow Creek Trail* 0.7 mi, or 0.6 mi on the *Yellow Creek Trail* from McGowan Mtn Rd (FR-324), gated Apr 15–Aug 15. Access from the N is by McGowan Mtn Rd, 3.1 mi from the Fernow Loop Rd (FR-701), and *Moore Run Trail*, 0.1 mi. If using the N access, park at the *Moore Run Trail* jct, go 0.1 mi to jct, R, for the *McGowan Mtn Trail*. Immediately cross a woods road and ascend steeply on rocky treadway to a large rock formation on the top of the ridge at 0.3 mi. At 1.1 mi pass L of the high point of McGowan Mtn (3912 ft) and turn SE. Sections of the trail are arbored by rhododendron. Red squirrels are frequently seen. Maple, ash, cherry, and yellow birch form a high canopy, and ferns form a velvet green ground cover. At 1.6 mi pass through a naturally sculptured sandstone formation. Enter a dense red spruce forest at 1.9 mi that continues for 0.7 mi. Descend rapidly on a footpath through hemlock and conifers to a RR grade at 2.7 mi. At 3.5 mi arrive at the end of the trail and jct with *Yellow Creek Trail*. It is 0.6 mi R to McGowan Mtn Rd, 3.7 mi N to the point of origin. (*USGS-FS Maps:* Parsons, Bowden. The trail has been relocated since the 1976 maps were printed.)

Turkey Run Trail (USFS #150)

- LENGTH: 5 mi

- DIFFICULTY: moderate

- FEATURE: wildlife

- TRAILHEADS AND DETAILS: The S access is by *Moore Run Trail*, 2.8 mi from the *Otter Creek Trail*, or 1.3 mi from the McGowan Mtn Rd (2.9 mi from Fernow Loop Rd, FR-701) in Fernow

Experimental Forest. Access from the N is on Fernow Loop Rd, 0.5 mi from *Big Springs Gap Trail* and 5.6 mi from downtown Parsons. If choosing the N access, park near the gated abandoned road. A registration box is near the gate. Follow the old road and ascend gradually in a forest of cherry and maple. Enter the Otter Creek Wilderness Area at 0.3 mi. Follow the old road through a forest of hardwoods around the E slope of McGowan Mtn and at 2 mi pass R of an old trail. At 2.3 mi take the L road fork, immediately cross Turkey Run, and switchback W. At 2.7 mi reach another road fork; turn L and climb to the ridge top. Ferns and mosses are plentiful. Leave the old road and enter an old skid trail at 3.1 mi. Continue ascent to the top of the ridge (3730 ft) and after 0.3 mi begin a slow descent through red spruce, hemlock, and rhododendron. Rejoin the old trail at 4 mi, continue descent (more rapidly) at 4.7 mi to the S terminus and jct with *Moore Run Trail* at 5 mi. Backtrack, make the loop R as described above, or descend L for other loops on the Otter Creek via the *Otter Creek Trail.* (*USGS-FS Map:* Parsons)

Middle Point Trail (1.6 mi; USFS #140); *Baker Sods Trail* (3 mi; USFS #132); *Little Black Fork Trail* (4.0 mi; USFS #134)

- LENGTH: 8.6 mi, ct

- DIFFICULTY: moderate to strenuous

- FEATURES: wildlife, botany

- TRAILHEADS AND DETAILS: Although these trails are not in the wilderness, they serve as access routes to the wilderness on *Yellow Creek Trail.* The relocated *Middle Point Trail* begins on the Stuart Memorial Drive (FR-91), 1.7 mi E from the Bickle Knob Recreation Area and 2.2 mi W from the Bear Haven Recreation Area. Park on the S side of the road, climb the bank, and follow the E slope of Stuart Knob in an open hardwood forest of huge oaks, maples, beech, and birches. A wide range of ferns, including cinnamon, hay-scented, Christmas, shield, and winged are on the trail. Wild lily-of-the-valley

(Malanthemum canadense) is among the ground cover.

After crossing a rocky ridge descend 800 ft in elev on a spur ridge N to the trail terminus in a saddle at 1.6 mi, and jct with the E and W *Baker Sods Trail*. To the L (W) the *Bakers Sods Trail* descends 0.2 mi to a jct, L, with the Rattlesnake Run Rd (FR-774). (FR-774 is a 2-mi walkout to the Stuart Memorial Dr where another L turn at 0.9 mi makes a loop of 4.7 mi to the point of origin.) On the *Baker Sods Trail* continue R at the Rattlesnake Run Rd jct and follow a timber road on the S slope of the mountain for 1.1 mi to the Baker Sods wildlife grazing fields, the trail's W terminus. Here it joins Baker Sods Rd (FR-798), a 3.8-mi walkout to Rocky Mtn High June Bug's Cabin at Shaver's Fork Rd (CO-6) and 5.6 mi L (S) on CO-6 to Stuart Campground. A turn R (E) on the *Baker Sods Trail* from the jct of the *Middle Point Trail* is 1.7 mi to its E terminus and jct with the *Yellow Creek Trail*. Along the way the trail is a scenic narrow footpath in an open hardwood forest, except for a brief use of an old RR grade in a descent to the jct with *Little Black Fork Trail*. Beyond the jct ascend and parallel the R of Little Black Fork, but cross it at 50 yds before the jct with the *Yellow Creek Trail*.

(The rarely hiked, 4-mi, unmarked *Little Black Fork Trail* descends within sight of the Little Black Fork in a deciduous forest interspersed with hemlock and rhododendron. It generally follows an old RR grade, but is frequently wet, rough, and rocky. At 0.6 mi is an overlook of the mouth of the North Fork of the Little Black. Pass a small waterfall at 1.1 mi and cross the creek at 1.4 mi, the first of five times en route. Ferns, mosses, and wildflowers are prevalent in the damp gorge. At 1.8 mi the stream disappears underground for 0.1 mi. Enter a black walnut grove at 2.1 mi. Reach Shaver's Fork Rd [CO-6] by Shaver's Fork at 4 mi. From here it is 1.5 mi upstream on CO-6 to the jct, L, with the Baker Sods Rd [FR-798] described above.) (*USGS-FS Map:* Bowden. The 1976 map needs updating on these trails.)

▶ HORSESHOE RECREATION AREA
(Tucker County)

Located beside Horseshoe Run in Lead Mine Valley, this attractive area has ten campsites with both flush and vault toilets, hand pump, and spigot water. Each campsite has a table and fireplace. There are 29 picnic units and large shelter for group occasions. Activities include fishing and swimming in the Horseshoe Run and hiking up both mountainsides. The season is May 20–September 10.

• ACCESS: From the W jct of US-219 and WV-72 in Parsons, go N 1.4 mi on WV-72, turn R on Holly Meadows Rd (CO-1), and go 5.9 mi to Horseshoe Run Rd (CO-7). Turn R and go 3.6 mi to the campground, L. For a NE access descend on Lead Mine Mountain Rd (CO-9) for 4.7 mi from US-219 to Lead Mine and 1.3 mi L to the campground, R.

• SUPPORT FACILITIES: Drive 1.3 mi NE on Horseshoe Run Rd to a country store in the community of Lead Mine.

Maxwell Run Trail (2.1 mi; USFS #157); *McKinley Run Trail* (1 mi; USFS #154)

• LENGTH: 6.2 mi, rt

• DIFFICULTY: moderate

• FEATURES: wildlife

• TRAILHEADS AND DETAILS: The *Maxwell Run Trail* is 1 mi SW from the campground on the Horseshoe Run Rd. Park opposite the trailhead. Enter the forest on the L side of the run on a footpath. Pass through a stand of white pine followed by a pasture, and at 0.2 mi follow a narrow footpath on a slope by the stream side. At 0.5 mi cross the S side of the stream near a small K-dam followed by another K-dam. Scenic cascades are at 0.7 mi and 0.9 mi. Pass through a wildlife grazing field, re-enter the forest, and cross the stream four more times on an old logging road. Pass two waterfalls and reach the trail's end at the Y of two runs. (The district plans to continue this trail 0.2 mi up Close Mtn to FR-903. A loop could then be made by walking 1.8 mi on FR-903 to *McKinley Run Trail* and a return to the campground for a circuit of 5.8 mi.)

The unblazed *McKinley Run Trail* begins where McKinley Run flows through the campground. Go upstream, ascend the highway embankment, go 150 yds on an old paved road, and ascend the slope L of a sycamore tree. Pass through rhododendron and a hardwood forest. Cross an old woods road and ascend on a blue-tagged footpath to the headwaters of McKinley Run after passing a hunter's deer stand. Ascend on a switchback to FR-903 at 1 mi. Backtrack or turn L and go 0.2 mi to a locked gate and to FR-16. Turn L on FR-16 and descend on the road through a scenic group of conifers and hardwoods to Horseshoe Run Rd for 0.6 mi. Turn L again and return to the campground for a loop of 2.2 mi. (*USGS-FS Map:* Lead Mine)

Horseshoe Run Nature Trail (0.5 mi) ; **Losh Run Trail** (2.3 mi; USFS #155) ; **Dorman Ridge Trail** (1.3 mi; USFS #153)

- LENGTH: 4.1 mi, ct

- DIFFICULTY: easy to moderate

- FEATURE: nature study

- TRAILHEADS AND DETAILS: At the S edge of the campground near site #2 is a trail design board. From here proceed on the *Horseshoe Run Nature Trail* through a forest of sycamore, hemlock, white pine, maple, ironwood, and yellow birch. Flowers include mandrake, jewelweed, and true forget-me-not *(Myosotis scorpioides)*. Ferns and ground ivy cover portions of the forest floor. After 0.4 mi the *Nature Trail* continues L for 0.1 mi to the Horseshoe Run. (Slightly upstream from the *Nature Trail* the construction of a footbridge over Horseshoe Run is planned for the *Losh Run Trail*.) After wading the creek, follow Losh Run upstream in a deep hollow with an open forest of yellow birch, white pine, hemlock, and oak. White snakeroot and ferns are along the trail. Ascend gradually, cross a number of drains, and at 0.8 mi enter a thick grove of rhododendron. Reach a saddle of Drift Ridge, L, at 1.5 mi. Continue R, pass W of a knob in the ridge and pass E of the headwaters of Mike's Run to ascend to a ridge crest and hemlock stand. At 2.3 mi reach a forest of white pine and the jct with *Drift Ridge Trail*, *Dorman Ridge Trail*, and *Mike's Run Trail*. A six-person shelter is L of this jct.

(The *Drift Ridge Trail* [no USFS #] and the *Mike's Run Trail* [USFS #156] are interrupted by a timber sale in the Dorman Tract that may last until 1990. Another disadvantage of hiking the 4 mi *Mike's Run Trail* is that the USFS does not have a right-of-way across private land at the S terminus to reach Lead Mine Rd.)

The *Dorman Ridge Trail* goes N for 0.4 mi through a hardwood forest to a field. Follow the trail through the field and a stand of white pine to a border of silverberry. Continue on an old farm road through fields where sections are growing up with young trees. Reach Lead Mine Mountain Rd (also called Hiles Run Rd) (CO-9) at 1.3 mi. Backtrack or use a vehicle shuttle. From here it is 0.7 mi W on CO-9 to Location Rd (CO-5) at a jct with three wooden crosses. It is 6 mi SW on Location Rd to the community of St George. For an E route on Lead Mine Mountain Rd descend 3.1 mi to Horseshoe Run Rd and turn R for 0.5 mi back to the campground. (*USGS-FS Maps:* Lead Mine, Saint George)

▶ OTHER TRAIL AREAS
(Tucker County)

Stonelick Trail *(3.4 mi, rt; USFS #137)*

This is a moderately difficult trail that follows an old isolated logging road. It is used frequently by ATVs, but the chance of seeing wildlife and camping outside the Fernow Experimental Forest makes it appealing. For the E terminus drive 5.1 mi from the Fernow Experimental Forest sign on US-219/WV-72 in downtown Parsons to the fork in the Fernow Loop Rd (FR-701) and go R for 1.5 mi to a jct R with FR-709. Go 0.2 mi on FR-709 to trail sign for a narrow parking space. Descend on two switchbacks to cross Stonelick Run at 0.4 mi. Vegetation is birch, cherry, oak, maple, basswood, hemlock, and rhododendron. White snakeroot and jewelweed are among the major wildflowers and an infrequent shrub is the Devil's walking stick (*Aralia spinosa*). At 1.3 mi is the MNF boundary line, but the trail is on a public right-of-way for 0.4 mi to Government Rd (CO-41) near Shaver's Fork. Backtrack. (*USGS-FS Map:* Parsons)

South Haddix Trail (USFS #126)

An isolated trail, the possible 4.5-mi *South Haddix Trail* has been segmented by timber roads and the district is analyzing its location for a possible change in termini. (The 1976 Montrose and the 1968 Parsons quad maps incorrectly show the trail as *Moore Trail* with the E terminus on private property at an underpass of the Western Maryland RR 1.5 mi W of Moore and the W terminus at FR-298.) The current access to the E terminus is to drive 4 mi S of Parsons on US-219 to Moore and turn off on South Haddix Rd (CO-219/10). Follow the road for 1.6 mi to a fork at Haddix Run South Branch. Parking here may be a problem because of space. Do not block either road or obstruct private property on the L. Hike past the gated FR-116 on the R and at 0.4 mi pass a water experiment station. Reach the trailhead at 0.5 mi, R. Ascend through rhododendron, oak, beech, maple, mountain laurel, and wildflowers for another 0.5 mi to the ridge crest. Turn L and follow the ridge for approximately 1.5 mi farther. Backtracking is recommended if trail direction becomes tenuous. (*USGS-FS Maps:* Parsons, Montrose)

▶ SECTION 2: GAULEY RANGER DISTRICT

Within the 157,913-acre Gauley Ranger District are four

developed campgrounds: Big Rock, Bishop Knob, Cranberry, and Summit Lake. Additionally, 23 numbered and restricted campsites exist along the Williams River and 12 on the banks of the Cranberry River. Both of these streams and the north fork of the Cherry are stocked with trout. Large and small game hunting is allowed in all areas except recreational areas, and bear hunting is not allowed in the Black Bear Sanctuaries. There are two developed picnic areas, North Bend and Woodbine. The district may be best known for the famous 750-acre Cranberry Glades Botanical Area, but equally significant are the 35,864-acre Cranberry Wilderness, the Highland Scenic Highway, and the Falls of Hills Creek. There is also another special place, the 26,000-acre Cranberry Back Country where for 50 yrs, without legal or designated status, the area has been traditionally closed to public motorized vehicles. The Back Country has nearly 75 mi of hiking trails and seven Adirondack shelters by the Cranberry River. Access to all of the above will be described further in this section.

Although hiking, backpacking, and camping are prominent on nearly 190 mi of trails, there are other activities for the outdoor sports enthusiast. For example, the lower Cranberry and the Gauley are suitable for canoeing, kayaking, and rafting. For cross-country skiing there are nearly 75 mi of trails, some marked with the standard diamond-shaped US Ski Association signs. Area information on outdoor sports for all seasons is available from the Richwood Chamber of Commerce. The chamber also has information on Richwood, the home of the National Ramp Association, which sponsors the annual Feast of the Ramson the first Saturday in April. A spring nature tour is the second Saturday in May and a Cranberry Glades tour is the second Saturday in July. (Chamber address: Main St, Box 587, Richwood, WV 26261, tel: 304-846-6790.) Exceptionally scenic vistas are on the Highland Scenic Highway, the *Forks of Cranberry Trail,* and the *Nature Trail* behind the Cranberry Mountain Visitor Center. The Cranberry Mountain Visitor Center (at the jct of WV-39/55 and WV-150, 6.3 mi W of US-219 at Mill Point) provides visitor information and audiovisual programs on the history and natural phenomena of the area. It is open daily, 9:30 A.M.–5 P.M., from Memorial Day to Labor Day, and weekends in May, September, and to the middle of October. From the center is a *Nature Trail* that begins E of the building and circles the mountain rim (elev 3605 ft) through a hardwood forest for remarkable vistas of the Greenbrier River Valley, Beaver Lick Mtn, and Bald Knob, Virginia. Some of the understory is striped maple and witch hazel (*Hamamelis virginiana*). The trail follows the *Pocahontas Trail* for 0.1 mi to a picnic area and loops back to the center parking area at 0.6 mi.

The Cranberry Glades Botanical Area receives its name from the cranberry (*Vaccinium macrocarpon* and other species) and from wet sphagnum bogs also called glades. The area is similiar to the arctic tundra of the Canadian bogs or "muskegs" in floristic composition, but dissimilar in that the West Virginia glades are unglaciated. The glades are the southernmost breeding area for a number of bird species. The area contains four glades; the 0.5 mi boardwalk *Cranberry Glades Botanical Trail* loops through two of them. Ten interpretive signs explain the flora and fauna, formation, geology, and future of this natural garden. Among the more than 100 identified plants are the snake mouth orchid (*Pogonia ophioglossoides*) and grass pink orchid (*Calapogon pulchellus*). Both bloom in late June or early July. Sundew (*Drosera rotundifolia*), monkshood (*Aconitum uncinatum*), and sarsaparilla (*Aralia nudicaulis*) also grow here. Access to the glades is 0.6 mi W on WV-39/55/150 from the visitor center to paved FR-102, R, for another 1.5 mi.

Another popular area for a short trail is at the Falls of Hills Creek Scenic Area, 5.3 mi from the visitor center on WV-39/55/150 and L for 0.2 mi to the parking area. From the parking area descend on the 0.8 mi round-trip *Falls of Hills Creek Trail* into a narrow sandstone and shale gorge covered by northern hardwood, hemlock, and rhododendron. Among the wildflowers are Dutchman's breeches (*Dicentra cucullaria*), trillium, wild orchids, and Canada violets. The 114-acre preserve has three waterfalls: 25-ft Upper Falls, 45-ft Middle Falls, and 63-ft Lower Falls (the second highest in the state). Above the Upper Falls the *Fork Mountain Trail* crosses the creek on its E route to the *Pocahontas Trail*. A landslide has destroyed a section of stairways and viewing platforms near the Lower Falls, resulting in a closed, dangerous route. The USFS is conducting an environmental assessment to determine reconstruction.

It is recommended that you write for, or pick up at the visitor center or district office, the "Recreation Guide for the Gauley District." It has information on activities as well as a map.

• ADDRESS AND ACCESS: District Ranger, Gauley Ranger District, PO Box 110, Richwood, WV 26261, tel: 304-846-2695. District office is 1 mi E of Richwood on WV-39/55/150. The visitor center is 21.4 mi E of the district office and 6.3 mi W from US-219 at Mill Point. (WV-55, the Highland Trace, is a 165-mi route from the West Virginia-Virginia border near Wardensville in Hardy County to Muddlety in Nicholas County. Named the Highland Trace by Margaret Temple West, a member of a task force appointed by Governor John D. Rockefeller IV, the scenic route is a guide to dramatize the state's skiing areas.)

• MAPS: Numbers 6-11

▶ **CRANBERRY GLADES BOTANICAL AREA**
  (Pocahontas County)

The glades area has two parking lots. The first is paved with asphalt at the entrance to the boardwalk trail described above, and the second is graveled, 0.9 mi downstream for an easy connection with the *Cow Pasture Trail* and the nonmotorized 16-mi Cranberry River Rd (FR-102/76) that connects with nine trails into the Cranberry Wilderness and the Cranberry Back Country.

Cow Pasture Trail (USFS #253)

- LENGTH: 6.7 mi

- DIFFICULTY: moderate

- FEATURES: wildlife, scenic Cranberry Glades

- TRAILHEADS AND DETAILS: From the paved parking lot walk up the entrance road for 0.2 mi to an old RR grade on the L. Pass the gate, enter the forest of birch and hemlock, and walk on a ground cover of buttercups. At 0.8 mi turn L at gate and go through a boggy area. Beavers have been active here. At 1.5 mi veer away from the glades into a hardwood forest, cross two streams, and enter an old cow pasture among sparse hawthorn and elder. There are scenic views here of the glades. Excellent area for bird-watching. Leave the old road and cross the South Fork of the Cranberry River at 3.5 mi. Cross a tributary at 4.1 mi and enter an old pasture. For the next mi cross tributaries, pass through pleasant pastures with beds of wild geranium *(Geranium maculatum)* and groves of yellow buckeye. After crossing a beaver dam area ascend to a ridge, descend into a boggy area, and cross a footbridge. Enter a hemlock stand and reach the Cranberry Rd (FR-102) at 6.5 mi. Turn L on FR-102 for 0.2 mi to a gate and the gravel parking area. Hike another 0.9 mi upstream to your point of origin for a loop of 7.8 mi. *(USGS-FS Map: Lobelia)*

▶ **CRANBERRY WILDERNESS AREA**
(Pocahontas and Webster Counties)

In 1983, Congress passed Public Law 97-466, which created the 35,500-acre Cranberry Wilderness. The area included 26,500 acres from the original Cranberry Back Country and 9000 additional acres. It is preserved forever without the sound of motorized vehicles or equipment. Trees will never be logged, minerals mined, or shelters built. Hunting, fishing, camping, hiking, and cross-country skiing will be allowed. There are nine hiking trails in the wilderness and some of them extend or connect with other trails outside the wilderness. The USFS has listed the following trails for "lower standard" maintenance to be maintained as funding permits: *County Line Trail, Big Beechy Trail, Tumbling Rock Trail, Forks of Cranberry Trail, District Line Trail, Laurelly Branch Trail, Middle Fork Trail, North Fork Trail,* and the *North-South Trail.* Because the bears chew painted or treated signs, the USFS is replacing signs with routed natural material.

Animal life in the wilderness includes 16 species of amphibians, 7 species of reptiles, 41 species of mammals, and 80 species of birds (among the most common are woodpeckers, vireoes, warblers, and sparrows, but the cardinal is not listed). More than 900 species of flora have been identified.

The USFS requests that all hikers and backpackers register at the access points and that campers carry a tent, as the shelters on the adjoining back country may be filled. Licenses are required for fishing and hunting. The weather is drastically capricious, requiring proper clothing. The area is usually wet, the summer temperature ranges from 40° to 70°, and in the winter reaches sub-zero temperatures with "white-outs" and deep snow. The nearest campground is the Cranberry Recreation Area described below.

At the NW edge of the Cranberry Back Country lies a scenic meadow campground by the Cranberry River. On carefully mowed lawns are 30 campsites with a picnic table and grill, hand pump drinking water, and vault rest rooms. Fishing, picnicking, camping, and hiking are its main activities. Because it is a popular campground, it fills up quickly, particularly in the spring and summer. Open March 15–December 8. The S terminus of the *North-South Trail,* the district's longest, is here.

• ACCESS: From Richwood at the jct of WV-39/55/150 and CO/FR-76 (across from Gales Restaurant) drive 12 mi on CO/FR-76 to the campground. (FR-76 beyond the campground is gated, restricted, and not open to vehicles.)

• SUPPORT FACILITIES: Motels, restaurants, banks, service stations, and shopping centers are in Richwood.

North-South Trail *(22.0 mi; USFS #688)*

- CONNECTING TRAILS:
  Lick Branch Trail (2.1 mi; USFS #212)
  Little Fork Trail (3.7 mi; USFS #242)
  Rough Run Trail (3.2 mi; USFS #213)
  Birch Log Trail (2.9 mi; USFS #250)
  Laurelly Branch Trail (3.4 mi; USFS #267)
  Tumbling Rock Trail (2.6 mi; USFS #214)
  North Fork Trail (6.6 mi; USFS #272)
  Middle Fork Trail (10 mi; USFS #271)
  Big Beechy Trail (5.4 mi; USFS #207)
  (District Line Trail 2.8 mi; USFS #248)

- TOTAL LENGTH: 64.7 mi

- DIFFICULTY: moderate to strenuous

- FEATURES: wildlife, botany, wilderness, geology

- TRAILHEADS AND DETAILS: The *North-South Trail* is unique and significant because it is as east-west in its distance as it is north-south, it is the district's longest trail, and it is the only continuous trail to connect two campgrounds. Additionally, it is a master trail route through the Cranberry Back Country and the Cranberry Wilderness with ten connecting trails in the Greenbrier District and three trails in the Marlinton District. Although the *North-South Trail* (formerly called the *Red and Black Trail*) is not a loop trail, the number of potential loops in its use is a hiker's dream. Elevation increase in the first 2 mi of the trail is 1040 ft and follows a ridge line of near 4000 ft elev for most of the distance.

From the Cranberry Campground parking area pass the FR-76 gate and trail signs, turn L, and ascend on a narrow footpath in a forest of beech, birch, cherry, maple, and poplar. Wildflowers such as Indian cucumber root *(Medeola virginiana)*, mandrake, and rose-colored twisted stalk are prevalent on the mountainside. At 0.5 mi begin the first of four switchbacks to the mountain ridge. At 1.6 mi and 2.1 mi cross tributaries of the Lower Twin Branch. A good campsite is R at 2.4 mi, followed by a jct with FR-272 (gated at Red Oak Knob). Cross the grassy road and ascend to an old woods road, which follows the ridge line through an open forest of tall cherry and maple. Ferns and trout lilies cover the path. Enter a short bog at 4 mi, followed by a mixed forest, which includes hemlock and red spruce. Arrive at the jct with *Lick Branch Trail*, R, at 4.7 mi. Water is 0.1 mi R.

(The 2.1 mi *Lick Branch Trail* drops 1050 ft in elev to FR-76 at the Cranberry River. Pass the confluence of cascading streams. At 0.4 mi pass an old pot-bellied stove among other signs of an old lumber camp. Follow an old RR grade to a seeded road at 1 mi, leave the road after 0.5 mi, and descend into a rocky area with hemlock. At 2.1 mi is a large, two-tiered waterfall at the trail terminus. It is 2.2 mi back to the Cranberry campground, a loop of 9 mi.)

Continue ahead on the *North-South Trail* and at 5.9 mi jct with the 3.7 mi *Little Fork Trail*, L.

(The *Little Fork Trail* descends N from the headwaters of Little Fork. At 1.1 mi cross the drain and stay on the E side through the gorge. Pass through stands of tall poplar, beech, yellow birch, cherry, and hemlock. Cross the creek at 3 mi and again at 3.3 mi. Reach the middle fork of the Williams River at 3.6 mi, wade, cross a flood plain for 0.1 mi, and jct with the N terminus of *Middle Fork Trail*, R. To the L is a cul-de-sac parking area, the terminus of FR-108. To the R is the W terminus of the *County Line Trail*. Trail loops can be made here for a return to the *North-South Trail*. At the parking area are five numbered, restricted campsites. FR-108 goes 0.5 mi to FR-86, a point on the state highway map listed as Three Forks of the Williams.)

The *North-South Trail* continues ahead on the ridge and at 6.4 mi is a jct with *Rough Run Trail*, R.

(The 3.2 mi *Rough Run Trail* descends 1000 ft in elev for 3.2 mi to FR-76 and the Cranberry River. After 0.2 mi the trail begins to follow, and subsequently cross, *Rough Run Trail* through rhododendron and hemlock for the first 1.8 mi. Follow an old RR grade as the trail leaves the stream and curves around the ridge spur to its exit at Little Rough Run for 3.2 mi.

Right on FR-76, it is 4.5 mi back to Cranberry Campground —
a loop of 14.2 mi.)

After another 0.9 mi on the *North-South Trail* jct with the
Birch Log Trail, R.

(The *Birch Log Trail* descends for 2.9 mi to FR-76 and to the
Cranberry River. It follows an old logging road along the Birch
Log Run through hemlock, oak, maple, and birch. Fern beds
are frequent. Cross Birch Log Run five times and smaller
drains in wet areas, particularly at 1 mi and 2.6 mi. On FR-76,
R, it is 9.1 mi to Cranberry Campground — a loop of 18.9 mi.)

Ahead on the *North-South Trail* ascend and descend slightly
for 0.9 mi to jct with the *Laurelly Branch Trail,* L, and enter the
Cranberry Wilderness Area at 8.2 mi.

(The 3.4-mi *Laurelly Branch Trail* descends on an old RR
grade with switchbacks through a hardwood forest to the middle fork of the Williams River and the abandoned FR-108, now
Middle Fork Trail. An exit downstream to FR-86 at the Williams
River is another 3.9 mi, or an ascent on the *Middle Fork Trail* is
6.1 mi to rejoin the *North-South Trail* 1.2 mi from the Highland
Scenic Highway, WV-150.)

Remaining on the *North-South Trail* the hardwoods become
increasingly mixed with red spruce and dense undergrowth,
mainly of rhododendron. Seeps are more frequent. At 10.2 mi
arrive at the N terminus of *Tumbling Rock Trail,* R.

(The 2.6 mi *Tumbling Rock Trail* descends and crosses the
stream a number of times. At 1.7 mi cross a tributary and
descend on a slope W of the stream. Reach FR-76 at the Cranberry River at 2.6 mi. To the R (N) it is 0.1 mi to Tumbling Rock
Shelter and 9.1 mi farther on FR-76 to Cranberry Campground — a 22-mi loop. It is 6 mi L (S) on FR-76 and FR-102
to Cranberry Glades parking area.)

For the next 4.5 mi of the *North-South Trail* the treadway has
more frequent seeps, rocky areas, and red spruce stands, which
form a canopy over moss-covered rocks, logs, and stumps. The
elev is between 4000 ft and 4400 ft. Reach a significant trail
intersection at 14.7 mi. The *North-South Trail* turns L (N) on the
old FR-76. To the R (S), FR-76 is *North Fork Trail,* which descends 6.6 mi to FR-102; straight ahead (E) is a 0.4 mi access

through a magnificent display of spruce and thick spongy moss to a parking area on the Highlands Scenic Highway, WV-150. (The access trail to WV-150 is an excellent point for a shuttle vehicle. Elev here is 4556 ft. North on WV-150 it is 5.6 mi to the Tea Creek Campground, and S on WV-150 it is 8.6 mi to the Cranberry Mtn Visitor Center.)

(The 6.6 mi *North Fork Trail,* formerly FR-76, descends through a beautiful forest, first of red spruce and gradually hardwood. At 2.5 mi the road crosses left fork and later north fork at 4.4 mi. White snakeroot, ferns, and cohosh border the road for the last 2 mi. Reach a jct with FR-102 at 6.6 mi. From here it is 4.3 mi upstream on FR-102 to the Cranberry Glades parking area.)

Continue on the *North-South Trail* on the abandoned FR-76, now growing over with red spruce from seedlings to Christmas tree size. Wildflowers are prominent in the open areas. At 15.9 mi reach a jct, L, with the *Middle Fork Trail.* The only sign here may be the old FR-108 sign.

(The 10 mi *Middle Fork Trail* follows down the stream by the same name, crosses a number of small drains and tributaries, and the main stream with a drop of 1930 ft to the fork of the Williams River parking area. Once a graded road and open for vehicular traffic, it is now returning to the wilderness it once was. Cascades, pools, moss-covered rocks, and hardwood forests provide immense beauty, another prize of the Cranberry Wilderness. At 6.2 mi jct, L, with the *Laurelly Branch Trail.* [The *Laurelly Branch Trail* ascends 3.5 mi to a jct with the *North-South Trail* described above.] At 7.5 mi jct R with the *Big Beechy Trail.* [The 5.4 mi *Big Beechy Trail* ascends steeply in a hardwood forest with rhododendron for the first 1.3 mi and then follows a ridge line to a jct with the *District Line Trail,* L, at 4.3 mi in a stand of large red spruce. It continues ahead on the ridge for another 1.1 mi to Sugar Creek Mtn and a jct with the *North-South Trail.*] The *Middle Fork Trail* crosses the scenic Beechy Run with a waterfall to the L and continues downstream. Pools, rock tiers, and cascades are scenic parts of the Middle Fork. At 8.6 mi cross a cement bridge. Among the hardwoods are witch hazel, bee balm, wild hydrangea, jewelweed, and flowering raspberry *(Rubus odoratus)*. At 10 mi the *Middle Fork Trail* ends at the jct with *Little Fork Trail, County Line Trail,* and the three forks of the Williams River parking area.)

From the E jct of the *Middle Fork Trail* the *North-South Trail* continues N for 1.1 mi to a jct with a spur trail R that leads out 0.1 mi to a registration box and parking area off the Highlands Scenic Highway, WV-150. The *North-South Trail* turns L up an embankment on the R of a wildlife grazing field. Reach the ridge crest at 17.4 mi. The treadway is one of red spruce needles, and in the summertime snow white Indian pipe rises from the lush green moss. At 18.1 mi jct with the *Big Beechy Trail,* L.

(As described above, the *Big Beechy Trail* follows the ridge line for 1.1 mi to a jct, R, with the *District Line Trail* and ahead for 4.3 mi to a descent and jct with the *Middle Fork Trail.* The 2.8-mi *District Line Trail* follows a high ridge line to a jct with the *County Line Trail* described below.)

The *North-South Trail* becomes a footpath and descends into a section of hardwoods and dense fern beds to skirt W of the Sugar Creek Mountain ridge at 18.6 mi. The treadway becomes increasingly rocky as the trail curves E and reaches a N rim at 20.5 mi. Descend on rugged and sometimes slippery rocks using care to follow the blue blazes. At 21.3 mi switchback L and descend steeply on a difficult treadway to FR-86 at 22.0 mi. Across the road is the Tea Creek Campground; to the R on FR-86 it is 1 mi to the Highlands Scenic Highway, WV-150. *(USGS-FS Maps:* Webster Springs SW and SE, and Woodrow do not show accurate trail locations.)

County Line Trail (11.2 mi; USFS #206); *District Line Trail* (2.8 mi; USFS #248)

- TOTAL LENGTH: 14 mi

- DIFFICULTY: strenuous

- FEATURES: wildlife, remote

- TRAILHEADS AND DETAILS: The *District Line Trail* and 9.2 mi of the *County Line Trail* (named for its proximity to Webster and Pocahontas counties) are in the wilderness. They can be used to form loops with the *Middle Fork Trail*, *Big Beechy Trail*, and the *North-South Trail*. The description below offers one of those options. At the trailhead parking area near the *Middle Fork Trail* at the end of FR-108 (0.5 mi off FR-86 at three forks of the Williams River), ascend gradually on the *County Line Trail* for 1.2 mi on the S slope of the mountain to the ridge crest. The forest is composed of birch, beech, poplar, hickory, and oak. Nettles and white snakeroot are prominent in the summertime. Follow the trail over a mixture of rocky footpaths, old woods roads, and rugged sections of the N slope to arrive at a rock formation at 2.1 mi. Cross drains at 3 mi and 3.8 mi. The Williams River can be heard, L (N). At 5 mi ascend on a rocky and mossy N slope. Sections of dense red spruce are here. Signs of bear and deer are at 5.9 mi in a cherry and maple forest. At 7 mi reach jct with *District Line Trail*, R, where bear have chewed former wire-framed signs.

(The 2.8 mi *District Line Trail* follows the ridge line R through hardwoods, red spruce, and hemlock to a jct with the *Big Beechy Trail*, where to the R a 16.6 mi loop can be made back to the point of origin by using 2.5 mi of the lower *Middle Fork Trail*. Or turn L on the *Big Beechy Trail* and go 1.1 mi to the *North-South Trail*.)

The *County Line Trail* turns L and at 7.6 mi reaches the ridge edge for a steep descent. From here there is a 1000 ft elev drop on 15 switchbacks with rugged treadway in a forest of cherry, maple, birch, and sparse hemlock to FR-86 and the Williams River at 9.2 mi. The *County Line Trail* is rarely used N of here. However, to continue, wade the river (if safe) and ascend 2 mi partially on an old RR grade by the Lower Bannock Shoals Run to *Turkey Mtn Trail*. Here the options would be to backtrack or hike R for 2 mi on the *Turkey Mtn Trail* and 4.4 mi on FR-135 to Tea Creek Campground on FR-86. (*USGS-FS Maps:* Webster Springs SW and SE, Bergoo)

Forks of Cranberry Trail (USFS #245)

- LENGTH: 5.7 mi

- DIFFICULTY: strenuous

- FEATURES: botanical study, geology

- TRAILHEADS AND DETAILS: The E trailhead is on Black Mtn at a parking area on the Highlands Scenic Highway (WV-150), 5.2 mi N of the Cranberry Mtn Visitor Center. Trail elev change is 1300 ft. Hike 0.2 mi to scenic view L of the Glades and the south fork of the Cranberry River drainage. Follow a rocky plateau for 1 mi through mountain ash *(Sorbus americana,)* rhododendron, mountain laurel, huckleberry, ferns, and spruce. Begin descent; pass through beds of trout lily and pass a spring, R, at 2.1 mi. Reach a rocky knoll at 2.2 mi with limited vistas; descend into a spruce and rhododendron stand. Pass large boulders and the "Elephant Rock" at 3.3 mi. Trail becomes overgrown; descend steeply in sections and under tall maple, cherry, and birch to reach the Cranberry River Rd (FR-102). (A turn R is 0,1 mi to jct R with the *North Fork Trail* [abandoned FR-76] and across the bridge of the north fork of the Cranberry River is an Adirondack shelter. From here it is 11.6 mi downstream to the Cranberry Campground.) Turn L and hike upstream on the Cranberry River Rd for 4.2 mi to a jct with the *Cow Pasture Trail* and the Cranberry Glades gravel parking area. (*USGS-FS Maps:* Hillsboro, Lobelia, Webster Springs SE)

▶ SUMMIT LAKE RECREATION AREA
(Greenbrier County)

High in the N corner of Greenbrier County is beautiful 43-acre Summit Lake (3388 ft). Adjoining it is a 33-site campground, one of the gateways to the Cranberry Back Country and an excellent base camp for planning hikes south of the Cranberry River and to the ridge line of Fork Mtn. The campground has hand pump water, tables, grills, and vault toilets (no hookups). Activities include boating (nonmotorized), fishing for trout, bass, and bluegill, and hiking. The campground is open March 15–December 8.

• ACCESS: From the town of Richwood drive 6.6 mi E on WV-39/55/150 to FR-77 on the L (5.8 mi from the district office). Drive 2 mi to the campground entrance.

• SUPPORT FACILITIES: Accommodations and shopping centers are in Richwood.

Summit Lake Trail

• LENGTH: 1.8 mi

• DIFFICULTY: easy

• FEATURE: lake vistas

• TRAILHEAD AND DETAILS: From campsite #1 follow the trail sign or from the lake parking area follow L around the lake on a blue-blazed trail into a forest of birch, oak, cherry, beech, and poplar. Rhododendron, ferns, club moss, and wildflowers are frequent. Cross a stream at 0.9 mi and another, Coates Run, on a footbridge at 1.3 mi. Pass the boat dock and complete the loop. (*USGS-FS Maps:* Webster Springs SW, Fort Mtn)

(In 1988 a short section of the *Pocahontas Trail* was relocated at Hills Creek; a number of short sections on the *Kennison Mtn Trail* were relocated for better cross-country skiing; and a major change in the *Frosty Gap Trail* placed its central route on the Frosty Gap Rd and shortened the NW terminus to jct with the *Pocahontas Trail*, 1.5 mi SE of Mikes Knob. Relocations have also been made on the *Fork Mtn Trail* near Desert Branch, both at its mouth and its headwaters.)

Pocahontas Trail (20.2 mi; USFS #263)

- CONNECTING TRAILS:
  Fisherman Trail (1.2 mi; USFS #231)
  Frosty Gap Trail (5.2 mi; USFS #235)
  Eagle Camp Trail (1 mi; USFS #259)
  (*Fork Mtn Trail* 21.4 mi; USFS #236)
  (*Kennison Mtn Trail* 9.7 mi; USFS #244)

- TOTAL LENGTH: 58.7 mi

- DIFFICULTY: easy to strenuous

- FEATURES: wildlife, wildflowers, history

- TRAILHEADS AND DETAILS: The W terminus of the 20.2 mi *Pocahontas Trail* is on gated Pocahontas Rd (FR-99), a 1 mi walk-in access. The E terminus is at the Cranberry Mountain Visitor Center parking area. It crosses the county lines of Nicholas, Webster, Greenbrier, and Pocahontas, as well as WV-39/55/150, and connects with a wide range of other trails for a short 1-mi hike to lengthy partial loops. Description begins here, not at its termini but at its jct with FR-77/99, because of its proximity to a developed campground.

  From Summit Lake Recreation Area drive or hike 1 mi on FR-77 to a saddle in the ridge at a parking area (3655 ft). Here is the jct with the *Pocahontas Trail*, Pocahontas Rd (FR-99), L, and the W boundary of the Cranberry Back Country. Also here is the W trailhead for the *Fisherman Trail*.

  (The *Fisherman Trail* was reconstructed by the YCC in 1979. It descends steeply for a drop of 900 ft in elev from the saddle into Pheasants Hollow, crosses the stream five times, and reaches the Cranberry River at 1.2 mi, its E terminus. Across the river is Pheasants Hollow Shelter and FR-76. The river can be waded at normal water levels. From here it is 5 mi downstream on FR-76 to the Cranberry Campground.)

  To hike L on the *Pocahontas Trail*, cross an open area and enter the forest by a large maple tree. Follow the E slope of the ridge through a hardwood forest. At 1 mi cross FR-99, and at 1.6 mi reach the Hanging Rock area, a tri-county point. Begin a gradual descent to cross Coats Run Rd (FR-786) at 2 mi. After curving N of the Hunter's Run headwaters and crossing a number of drains, join a wildlife road at 3.5 mi. A spring is on the L at 3.7 mi. Reach the W terminus of the trail at FR-99 at 4.2 mi. Backtrack or turn L on FR-99 and hike 1 mi to the gate and vehicle access. It is 6.1 mi from the gate to Richwood. Or turn R for 0.3 mi to a jct L with *Barrenshe Trail* and hike 4.5 mi to FR-76. It is another 4.5 mi L on FR-76 to Richwood.

To hike R on the *Pocahontas Trail* at the FR-77/99 jct enter the forest on an old woods road near an old building foundation. Ascend and follow the ridge line (and the Cranberry Back Country border) through a forest of beech, cherry, maple, oak, hemlock, and rhododendron. At 0.6 mi and 1.3 mi are boggy areas. Reach a clear-cut area at 1.9 mi and continue through the cut for 0.8 mi. There is another wet area at 3.2 mi. At 3.5 mi cross FR-77 and join FR-77 at 4.2 mi for 0.1 mi before turning R into the woods. (FR-77 ends 1.3 mi at Mike's Knob, 4240 ft.) The W terminus of the 5.7-mi *Frosty Gap Trail* is here.

(*Frosty Gap Trail* begins at the sharp bend in the road that ascends to the top of Mike's Knob. It is an undulating ridge trail, almost exclusively between 4000 ft and 4400 ft elev for its entire distance. It follows old RR grades and timber routes, but is overgrown in spots. It is signed as both a hiking and cross-country ski trail. From FR-77 it parallels the *Pocahontas Trail* SE for 1.5 mi to a spur connection, after which it turns more to the E through a red spruce forest. At 5.2 mi it crosses Dogway Rd [FR-232], gated to the L but open to the R for vehicle access 1.2 mi from WV-39/55/150. Straight ahead, the trail goes 0.5 mi to its E terminus with *Kennison Mtn Trail*.)

Continue ahead on the *Pocahontas Trail*, which parallels the *Frosty Gap Trail* for 1.5 mi to a spur connection, L, at 6.8 mi. Descend slightly, turn S around a knob to a switchback for a descent on the SE slope. Reach the jct with the *Eagle Camp Trail*, R, at 8.2 mi.

(*Eagle Camp Trail* is a 1 mi access route between *Pocahontas Trail* and WV-39/55/150. It follows W of the Left Branch drainage on a gradual descent through a mined forest to the North Fork of the Cherry River. In normal weather the river can be crossed on a fallen log. Across the river in a small field is a parking area. It is 10.1 mi W on the highway to the Summit Lake Campground and 13.9 mi to the district office.)

On the *Pocahontas Trail* cross the headwaters of the Left Branch at 8.4 mi and begin a 2-mi S and E curve around the slopes of Yew Mtn. A number of places are wet, such as a 0.3-mi section near the Left Branch and spots where there is natural drainage from the slope. The forest is chiefly hardwood with rhododendron a part of the understory. At 10.4 mi arrive at WV-39/55/150 and a small parking area. From here it is 16 mi R on the highway to the district office and 4.5 mi L to the Cranberry Mountain Visitor Center. Cross the road, descend to and rock hop (in normal weather) Hills Creek to a dense meadow where red bee balm *(Monarda didyma)* grows. Cross a tributary and enter a garden-like area of rhododendron, hemlock, and wood shamrock. Ascend steeply on the N slope of Spruce Mtn and reach a jct, R, with the terminus of *Fork Mtn Trail* at 12 mi. Bears have damaged the trail signs.

(The 21.4-mi *Fork Mtn Trail* descends W on the N slope of Spruce Mtn for 2.4 mi to Falls of Hill Creek Scenic Area, and beyond it ascends SW to Rocky Knob, where it turns W on the Fork Mtn ridge line. Its W terminus is on WV-39/55/150 at the North Fork of the Cherry River bridge, 1.1 mi E of the district office. It could serve as a long partial loop to return within 6.8 mi of the Summit Lake Campground. See details below.)

Ahead on the *Pocahontas Trail* at 12.5 mi turn sharp L; intersect with Spruce Mtn Rd (an old woods road) at 12.9 mi (4000 ft). Bear tracks are often seen in this area, particularly near drains. Forest is cherry, oak, maple, birch, and, infrequently, red spruce. Among the wildflowers are a species of green unfringed *(Habenaria)* orchids. Arrive at the S terminus jct of *Kennison Mtn Trail* at 13.4 mi.

(The *Kennison Mtn Trail* ascends slightly, curves around Blue Knob, descends through a hardwood forest, and crosses WV-39/55/150 at 1 mi on its way to the Cranberry River and a jct with the *Frosty Gap Trail*. See description below. Use of these two trails can form a loop of 28.6 mi back to Summit Lake.)

Continuing on the *Pocahontas Trail*, go through a boggy area and R of a field at 13.8 mi; make a sharp L at 14.1 mi. Bears have damaged the trail signs. After 0.3 mi begin E descent on four switchbacks through tall hardwoods. An understory is dense with jewelweed, ferns, striped maple, cohosh, nettles, love vine, and squaw root *(Conopholis americana)*. Reach a picnic area and join the *Visitor Center Nature Trail* at 15.8 mi. At 16 mi arrive at the E terminus of the visitor center parking area. A few yds E on the *Nature Trail* provides a magnificent view of the Greenbrier River Valley and the Allegheny Mtns. (*USGS-FS Maps:* Webster Springs SW, Lobelia, Fork Mtn)

Kennison Mountain Trail *(USFS #244)*

* LENGTH: 9.7 mi

* DIFFICULTY: strenuous

* FEATURES: outstanding spruce forest, isolation

* TRAILHEADS AND DETAILS: The S trailhead is at the Blue Knob jct with the *Pocahontas Trail*, 2.6 mi W of the visitor center, but 1 mi S of its crossing at WV-39/55/150. At this point on the highway it is more likely to be used N than from its S terminus. A rarely used trail, it has at least a dozen overgrown sections and no water except at a small drain 2 mi from the highway. Its attractiveness, however, is in its open hardwood areas, dense hemlock, red spruce and rhododendron stands, sections of ferns and wildflowers, and wildlife. If hiking the entire trail, begin at the visitor center on the *Pocahontas Trail*. After descending from the *Pocahontas Trail* for 1 mi, cross the highway and soon ascend for 0.7 mi to the S of the Kennison Mtn range (4445 ft). Jct with *Frosty Gap Trail* at 2.1 mi. (At this point a loop could be made on *Frosty Gap Trail* to its first spur connection with the *Pocahontas Trail* and a turn S for a return to the point of origin at the visitor center for 18.7 mi.) Continue ahead through large stands of spruce forest with segments of hardwoods, hemlock, and rhododendron for 6 mi on slight change in contour levels. Except in rainy seasons, the treadway is generally dry. At 8.3 mi descend a 1000-ft drop in

elev to the S bank of the Cranberry River. Wading is necessary to reach FR-76 on the N side of the river to Houselog Run shelter at 9.6 mi. On FR-76 (where vehicle traffic is not allowed) it is 8 mi N to Cranberry Campground and 8 mi SE to Cranberry Glades parking area. (*USGS-FS Maps:* Webster Springs SE, Lobelia)

Fork Mountain Trail *(21.4 mi; USFS #236)*

• CONNECTING TRAILS:
Big Run Trail (1 mi; USFS #237)
Falls of Hill Creek Trail (0.8 mi, rt)
(*Pocahontas Trail,* 20.2 mi; USFS #263)

• TOTAL LENGTH: 43.4 mi

• DIFFICULTY: easy to strenuous

• FEATURES: wildlife, botanical study, Falls of Hill Creek Scenic Area

• TRAILHEADS AND DETAILS: From the district office drive E for 1.1 mi on WV-39/55/150 to the trailhead across the north fork of the Cherry River bridge. (It is 6.8 mi W from Summit Lake Recreation Area.) Enter the forest at the bridge in a low area on an old RR grade and follow the easy blue-blazed trail downstream. At 0.1 mi is a precipitous passage by the river. At 1.3 mi turn L, rock hop Desert Branch, and gradually ascend on a logging road. A wide range of botanical species include maple, cucumber, poplar, yellow birch, cherry, wood shamrock, rhododendron, orchids, club mosses, bee balm, ferns, blue-bead lily *(Clintonia borealis)*, bellwort, blue and black cohosh, and meadow parsnip *(Zizia trifoliata)*. At 1.6 mi rock hop the stream and ascend twice to old RR grades before passing L of a beaver dam at 2.8 mi. Possible campsites here. Wildlife frequently seen. Cross small stream at the E end of the glade at 3.4 mi, cross FR-946 at 3.6 mi, and ascend to Fork Mtn ridge at 4.1 mi. (FR-946 is being developed for a timber sale and is not open for traffic from its locked gate entrance on Spencer Run Rd, CO-39/17.) Follow the ridge line, pass N and above Shiras Run headwaters through a forest of cherry, maple, and beech. Turn S at 5.6 mi in a rocky area. Hike on the E slope for 1.6 before taking a more SE direction. Reach the N slope of Rockcamp Knob (3933 ft) at 8.7 mi. In a more E direction, on rocky treadway, arrive at *Big Run Trail* jct, L, at 10.6 mi.

(The *Big Run Trail* is a 1-mi access spur that descends steeply and partly on an old RR grade on the E side of Big Run to WV-39/55/150. Parking space is narrow here. It is 11.1 mi W on the highway to the district office.)

Continue SE on rocky, sometimes extremely rocky, treadway for 1.5 mi before turning S. After another 2.4 mi turn E on the slope. The land has sections of wet areas, large rocks covered with thick moss, rhododendron thickets, and patches of moosewood *(Virburnum alnifolium)*. Deer, wild turkey, and red squirrel are frequently seen. At 15.1 mi ascend to the ridge line on an old woods road and turn L. (The woods road continues R to a private property road.) Follow the ridge and reach the S terminus of FR-223 at 16 mi. Cross the road and parallel the Quiggly Rd (a private road R) for 0.9 mi to a woods road L. Leave the mountain ridge at 16.9 mi in a forest of beech, maple, cherry, and sparse red spruce. Understory is ferns, striped maple, moosewood, woodland sunflowers, and pink turtlehead. Cross a small stream at 18.2 mi and jct with the *Falls of Hill Creek Trail* at 18.9 mi. (To the L it is 125 yds to the Falls of Hill Creek Scenic Area parking lot and 0.2 mi out to WV-39/55/150; to the R the *Falls of Hill Creek Trail* descends for 0.4 mi to the middle falls.) Continue ahead for another 125 yds to the Upper Falls and a sharp turn L. Go upstream, rock hop, and ascend in a forest of rhododendron, hemlock, and yellow birch. At 19.9 mi cross a small drain in a ravine; treadway is rocky and mossy. At 21.1 mi descend to an old RR grade and arrive at the E terminus of the trail and jct with the *Pocahontas Trail* at 21.4 mi. From here it is 4 mi R on the *Pocahontas Trail* to the Cranberry Visitor Center or L it is 1.6 mi to WV-39/55/150. (*USGS-FS Maps:* Richwood, Fork Mtn, Lobelia)

► BISHOP KNOB RECREATION AREA
(Webster County)

Located 11.7 mi N of Richwood, this area has 61 campsites in a spacious hardwood forest, hand pump water, and vault toilets. Each campsite is equipped with picnic table, lantern post, and grill. The campground is open March 1–December 1.

• ACCESS: From jct of WV-39/55/150 and Cranberry Rd (CO-76) (across the road from Gales Restaurant) in Richwood, drive N on Cranberry Rd and reach Big Rock Recreation Area at 5.7 mi. (Right it is 7 mi to Cranberry Recreation Area.) Turn L on FR-81 and drive 6 mi to FR-101; turn R on FR-101 to entrance, R.

• SUPPORT FACILITIES: (The same as for Summit Lake Recreation Area.)

Adkins Rockhouse Trail *(2.1 mi; USFS #228)*; *Cranberry Ridge Trail* *(5.8 mi; USFS #223)*

• LENGTH: 7.9 mi, ct

• DIFFICULTY: moderate

• FEATURES: black cherry seed orchard, wildlife

• TRAILHEADS AND DETAILS: These trails connect on FR-81, 0.3 mi S from the jct of FR-81 and FR-101 at Bishop Knob Recreation Area. Hike W on blue-blazed *Adkins Rockhouse Trail* near the fence of the Black Cherry Seed Orchard. Descend gradually to a timber road at 0.6 mi. At 1.3 mi follow the N side of Adkins Rockhouse Branch on an old RR grade. Cross a tributary at 1.6 mi and reach the Gauley River Rd (FR-234) near the Gauley River at 2.1 mi. Backtrack or use vehicle shuttle. (To the W trailhead drive FR-101, 3.1 mi from the Bishop Knob campground, to FR-234 and turn L. Drive 5.1 mi S to trailhead, L.)

The *Cranberry Ridge Trail* begins opposite the road from *Adkins Rockhouse Trail*. Cross a damp area and at 0.6 mi pass a spur trail, L, to Bishop Knob campsite #44. Follow an old woods road through a hardwood forest and begin a gradual descent at 1.3 mi. At 2.1 mi the headwaters of Glade Run flow partially underground. At 2.5 mi pass E of a scenic lake and follow the road across Glade Run, S of the dam. Ascend and veer L off the road at 3.1 mi. (A gated road ahead leads out 0.6 mi to FR-81.) Ascend steeply, pass over a hill with red spruce to the R and arrive at FR-84 at 3.8 mi. Cross FR-81 and follow a ridge line through a hardwood forest. Some clear-cuts of timber are on the L. Painted trillium *(Trillium undulatum)* are on this ridge. At 5.7 mi reach a logging road, turn L and reach the SW end of the trail at 5.8 mi on CO-7/6. (Left on CO-7/6 it is 0.6 mi to the trailhead of *Hinkle Branch Trail,* 2.1 mi to FR-81, and 7.4 mi back to Bishop Knob camping area.) *(USGS-FS Map: Camden on Gauley, Webster Springs SW)*

Hinkle Branch Trail *(USFS #219)*

• LENGTH: 2.4 mi, rt

• DIFFICULTY: moderate

• FEATURES: wildflowers, Cranberry River

• TRAILHEAD AND DETAILS: From the jct of FR-76 and FR-81 at Big Rock Campground it is 0.7 mi on FR-81 to CO-7/6. Turn L, go 1.5 mi to a small parking area across Hinkle Branch. Follow the blue-blazed trail downstream under tall birch, beech, and hemlock. Large colonies of club moss, mandrake, and wild lily-of-the-valley are prominent. Cross the stream at 0.4 mi, descend to another old road in a halcyon glen near the branch at 0.8 mi. Reach the bank of the Cranberry River at 1.2 mi. Backtrack. *(USGS-FS Map: Camden on Gauley)*

Barrenshe Trail *(USFS #256)*

- LENGTH: 4.5 mi

- DIFFICULTY: moderate

- FEATURE: Barrenshe Run cascades

- TRAILHEADS AND DETAILS: From the jct of FR-81 and FR-76 at Big Rock Campground drive 1.4 mi S on FR-76 (4.5 mi N from Richwood) to *Barrenshe Trail.* Park on the W side of the road. The blue-blazed trail ascends on the road bank, E, to follow an old RR grade upstream by large beds of foamflower *(Tiarella cordifolia)* to cascades of Barrenshe Run. Turn L, ascend steeply to the ridge at 0.7 mi, veer R, and follow an undulating ridge line with oak, hemlock, maple, and locust for 3 mi. Striped maple is frequent as an understory. Curve on the N slope of Briery Knob (3765 ft). Reach gated FR-99 at 4.5 mi. Backtrack or go R on FR-99 for 0.3 mi to the *Pocahontas Trail* (see connecting information below) on the L. Another option is to continue on FR-99 for 1 mi to gate and vehicle access, and 3.7 mi on Country Club Rd to jct with FR-76. *(USGS-FS Maps: Camden on Gauley, Webster Springs)*

▶ OTHER TRAIL AREAS
(Webster and Pocahontas Counties)

Turkey Mtn Trail *(20.5 mi; USFS #209)*; Twin Branch Trail *(1.5 mi; USFS #205)*; County Line Trail *(North Section, 2 mi; USFS #206)*

These trails are rarely used; they need maintenance and the USFS is considering a partial relocation of the *Turkey Mtn Trail.* For hikers who wish an isolated area, the following access description should be of assistance until the changes are complete. The nearest campground W is Bishop Knob and E is Tea Creek. From the E edge of the town of Cowen at jct of WV-20 and Williams River Rd (CO-46), drive 3.6 mi on CO-46 to Sawyer Run Rd (FR-735), L. From Bishop Knob Campground drive W on FR-101 to Williams River and jct with CO-46 at Dyer. Turn L on CO-46 and go 0.8 mi to FR-735 and park at gated road on R, *Turkey Mtn Trail*'s W terminus. The trail is blue-blazed and ascends gradually NE for 2.5 mi through a hardwood forest. Reach the forest boundary and begin a S direction to a jct with a number of old timber roads at 4.6 mi. For the next 5 mi meander E and S along the ridge line; ignore old roads and jeep passages on the R or L, and reach White Oak Fork Rd (FR-133) at 9.6 mi. (It is 3.1 mi SW on FR-133 to FR-86, which parallels the Williams River.) Continue on the ridge along the forest boundary in a hardwood forest. Ferns, club mosses, and such wildflowers as Bowman's root are frequent. Deer, wild turkey, and grouse are often seen. At 13 mi reach jct with *Twin Branch Trail*, R. (The 1.5 mi *Twin Branch Trail* descends along the Upper Twin Branch to the Williams River. Crossing to FR-86 may be difficult.) On the *Turkey Mtn Trail* jct with the N terminus of the *County Line Trail* at 18.5 mi. (The *County Line Trail* descends 2 mi on an old RR grade by Lower Bannock Shoals Run to the Williams River. Crossing may be difficult to FR-86 for completing the other 9.2 mi.) The *Turkey Mtn Trail* reaches a tricounty corner — Webster, Randolph, and Pocahontas — at 19.1 mi. Follow a jeep road SE on the ridge to FR-135 at 20.5 mi, the E end of the trail. Gated and locked FR-135 was severely damaged by the flash floods in 1984, and a 4.4 mi walk may be necessary down the mountain to the Tea Creek Campground and FR-86. (*USGS-FS Maps: Webster Springs SW and SE, Bergoo, Woodrow, Sharp Knob*)

▶ SECTION 3: GREENBRIER RANGER DISTRICT

In comparison to the other districts, the Greenbrier is the largest (199,723 acres), has more than two or three times as many miles of forest roads (408 mi), and the longest section (48 mi) of the *Allegheny Trail*. There are 96.9 mi of other trails. In addition to its size, it also leads in having the most headwater sources to some of the major rivers. Often called the "Birthplace of Rivers," the Tygart, Shaver's, Glady, and Laurel flow

N to the Monongahela River; the east and west forks of the Greenbrier start S to the New River, and the Elk begins W to the Kanawha River; the Jackson drains E to the James River, and the south branch of the Potomac flows NE. The district also has more nesting birds (104 species) in the 12,195-acre Laurel Fork Wilderness than any other MNF wilderness and the largest preserve (148-acres in the Gaudineer Scenic Area) of virgin red spruce and northern hardwood. The USFS is considering the designation of former RARE II areas, those that did not become wilderness areas, as semi-primitive, non-motorized localities. Logging roads and mining would be prohibited.

Recreation areas include three picnic grounds and two campgrounds. One picnic area is Old House Run on US-250, 2.5 mi E from WV-28 in Thornwood, and another is nearby at Buffalo Fork Lake on FR-54, 2.4 mi off WV-28 in Thornwood. (North on WV-28, 5.6 mi from Thornwood, is the Locust Springs Picnic Area on FR-60 in the George Washington National Forest.) The other picnic area is on Gaudineer Knob (4440 ft) on FR-27, 2.3 mi off US-250/WV-92 and 7.4 mi W of the Ranger Station in Bartow. The Gaudineer area was dedicated in 1937 in honor of D. R. Gaudineer, a ranger for 12 yrs in the MNF, who sacrificed his life in an attempt to save others. Farther N, 0.8 mi, on FR-27 is the parking area, R, for the *Virgin Spruce Trail*, a 0.5-mi interpretive loop that has exceptionally tall maple, beech, cherry, ash, birch, and spruce. An understory and ground cover has mooosewood, rhododendron, new growth spruce and birch, wood shamrock, trillium, and foamflower. Campgrounds are Laurel Fork (six sites) on FR-423, 1.5 mi off FR-14, and Island Creek (four sites) on WV-28, 0.8 mi N from the S entrance of FR-14.

The W boundaries of the district are the Tygart Valley, a broad and beautiful farming area that invites an artist's brush, and a section of Glady Fork on the N panhandle. Across the N border is US-33, and the E boundary follows directly S from US-33 near Job to WV-28 and S along the Virginia state line to the Marlinton Ranger District. The S boundary is SE from Valley Head in the W to the N boundary of Seneca State Forest and to the Virginia state line in the E, N of Paddy Knob.

• ADDRESS AND ACCESS: District Ranger, Greenbrier Ranger District, Bartow, WV 24920, tel: 304-456-3335. In Bartow, 0.3 mi W on US-250/WV-92 from its jct with WV-28/92.

• MAPS: Numbers 12-19

▶ MIDDLE MOUNTAIN AREA
(Randolph and Pocahontas Counties)

On the main ridge of Middle Mountain (over 3500 ft in elev) is FR-14, engineered to wave like a colorful banner in the wind for 26.5 mi from Wymer in the N to Burner Mtn in the S, before it descends to Fivemile Hollow for 4 mi to the National Youth Science Camp at WV-28, N of Thornwood. Tall black cherry, red and sugar maples, yellow birch, green ash, beech, and other hardwoods, which Dr. Maurice Brooks said had "leafy crowns," tower over open gentle understories. Deer, grouse, and wild turkey are often seen crossing the road. Trail signs indicate the frequent descent to deep and damp shady paths under conifers and rhododendron. And for 12 mi on the E side of the road the forest is forever preserved in the Laurel Fork Wilderness. For those who love the splendor of the decid-uous forest and cannot go hiking, a leisurely drive on this road is the next best thing.

If you see Middle Mtn from the air, you can understand why it is named Middle Mtn. It is between Shaver's Mtn, W, and Rich Mtn, E, but beyond those ranges are Cheat Mtn and another Rich Mtn in the W, and Spruce Mtn, Fork Mtn, and Shenandoah Mtn in the E, all appearing as huge garden rows with natural irrigation between. This view, if none other of the topography, sustains Louise McNeill's "The Forest": "And shadowed in the distance . . . From Allegheny westward there is rolled . . . As God first planted when the hills awoke." Be-cause the Middle Mtn trails are linear in their directions, some will be described in connecting groups to offer the use of the forest roads for circuit routes. The USFS reports that all trails are maintained every three or four yrs, with the exception of those in the Laurel Fork Wilderness Area, which receive less attention.

• ACCESS: The N entrance is from Wymer on FR-14 at the jct with US-33. The S entrance is from Thornwood on FR-14 at the jct with WV-28, and from the E there is Dry Fork Rd (CO-40), 5 mi from Osceola (Sinks of Gandy). A W route is from Glady on Elliots Ridge Rd (CO-22).

• SUPPORT FACILITIES: A former CCC camp, the Laurel Fork Campground has six campsites, hand water pump, tables, and vault toilets in the middle of the Laurel Fork Wilderness Area. In Bartow there is a motel, a restaurant, grocery stores, a service station, and a post office. The nearest commercial campground with full service is 3 mi S of Bartow on WV-28/92. Address: Boyer Station, Rt, 1 Box 51, Arbovale, WV 24915, tel: 304-456-4667.

Laurel River Trail *(17.2 mi; USFS #306)*

• CONNECTING TRAILS:
Stone Camp Trail (1.5 mi; USFS #305)
Middle Mountain Trail (1.2 mi; USFS #307)
Forks Trail (1.1 mi; USFS #323)
Beulah Trail (4.2 mi; USFS #310)
Camp Five Trail (1.6 mi; USFS #315)

• TOTAL LENGTH: 26.8 mi

• DIFFICULTY: moderate to strenuous

• FEATURES: Laurel Fork Wilderness, wildlife, plant life

• TRAILHEADS AND DETAILS: (Because of the damage caused by the 1985 floods, a few short segments of the *Laurel River Trail* may be relocated.) The N entrance of the *Laurel River Trail* is on the S side of Beaverdam Run, on FR-14, 5 mi S of Weymer and US-33. After 3.4 mi the trail enters the Laurel Fork Wilderness. (On FR-14 the Laurel Fork Wilderness begins 2.6 mi S of Beaverdam Run.) The Laurel Fork Wilderness is in two sections: the North with 6081 acres and the South with 6114 acres. They were established by a Congressional public law in January 1983. The E boundary is on the slope of Rich Mountain and the W border is on the E side of FR-14 along the Middle Mtn ridge. Forming the S border is Burner Mtn and the headwaters of Laurel Fork, a trout stream that flows N through the center of Dry Fork in the Cheat District. Between the two sections are ten acres of nonwilderness on FR-423 for a semiprimitive Laurel Fork Campground. The wilderness has a number of wildlife species that are not found in the other MNF district wildernesses. They are the hellbender *(Crypto-branchus alleganiensis)* and the mud puppy *(Necturus maculosus)* among 19 species of amphibians; the Eastern box turtle *(Ter-rapene carolina)* and the milk snake *(Lampropeltis triangulum)* among 15 species of reptiles; the red bat *(Lasiurus borealis)* and the least weasel *(Mustela nivalis)* among 38 species of mammals; the hooded merganser *(Lophodytes cucullatus)*, the red-shoul-dered hawk *(Bauteo platypterus)*, the yellow-billed cuckoo *(Coc-cyzus americanus)*, the willow flycatcher *(Empidonax traillii)*, the least flycatcher *(Empidonax minimus)*, the brown thrasher *(Toxos-toma rufum)*, the cedar waxwing *(Bombycilla cedrorum)*, the bobolink *(Dolichonyx oryzivorus)*, and the dickcissel *(Spiza ameri-cana)* among 104 species of nesting birds. Both the copperhead and the rattlesnake are found in the hardwood and pine ecosystems. The rattlesnake is also found in the red spruce ecosystems.

To hike the 9.6 mi N section of the *Laurel River Trail* park on the N side of Beaverdam Run near the entrance to *McCray Ridge Trail* and walk 0.1 mi S on FR-14 to a seeded woods road, L, and enter a forest of maple, cherry, and birch. Parallel the stream by an open area of old beaver dams, glades, and vegetation such as ninebark *(Physocarpus opulifolius)*, meadowsweet *(Spirea latifolia)*, fireweed, and cinnamon fern. At 0.3 mi leave the road, turn sharply L, and enter a section of hemlock, spruce, and rhododendron. Pass L of a rocky area and at 1.2 mi reach the river bank. Campsites are here. Go upstream through a flood plain to a crossing of Laurel Fork at 1.4 mi. The river can be waded in normal weather. After crossing the river the trail goes upstream for 8.2 mi to Laurel Fork Campground. It follows short sections of footpaths and some old RR grades, but mainly a woods road. After crossing Bennett Run, return to the side of the river but soon veer away. Reach a pipeline clearing and Mud Run at 2.8 mi. Here is the N boundary of the Laurel Fork Wilderness. Deer are frequently seen here. Turn R and follow the pipeline swath for 0.2 mi. Turn L and gradually ascend and then descend on the old road through rhododendron and mountain laurel. Cross Stone Camp Run at 4.1 mi (this is an E tributary and not the Stone Camp Run with the trail). Cross Scale Lot Run after another 0.5 mi and pass through a forest of hemlock. At 5.3 mi reach a jct with the *Stone Camp Run Trail*, R, in a meadow of bellflower, ironweed, asters, and golden Alexanders.

(The 1.5 mi *Stone Camp Run Trail* [650 ft gain in elev] crosses the river. Follow the blue-blazed trail up a deep hollow on portions of an old RR grade that weaves back and forth across the stream. Treadway is wet in sections. Black cohosh, ferns, and saxifrage grow on the trailsides. Conifers are infrequent in a forest of beech, cherry, birch, and maple that become unusually tall from 1.2 mi to the top of the Middle Mtn ridge and jct with FR-14. It is 3.8 mi N on FR-14 to the beginning of *Laurel River Trail* for a loop of 10.6 mi.)

Ahead on the *Laurel River Trail*, immediately after the jct with the *Stone Camp Run Trail*, cross Three Bear Run and follow a generally straight trail for 1.8 mi. Campsites are along the way. There are considerable signs of beaver activity on the W side of the river. Cross Bill White Run at 6.4 mi and Adamson Run at 7.1 mi. At 8 mi reach the jct with the blue-blazed *Middle Mtn Trail*, R.

(On the *Middle Mtn Trail* descend from the road, cross a small boggy area in hardwoods of maple and ironwood for 0.1 mi, and wade across Laurel Fork. Follow an old woods road in a hardwood forest to the stream's headwaters at 0.8 mi. Ascend on a footpath of switchbacks to the W terminus at FR-14. Elevation gain is 584 ft. The FR is too narrow to park here, thus parking is necessary 0.2 mi S at the jct with FR-422. It is 6.5 mi N on FR-14 to the N entrance of the *Laurel River Trail*.)

Continuing on the *Laurel River Trail,* pass through a stand of hemlock and join an old RR grade at 8.7 mi. Reach the river bank where large hawthorn grow on the edge. Cross Five Lick Run, and pass through a grassy field with wildflowers to re-enter the forest. At 9.2 mi arrive at a parking area on Dry Fork Rd (CO-40). Turn R and go 0.4 mi on CO-40 to the bridge and cross the bridge to the Laurel Fork Campground. Here is the S terminus of the N section of the *Laurel River Trail.*

The Laurel Fork Campground has six campsites, hand water pump, tables, and vault toilets on the W side of the river. Primitive camping is also allowed anywhere in the adjoining open areas. (The USFS has plans to reconstruct the campground when funds become available.) The managed season is from April 15 through November. The nearest grocery store, post office, and gasoline (open 11 A.M.–3 P.M., Monday–Saturday) is in Glady, 6.2 mi on FR-423 W for 1.5 mi, FR-14 N for 0.3 mi, and FR-422 W for 2.5 mi to Elliots Ridge Rd (CO-22). Wymer also has a grocery store, post office, and gasoline; they are open each day with more hours. (See other support facilities above.)

The 7.6 mi S section of the *Laurel River Trail* is within the Laurel Fork Wilderness and receives low standard maintenance, but some improvements were made in 1984 by the Sierra Club. Nevertheless, the trail is well-blazed, scenic, and generally easy on old RR grades, forest roads, and foot trails. From the Laurel Fork Campground go upstream by the restrooms and enter the forest in a red pine grove. Pass remnants of a water supply used by the CCC in the 1930s and reach a jct, R, with *Forks Trail* at 0.6 mi.

(The 1.1 mi *Forks Trail* ascends in a hollow and a S slope in a hardwood forest for 0.6 mi to FR-14. It crosses FR-14 and descends for 0.5 mi on a spur ridge and hollow of hardwoods, ferns, and club mosses to a gated gas well access road, FR-183. Here it could be used as a loop S on FR-183 to the *Beulah Trail* and a return to the *Laurel River Trail* and *Forks Trail* jct for 4.6 mi, or FR-14 could be used for 0.9 mi to make a shorter loop of 3.5 mi.)

On the *Laurel River Trail,* cross a small drain in a meadow with scattered hemlock, pass a patch of skunk cabbage, and ascend slightly on a rocky area. To the L are sections of rapids and pools in the river. Reach a jct, R, with the *Beulah Trail* at 1.5 mi.

(The scenic 4.2 mi *Beulah Trail* ascends 440 ft in elev for 0.9 mi to cross FR-14 on its way to FR-44 where it provides the only practical trail route from this area to Shaver's Mtn. Ascend on a partial old RR grade in a hardwood forest. At 0.5 mi it passes a water hole, favored by deer and surrounded by beds of ferns and wood shamrocks. It crosses FR-14 and can be used as a loop trail with the *Forks Trail* described above, or it can be used as access to FR-44 and Shaver's Mtn. It is described in more detail below.)

Continue ahead on the *Laurel River Trail* on a more open slope and make a horseshoe curve near the mouth of Crawford Run, a tributary E of Laurel Fork, at 2.2 mi. Cross a number of drains where hemlock and spruce dominate, and arrive at the jct of *Camp Five Trail*, R, at 4.1 mi near a stand of red pine.

(The 1.6 mi *Camp Five Trail* ascends gently along Camp Five Run to FR-14. Outstanding features of this lush area are large fern and club moss beds, and a charming mixture of hardwoods and conifers. Grouse and songbirds are prominent. Pass an inactive beaver dam at 0.2 mi and a small impoundment near the Middle Mountain Cabins at 1.4 mi.)

On the *Laurel River Trail* follow a grassy trail past old beaver dams, L. At 4.4 mi cross Laurel Fork (for the first time since the campground). It can be rock hopped in normal weather. Leave the old RR grade on a slope; pass more old beaver dams. Summer butterflies are copious here. At 4.7 mi pass the remains of a large sawdust pile and enter a spruce and red pine grove. Pass through a boggy area at 5.1 mi. Prairie cord grass *(Spartina pectinata)*, bulrush, sedge, and speckled alder are prevalent. Because of beaver dams, the trail may be difficult to follow through swamps and high water. A departure from the trail to find a suitable crossing upstream may be necessary. The open area is scenic and wild turkey are often seen. At 5.3 mi curve away from the main stream and ascend into a forest of conifers, maples, and birch. Join a seeded road (gated FR-97) at 6.3 mi. A section of the forest here has been set aside for testing and demonstrating silviculture practices for Allegheny hardwoods. Reach FR-14 at 7.6 mi. It is 10.5 mi S on FR-14 to WV-218 near Thornwood, and 1.4 mi N on FR-14 to *Camp Five Trail*, where a loop of 6.5 mi can be made for a return to the *Laurel River Trail* jct. (*USGS-FS Maps:* Glady, Sinks of Gandy, Whitmer)

McCray Ridge Trail (USFS #302)

- LENGTH: 4.7 mi

- DIFFICULTY: easy to moderate

- FEATURES: Glady Fork, wildlife, scenic

- TRAILHEADS AND DETAILS: The *McCray Ridge Trail*, rather than crossing the ridge, follows the McCray Creek that runs from Middle Mtn to Glady Fork. Its steady contour is between 2800 and 3000 ft the entire distance. It is the only trail that directly connects Middle Mtn to the *Allegheny Trail*. The E terminus is 5 mi S of Weymer on FR-14 to a parking area a few yds N of Beaverdam Run, at a gated road of the Columbia Gas Trans Corp. Follow the blue-blazed trail on the road through an assorted hardwood forest with scattered hemlock and red spruce; pass L of a wildlife food plot and R of the Beaverdam Run glades. Slightly ascend and reach a jct with a woods road, R, at 1.1 mi. Cross an old RR grade and descend gently on an old road for 0.5 mi to a jct; turn L to parallel McCray Creek. Cross a pipeline swath at 2.3 mi and remain on the L side of the stream. Pass through a mixture of hardwood, hemlock, and rhododendron. At 3.5 mi reach a jct with the *Allegheny Trail*. Turn L on jointly running trails for 0.5 mi, where *McCray Ridge Trail* descends R to the Glady Fork. Wading will be necessary, and impossible during spring runoffs or other high water. Across the river, follow upstream for 0.4 mi, veer R and parallel a drain on a footpath, pass through a hemlock grove, and reach the W terminus at Glady Fork Rd (CO-27) at 4.7 mi. It is 4.3 mi L to Glady and 5.1 mi R on

CO-27 to Alpena and US-33. (*USGS-FS Map:* Glady)

Beulah Trail (*4.2 mi; USFS #310*); **County Line Trail** (*4.1 mi; USFS #311*)

- LENGTH: 8.3 mi, ct

- DIFFICULTY: moderate to strenuous

- FEATURES: wildlife, scenic forest, gas wells

- TRAILHEADS AND DETAILS: In John Bunyan's *Pilgrim's Progress*, the land of Beulah was a tranquil land of peace and rest. The *Beulah Trail* has been named correctly. Its E trailhead is at the jct with the scenic *Laurel River Trail* (1.5 mi S from the Laurel Fork Campground). It ascends W in a moist glen where hardwoods shade the fern beds, mossy rocks, and cascading tributary. At 0.5 mi it passes a small water hole, favored by deer, and ascends a S slope to reach FR-14 at 0.9 mi. (It is 0.9 mi N on FR-14 to a jct with the *Forks Trail,* and 3.9 mi S on FR-14 to a jct with *Camp Five Trail.*) Across the road it descends steeply on a N slope to a cove and drain at 1.2 mi. Birch and maple are the dominant hardwoods. Colorful and poisonous baneberry *(Actaea pachypoda)* is seen among the rich fern beds. Reach FR-183 (a gated gas well access road) at 1.5 mi and turn L. To the R on FR-183 it is 1 mi to the W terminus of *Forks Trail.*) Follow the road as it parallels the east fork of Glady Fork on a long scenic horseshoe curve past gas lines to gated FR-183B at 1.9 mi. Follow the road for 1.1 mi to a jct uphill with the N terminus of the *County Line Trail.* Here the *County Line Trail* follows the road and the *Beulah Trail* turns a sharp R on a footpath to descend in an open hardwood forest. Cross two drains where wildlife is frequently seen and gradually descend on a N slope to the main stream crossing at 4.1 mi. Reach FR-44 at 4.2 mi. (It is 0.5 mi L on FR-44 to the *High Falls Trail,* and 3.5 mi R on FR-44 to Glady.)

At the N terminus of the *County Line Trail* at the jct with the *Beulah Trail,* hike up the road (FR-183-B) to the crest of the ridge and descend to a curve where the road ends at a gas well and the blue-blazed trail remains on the ridge at 0.5 mi. Ascend to the first (3610 ft) of five major knobs on Little Beaver Mtn, a ridge of hardwoods that is shaped like a crescent high above the headwaters of the east fork of the Glady Fork. Arrive at the unmarked county line of Randolph (L) and Pocahontas (R) at 2 mi. After a plateau begin a descent on switchbacks into an impressive open cove of cherry and maple to cross an old RR grade in a saddle at 2.5 mi. Ferns and wildflowers are abundant and a drain begins on the L. Ascend on two switchbacks to a knob (3686 ft), descend to another saddle, and ascend again to another knob. At 3.7 mi reach a clearing with a gas well and a pipeline crossing at the end of FR-35A. There is plenty of space here to park. The trail's S terminus is 0.4 mi farther down the road to a jct in a sharp curve with Snorting Lick Rd (FR-35). To the L it is 0.7 mi to FR-14. (The *USGS-FS Maps,* Widell [1977], Sinks of Gandy [1970], and Glady [1976] do not show trail relocations.)

Lynn Knob Trail *(3.9 mi; USFS #317)*; Hinkle Run Trail *(3.4 mi; USFS #367)*

- LENGTH: 7.3 mi, ct

- DIFFICULTY: moderate to strenuous

- FEATURES: scenic, diverse animal and plant life

- TRAILHEADS AND DETAILS: These two N–S trails are grouped because they connect on FR-17. The N terminus of the *Lynn Knob Trail* is on Middle Mtn Rd (FR-14), 11 mi N on FR-14 from WV-28 near Thornwood and 19.5 mi S on FR-14 from US-33 at Weymer. FR-14 is too narrow for vehicle parking at the trailhead. Park 0.4 mi S near the gated Elklick Run Rd (FR-179). It is 0.6 mi on FR-179 to where the trail crosses the road.

At the trailhead, ascend to a knob (3935 ft) at 0.2 mi and turn SW on a wide trail on a high ridge of hardwoods with excellent views when the leaves are off. Cross Elklick Run Rd at 0.8 mi and ascend to Lynn Knob (3990 ft) in a beech and cherry forest at 1.2 mi. Deer, turkey, red squirrel, and grouse are often seen here. At 2.6 mi begin a descent, steep in sections, on switchbacks. Reach an old logging road at 3 mi and descend through a beautiful maple forest. Pass a number of drains with ferns and club moss. Arrive at the S terminus at the Little River Rd (FR-17) at 3.9 mi. (It is 1.4 mi E to FR-14 and 4.2 mi W to FR-44.)

Across the road is the N terminus of the *Hinkle Run Trail.* Descend slightly on a grassy road, make a sharp L, cross a small stream, rock hop or wade the Little River at 0.1 mi. Liverwort grows on mossy rocks. Parallel the stream for 0.5 mi to the mouth of Hinkle Run. Pass R of an open field at 0.8 mi. After the third crossing of Hinkle Run, leave the stream and parallel a tributary drainage from the SE. Cross a stream at 2.3 mi. Ascend to a grassy grazing field at 2.7 mi and pass through a variety of wildflowers, including butter-and-eggs *(Linaria vulgaris),* a "honey guide" for insects. At 2.8 mi reach an old logging road and turn R. Ascend on the road to a curve where the road levels on a grassy treadway through birch and maple, and for the last 0.1 mi, a red pine plantation. Here is the S terminus at the jct of FR-14 and FR-15. Elevation gain is 646 ft. (It is 5 mi L on FR-14 to FR-17 and 4 mi R on FR-14 to WV-28.)

Burner Mountain Trail *(USFS #322)*

- LENGTH: 3.6 mi

- DIFFICULTY: moderate

- FEATURE: nature study

- TRAILHEADS AND DETAILS: The E trailhead of the *Burner Mtn Trail* is 1 mi S on FR-14 from the jct of FR-14 and FR-15 at the S terminus of the *Hinkle Trail.* (However, at the FR jct there is a spur access trail up the Burner Mtn ridge for 0.7 mi to the *Burner Mtn Trail.* A posted, seeded road is unmarked and unblazed through a forest of red pine, hawthorn, cherry, and maple. It passes through a wildlife food plot on the ridge top to join the blue-blazed *Burner Mtn Trail.*) From the jct of WV-

28 and FR-14 at the National Science Youth Camp, drive up
FR-14 for 3 mi to the trailhead sign, L, and parking on the R.
Ascend Burner Mtn on the wide pathway and reach the ridge
top at 0.2 mi. Pass L of the wildlife food plot described above
and follow the blue-blazed trail on the ridge line of 4000 ft or
more elev. Treadway is on a wide woods road. The forest has
maples, ash, oak, cherry, birch, spruce, ferns, and wildflowers.
The wildlife includes deer, turkey, red squirrel, owls, and
songbirds. At 1.1 mi pass an old woods road L; begin a slight
ascent and reach a knob (4285 ft) at 2 mi. After 0.2 mi turn W,
then NW, and finally N in a slight descent on the ridge. Enter
a red pine grove at 3.4 mi and a grassy area at the trailhead on
FR-15. From here it is 0.6 mi L to the *Span Oak Trail* and 4.1 mi
R to FR-14. (*USGS-FS Maps:* Thornwood, Durbin)

Span Oak Trail (USFS #321)

• LENGTH: 3.7 mi

• DIFFICULTY: strenuous, elev gain 1175 ft

• FEATURES: nature study

• TRAILHEADS AND DETAILS: From US-250 on Highland Street
in Durbin go N on FR-44 for 7 mi to trailhead on R (before the
Little River bridge and FR-17 jct). (It is 16.2 mi N on FR-44 to
Glady.) Follow the blue-blazed trail on an old wagon road
through red pine, maple, birch, and serviceberry, past attractive views of the Little River. Cross a small drain at 0.3 mi and
ascend gradually through cherry, witch hazel, rhododendron,
and ferns. Turn R at 0.4 mi on an old RR grade and pass the
site of a former RR trestle at 0.6 mi. Turn off the RR grade;
ascend to the top of the ridge at 1.1 mi. Follow the ridge in a
gradual climb for 2.6 mi through a beautiful forest of birch,
maple, cherry, and oak. Deer, turkey, grouse, owls, and songbirds frequent the ridge. At 3 mi parallel FR-477, pass a
wildlife food plot and reach the E terminus for 3.7 mi at FR-15.
(FR-15 is usually rutted and narrow.) It is 0.6 mi L on FR-15 to

Burner Mtn Trail and 4.1 mi farther on FR-15 to FR-14. (*USGS-FS Map:* Durbin)

▶ ISLAND CAMPGROUND AREA
(Pocahontas County)

This small picturesque campground is on an island of the east fork of the Greenbrier River at the SW toe of Poca Ridge and the mouth of Long Run. It has only four campsites with tables and vault toilets, but it is an excellent base for hiking the *East Fork Trail* and the nearby trails.

• ACCESS: In Bartow, at the jct of US-250 and WV-28/92, drive N on WV-28 for 4.7 mi to entrance, L.

• SUPPORT FACILITIES: In Bartow there is a motel, restaurant, service station, post office, and grocery stores. The nearest commercial campground with full service is 3 mi S of Bartow on WV-28/92. Address: Boyer Station, Rt 1, Box 51, Arbovale, WV 24915, tel: 304-456-4667.

East Fork Trail *(USFS #365)*

• LENGTH: 7.9 mi

• DIFFICULTY: easy

• FEATURES: scenic, botanical study

• TRAILHEADS AND DETAILS: This luxuriant luminous pathway is a paradise for wildflower enthusiasts. From the ragwort and violets of springtime to the wreath goldenrod *(Solidago caesia)* in the fall, there is color, fragrance, and beauty. At the S trailhead in Island Campground, enter at the trail sign and follow an old RR grade through a hemlock grove for 0.3 mi to parallel the east fork of the Greenbrier River. The stream has both native and hatchery trout. It is one of those streams observed by poet laureate Roy Lee Harmon in *Summer River:* "For carefree days, for happiness sublime, I know that there are things to find, along a summer river any time." Yellow birch, beech, hemlock, ironwood, maple, alder, and red spruce are along the trail. Reach an island at 0.7 mi, but hike on the E bank if the water is high. At 2 mi cross a tributary and pass through a field with St John's wort, asters, elderberry, and golden Alexanders. Although the blue blazes indicate a fording of the stream at 2.4 mi, the forest is open enough to hike 0.3 mi to rejoin the trail without crossing. Make a horseshoe turn after another 0.3 mi but soon return to a N direction. At 4 mi begin a longer curve on the mountainside to small meadows and a red pine plantation. Rock hop Abe's Run and immediately arrive at Abe's Run Rd (FR-51). Here is an open area good for campsites. To the R, it is 2.4 mi to WV-28 and 4 mi farther S to Island Campground. To the L is a cement bridge and gate. Serviceberry, wildflowers, and ferns are prominent. Continue upstream on a pleasant path through a number of red spruce borders. At 5.8 mi cross Burning Run and at 6.8 mi cross Simmons Run. For the last 0.8 mi the trail is close to the stream bank. Wildflowers and mosses are prolific. At 7.9 mi reach the N terminus of the trail and jct with the Pigs Ear Rd (FR-254). It is 1.6 mi E to FR-103 and 1.9 mi farther to WV-28 for a total return R on WV-28 of 9.3 mi to Island Campground. (*USGS-FS Map:* Thornwood, Sinks of Gandy)

Smoke Camp Trail *(USFS #324)*

* LENGTH: 2.6 mi, rt

* DIFFICULTY: strenuous, 1327 ft elev gain

* FEATURE: Rothkugel Forest Plantation

* TRAILHEADS AND DETAILS: From Island Campground, drive S on WV-28 for 2 mi to the Max Rothkugel sign, L, and park. Walk S on WV-28 for a few yds to the trailhead, L. Ascend into the forest where in 1907 Rothkugel planted Norway spruce, European larch, and black locust under the supervision of George F. Craig, a close friend of the famous forester Gifford Pinchot. Originally, Craig acquired 13,000 acres; later, 9965

acres became one of the first tracts for the MNF. At the lower elev are conifers, but after 0.6 mi enter a hardwood forest of cherry, beech, ash, and maple. Pass a spring at 0.8 mi. Ascend steeply on a N slope, reach a ridge line, and exit at the E terminus with Smoke Camp Rd (FR-58) at 1.8 mi. To the R is the site of the former Smoke Camp fire tower. Backtrack. (FR-58 is closed from April to mid-August for wildlife protection. The road connects with Long Run Rd, FR-57, which begins 0.1 mi S on WV-28 from Island Campground.) (*USGS-FS Map:* Thornwood)

Buffalo Fork Lake Trail (USFS #368)

- LENGTH: 1.1 mi

- DIFFICULTY: easy

- FEATURES: scenic, wildflowers

- TRAILHEADS AND DETAILS: Access is from the jct of WV-28 and FR-54, 1.3 mi N on WV-28 and US-250 jct, and 2.3 mi S from Island Campground. Drive 2.4 mi on FR-54 to parking area L, midway of Buffalo Fork Lake. The 22-acre impoundment was completed in 1969. Swimming, motorboats, and the use of live minnows for fishing are prohibited. Facilities include picnic area, vault toilets, and drinking water. Hike down the road, cross the dam, and enter the forest. At 0.7 mi reach a boardwalk and a bridge in a marshy area. (The bridge over Buffalo Fork may be washed out.) Reach the road and return to the parking area. Vegetation on the trail includes hemlock, beech, birch, trillium, club mosses, Columbine, and waterleaf (*Hydrophyllum virginianum*). (*USGS-FS Map:* Thornwood)

▶ SHAVERS MOUNTAIN AREA
(Randolph and Pocahontas Counties)

Shaver's Mtn is a long (over 20 mi), high (4000 ft), narrow (3 mi), remote, and scenic SW–NE ridge between two rivers. On its ridge line are the former *Shavers Mtn Trail* and *North-South Trail,* now the *Allegheny Trail* (see Chapter 11). For 10 mi on the S half, the county line of Randolph (W) and Pocahontas (E) weaves across the ridge top, and on the E slope for this same distance there is an 0.8-mi-wide swath of private land. On the E slope the elev drops 1000 ft for 1.5 mi to the West Fork of the Greenbrier River that flows S, and on the W slope the elev drop is 500 ft for 2 mi to the Shaver's Fork that flows N. Wildlife, particularly bear and deer, is abundant in a forest of mixed hardwoods, spruce, hemlock, and pines. The Gaudineer Knob Picnic Area is 2.3 mi into the forest on FR-27 from US-250/ WV-92, and it is another 0.8 mi on FR-27 to the Gaudineer Scenic Area and *Virgin Spruce Trail* described in the introduction to this section.

The *Allegheny Trail* follows the ridge in forest property for 20.4 mi. Its N access is in Glady and the S access is on US-250/ WV-92, 2 mi W of Durbin. It has two shelters, one vehicle access point, and three foot trail access points on this long stretch. The farthest N is the *High Falls Trail* from FR-44. In the S is *Johns Camp Run Trail* from FR-317; at the Gaudineer Scenic Area it touches FR-27, and near the jct of FR-27 and US-250/WV-92 there is a 0.2 mi spur trail for an access. The only vehicle access to the ridge is on FR-27, 4 mi W of Durbin.

• SUPPORT FACILITIES: Slightly SE and across the road from the Gardineer Rd (FR-27) entrance off US-250/WV-92 is a seasonal motel, restaurant, and public telephone. In Durbin, 4 mi E on US-250/WV-92 there is a service station, grocery store, restaurant, and laundromat.

High Falls Trail (USFS #345)

• LENGTH: 5 mi, rt

• DIFFICULTY: moderate to strenuous

• FEATURES: scenic, beaver dam, High Falls

• TRAILHEADS AND DETAILS: Entrance to the E terminus is on FR-44, 4 mi S of Glady and 19 mi N on Little River Rd (FR-44) from Durbin. The road is too narrow for parking at the trail-head but there is space nearby, N on the W side of the road. Follow the blue blazes on an old woods road in a wet area and cross the west fork of Glady Fork at 0.2 mi. A beaver dam is upstream. Cross the abandoned Western Maryland RR at 0.4 mi. Pass through a pasture with grasses, hawthorn, and wild-flowers such as depford pink, daisy, and self-heal. Cross a stream and then enter the forest at 0.5 mi. Deer, raccoon, turkey, and numerous songbirds have been seen here. Climb a stile and ascend steeply in a wet area to an intersection with the *Allegheny Trail* at 1 mi in a forest of maple and cherry. (On the *Allegheny Trail* it is 1.1 mi S to Widell shelter and 8.3 mi to Johns Camp shelter. It is 5 mi N to Glady.) Continue ahead, W, descend, cross Deer Lick to a S slope, and reach the Western Maryland RR after 1 mi. Elevation drop is 700 ft. Turn R and follow the RR 0.5 mi to a horseshoe bend in Shavers Fork to scenic High Falls (approx 12 ft high) at 2.5 mi. Backtrack. (*USGS-FS Maps:* Wildell, Beverly East)

Johns Camp Run Trail (USFS #341)

- LENGTH: 0.8 mi

- DIFFICULTY: easy

- FEATURE: wildlife

- TRAILHEADS AND DETAILS: From the jct of US-250/WV-92 and FR-27, 4 mi W of Durbin, take FR-27 for 6.1 mi to jct with FR-317, R. Drive 0.5 mi on FR-317 to a dead-end. Begin the trail on a wet old woods road that parallels Johns Camp Run. The forest is mainly birch and spruce. At 0.7 mi cross a small stream and follow a footpath to the *Allegheny Trail* and Johns Camp shelter. There is evidence that deer, red squirrels, chip-munks, raccoons, and other small animals frequently visit this campground. On the *Allegheny Trail* S it is 9.5 mi to US-250/WV-92; N, it is 8.3 mi to jct with *High Falls Trail*. (*USGS-FS Map:* Wildell)

►CHEAT MOUNTAIN AREA
(Randolph County)

The high, scenic Cheat Mtn area is the westernmost section of the district. Altitudes range from 3700 ft to 4200 ft on its long ridge line. Its W drainage is to the Tygart River and its E waters flow to the trout-filled Shavers Fork. The mountain range is rich in timber, minerals, vascular plants, and wildlife, particularly bear, deer, and turkey. There is a 5.5 mi "Fish-for-Fun" section of Shavers Fork, from Whitmeadow Run downstream to McGee Run, which is stocked twice annually. Four trails have their W termini on the Cheat Mountain Rd (FR-92), the main artery across the ridge. The trails descend like tributaries to Shavers Fork. One other trail, *Chestnut Ridge Trail*, has its E terminus on FR-92 and goes down the W slope. There are no designated campgrounds or picnic areas, but there are excellent campsites on the trails and the back country roads.

• ACCESS: The S access is at the jct of FR-92 and US 250/WV-92 at Cramer Top (3803 ft), 9.8 mi W of Durbin and 8.4 mi E of Huttonsville. The N access to FR-92 is by Back Road (CO-37), which begins 1.6 mi S of Beverly on US-219/250.

• SUPPORT FACILITIES: Motels, restaurants, service stations, banks, grocery stores, and a post office are in Huttonsville and in or near Durbin.

Stonecoal Ridge Trail *(USFS #360)*

• LENGTH: 3.8 mi

• DIFFICULTY: moderate

• FEATURE: wildlife

• TRAILHEADS AND DETAILS: From the jct of US-250/WV-92 and FR-92, drive N on FR-92 for 3.2 mi to the W trailhead, R. Follow the ridge with some undulations in a mixed forest dominated by red spruce. Deer and turkey are seen at the wildlife food plots, such as at 1.8 mi, and chipmunks are prevalent throughout. Ferns, mosses, and new growth are common ground covers. From 2.2 mi the blazes may be absent, but the trail begins a descent on the S slope of the ridge toward a drain. At 3.1 mi curve away from the stream and reach FR-760 at 3.8 mi. Turn R and descend on gated road to FR-209, the E trailhead. Across the road is a thick stand of rhododendron by Shavers Fork. The exit is 1 mi upstream on FR-209 to US-258/ WV-92, 2.5 mi E of FR-92. (*USGS-FS Maps:* Mill Creek, Wildell)

Chestnut Ridge Trail (USFS #327)

- LENGTH: 5.5 mi

- DIFFICULTY: strenuous, 1548 ft elev gain

- FEATURES: scenic, wildlife

- TRAILHEADS AND DETAILS: The E trailhead is on FR-92 (opposite the jct with FR-47), 4.2 mi from US-250/WV-92. Descend in a hardwood forest of cherry, maple, and yellow birch with sparse conifers on a rocky and sometimes wet, eroded treadway for 0.7 mi to FR-1560. Turn R. (At 0.8 mi the abandoned and unmaintained *McGee Run Trail* is L.) Follow FR-1560 for 0.7 mi and turn L on an old woods road along Chestnut Ridge. At 2.4 mi is jct with *Laurel Run Trail*, L. (The *Laurel Run Trail* is no longer maintained by the USFS.) Deer, turkey, and grouse are often seen on the ridge. Pass through a wildlife food plot at 2.6 mi. ATVs use the trail. Turn L at 4 mi on a footpath and descend to a secluded cabin with a scenic view at 4.1 mi. Cross another ATV route at 4.3 mi. Leave the ridge, L, and descend in a cove of nettles, white snakeroot, wild azaleas, and ferns. At 4.9 mi arrive at a drain and pass through a mixed forest with poplar, dogwood, bush dogwood, and locust. Wild sunflowers, goldenrod, asters, and vines grow in the meadow. Arrive at Shavers Run Rd (CO-39/1) and a wooden bridge over Shavers Run at 5.5 mi, the trail's W terminus. Access here is from the town of Mill Creek at the jct of US-219/250/WV-92 and Back Road (CO-39) at the Mill Creek Methodist Church.

Follow CO-39 over the Tygart River bridge and go 0.6 mi to Mud Run Rd (CO-39/2), R (old barn is L). Follow Mud Run Rd for 2 mi and turn R on Shavers Run Rd (CO-39/1). After another 0.8 mi reach trailhead, R. (*USGS-FS Map:* Mill Creek)

Whitemeadow Ridge Trail (USFS #361)

* LENGTH: 4.6 mi

* DIFFICULTY: moderate

* FEATURES: wildlife, scenic

* TRAILHEADS AND DETAILS: The trail entrance is 1.4 mi N on FR-92 from the *Chestnut Ridge Trail* at FR-92 and FR-47 jct. Follow the blue blazes, though some are faint, uphill on a wide seeded road to a knob at 0.4 mi. Turn L on the ridge that remains about 4000 ft in elev for 2.3 mi. The forest has birch, maple, red spruce, and hemlock. Wildlife is prominent. Sections of the trail are unblazed. At 2.7 mi begin a descent that becomes steeper after 0.5 mi. On a rocky treadway, descend to an old RR grade at 3.6 mi. Bear have been sighted here. (To the L is an access route through a birch and rhododendron forest for 0.5 mi to the E terminus of FR-49 at scenic Shavers Fork.) A turn R on the old unblazed RR grade leads through a verdant, tranquil, and sometimes gardenlike route of rhododendron, birch, ferns, mosses, and the sound of the river. After 1 mi reach the E terminus of the trail and the E terminus of FR-47. Here is an excellent campsite area near the trout-stocked Shavers Fork. It is 2.2 mi on FR-47 up Whitemeadow Run to FR-92. (*USGS-FS Maps:* Mill Creek, Wildell)

(The new 26-mi *West Fork Trail* is being developed on the old Western Maryland RR from Glady to Durbin. It can be used for hiking, bicycling, and skiing. Call the Ranger Station for more information, 304-456-3335.)

Crouch Ridge Trail (2.9 mi; USFS #362); *Turkey Trail* (0.7 mi; USFS #364)

- LENGTH: 3.6 mi, ct

- DIFFICULTY: moderate

- FEATURE: wildlife

- TRAILHEADS AND DETAILS: The W trailhead is a few yds N on FR-92 at jct of FR-92 and FR-49. Follow the ridge line over knobs. In sections, walking is rough over rocks and roots. Ferns are copious and the forest is red spruce, hemlock, birch, and maple. At 2 mi reach a fork in the trail: *Turkey Trail* goes L and *Crouch Ridge Trail* goes R. (The *Turkey Trail* descends 0.7 mi in a damp ravine area to cross Yokum Run and exit at FR-188.) To the R is a new gated road for coal mining that has access across Shavers Fork to the Western Maryland RR. (To the L on FR-188, go 0.5 mi to a parking area and pass the jct with *Yokum Ridge Trail*, R, on the way. From here it is 1.9 mi on FR-188 to FR-92.) Continue descent on *Crouch Ridge Trail*, cross a number of wet spots, and pass through a forest of exceptionally tall and large red spruce in an open forest. Rock hop Crouch Run and reach FR-49 at 2.9 mi. To the L it is 1.2 mi E to the road's terminus at Shavers Fork. To the R it is 2.7 mi up Crouch Run to jct with FR-92. (*USGS-FS Maps:* Mill Creek, Wildell)

Yokum Ridge Trail (1.4 mi; USFS #365); *Yokum Ridge Spur Trail* (0.8 mi; USFS #369)

- LENGTH: 2.2 mi, ct

- DIFFICULTY: moderate

- FEATURES: wildlife, scenic

- TRAILHEADS AND DETAILS: From FR-92 and FR-188 jct, drive N on FR-92 for 0.9 mi to trailhead, R. Enter forest of red spruce, maple, birch, and cherry with understory of new growth and ferns. Club moss and other mosses form a ground cover. At 0.9 mi is a trail fork. The *Yokum Ridge Trail* goes L.

(An old damaged sign indicates the L fork is the *Bear Trail*, but the USFS has taken this off their list for maintenance.) (To the R the unblazed, 0.8-mi *Yokum Ridge Spur Trail* descends through a forest of tall red spruce, birch, and maple. At 0.6 mi pass through a boggy area to an open grassy area that has a good campsite. Follow an old RR grade over remnants of bridges, cross Yokum Run in a damp, dark green mossy area to reach FR-188 at 0.8 mi, the trail terminus. To the R it is 0.2 mi to a parking area and 1.9 mi farther on FR-188 to FR-92.) On the *Yokum Ridge Trail* descend through a beautiful forest of tall maple, red spruce, and beech where wood shamrock and moosewood are abundant. Turkey, deer, and bear are in the area. Pass R of a small stream and ravine and descend to exit at 1.4 mi. To the R is the river bank of Shavers Fork. To the L it is 50 yds to a cul-de-sac, the E end of McGee Run Rd (FR-210), and 1.8 mi W to FR-92. At FR-92 it is 9 mi S to US-250/WV-92. (*USGS-FS Map:* Wildell)

▶ **OTHER TRAIL AREAS**
(Pocahontas County)

Rattlesnake Trail *(2.5 mi; USFS #366);* **North Fork Trail** *(2.9 mi; USFS #333)*

• LENGTH: 5.4 mi, ct

• DIFFICULTY: *North Fork Trail* is moderate; *Rattlesnake Trail* is strenuous with 1548 ft elev gain

• FEATURE: nature study

• TRAILHEADS AND DETAILS: The USFS is considering major improvements in the treadway of these trails and possibly a new trail for an E loop route. To reach the W trailheads, turn off WV-28/92 in Arbovale on Back Draft Rd (CO-6), opposite the National Radio Astronomy Observatory, and drive 0.6 mi. Turn L on North Fork Rd (CO-6/1) and go 1.6 mi to a fork in the road. Veer L on gravel road for 0.4 mi to FR-197. Cross cement bridge over North Fork of Deer Creek, pass L of Sutton Run Rd (FR-1678), and reach the end of FR-197 at a group of hunter's cabins after 1.4 mi.

Begin the *Rattlesnake Trail*, R, on the abandoned FR and cross Tacker Run at 0.2 mi. Through hemlock, witch hazel, maple, and birch reach Rattlesnake Run at 0.5 mi. Turn L up Rattlesnake Hollow and ascend steeply on four switchbacks to a ridge line at 1.2 mi. Deer, grouse, turkey, skunk, and red squirrel are on this trail. Continue constant ascent in oak, hickory, ash, beech, cherry, and mountain laurel for another 1.2 mi to a grassy area and Elleber Sods Rd (FR-1681). Ahead 0.1 mi is Elleber Knob (4595 ft) with superb views of Deer Creek Valley, Little Mtn, and other distant ridges. Backtrack or plan vehicle shuttle. To the R, FR-1681 is 9 mi to US-250 at the West Virginia-Virginia state line, on the Virginia side. There are two gates on the road; the first (usually open), is 1 mi from US-250, and the other gate, 1 mi E of Elleber Knob, is closed except for the fall game season.

The *North Fork Trail* goes upstream by the North Fork. Cross Tacker Run at 0.1 mi in a hemlock and maple forest. Cross an overflow of North Fork, R of gentle section of cascades. Follow an old RR grade and pass R of another old RR grade at Block Run at 0.8 mi. At 1.6 mi there are sections that are eroded and need relocating. There are a number of beaver ponds here; deer and raccoon tracks are noticeable. Cross the North Fork a number of times and reach the Elleber Sods Rd (FR-1681) at 2.9 mi, the NE trail terminus. Here is the confluence of North Fork and Elleber Run. Backtrack or use a vehicle shuttle 2.2 mi S on FR-1681 from US-250 at the West Virginia-Virginia state line. It is 7 mi W on US-250 to the jct with WV-28 near Thornwood. (*USGS-FS Maps:* Green Bank, Hightown)

Peters Mountain Trail (5.5 mi; USFS #359); **Bar Ford Trail** (1.5 mi; USFS #370)

- LENGTH: 7 mi, ct

- DIFFICULTY: moderate

- FEATURE: nature study

- TRAILHEADS AND DETAILS: The E trailhead for *Peters Mtn Trail* is on WV-92, 0.6 mi S of jct with WV-7. The W trailhead is on WV-7, 0.6 mi E from the Greenbrier River bridge in Cass. On WV-92 (2610 ft) ascend gradually from the trail sign on a blue-blazed trail through white oak, white pine, hickory, and dogwood to the ridge top at 0.2 mi. Wintergreen, Indian plantain, wild azalea, and thyme-leaved speedwell *(Veronica serpyllifolia)* border the trail. Descend and ascend knobs, first in a SW direction, then W, and then S to a fork at 2.7 mi (3078 ft) with *Bar Ford Trail.*

(*Bar Ford Trail* forks R and descends to Clay Hollow where it follows the stream to its mouth at Deer Creek at 1 mi. Follow upstream on the R of Deer Creek to creek crossing. Only a cable remains of a former cable line crossing; wading is necessary. Ascend steeply on a large rock formation to a sharp curve on WV-7, 1 mi E from the Greenbrier River bridge in Cass.)

Continue L on the *Peters Mtn Trail*, which undulates through a hardwood forest with scattered Virginia pine and evidence of wildlife. At 4.3 mi curve N and begin descent at 4.6 mi. Wade across Deer Creek at 5.4 mi and ascend to WV-7, 0.6 mi E from the Greenbrier River bridge in Cass. If entering the trail here and the trail sign is missing, look for a mailbox belonging to O.J. Beck, across the road from a green cement block house. Parking is difficult here. (*USGS-FS Maps:* Cass, Clover Lick, Green Bank)

▶ **SECTION 4: MARLINTON RANGER DISTRICT**

The Marlinton Ranger District has 131,943 acres and 213 mi of system forest roads. Its W boundary adjoins the Gauley

Ranger District along the Highland Scenic Highway (WV-150) for 13.3 mi from the Cranberry Mountain Visitor Center to the Williams River. This area also includes the Tea Creek drainage, the remote Gauley Mtn range, and such magnificent high points as Sharp Knob (4532 ft), Little Spruce Knob (4128 ft), Big Spruce Knob (4673 ft), Gauley Peak (4584 ft), and Red Spruce Knob (4703 ft). The Greenbrier Ranger District is on the N boundary from Valley Head to Cass and the N edge of Seneca State Forest. On the E boundary it adjoins the George Washington National Forest along the Virginia-West Virginia state line on the Allegheny Mtn ridge. The S border is from the Calvin Price State Forest to High Top on the state boundary and adjoins the White Sulphur Ranger District. The *Allegheny Trail* runs N–S for 32 mi through the E center of the district (see Chapter 11). Trails such as the *Baldwin Trail* and the *Leatherwood Trail* are significant examples of remoteness. The district has four semiprimitive recreational areas with campgrounds, none of which it plans to expand. They are Bird Run, Day Run, Pocahontas, and Tea Creek, open year-round, but snow usually closes them from late December to mid-March. There are more than 75 mi of hiking trails and 32 mi of the *Allegheny Trail*.

- ADDRESS AND ACCESS: Marlinton Ranger District, Marlinton, WV 24954, tel: 304-799-4334. The office headquarters are at the E edge of Marlinton on WV-39.

- MAPS: Numbers 6, 9, 20, and 21

▶ BIRD RUN RECREATION AREA
(Pocahontas County)

This area has a level campground with 12 shaded campsites in a forest of tall conifers and hardwoods on the E side of cascading Bird Run. There are vault toilets and a hand water pump for drinking water. Open all year. The campground is the former CCC Camp Copperhead, established in 1935.

• ACCESS: At the jct of WV-92/84 in the community of Frost, take WV-84 E 1.6 mi. From Virginia take VA-84 W from Vanderpool. The area is 3.1 mi W from the state line.

• SUPPORT FACILITIES: The nearest store for gas and groceries is Gray's at the Frost crossroads, WV-92/84.

Bird Run Trail (USFS #486)

• LENGTH: 4 mi

• DIFFICULTY: strenuous, 1792 ft elev gain

• FEATURE: wildlife

• TRAILHEADS AND DETAILS: Formerly *Paddy Knob Trail* (USFS #431), the trail leaves the Bird Run Campground at site #7 and follows a wagon and timber road, which crosses Bird Run five times in the first mi. You can usually rock hop the stream, but rainfall may require wading. Red squirrel, grouse, wild turkey, and deer are frequently seen. The forest is mainly hemlock, white pine, oak, hickory, and maple with an increase of mountain laurel in the higher elev. After crossing the main stream for the last time, begin a more gradual ascent on a grassy arboreous treadway to the headwaters of a tributary. Cross drains at 1.7 mi and 2 mi, and begin a steep ascent. Turn N at the stream's headwaters at 2.9 mi. At 3.1 mi curve L, then R, on two switchbacks. Exit at the trail sign on FR-55 at 4 mi. It is 0.1 mi L to a spur entrance road, R, at Paddy Knob (4477 ft), the site of a dismantled lookout tower. Wildflowers flourish here. Backtrack. A vehicle shuttle is 3 mi N on FR-55 to WV-84, L, and 3 mi back to the campground. (*USGS-FS Map:* Paddy Knob)

Sugar Camp Trail (USFS #406)

- LENGTH: 4.1 mi

- DIFFICULTY: strenuous, elev gain 1235 ft

- FEATURE: nature study

- TRAILHEADS AND DETAILS: From the Bird Run Campground go W on WV-84 for 1.6 mi to the jct of WV-84/92 at Frost. Turn R and go 1.5 mi on WV-92 to the trail entrance, R. The blue-blazed trail is a former limited vehicle access road for maintaining wildlife food plots across Sugar Camp Mtn to FR-55. The ascending, crooked trail-road is being reconstructed for the first 2.1 mi. Along the way is one of the district's most spectacular forest displays of flame azalea (*Rhododendron calendulaceum*) in rich shades of orange, coral, xanthous, and aureate yellow. Adorning them are pink-white mountain laurel, an oak and hickory forest, scattered hemlock and Virginia and white pines. Deer pass through from the grazing fields to the streams on each side of the ridge. At 2.5 mi the trail straightens out and ascends on the ridge crest to a locked gate 0.1 mi before the E terminus at 4.1 mi. Large Solomon's seal and *Trillium grandiflorum* grow here. Backtrack or use a vehicle shuttle for 2.1 mi R on FR-55 to WV-84 and R for 3 mi to Bird Run Campground. (*USFS-FS Map:* Paddy Knob)

▶ POCAHONTAS RECREATION AREA
(Pocahontas County)

The Pocahontas Recreation Area is in the SE corner of the district and accessible to nearby trails in the White Sulphur District also. It is 4 mi SE of famed Minnehaha Springs and Camp Minnehaha, where the mineral springs bubble from the hillside between Kapp Creek and Douthat Creek. The area was named to honor Minnehaha (meaning "laughing water"), wife of Dakota Indian Hiawatha in Longfellow's fictional *The Song of Hiawatha*. The recreation area is cloistered in rhododendron and exceptionally tall hemlock and white pine. There are ten campsites with picnic tables, vault toilets, and a manual water pump for drinking water.

• ACCESS: From the jct of WV-39/92 at Remel Forest Plantation, go S for 1.8 mi on WV-92 to entrance, L.

• SUPPORT FACILITIES: The nearest general store for groceries, gasoline, and public telephone is in Minnehaha Springs, 4 mi NW on WV-39/92.

Two Lick Trail (USFS #456)

• LENGTH: 4.3 mi

• DIFFICULTY: moderate

• FEATURES: remote, botany

• TRAILHEAD AND DETAILS: At the entrance of the Pocahontas Campground, at the immediate L, follow a blue-blazed foot trail and cross a footbridge over Cochran Creek in a hemlock forest. After 0.1 mi the trail forks around the headwaters of Two Lick Run. If turning R, after 0.2 mi pass through beds of club mosses such as *Lycopodium flabelliforme* and *Lycopodium obscurum*. Ascend a ridge in a hardwood forest with sparse Virginia and white pine, and at 1.6 mi turn sharply L to the side of another ridge. After a rocky footway, descend and ascend slightly between the ridges and turn L again at 2.6 mi for a descent by switchbacks to Two Lick Run. Pass L of a grazing field at 4.1 mi and complete the loop at 4.3 mi. (*USGS-FS Map:* Mountain Grove)

Laurel Creek Trail (8 mi; USFS #466); Lockridge Mountain Trail (6.7 mi; USFS #407)

• TOTAL LENGTH: 14.7 mi

• DIFFICULTY: moderate

• FEATURES: nature study, history, remote

• TRAILHEADS AND DETAILS: The *Laurel Creek Trail* is one of three National Recreation Trails in the MNF. It was constructed in 1975 by the Older American Workers under the supervision of the USFS. From the Pocahontas Campground drive N 2.3 mi on WV-92 to a jct with WV-39. Turn L and go 0.4 mi to the Rimel parking circle and picnic area, R. (From Minnehaha Springs drive S on WV-39/92 for 3.6 mi.) Follow the blue-blazed trail R, cross the *Lockridge Mtn Trail* (road) and reach an old RR grade at 0.4 mi. Proceed upstream, L of the trout-stocked Laurel Creek, on a wide grassy trail under a magnificent canopy of hemlock, oak, and white pine. The route is bordered by rhododendron, witch hazel, and hay-scented fern. Cross streamlets from the L; enter a long meadow at 1.1 mi. At 2.2 mi there is a skunk cabbage patch. Turn L off the grassy road at 2.7 mi by Lockridge Run. (To the R it is 2.3 mi on an old, part overgrown logging road upstream to the Virginia state line and FR-55.) Begin ascent at 3.8 mi into a timber clear-cut area. Curve S around the slope and pass an Adirondack shelter, R, at 4.5 mi. Continue to curve around a number of Lockridge Mtn spur ridges in a hardwood forest to cross *Lockridge Mtn Trail* (road) at 7.5 mi. Begin a descent to a drain and reach the parking area at 8 mi.

The *Lockridge Mtn Trail* is a forest road currently being repaired and widened to be used for a timber sale. Entrance is 0.2 mi W of the WV-39/92 jct and 0.3 mi E from the Rimel parking area. Cross *Laurel Creek Trail* at 0.2 mi and ascend; mountain laurel and wild pink are on the road banks. Reach an intersection with *Laurel Creek Trail* at 1.1 mi. At 3.2 mi pass L of the shelter described above. Continue NE on the ridge in a hardwood forest to a sharp R at 6.3 mi, and reach FR-55 at 6.7 mi. Backtrack. (*USGS-FS Map:* Minnehaha Springs)

Middle Mountain Trail (*North Section, USFS #408*)

* LENGTH: 4.6 mi

* DIFFICULTY: moderate

* FEATURES: flora and fauna

* TRAILHEADS AND DETAILS: (The 13.4 mi S section is described in the White Sulphur District, Section 6.) Entrance to the N trailhead is across the road (WV-39/92) from the Rimel parking circle and trailhead for the *Laurel Creek Trail*. Follow the blue blazes through a stand of white pine for 0.1 mi to Laurel Creek. Rock hop or wade because the footbridge has been washed out. (The USFS does not plan to replace the bridge due to budget constraints. During high water, another access is possible by entering the pine forest in the SW corner of WV-39/92 jct and hiking downstream 0.5 mi to cross Cochran Creek near its confluence with Laurel Creek.) Begin ascent on a well-graded treadway through a garden of violets and ferns — Christmas, sensitive, maidenhair, cinnamon, and hay-scented. Tall hemlocks drape over rhododendron before the trail enters an oak forest with mountain laurel. At 0.5 mi reach jct with a grassy road. Turn R and continue ascent. The air is filled with the medicinal odor of pennyroyal. Reach Middle Mtn crest line and wildlife waterhole at 1.5 mi and follow SW. Pass another wildlife waterhole and food plot at 2.5 mi, and at 3.5 mi arrive at a shelter. (There is a lack of water on the ridge crest.) At 4.4 mi reach a jct with the newly constructed Divide Rd (FR-790), which descends E for 3 mi to a gate at WV-92. The trail ascends 0.2 mi farther to the White Sulphur District where the trail number changes from 408 to 650. Backtrack, hike down the Divide Rd, or continue ahead. (*USGS-FS Maps:* Minnehaha Springs, Mountain Grove, Lake Sherwood)

▶ BEAVER CREEK AREA
(Pocahontas County)

Beaver Trail *(USFS #458)*

- LENGTH: 2.8 mi, rt

- DIFFICULTY: strenuous, 1165 ft elev gain

- FEATURE: panoramic view

- TRAILHEADS AND DETAILS: From the jct of Beaver Creek Rd (CO-21) and Pyles Mtn Rd (CO-21/4), at the E entrance of Watoga State Park, go N on Beaver Creek Rd for 1.8 mi to a curve L and a cabin R. (Request permission from the occupant of the cabin to park near the unmarked trail entrance.) Follow the private road, pass R of a house, reach the forest boundary, and cross Mary Sharp Run footbridge at 0.3 mi. Among the flora are hemlock, white pine, rhododendron, trailing arbutus, wintergreen, fern, oak, and maple. Cross the creek again at 0.7 mi, turn sharp L, and ascend steeply to crest of a ridge. Ascend steeply on switchbacks to the top of Beaver Lick Mtn (3645 ft; Beaver 2 on the topo map), site of a dismantled firetower, for a superb panoramic view at 1.4 mi. Backtrack. (A parking area is here, accessible during the hunting season on Beaver Lick Tower Rd [FR-343]. See Middle Mtn Area in Section 6, White Sulphur District.) (*USGS-FS Maps:* Marlinton, Lake Sherwood)

Beaver Creek Trail

- LENGTH: 0.4 mi

- DIFFICULTY: easy

- FEATURE: scenic

- TRAILHEADS AND DETAILS: At the Beaver Campground on the E side of the Watoga State Park, drive to campsite #27 and gate. (The trail formerly began here and went 2.1 mi to FR-343.) If the gate is open, drive upstream to a large meadow (a former light plane landing strip) in the Calvin Price State Forest. At 0.1 mi reach a jct, R, with *Jacob's Well Trail*, which goes W into Watoga State Park. After another 0.3 mi, park at the graveled cul-de-sac. Rock hop Beaver Creek and follow an old wagon road through a scenic and dark forest of hemlock, maple, and rhododendron for 0.4 mi to a jct with the *Allegheny Trail* R and L. (The *Allegheny Trail* is being relocated here to follow the *Jacob's Well Trail*.) A turn L on the *Allegheny Trail* is 1.3 mi up the hollow and ascends the headwaters to Beaver Lick Tower Rd (FR-343), the boundary of White Sulphur District. (*USGS-FS Map:* Lake Sherwood)

▶ HIGH ROCK AREA
(Pocahontas County)

High Rock Trail

• LENGTH: 3.2 mi, rt

• DIFFICULTY: moderate

• FEATURE: scenic

• TRAILHEADS AND DETAILS: From the Cranberry Mtn Visitor Center, drive on the Highlands Scenic Highway (WV-150) for 3.3 mi to a parking area, R. Trail enters open woods of maple, beech, and oak with a ground cover of ferns, trillium, blue bead lilies, and other wildflowers. Follow the High Rock ridge, cross an old timber road at 1.3 mi, and reach a precipitous rock formation for a splendid view at 1.6 mi. A chestnut fence is a protective barrier at a cliff. Views are of Bald Knob (4289 ft), directly ahead, and in the far distance, the Beaver Lick Mtn and the Allegheny Mtns. Backtrack. (*USGS-FS Map:* Hillsboro)

Cranberry Overlook Trail

- LENGTH: 0.5 mi, rt
- DIFFICULTY: easy
- FEATURE: cranberry glades

- TRAILHEAD AND DETAILS: From the *High Rock Trail* parking area described above, go N 1.5 mi to another parking area, R. Follow the sign and ascend through birch, maples, moosewood, and ferns to a spectacular view of the Cranberry Glades Botanical Area and Kennison Mtn range. Backtrack. (*USGS-FS Map:* Hillsboro)

▶ TEA CREEK RECREATION AREA
(Pocahontas County)

Here is a rich meadow filled with the spring fragrance of black locust and apple tree blossoms. Once an old logging camp with a church and school, it now is a campground with yellow buckeyes, elderberries, raspberries, and wild plums growing by the entrance. Canada lily (*Lilium canadense*) grows by the stream banks. The area is bordered on the E and the S by the splashing waters of Tea Creek and the trout-filled Williams River. Towering 1000 ft above it are Sugar Creek Mtn, Turkey Mtn, and Tea Creek Mtn. The campground is open all year with 29 camping sites, tables, vault toilets, and a hand pump for drinking water. In addition to the immediate trails, across the entrance road is the N terminus of the *North-South Trail* from the Gauley Ranger District.

- ACCESS: At the jct of WV-150 and WV-39/55, at the Cranberry Mtn Visitor Center, drive N on WV-150 for 13.3 mi to FR-86, turn W, and drive 1 mi to the campground entrance, R, over a cement bridge.

- SUPPORT FACILITIES: In Marlinton, 15.5 mi E on WV-150 and S on US-219, there are banks, shopping centers, restaurants, motels, and service stations.

Tea Creek Trail (6.4 mi; USFS #454); **Right Fork of Tea Creek Trail** (3 mi; USFS #453); **Tea Creek Mtn Trail** (4.6 mi; USFS #452); **Gauley Mtn Trail** (5.4 mi; USFS #438)

- LENGTH: 20.8 mi, ct

- DIFFICULTY: strenuous

- FEATURES: wildlife, rugged, wildflowers

- TRAILHEADS AND DETAILS: These trails may be overgrown in sections, as they are maintained usually every three to four years. They are described as a group for loop connections. There are three spur trails. The *Tea Creek Trail* was severely damaged by the 1981, 1984, and 1985 floods and sections have been washed out, rendering the trail impassable during wet periods. It is recommended by the district ranger that only experienced hikers undertake this route to the other trails. From the Tea Creek Campground parking area, follow the signs across the Tea Creek footbridge on an old RR grade. To the immediate L is the *Tea Creek Trail*. Follow upstream on a steep embankment through a forest of ironwood, maple, beech, and yellow birch on portions of an old RR grade. Wildflowers include purple-fringed orchids (*Habenaria psycodes*), wood betony, and yellow root. At 1 mi is an old beaver dam in a low area, partially washed out and easily flooded. At 1.5 mi is a flat area between the trail and the creek that makes for good campsites. Cross a number of washouts and at 2.5 mi reach a fork in the creek. To the R is the *Right Fork of the Tea Creek Trail*.

(The *Right Fork of the Tea Creek Trail* also follows portions of an old RR grade, crosses the winding fork a number of times since the damage by the flash floods, but specifically at 1.3 mi and 1.9 mi. There are sections of concentrated rhododendron and conifers. At 3.2 mi reach the jct with the *Tea Creek Mtn Trail*, R, and a 0.6 mi spur trail to the *Gauley Mtn Trail*, L. A loop on the 4.6 mi *Tea Creek Mtn Trail* will bring you back to the Tea Creek Campground after a total of 10.2 mi. The *Tea Creek Mtn Trail* and the *Gauley Mtn Trail* are described below.)

Continue up the *Tea Creek Trail*, crisscrossing the stream by rock hopping at least eight times, and since the flood, the washouts have added other crossings. At 4.5 mi is a marshy area. Leave the stream and ascend on an old RR grade switchback to pass a rock overhang formation at 5 mi. At 5.4 mi is a spur trail jct, R. (The 0.6-mi spur trail is a shortcut to the *Gauley Mtn Trail* described below.) Continue the ascent, cross drain, and climb strip mine bank to reach an Adirondack shelter for six persons at 5.7 mi. Bear, deer, wild turkey, hawks, owls, chipmunks, and red squirrels have been seen in this area. Follow an easy treadway with carpets of club mosses through red and Scotch pine to a small strip mine pond at 6.3 mi. In the pond are red-spotted newts *(Notophthalmus viridescens)*. Arrive at Sharp Knob Rd (FR-24) at 6.4 mi. (Left on FR-24 it is 7.1 mi to *Leatherwood Trail*, and R on FR-24 it is 0.2 mi to the entrance, R, of the *Gauley Mtn Trail*. Farther down the mountain on FR-24 it is 3.6 mi to US-219, 2.4 mi S of Slaty Fork.)

On the *Gauley Mtn Trail* climb an earthen barrier and follow an old RR grade through yellow birch, maple, and red spruce. The treadway is frequently wet. Elevation remains steady — between 4200 ft and 4400 ft for the entire distance. At 0.9 mi, R, is a jct with a 0.6 mi spur trail that leads R to *Tea Creek Trail*. Ahead, reach a wildlife field at 1 mi, at 2 mi, and at 3.7 mi. The wildflowers on the trail include wood shamrock, foamflower, blue bead lily, and painted trillium. Mosses, ferns, and club mosses are prominent. At 5 mi reach a jct with a spur trail, R. (The 0.6-mi spur trail is a connector to the Y of *Right Fork of Tea Creek Trail* and the *Tea Creek Mtn Trail*. Along its rocky treadway are wildflowers, thick moss, and streamlets. It also passes L of multiple beaver dams.) The *Gauley Mtn Trail* continues ahead, crosses a stream, and, at 5.4 mi, reaches a parking area at WV-150. From here it is 3.7 mi R (S) on WV-150 to the jct with the Williams Creek Rd (FR-86) and the Tea Creek Campground.

To hike the *Tea Creek Mtn Trail* follow the connecting spur and take a L at the jct with the *Right Fork of the Tea Creek Trail*. Cross a ravine and ascend on a rocky treadway with switchbacks. (At 0.3 mi is a blue-blazed spur trail, L, that leads out through an overgrown trail for 0.2 mi to WV-150. Its exit is by a large maple 50 ft S from the Little Laurel Overlook sign.)

Reach the crest of the mountain ridge in a forest of red spruce and yellow birch. Follow the high crest where a number of outcroppings provide scenic views of the Williams River drainage and peaks such as Big Spruce Knob and Red Spruce Knob. At 2.6 mi on a knoll begin a descent (1348 ft loss in elev) on the ridge for 2 mi to a jct with the *Williams River Trail* at 4.6 mi. To the R it is 0.1 mi to the Tea Creek Campground. The total distance for the longest loop is 16.8 mi. (*USGS-FS Maps:* Woodrow, Sharp Knob)

Williams River Trail (USFS #487)

- LENGTH: 3 mi

- DIFFICULTY: easy

- FEATURE: Williams River deadwater

- TRAILHEADS AND DETAILS: From the Tea Creek Campground follow the trail sign across the Tea Creek on a footbridge to a jct L with the *Tea Creek Trail* and a few yds farther with the *Tea Creek Mtn Trail* on an old RR grade. Pass through a hardwood forest and open fields on the N side of Williams River. At 1 mi pass under WV-150 bridge and reach a spur trail at 1.2 mi to a nearby parking area. Continue ahead and pass the William River deadwaters; cross Little Laurel Creek at 2.4 mi and enter Handley Public Hunting and Fishing Area to join Williams River Rd (CO-17/1) at 3 mi, the E terminus. Backtrack or use a vehicle shuttle by driving on FR-86 E from the campground to jct L with CO-17/4 and to CO-17/1 for a total of 9.2 mi. (*USGS-FS Map:* Woodrow)

▶ SHARP KNOB AREA
(Randolph and Webster Counties)

Leatherwood Trail (5 mi; USFS #434); Baldwin Trail (4.5 mi)

- LENGTH: 19 mi, rt

- DIFFICULTY: moderate to strenuous

- FEATURES: wildlife, isolated, scenic

- TRAILHEADS AND DETAILS: To reach these remote trailheads, drive 8.9 mi on FR-24 from the jct of US-219/FR-24 (7.2 mi N of US-219/WV-150 jct or 2.4 mi S of Slaty Fork post office on US-219). The road is severely eroded and rocky for its 3.8 mi ascent to the top of Gauley Mtn. Here it turns N and becomes generally level on a 4000-ft elev plateau, but it has large depressions and ruts. At 5.5 mi turn R at a sharp fork (FR-368 is L), pass R of Sharp Knob, and reach a forest gate at 6.9 mi. If the gate is unlocked, drive another 2 mi to *Leatherwood Trail* entrance, L.

Begin the unblazed and unmarked *Leatherwood Trail* at 4348 ft elev on a grassy old wagon road. The forest is lush, damp, and scenic with red spruce, yellow birch, rhododendron, mountain laurel, and ferns. At 1 mi pass through the first of four wildlife food fields. Deer, grouse, and wild turkey are often seen on the trail. At 1.6 mi the forest becomes more of hardwoods and hemlock, and the trail has more undulations. Leave the ridge for the S slope at 3.4 mi and pass under an abandoned power line at 3.5 mi. There is an intermittent spring, R, at 3.7 mi and nearby campsites in a maple forest. Here there is also a fork in the trail. Ahead is a 20-acre scenic field with waving grasses, yellow hawkweed, fireweed (*Epilobium angustifolium*), milkweed, self-heal, daisy, and silverberry, and the vanished homesite of Moriah Green at 4 mi. On the R trail fork (used frequently by ATVs) descend into the hollow, cross the left fork of Leatherwood Creek and terminate the trail at the forest boundary at 5 mi. (Private trail continues to strip mining roads.) Backtrack.

The unblazed and unmarked *Baldwin Trail* (also called *Ber-*

goo Creek Trail) is 0.9 mi farther N on FR-24, L. The trail is a former RR grade now usable, but rocky, for hiking and 4WD vehicles. Begin at 4229 ft elev and descend gradually to an elev of 3200 ft at the W terminus. The trail follows the N slope of a ridge. Wildlife is frequently seen, including bear and owls. The forest is chiefly hardwoods such as black cherry, yellow birch, and maple. At 2 mi, R, there is a row of iron stakes and other remnants of timber harvesting 80 years ago. Ferns, meadow parsnip, and white snakeroot are on the roadsides. At 4.5 mi reach the forest boundary. The old road continues ahead through private property to coal mines. Backtrack. (*USGS-FS Map:* Sharp Knob)

▶ SECTION 5: POTOMAC RANGER DISTRICT

Each district has its special significance, but none excels the 134,482 acres of mountains and meadows in the Potomac District. It is named for the Potomac River, whose North Fork of the South Branch flows NE through the Allegheny Mtns. Its N boundary is N of the Dolly Sods Wilderness Area. On the W the line follows the waters of Dry Fork to border both the Cheat and the Greenbrier districts. The S boundary is the West Virginia-Virginia state line and the George Washington National Forest, and the E border is along US-220 N from near Franklin to Petersburg. It is the only district in the MNF that had "pioneer zones." The three zones all occur in the Spruce Knob-Seneca Rocks National Recreation Area with a total acreage involving both public and private lands. Seneca Creek has 11,000 acres, 90 percent of which are under the administration of the USFS; Hopeville Gorge has 4500 acres with 84 percent under the control of the USFS, and Smoke Hole has 5800 acres with 40 percent under the control of the USFS. The new MNF Draft Plan does not include these pioneer zones, but does list them under a management policy that emphasizes a semiprimitive, nonmotorized recreational environment.

More than 140 mi of superb trails and 108 mi of winding forest service roads grace the district's priceless scenery from the state's highest point on Spruce Knob (4861 ft) to the pristine depths of Red Creek gorge in Dolly Sods. The district's natural monuments of sandstone such as Champe Rocks, Seneca Rocks, Eagle Rock, Chimney Rock, and Bear Rocks are only a few of the many geological formations. Within the district boundary, but not in the forest, are two commercially owned caverns — Seneca and Smoke Hole — both on WV-28. Between the forest properties are rich, cultivated bottom lands with crops, cattle, and sheep on manicured farms. Country stores, country roads, and country homes remind the hiker that those whom Jack Weller characterized as "yesterday's people" have a heritage as stable as the sandstone mountains.

The district has three recreation areas with campgrounds: Big Bend (45 units), Red Creek (12 units), and Spruce Knob (45 units). Seneca and Smoke Hole Campgrounds were destroyed in the November 1985 floods. There are no plans to reopen them. Big Bend Campground was isolated, thanks to severe access-road damage, but has reopened. None of these have electrical or water hookups, and Judy Springs is a walk-in primitive camp. For the purpose of trail grouping, trails are described below in three geographical areas: Seneca Rocks Area, Dolly Sods Area, and Spruce Knob Area. The longest trail is the 23.8 mi *North Fork Mtn Trail,* and the shortest is the 0.3 mi *Northland Loop Trail.*

- ADDRESS AND ACCESS: District Ranger, Potomac Ranger District, Rte 3, Box 240, Petersburg, WV 26847, tel: 304-257-4488. The location is 2 mi W of Petersburg on WV-28.

- MAPS: Numbers 22-28

▶ SENECA ROCKS NATIONAL RECREATION AREA (Grant and Pendleton Counties)

Within the area boundaries are Seneca Rocks Visitor Center on WV-28/4 at the Mouth of Seneca and two recreation areas — Big Bend Campground and Smoke Hole Picnic Area — both in the Smoke Hole Canyon on Smoke Hole Rd (CO-2).

"Seneca" is thought to be an Indian word meaning stone or rock.

Big Bend is a large horseshoe bend of the North Fork of the South Branch of the Potomac River in a tranquil meadow rimmed by a high ridge of Cave Mtn. There are 45 campsites with picnic tables, grills, and tent pads. Drinking water and flush toilets are available from mid-April to October 1. Fishing is allowed. *Big Ben Trail* loops around the campground. One easy entrance is on the grated service road at campsite #12, toward the river. Turn L and hike through a border of oak, walnut, sycamore, and papaw by the river. At 0.4 mi pass an old log cabin site; ahead, cross the campground road and ascend to a knob for scenic views of the river bend. Descend and pass by rock formations, enter the edge of a meadow, and return to the point of origin at 1.4 mi.

• ACCESS: From the jct of US-220 and Smoke Hole Rd (CO-2) in the community of Upper Tract, take Smoke Hole Rd for 4 mi to Smoke Hole Picnic Area and 5 mi farther to Big Bend Campground.

• SUPPORT FACILITIES: There is a general store at the jct of CO-2 and FR-79, 0.3 mi N of the Smoke Hole Campground, near St George's log-cabin Methodist Church, built in the 1850s. In Franklin, 16.5 mi farther S on US-220, are motels, restaurants, banks, service stations, and stores.

South Branch Trail *(USFS #539)*

• LENGTH: 3.5 mi

• DIFFICULTY: moderate

• FEATURES: scenic, history

• TRAILHEADS AND DETAILS: From Big Bend Campground drive S on Smoke Hole Rd for 5 mi to Smoke Hole Picnic Area, L. From the parking area walk back to the picnic entrance and ascend on E slope for 0.5 mi to the N slope of the mountain and cross an old wagon road at 0.6 mi. The area has oaks, hickory, dogwood, maple, beech, ferns, redbud, and wildflowers. At 1.2 mi reach opening swath from gas pipeline and a power line opening at 1.4 mi. Scenic views W of North Fork Mtn. Near a stand of red cedar and Virginia pine bloom blue viper's bugloss *(Echium vulgare)*. Reach an open farm road and sink hole at 1.8 mi. Cross an abandoned farm field and descend on a jeep road. At 2.5 mi turn L off the road and descend through mountain laurel and rhododendron to the river. Follow upstream on a rocky area, cross footbridge, and complete the loop trail at 3.5 mi in the picnic area. *(USGS-FS Map: Upper Tract)* (From Smoke Hole Picnic Area, S on Smoke Hole Rd for 0.5 mi, is the legendary Smoke Hole Cave used by Indian and early settlers for curing meats. The 0.3 mi climb is exceptionally steep and slippery. Take a flashlight.)

North Fork Mountain Trail *(23.8 mi; USFS #501)*

- CONNECTING TRAILS:
  Redman Run Trail (1.6 mi; USFS #507)
  Landes Trail (1.4 mi; USFS #502)

- TOTAL LENGTH: 26.8 mi

- DIFFICULTY: moderate to strenuous

- FEATURES: superb vistas, wildlife, wildflowers, Chimney Top

- TRAILHEADS AND DETAILS: If hiking the *North Fork Mtn Trail* from the S, park on the N side of US-33 at the top of North Fork Mtn (3592 ft), 5 mi E of Judy Gap and 9 mi W of Franklin. The district's longest trail follows the E and leeward slope of North Fork Mtn near the ridge line, except occasional sections on the ridge top. For 4.6 mi the trail is on sections of private land. At the N end the trail leaves the ridge and rapidly descends NE to FR-74. It is generally rocky through a hardwood forest with scattered stands of Virginia pine and does not have any springs or streams on its immediate route. Scenery is more than spectacular.

After 0.4 mi the mossy jeep road through hardwoods becomes a footpath. Excellent views of Germany Valley and

Spruce Mtn are L. (Germany Valley was the site of Hinkle's Fort, built in 1761–62. It was the last defense post after the Shawnee Indians had destroyed Fort Upper Tract and Fort Seybert in April 1758.) At 2.1 mi the foot trail becomes a woods road, which is less rocky. The road becomes more rocky and wider at 2.9 mi. At 3.3 mi pass under a power line; timbering is noticeable on the L for the next 0.7 mi. At 4 mi are large chestnut oaks and black birches with striped maples as part of the understory. Reach jct at 4.3 mi; timber road L descends 2 mi to Germany Valley and the timber road R descends 2.3 mi to Reeds Creek Rd (CO-8). (A spring, L, is 0.8 mi down the mountain on this road.)

A clearing and turnaround is at 4.5 mi and a hang-gliding ramp is on the W side of the ridge line. (Vehicle access to this point is from a private road on the W slope.) The trail becomes a footpath; skirt E of a rocky knob on private lands. Trail is well designed and naturally decorated with ferns, mosses, lichens, spring beauty (*Claytonia*), mountain laurel, and blueberries. Vista at 5.8 mi. White markers on L at 7.5 mi indicate development on private property, a disturbing obstruction to the amenity of the trail. Ascend steeply through dense area of mountain laurel, Virginia pine, wintergreen, and bracken. Overview at 8.2 mi with superb view of Seneca Rocks. Skirt E of High Knob, continue through open woods and for the only time on the trail cross the ridge line and descend slightly on the W slope to a saddle at 9.5 mi. Here the trail is an old woods road that leads into a jeep road. Ascend steeply and at 10 mi reach pipeline swath and gravel road. At 10.5 mi pass a radio tower, the highest point on the trail (3795 ft), and descend on FR-79 to reentry of forest at 11.9 mi. (FR-79 is passable for passenger cars. It is 3.5 mi farther down the mountain on FR-79 to Smoke Hole Rd for exit N on FR-74 to WV-28 or S on CO-2 to US-220.) A large rock formation and numerous wildflowers, including thousands of spring beauty that bloom in April, are at 14.2 mi. An abandoned trail (1.5 mi *Kimble Trail*) is jct R at 14.3 mi. Ascend to ridge at 14.8 mi. Pass huge ant hills at 14.9 mi. The trail forks at 15.7 mi with *Redman Run Trail*, R.

(At first the *Redman Run Trail* descends gradually but becomes steep near the N terminus for 1.6 mi to FR-74 [also called Smoke Hole Rd]. Here are a hikers' sign and USFS boundary markers in a young forest of ash and locust. It is 4.7 mi from here N on FR-74 to the N trailhead of *Landes Trail*, and 2 mi farther to N trailhead of the *North Fork Mtn Trail*.)

Continue ahead, pass E of large rock formation, descend below 3000 ft elev, then begin a steep ascent at 1.6 mi and reach a rhododendron thicket at 17.2 mi near the ridge line. There is a large section of wild azaleas here. At 18.7 mi, L, is a huge honeycombed sandstone wall with two other rock monoliths. Overlook is impressive. Pass through open hardwood forest and weave from E slope to ridge for over 1 mi. Reach fork with *Landes Trail*, R, at 20 mi.

(The 1.4 mi *Landes Trail* descends on grassy switchbacks and is steep in spots on rocky treadway set in moss. Reach the N terminus in oaks and stands of maple on FR-74 near a hikers' sign. It is 2 mi N on FR-74 to N jct of the *North Fork Mtn Trail*.)

Ahead on the *North Fork Mtn Trail* reach the ridge top and a lookout at 20.3 mi. At 21 mi arrive at a small plateau. At 21.1 mi, a 0.1 mi spur trail is L to Chimney Top, with exceptional scenic views of Fore Knobs and the Dolly Sods Wilderness. Back on the main trail, descend by switchbacks, cross large rock formation in steep area at 21.5 mi. Pass a lookout at 22 mi for view of New Creek Mtn and NE canyon below. Continue on switchbacks and reach FR-74 at 23.8 mi. It is 0.3 mi N on FR-74 to WV-28. The November 1985 flood washed away the Smoke Hole Rd (FR-244) bridge at the WV-28 jct. An inquiry should be made to the district office to determine when a new bridge will be open for vehicular traffic. (*USGS-FS Maps:* Circleville, Franklin, Upper Tract, Hopeville, Petersburg West)

Seneca Rocks West Side Trail *(1.7 mi)*

• LENGTH: 2.4 mi rt

• DIFFICULTY: strenuous to easy

• FEATURES: impressive vistas, history

• TRAILHEADS AND DETAILS: This new trail replaces the old trail that followed an old woods road around the S face and up a steep scramble trail near the E face of Seneca Rocks. Parts of the old trail, including the swinging bridge, were washed away in the 1985 flood. The Seneca Rocks Visitor Center was also damaged by the flood, but it has been restored, and a campground has been constructed near the visitor center. From the visitor center, the *Seneca Rocks West Side Trail* leads to a new swinging bridge to cross the north fork of the south branch of the Potomac River. From there it meanders and ascends to a viewing platform near the N peak of Seneca Rocks. There are several signs along the way that explain the natural feature and the history of the area. The trail is designed for everyone who desires a safe climb (900 ft elev change) to the top of Seneca Rocks. (Seneca Rocks is popular for rock climbers. Hikers should stay away from the climbing areas. There have been fatalities.)

The Seneca Rocks Visitor Cneter provides an information staff, exhibits, films, and programs on the Seneca Rocks and the nearby area. A picnic area is also provided. Outdoor display markers record some of the geological history of West Virginia. For example, it is estimated that the state was at the bottom of a vast sea 450 million years ago. Layer upon layer of silt, sand, and gravel became 50,000 ft deep. Such compressions became beds of rock. About 250 million years ago the pressure from the earth lifted the former sea's area to some of the highest mountains in North America. Rivers carved the uplifted plains into valleys and ridges so that what we see today are the foundations of the original mountains. In the process some hard ridges of sandstone, such as Seneca Rocks, were slower in wearing down.

• ADDRESS AND ACCESS: Seneca Rocks Visitor Center, Seneca Rocks, WV 26884, tel: 304-567-2827. The center is open Memorial Day through Labor Day, M–F 9 A.M.–6 P.M. and year-round Sat–Sun, 9 A.M.–4 P.M. It is located on WV-28/4, near its jct with US-33 at Seneca Rocks.

▶ SPRUCE KNOB NATIONAL RECREATION AREA
(Randolph and Pendleton Counties)

Within this system are 17 individual trails, all of which connect with at least one other trail, for a network of over 60 mi. The two longest trails — the 7.9 mi *Allegheny Mtn Trail* and the 8.3 mi *Seneca Creek Trail* — could be longer, but a chunk of private property limits their continuity. The trails are described in groups for loop options, and the Spruce Knob Lake Campground is chosen as a main base for camping. It has 45 sites, some of which are slanted on a hillside and require prop blocks for RVs. There are vault toilets, hand water pumps, picnic tables, and grills. The season is March 1 through December. Nearby is the 25-acre Spruce Knob Lake (3840 ft), the highest lake in the state. Only campers may moor their nonmotorized boats on the lake. Swimming is prohibited. Trout, bass, and sunfish are stocked. Across the road from the campground entrance is the 0.5 mi *Short Trail*, a walk-through in a beechnut grove and past a row of red spruce and other conifers to FR-112. (Across the road is the *Gatewood Trail*, an interpretive site that is in the process of being refurbished and updated.) Backtrack or make a 1 mi loop, L, to return on the road.

The area's northernmost campground, Seneca Recreation Area on Whites Run Rd (CO-33/3), 2.5 mi W of Onega off US-33, was destroyed in the November 1985 floods. A primitive walk-in campground (Judy Springs) is on the *Seneca Creek Trail* and is described below.)

• ACCESS: To reach Spruce Knob Lake Recreation Area from the N, take Whitmer Rd (CO-29) S from US-33 (1 mi W of

Harmon) to Whitmer for 8.3 mi. From Whitmer continue S on Whitmer Rd for 10.3 mi and turn L on FR-1 for 2.5 mi to the campground. A route from the S is on Sawmill Run Rd (CO-28/10), (2.8 mi S of Cherry Grove on WV-28). Ascend on a crooked road for 8.6 mi to FR-112 and follow the campground signs for another 1.3 mi. From the E, take Briery Gap Rd (CO-33/4 at Gateway General Store, 1 mi N of Judy Gap) off US-33, for 2.5 mi to FR-112 and follow the campground signs for another 14 mi.

• SUPPORT FACILITIES: The nearest stores for groceries, gasoline, and hunting and fishing licenses are Sites Community Store in Whitmer, 12.8 mi N (tel: 304-227-9928), and Gateway General Store on US-33, 16.5 mi E on FR-112 (tel: 304-567-2810).

Big Run Trail *(3.1 mi; USFS #527);* **North Prong Trail** *(2.8 mi; USFS #528);* **Leading Ridge Trail** *(5.2 mi; USFS #557);* **Elza Trail** *(2 mi; USFS #556);* **Bee Trail** *(1.9 mi; USFS #555)*

• TOTAL LENGTH: 15 mi

• DIFFICULTY: moderate

• FEATURES: wildlife, wildflowers, bird-watching

• TRAILHEADS AND DETAILS: These trails are grouped because of their circuit potential. (Footbridges may be washed away by flash floods, but the Gandy Creek can be waded in normal conditions.) From the Spruce Knob Lake Campground, drive E on FR-1 for 0.6 mi to jct with FR-112, turn L, and drive another 0.5 mi to a side road, L. Here is the SE terminus of *Big Run Trail,* L, and the S terminus of the *Allegheny Mtn Trail,* R. The *Big Run Trail* descends NW to its terminus at Gandy Creek and Whitmer Rd. (The 7.2-mi *Allegheny Mtn Trail* follows N on a gated wildlife road along the ridge line. It is described below.)

On the *Big Run Trail* descend gradually through a forest of tall yellow birch, beech, cherry, and red and striped maple. At 0.2 mi a drain begins on the L; it becomes the S tributary of Big Run. At 1.5 mi the *North Prong Trail* connects from the R, near the confluence with Big Run, in a grassy meadow of old apple trees and wildflowers. Follow the *Big Run Trail* downstream partly on an old RR grade for another 1.6 mi and rock hop the stream frequently. A number of good campsites are along the way; others have been washed away by the floods. Exit the forest at 2.9 mi in a wildlife grazing field. Cross the Gandy Creek footbridge, or wade to the parking area on Whitmer Rd (CO-29) at 3.1 mi. Backtrack or, if using a shuttle, it is 6.1 mi S on Whitmer Rd and FR-1 and 112 to the point of origin. If a loop is preferred, some of the options are described below.

From the parking area walk N on Whitmer Rd (downstream) for 0.4 mi to the entrance of the *Leading Ridge Trail,* R. Cross the Gandy Creek footbridge, or wade and reach a gated wildlife road at 0.1 mi. Ascend on an excellent treadway through a fine forest of cherry, maple, and hemlock to a horseshoe curve at 0.9 mi. In the summer, fritillary butterflies are seen on roadside banks with wildflowers. At 2 mi is a grazing field. Continue a mild ascent through open woods predominated by beech to another wildlife plot and intersection with the *Elza Trail* and *Bee Trail* at 2.9 mi. Deer are likely to be seen here. If you turn R on the *Elza Trail,* descend on a wildlife road through an open forest and grazing field for 0.5 mi to its E terminus and jct with the *North Prong Train* at a vehicle wooden bridge; turn R, downstream, and go 1.2 mi farther to jct with, and return on, the *Big Run Trail* to complete a loop of 9.6 mi.

(To the L of the *Leading Ridge Trail,* the 1.5 mi W section of the *Elza Trail* and its connecting 1.9 mi *Bee Trail* descend to Whitmer Rd.) If you continue ahead on the *Leading Ridge Trail,* ascend through a hardwood forest for 2.3 mi to the *Allegheny Mtn Trail,* turn R on the *Allegheny Mtn Trail* for 2.8 mi, and return to the point of origin for a loop of 11.5 mi.

A third loop option that is also 9.6 mi is to walk downstream on the Whitmer Rd for 1.8 mi from the *Big Run Trail* parking area to the W terminus of the *Elza Trail,* R. Cross a footbridge over or wade across the Gandy Creek, and enter a grassy area with hay-scented ferns for 0.1 mi. Cross a small stream at 0.5 mi in a hollow of hardwoods, ferns, and club mosses. Pass the headwaters; at 1.5 mi jct with the *Bee Trail,* L, immediately before a jct with the *Leading Ridge Trail*. From here follow the *Elza Trail* S for 0.5 mi to the *North Prong Trail* and the *Big Run Trail* as described in the first option.

A fourth circuit option of 10.7 mi is to walk downstream on Whitmer Rd 2.5 mi from the *Big Run Trail* parking area to the W terminus of the *Bee Trail,* R. Cross a footbridge over or wade across the Gandy Creek; enter a meadow of ferns and wildflowers before passing through a red spruce grove at 0.2 mi. Ascend on the R side of the cascading Bee Run. At 0.8 mi leave the old woods road and turn R on a footpath across a ridge slope. Pass stream headwaters at 1.1 mi and jct with the *Elza Trail* and *Leading Ridge Trail* at 1.9 mi. From here follow the *Elza Trail* S to the *North Prong Trail* and the *Big Run Trail*.

The use of these trails and Whitmer Rd, which parallels Gandy Creek, is enhanced because the rushing Gandy Creek has rainbow and brook trout, meadows filled with warblers, sparrows, and small game fowl, and a wide range of plant life. In July, hundreds of monarch butterflies are on the milkweeds and edible, ripe pome-red berries droop from the shadbush *(Amelanchier arborea)*.

If the 2.8 mi *North Prong Trail* is chosen for a short loop after the 1.5 mi descent on the *Big Run Trail*, turn R at the meadow jct. Pass through 100 yds of ferns, grasses, and wildflowers such as bee balm, sunflowers, thistle, fleabane, asters, wild basil, and musk mallow *(Malva moschata)*. Cross Big Run a number of times and pass through other small meadows. Excellent spaces for campsites. At 1.2 mi is jct, L, with the *Elza Trail*. (The *Elza Trail* crosses a vehicle wooden bridge to ascend to and cross *Leading Ridge Trail* described above.) The *North Prong Trail* continues upstream on the wildlife road and at 1.9 mi veers away from the stream for an easy ascent to the *Allegheny Mtn Trail* at 2.8 mi. A return, R, on the *Allegheny Mtn Trail* for 2.3 mi to the point of origin on FR-112 is a 6.6 mi loop. *(USGS-FS Maps:* Spruce Knob, Whitmer)

Allegheny Mountain Trail *(7.9 mi; USFS #532)*

- CONNECTING TRAILS:
  Tom Lick Trail (1.1 mi; USFS #559)
  (North Prong Trail, 2.8 mi; USFS #528)
  (Leading Ridge Trail, 5.2 mi; USFS #557)
  Swallow Rock Trail (3.2 mi; USFS #529)
  Bear Hunter Trail (1 mi; USFS #531)
  Spring Ridge Trail (3.2 mi; USFS #561)
  (Horton-Horserock Trail, 6.2 mi; USFS #530)
  Little Allegheny Mountain Trail (4.5 mi; USFS #535)

- TOTAL LENGTH: 32.1 mi

- DIFFICULTY: moderate to strenuous

- FEATURES: scenic, wildlife, plant life

- TRAILHEADS AND DETAILS: The directions to the S terminus
of the *Allegheny Mtn Trail* from the Spruce Knob Lake Campground are the same as described above for the *Big Run Trail.*
Follow the *Allegheny Mtn Trail* by the gated wildlife road
through beech, yellow birch, cherry, red maple, and oak with
slight elev change from 4000 ft. A wildlife field, R, is at 0.9 mi,
and a wildlife road, L, is at 1.6 mi. Autumn colors are outstanding. At 2.1 mi is jct, R, with the *Tom Lick Trail.*
  (The *Tom Lick Trail* descends 1.1 mi on the N side of the Tom
Lick Run to Seneca Creek, where it crosses on a footbridge to
a jct with the *Seneca Creek Trail.*)
  Ahead on the *Allegheny Mtn Trail* reach a fork and jct with the
signed *North Prong Trail,* L, at 2.3 mi in a grassy open area.
Water sources are near on both sides of the ridge.
  (The 2.8 mi *North Prong Trail* passes through a wildlife clear-
ing by a grove of red pine, descends, and connects with the *Elza
Trail* and the *Big Run Trail* described above.)
  Continuing on the *Allegheny Mtn Trail* reach a jct with the
Leading Ridge Trail, L, at 2.8 mi.
  (The 5.2 mi *Leading Ridge Trail* is a wildlife road that follows
a ridge line to a wildlife clearing at 2.3 mi for an intersection
with the *Elza Trail* and the *Bee Trail.* It continues through the

clearing and descends to Camp Seven Hollow for an exit at the Gandy Creek and Whitmer Rd as described above.)

At 3.3 mi on the *Allegheny Mtn Trail* reach a clearing and crossing with the signed *Swallow Rock Trail.*

(The 3.2 mi *Swallow Rock Trail* goes R for 0.9 mi to the *Seneca Creek Trail*, and L for 2.3 mi to the Gandy Creek and Whitmer Rd. West on the trail descend through a hardwood forest to the drainage of Swallow Rock Run, where a breeze is almost constant. At 1.5 mi pass L of a N tributary. Bordering the trail are bellflowers, white snakeroot, ferns, and club mosses. Rock hop the stream at 2.1 mi, and turn sharp R into a good campsite area. Ascend through a rhododendron stand and descend to Whitmer Rd on the N side of the road bridge at a parking area. This area is part of the Gandy Creek Experimental Stream Improvement Project and is 4 mi S of Whitmer. It is 1.4 mi N of the *Bee Trail* entrance, another possibility for a circuit hike.)

Continue N on the *Allegheny Mtn Trail* on the leeward side of the ridge and reach a clearing, L, and jct, R, with *Bear Hunter Trail* at 4.7 mi.

(The *Bear Hunter Trail* descends E through a remarkably open forest of tall cherry, beech, maple, and ash for 0.3 mi. Large patches of blue cohosh are part of the sparse ground cover. Cross a small stream at 0.8 mi and reach Judy Springs Walk-in Campground and *Seneca Creek Trail* at 1 mi. A circuit trail of 10.9 mi can be made here by following *Seneca Creek Trail* S to *Tom Lick Trail* and back to the *Allegheny Mtn Trail* for a return to the point of origin.

Ahead on the *Allegheny Mtn Trail* ascend gradually to a higher ridge level. At 5 mi is a view, R, of Spruce Mtn, and at 5.4 mi is a thick grazing field, L, with wild basil, butter-and-eggs, yarrow, and silverberry. Wild turkey, deer, grouse, and raccoon are often heard or sighted in this area. Exit from the forest to the end of the road at 6.2 mi in a grazing field where the signed *Spring Ridge Trail* (wildlife road) is L and the *Allegheny Mtn Trail* descends steeply through the L side of the field.

(The *Spring Ridge Trail* has an easy treadway and passes through two grazing plots in the first 1.2 mi before descending on the N slope of the ridge. Curve R at 2 mi from the ridge line and curve L at 2.2 mi for a continuation of the N slope. A drain begins on the R. At 2.6 mi curve L into a scenic hollow and cross a small drain where hemlocks are part of the hardwood forest. Reach a locked post gate and the Whitmer Rd at 3.2 mi. From here it is 0.8 mi N on Whitmer Rd to the *Horton-Horserock Trail* W entrance and 2 mi N to the town of Whitmer.)

(The 6.2 mi *Horton-Horserock Trail* descends W for 2.4 mi to the Whitmer Rd and E for 1.1 mi to the *Seneca Creek Trail*. A separate description is detailed below.)

Although 4WDs have been using the *Allegheny Mtn Trail* from its S entrance, their use is more noticeable here as the *Allegheny Mtn Trail* becomes more of a footpath. Descend into a saddle and ascend to the ridge line through a hardwood forest and reach a jct, R, with the *Little Allegheny Mtn Trail* at 7.9 mi. To avoid trespass problems on the *Allegheny Mtn Trail* to a private property road, take the *Little Allegheny Mtn Trail* to Whites Run Rd (CO-33/3).

The *Little Allegheny Mtn Trail* follows a ridge line 2 mi to a gas pipeline crossing. Here are vistas of the Seneca Creek Valley and Kisamore Mtn (E) and the Dry Fork area (W). Follow the ridge, gradually descending through scenic sections of mountain laurel, Virginia and white pine, birch, oak, hemlock, huckleberry, wintergreen, and wild orchids. A number of outcrops on the ridge spine provide scenic views of the valleys. At 2.5 mi is one of a number of small saddles. On the R, and far below, the sound of Seneca Creek is audible. Continue the descent and begin the first of four switchbacks in groves of rhododendron at 3.3 mi. At 4.4 mi is jct with a 60-yd spur trail R to Seneca Creek Rd (FR-1580) and a huge (9 ft in circumference) apple tree. Turn L and cross a footbridge over Whites Run to Whites Run Rd at 4.5 mi. A parking area is 0.1 mi downstream. It is 1.6 mi from here downstream to the former Seneca Creek Campground and another 0.5 mi to US-33. The nearest store for groceries, gasoline, and a post office is Phares Store in Onego, 2.7 mi E (from the former campground) on US-33 (tel: 304-567-2285). (*USGS-FS Maps*: Spruce Knob, Whitmer, Onego)

Horton-Horserock Trail (USFS #530)

- LENGTH: 6.2 mi

- DIFFICULTY: strenuous

- FEATURES: scenic, history, nature study

- TRAILHEADS AND DETAILS: The trail receives its name from its termini — the NW trailhead on Whitmer Rd near the community of Horton (2839 ft) and the SE terminus with *Huckleberry Trail* on the W slope of Horse Rock (4536 ft). It connects with a number of trails for a wide range of loop choices, and its variety of scenery is impressive.

For the W trailhead, park in the parking area on Whitmer Rd, 1 mi S of Whitmer at the Potomac Cooperative Wildlife Management Area sign. Follow an old wagon road into the forest, remain R of the Lower Two Spring Run, and cross over an earthen barricade. The forest is mainly beech, maple, and birch with a few hemlocks. Rock hop the stream at 1 mi and again at 1.1 mi. Curve more to the SE at the confluence of the two runs at 1.5 mi and again at 1.1 mi. For the next 0.5 mi the stream disappears twice underground. The area is exceptionally scenic in the autumn; good campsites at 2.1 mi. Ascend steeply on rocky and eroded treadway to jct with *Allegheny Mtn Trail* at 2.4 mi. (It is 6.4 mi R on the *Allegheny Mtn Trail* to FR-112 and 6 mi L to Whites Run Rd. The correct distance for the Judy Springs sign is 2.6 mi.) Continue E at the sign and descend 800 ft in elev for 1.1 mi on the E slope of the ridge to Seneca Creek. On the descent are scattered views of Spruce Mtn range. (The 1968 Whitmer topo map has an incorrect trail drawing of this descent.) Cross Seneca Creek on a footbridge (rock hop or wade if the footbridge is washed away) and jct with the *Seneca Creek Trail* on an old RR grade. (To the L it is 3.3 mi to the N terminus of *Seneca Creek Trail* and to the R it is 5 mi to the S terminus at FR-112.) The *Horton-Horserock Trail* turns R and on the *Seneca Creek Trail* for 0.2 mi before ascending L at the beautiful Upper Seneca Creek Falls. (Across the footbridge and upstream it is 1.4 mi to the Judy Springs camping area.) Climb the bank to an old RR grade, turn R, and go 0.1

mi to a sharp turn L, upstream. Ascend in an open hollow of maple and a treadway of wood shamrock. Large black cohosh have floral stalks like a candelabra. At 4.1 mi turn R and follow cairns through a grazing field that has an immense display of summer wildflowers. Enter an open forest on a rocky treadway and ascend to a jct, R, with the *Judy Springs Trail* at 4.9 mi. (The *Judy Springs Trail* descends 0.7 mi to Judy Springs Campground and connects with the *Seneca Creek Trail*.) Continue ascent on an old rocky road to the *Lumberjack Trail*, R, at 5.6 mi, and arrive at the trail's S terminus with a jct to the *Huckleberry Trail* at 6.2 mi. (*The Lumberjack Trail* is an old RR grade that has its S terminus at FR-112, and the *Huckleberry Trail* ascends to the ridge top of Spruce Mtn and has a S terminus at the parking lot on Spruce Knob. Both trails are described below.) (*USGS-FS Maps:* Whitmer, Onego)

Seneca Creek Trail *(5 mi; USFS #515)*

- CONNECTING TRAILS:
  (*Tom Lick Run Trail*, 1.1 mi; USFS #559)
  (*Swallow Rock Trail*, 3.2 mi; USFS #529)
  Judy Springs Trail (0.7 mi; USFS #512)
  (*Bear Hunter Trail*, 1 mi; USFS #531)
  (*Horton-Horserock Trail*, 6.2 mi; USFS #530)

- TOTAL LENGTH: 17.2 mi

- DIFFICULTY: easy to strenuous

- FEATURES: scenic, waterfalls, nature study, Judy Springs, RR history

- TRAILHEADS AND DETAILS: From the Spruce Knob Lake Campground drive 2.6 mi E on FR-1 and FR-112 to the parking area on L. Before beginning the hike it is advisable to read the information board at the trail entrance. You will be entering a previous USFS Seneca Creek Pioneer Zone that provides only nonmotorized recreation facilities. The former 13 mi *Seneca Creek Trail* now dead-ends after 5 mi at the *Horton-Horserock Trail* jct. The Lower Falls of Seneca are on private property. The owner has requested that his name and address not be published, but you may contact the district ranger for information on how to receive permission for the entire hike. All of the footbridges and parts of the trail were washed away in the 1985 floods. There are no immediate plans to restore all the bridges. Hiking will require rock hopping or wading.

From the parking area pass through a gated forest road; descend gently through a forest of hardwood and hemlock. Serviceberry and gooseberry are on the road banks. Cross Trussel Run, a streamlet at 0.5 mi, pass an old beaver dam, and at 0.9 mi jct L with the moderate 1.1 mi *Tom Lick Run Trail*. (The *Tom Lick Run Trail* ascends to connect with the *Allegheny Mtn Trail*.) At 2.1 mi cross Beech Run, another small stream. Jct with the 3.2 mi *Swallow Rock Trail* L at 2.2 mi. (The *Swallow Rock Trail* is a moderate trail that ascends 0.9 mi to cross the *Allegheny Mtn Trail* and descend to Whitmer Rd.) Cross Seneca Creek on a footbridge (or rock hop) at 3 mi and reach Judy Springs Campground at 3.4 mi. Facilities here include an effusive hand water pump and multiple gravel paths to campsites in the meadow near old apple trees and in the forest. Across the footbridge is the *Judy Springs Trail*, L, and a 300-ft path, R, to Judy Springs, a gushing fount of water from the rocky mountainside in a cove of hemlock, birch, fern, and liverwort. (Judy is the surname of pioneer families who first lived in the area.)

(The *Judy Springs Trail* ascends through the forest for 0.2 mi, over a stile to a grazing field, and follows cairns up the mountainside to the NE corner. This is an exceptionally resplendent area any season of the year. In the summer there are St John's wort, daisy, red clover, wild basil, deptford pink, birdfoot's-trefoil *[Lotus corniculatus]*, and bittersweet nightshade *[Solanum dulcamara]*. Song sparrows, indigo buntings, and fritillary butterflies frequent the field. Reach the end of the trail at 0.7 mi at a jct with the *Horton-Horserock Trail* described above. Backtrack or turn L on the *Horton-Horserock Trail* and descend for 1.2 mi, connect with the *Seneca Creek Trail,* and hike upstream for 1.4 mi to the campground for a loop of 3.3 mi.)

At the hand water pump continue downstream on the *Seneca*

Creek Trail and jct with the *Bear Hunter Trail,* L, at 3.5 mi. (The
1 mi *Bear Hunter Trail* is a strenuous ascent by a small stream
through hemlock and birch to the *Allegheny Mtn Trail* described
above.) Continue on the old RR grade by cascades and an ideal
bathing pool. Cross a footbridge (or rock hop) at 3.7 mi and
again at 4.1 mi. As the canyon becomes narrower, the number
of echoes of waterfalls increases. Birch, beech, and rhododendron cover the canyon walls. At 4.8 mi arrive at the most
spectacular section of the trail, where it spans a tier of the
Upper Falls of Seneca. Across the creek is a R jct with the
Horton-Horserock Trail, but the L jct is 0.2 mi farther downstream on the *Seneca Creek Trail.*

(The SE section of *Horton-Horserock Trail* ascends a steep
bank at the bridge and goes to its terminus at the *Huckleberry
Trail,* and the NW section crosses Seneca Creek and ascends to
cross the *Allegheny Mtn Trail* as described above.)

Continue downstream on the *Seneca Creek Trail* on the old
RR grade. Campsites are frequent. Seneca Creek has native
trout and is a desirable area for anglers. At 5.3 mi cross the
creek where once a RR trestle flanked the canyon wall. Cross
the cascading creek again at 5.4 mi and twice more on the
gradual descent to the forest boundary and N terminus at
8.3 mi. Backtrack. (*USGS-FS Maps:* Spruce Knob, Whitmer,
Onego)

Whispering Spruce Trail (0.5 mi); **Huckleberry Trail** (3.2 mi;
USFS #533); **Lumberjack Trail** (3.3 mi; USFS #534)

- LENGTH: 7 mi, ct

- DIFFICULTY: easy to moderate

- FEATURES: panoramic, heath meadows, nature study, RR
history

- TRAILHEADS AND DETAILS: Spruce Knob (4861 ft), the state's
highest point, is 8.3 mi E from the Spruce Knob Lake Campground and 11.7 mi W from US-33 near Judy Gap. From the
parking area follow the signs on the interpretive loop *Whisper-*

ing Spruce Trail to the observation tower. From the deck are views E to North Fork Mtn range and 38 mi beyond to the Shenandoah Mtn range. The N views include Picea Peak (4613 ft), Little Middle Mtn, and Roaring Plains. Scenery to the W spans the Middle Mtn range, Cunningham Knob (4450 ft), Spruce Knob Lake, Big Run Grazing Area, Yokum Knob (4300 ft), Pharis Knob (4674 ft), and numerous spur ridges and valleys. The S views are to Hunting Ground Mtn and the Big Mtn range. Continue on the trail through spruce whose limbs are missing on the W side because of the constant and often harsh winds. There are magnificent views at the outcroppings. Rose azalea, fireweed, pink lady's slipper, mountain ash, deciduous hollies, and Minnie-bush *(Menziesia pilosa)* provide seasonal beauty. Return to the parking area.

To hike the *Huckleberry Trail* begin at the N side of the parking area at the trail sign. The treadway is rocky through spruce, mountain laurel, bleeding heart, huckleberry, and Canada dogwood *(Cornus canadensis)*. At 0.2 mi is a faint trail, R, with white blazes, for 150 yds to a spring. Excellent vistas are at 1 mi and a heath meadow continues for 0.3 mi. At 1.9 mi are remains of a small plane crash, L. Shift more to the W side of Spruce Mtn and enter another heath meadow of ferns, grasses, and huckleberry with views W at 2.6 mi. At 3.2 mi arrive at the N trail terminus and jct with *Horton-Horserock Trail*.

If hiking the *Lumberjack Trail,* descend on the *Horton-Horserock Trail* for 0.6 mi to jct. On the rocky and eroded descent, pass an open field with a large patch of false hellebore *(Veratrum viride)*, a poisonous plant that according to legend was used to select Indian chiefs. If a man survived its consumption, he was considered to be a potential chief. Turn L at the *Lumberjack Trail* jct. (The *Horton-Horserock Trail* continues NW to a jct with the *Judy Springs Trail* and Seneca Creek, and on to the *Allegheny Mtn Trail* to end at Whitmer Rd, as described above.) The *Lumberjack Trail* follows an old RR grade its entire length along the W slope of Spruce Mtn. After 0.4 mi you will notice old RR crossties in a wet area, the first of 12 places, including 1 mi, 1.7 mi, 2 mi, and 2.6 mi. There is some evidence of RR trestles. For example, at 1.5 mi yellow birch grows from a rotted log foundation. The RR banks must be followed in a number of areas because of the continuous drainage from the mountainside. Deer and wild turkey are frequently sighted in the hardwood forest of birch and maple. Mountain lettuce (*Saxifraga micranthidifolia*) and orchids in the *Habenaria* genus grow here. Cross the last streamlet at 2.9 mi and arrive at FR-112, the S terminus, at 3.3 mi. From here it is 5.2 mi L on FR-112 and 104 to Spruce Knob parking area and 0.6 mi R to the parking area of *Seneca Creek Trail*. (*USGS-FS Maps:* Spruce Knob, Whitmer)

Back Ridge Trail (USFS #526)

- LENGTH: 4.6 mi

- DIFFICULTY: strenuous, elev gain 1451 ft

- FEATURES: scenic, nature study

- TRAILHEADS AND DETAILS: Isolated from the connecting trails described above, the N terminus of *Back Ridge Trail* is 4.1 mi S of the Spruce Knob Lake area using FR-112 and Sawmill Run Rd (CO-28/10). The S terminus is on the W side of the bridge over Big Run on WV-28. Between the termini it is 0.5 mi E on WV-28 and 5.8 mi N on Sawmill Run Rd. If hiking S, park across the road from private property and a Woodlands Institute sign (3963 ft). The trail, overgrown in sections, follows the ridge line along the USFS boundary with some views E. At 1 mi begin a slight descent and skirt the W edge of the ridge. The Big Run Falls, deep in the canyon, can be heard to the R, at 1.5 mi. Follow portions of logging roads with mountain laurel and new growth of oaks and beech. Begin a descent, at first gradually, then steeply, on rocky treadway and reach Big Run at 3.1 mi. Rock hop and jct with old RR grades damaged by flooding. Fishermen use both the R up Big Run and L up Collar Hollow Run. The forest here is chiefly birch, beech, hemlock, and rhododendron. Turn L, downstream, and after 0.1 mi cross Collar Hollow Run. Rock hop or wade Big Run twice more, the last time at 3.9 mi, where the grade becomes wider. Jewelweed and ground ivy *(Glechoma hederacea)*, a creeping herb, are plentiful. Pass a number of small K-dams. Reach WV-28 at 4.6 mi. Parking space is 0.1 mi R on the L side of the highway. (*USGS-FS Maps:* Spruce Knob, Snowy Mountain)

▶ **DOLLY SODS AREA**
(Tucker, Grant, Randolph, and Pendleton Counties)

The name of Dolly Sods developed from that of the Dahles, a pioneer family who grazed their livestock on sods, meaning "grassy grounds" or pastureland. In 1975, Congress passed the Eastern Wilderness Act that set aside two areas as wilderness in the MNF. One was the Dolly Sods Wilderness with 10,215 acres and the other was the 20,000-acre Otter Creek Wilderness in the Cheat District. Adjoining the E boundary of Dolly Sods Wilderness is the 2400-acre Dolly Sods Scenic Area, which also has restricted usage. On the S boundary, S of FR-19, are more than 11,000 acres of forest on the Flatrock and Roaring Plains. It has a geological, botanical, and wilderness character similar to the other areas, but lacks the same types of restrictions. These combined areas are served by one campground, one picnic area, and an interpretive trail, all of which are outside the wilderness. The Dolly Sods Picnic Area is on FR-19, 0.6 mi SW of the jct with FR-19 and 75. The Red Creek Campground on FR-75 is 5.5 N of the picnic area on FR-75, and the *Northland Loop Trail* is 0.4 mi S of the Red Creek Campground on FR-75. The 0.3 mi interpretive trail has stations explaining the flora and how birds and animals use the seeds and fruits, conglomerate rock formations, heath plateaux and bogs with alder thickets. At 0.1 mi on the trail a boardwalk provides views of a glade in Alder Run.

The remote and rugged Dolly Sods Wilderness is a popular area for hiking more than 25 miles of trails through northern hardwood and conifer forest, near cascading streams, over rocky plateaux, and around glades and beaver dams. Although permits are not required, it is recommended by the USFS that someone outside the wilderness know where you are hiking and that you hike with one or more companions. The area is usually wet; there is more than 55 inches of precipitation annually and preparations should be made for rain, thunder, snow, and wind storms. The use of motorized equipment is prohibited and, unless specified otherwise, camping should be 100 ft away from streams and trails and farther away from roads. The rule of "pack it in, pack it out" should be followed devoutly. Horse travel is not suitable.

The wilderness is replete with wildlife — 17 species of amphibians; 6 species of reptiles (poisonous ones are copperhead and rattlesnake); 38 species of mammals; and 82 species of nesting birds, some of which are not seen in the state's other wilderness areas. These species include the marsh hawk *(Circus cyaneus)*, upland sandpiper *(Bartramia longicauda)*, meadowlark *(Sturnella magna)*, kingbird *(Tyrannus tyrannus)*, raven, prairie warbler, and Canada goose. The altitude range, from 2620 to 4122 ft, provides an environment for hundreds of vascular plant species. Sundew *(Drosera rotundifolia)*, cotton grass *(Eriphorum virginicum)*, and speckled alder *(Alnus rugosa)* are some of the plants found in the sphagnum bogs. The wilderness is returning to its natural state after a history of farming, lumbering, and military ordinance exercises in WW II. Also returning to its natural state is the Flatrock and Roaring Plains Area, with the exception that a timber road is planned and the multicolored flagging by surveyors indicates ominous alternative corridors.

• ACCESS: At the jct of WV-28 and Jordan Run Rd (CO-28/7), near the Smoke Hole Caverns (9 mi W of Petersburg), take CO-28/7 N for 1 mi, turn L on FR-19 and go 6 mi to jct with FR-75. Trailheads are both R and L. From the W at jct of WV-32 and Laneville Rd (CO-45) drive 5.8 mi to FR-19 at the North Fork of the Red Creek bridge.

• SUPPORT FACILITIES: The Red Creek Campground, 4.9 mi from the jct of FR-19 and FR-75, has 12 campsites, hand pump drinking water, tables, grills, and vault toilets. It is open April 1 through December. The nearest campground with electrical and water hookups, and hot showers is at Canaan Valley State

Park on WV-32 (tel: 304-866-4121), 7.5 mi W from the Red Creek bridge (see Chapter 6). The nearest general grocery store is immediately S on WV-32 at the WV-32 jct with the Laneville Rd entrance to Dolly Sods.

Red Creek Trail *(6.1 mi; USFS #514)*

* CONNECTING TRAILS:
  High Water Trail (0.8 mi; USFS #552-A)
  Little Stonecoal Trail (1.8 mi; USFS #552)
  Dunkenbarger Trail (1.6 mi; USFS #558)
  Big Stonecoal Trail (4.4 mi; USFS #513)
  Rocky Point Trail (1.8 mi; USFS #554)
  Fisher Spring Run Trail (2.3 mi; USFS #510)
  Rohrbaugh Plains Trail (3.5 mi; USFS #508)
  Wildlife Trail (1.2 mi; USFS #560)
  Breathed Mtn Trail (2.5 mi; USFS #553)
  Blackbird Knob Trail (2.2 mi; USFS #511)

* TOTAL LENGTH: 28.2 mi

* DIFFICULTY: moderate to strenuous

* FEATURES: Red Creek drainage, history, nature study

* TRAILHEADS AND DETAILS: These trails are described in a group, as if branches from a tree. The trunk is *Red Creek Trail* with its base entrance on FR-19 at Red Creek. The other trails extend out to five additional access points — one on FR-19, one on FR-80, and three on FR-75. A number of circuits can be arranged; some are described below.

Before you begin the trails there are three conditions that require attention. One is the danger of flash flooding on the low areas along Red Creek. Because of the steep canyon walls, level space for camping is mainly confined to low areas beside Red Creek, and that space is limited. Some of the desirable sites were washed away or damaged in the November 1985 (or previous) floods. All the footbridges have been washed away over a period of time and there are no plans to rebuild them. Red Creek is not fordable on the *Red Creek Trail*, near Fisher

Spring Run, nor on the *Little Stonecoal Trail*, nor on the *Big Stonecoal Trail* during high water. An alternate route, the *High Water Trail*, was severely damaged for 0.2 mi on a flood plain in the 1985 floods. The *High Water Trail* begins at the W end of the Red Creek bridge on FR-19 (across the creek from the *Red Creek Trail* parking area), and ascends steeply for 0.1 mi to an old RR grade. It turns R and reaches Little Stonecoal Run and *Little Stonecoal Trail* at 0.8 mi. Additionally, in a flood stage, three tributaries, including Fisher Spring Run, on the E side of Red Creek, are not fordable in a flash flood.

Another concern is that some old mortar shells remain in the area from WW II military exercises. Two were detonated by bomb squads in 1985 and one as late as January 2, 1986. If you find one, the USFS requests that you do not touch it, but visibly mark the site, draw a map, and report your find in person or by telephone to the district office in Petersburg.

The other concern is that hikers using *Red Creek Trail* as an extension to the *Blackbird Trail*, which is on private property, or using the *Blackbird Trail* from FR-75 near the Red Creek Campground to reach the *Red Creek Trail* must secure a required privilege pass by applying to CSK Resources, Inc., P.O. Box 218, Thomas, WV 26292, tel: 304-463-4113, or by contacting the local Thomas or Davis Volunteer Fire Departments. The pass fee is dependent on whether the hiker is from Tucker County, in-state, or out-of-state. The request should be made well in advance of planned transit.

To follow the *Red Creek Trail*, park at the parking area near the Wildlife Manager's cabin on FR-19, the E side of Red Creek Bridge. (It is 5.8 mi E from WV-32 on the Laneville Rd [CO-45] and 10.7 mi W from WV-28 on FR-19.) Hike upstream on an old RR grade under tall hemlock, birch, maple, cherry, and poplar. Rhododendron forms an understory in sections. Club mosses and ferns are among the ground covers. At 0.5 mi jct with *Little Stonecoal Trail*, L.

(To hike *Little Stonecoal Trail*, go 0.1 mi to Red Creek, wade, and parallel E of cascading Little Stonecoal Run. Ascend steadily for 1.3 mi on an old wagon road through maple, birch, poplar, and ash. The slope to the gorge is precipitous. Some of the cascades are arbored with rhododendron. After an elev gain of 1000 ft, jct with the *Dunkenbarger Trail*, R. *Little Stonecoal Trail* continues for 0.4 mi to its W terminus at the forest boundary. The 1.6-mi *Dunkenbarger Trail* crosses the Coal Knob plateau through a spruce forest with thick rhododendron, mountain laurel, and mosses. Wet spots in the trail are usual. Rock hop Dunkenbarger Run at 0.9 mi, where deer and bear are occasional visitors. Reach a jct with *Big Stonecoal Trail*. It goes L for 2.5 mi to its N terminus at FR-80 and jct with *Breathed Mtn Trail*, or go R for 1.9 mi downstream to rejoin the *Red Creek Trail* as described below.)

After 1 mi on the *Red Creek Trail* there is evidence of past floods that have rechanneled the river and washed away beaver dams and sections of the old RR grade. At 1.5 mi reach a jct with *Big Stonecoal Trail*, L.

(To hike the 4.4-mi *Big Stonecoal Trail*, wade Red Creek and parallel E of the cascading stream of Stonecoal Run in a steady ascent to a jct with *Rocky Point Trail*, R, at 1.3 mi. [The *Rocky Point Trail* goes 1.8 mi to a jct with the *Red Creek Trail*.] Ahead, the *Big Stonecoal Trail* follows the old RR grade. At 1.7 mi pass R of a waterfall, at 1.8 mi rock hop Stonecoal Run, and at 1.9 mi jct with *Dunkenbarger Trail*, L. For the next 2 mi the treadway is generally wet, mossy, and sometimes rocky on and off the old RR grade. The deciduous forest is mixed with groves of red pine and spruce. Cross the stream again at 2.1 mi, 3.2 mi, and 3.9 mi. There may be active beavers at 3.3 mi. At 3.9 mi begin ascent of rocky area to the N terminus of the trail and jct with FR-80, L, and W terminus of *Breathed Mtn Trail*, R. This area is a frequent campsite for those who enter on FR-80, though FR-80 is severely eroded and passable only with a 4WD vehicle. It is 3.2 mi out to Freeland Rd [CO-37], which makes a jct with WV-32 E of Canaan Valley State Park. *Breathed Mtn Trail* goes 2.5 mi E to a jct with the *Red Creek Trail*.)

Continue upstream on the *Red Creek Trail* from the jct with *Big Stonecoal Trail*, but leave the flood plain and ascend to a mountainside footpath to cross the top of a waterfall at 2.1 mi.

At 2.5 mi cross another cascading tributary (impossible to rock hop in high water) and reach a jct with *Fisher Spring Run Trail*, R, at 3.2 mi.

(The *Fisher Spring Run Trail* ascends 2.3 mi to an access point on FR-75, an elev gain of 1000 ft. Ascend, cross Fisher Spring Run at 0.4 mi [not passable in high water], and ascend on seven switchbacks N of the cascading stream. Reach a jct with the *Rohrbaugh Plains Trail*, R, at 1.2 mi. Stream runs underground in the area. Continue upstream; at 1.6 mi veer R from the stream and ascend in a rocky treadway, sometimes wet. Birch, beech, and maple are prominent. At 2.1 mi pass a small clearing and reach FR-75 parking area at 2.3 mi. From here it is 2 mi N on FR-75 to Red Creek Campground.)

(On the *Rohrbaugh Plains Trail*, from the jct with *Fisher Spring Run Trail*, follow the old RR grade for 0.4 mi to jct, L, with the *Wildlife Trail*. [The 1.2-mi *Wildlife Trail* is an abandoned FR that was used for maintaining wildlife food fields. It is now an easy graded access trail from a parking area on FR-75, 2.2 mi N from the *Rohrbaugh Plains Trail* S terminus at the Picnic Area, and 1.3 mi S from the *Fisher Spring Run Trail* on FR-75.] Continue on the *Rohrbaugh Plains Trail* past a wildlife food plot at 0.6 mi and a large field at 0.8 mi. Reach scenic outcroppings at 0.9 mi, where for 0.2 mi there are views of Red Creek Canyon and the Stonecamp Mtns. Cross three drains, pass through sections of hemlock and spruce, boggy areas, and open grassy fields before crossing the last drain at 2.7 mi. Cross an old woods road and exit at FR-75 at 3.5 mi near the Picnic Area.)

To continue on the *Red Creek Trail* from the jct with the *Fisher Spring Run Trail*, make a short descent to Red Creek and wade or rock hop near the blue blazes at 3 mi. Go upstream in a campsite area under hemlock, ash, and birch, and ascend to a jct with *Rocky Point Trail*, L, at 3.6 mi.

(The *Rocky Point Trail* is an old RR grade, exceptionally rocky in places. When the tree leaves are off there are views of Fisher Spring Run falls and the rock formations on the canyon rim of Rohrbaugh Plains. At 1 mi the trail curves R at the enormous sandstone cliffs of Breathed Mtn. Thoreau observed in his hikes that the finest stone cutters were not of copper or steel, but of "air and water working at their leisure with a liberal allowance of time." A good example is here on Pottsville sandstone. A climb to some of the higher rock formations provides a magnificent view of Red Creek Canyon, Stonecoal Gorge, Coal Knob, and as far SW as Roaring Plains. Bear have been seen on the trail from here to the *Big Stonecoal Trail* jct at 1.8 mi. A return to the point of origin at the Red Creek parking area can be made here by turning L on *Big Stonecoal Trail*, downstream to the *Red Creek Trail*, and to the Red Creek parking area for a circuit of 8.2 mi. Or a longer loop can be made by going upstream to meet *Dunkenbarger Trail*, turning L, jct with *Little Stonecoal Trail*, and returning to the Red Creek parking area for a loop of 9.6 mi.)

To continue on the *Red Creek Trail*, follow the canyon on the old RR grade in a deciduous forest and reach a jct with *Breathed Mtn Trail* at 5 mi.

(The 2.5-mi *Breathed Mtn Trail* ascends steeply and reaches a boggy plateau at 0.3 mi. Numerous beaver ponds are R of the scenic and mesic trail for the next 1 mi. The forest is mixed with fir, spruce, yellow birch, maple and cherry, rhododenron, and mountain laurel. Red pine plantations are at 0.8 mi and 1.1 mi. *Lycopodium* and sphagnum are profuse. Cross the headwaters of Stonecoal Run at 2.3 mi and reach the W terminus of the trail; jct with *Big Stonecoal Trail* and FR-80, described above. A loop can be made here on the *Big Stonecoal Trail* to rejoin the *Red Creek Trail* for a return to the parking area at the Red Creek bridge for a total of 13.5 mi, or 13.8 mi if using the *High Water Trail*.)

Continue on the *Red Creek Trail* and pass over some old RR grade ties with spikes. Reach the confluence of the left fork of Red Creek and Red Creek at 5.2 mi. Rock hop the left fork to a popular campsite area and follow the blue blazes upstream, L. At 5.3 mi leave the creek bank and ascend steeply into a red spruce forest. Arrive at the boundary of private property, CSX Resources, at 5.6 mi, and leave the Dolly Sods Wilderness Area. Follow the trail through an open field of blueberry, minniebush, wintergreen, wild flowers, and mountain laurel. Reach the N terminus of the *Red Creek Trail* at 6.1 mi and jct with the *Blackbird Knob Trail*. Backtrack, or follow the *Blackbird Knob Trail*, R.

If taking the *Blackbird Knob Trail*, follow a pleasant trail through a hardwood forest to an open area where deer and grouse are frequently seen. Rock hop or wade Red Creek at 0.5 mi and Alder Creek at 1.1 mi. Ascend gradually in open areas, leave the private property of CSX Resources at 1.4 mi, and reenter the MNF. Follow the path to a rock outcropping with spruce, ferns, and blueberry at 1.8 mi; descend slightly and reach FR-75 at 2.2 mi for a total mileage of 8.3 mi from the Red Creek bridge on FR-19 and an elev gain of 1267 ft. Across the road is the parking area and to the R is the Red Creek Campground. (*USGS-FS Maps:* The Blackbird Knob, Blackwater Falls, Laneville, and Hopeville topos [1967-1969] have a number of incorrect trail routes.)

South Prong Trail *(5.9 mi; USFS #517);* Boar's Nest Trail *(2.7 mi; USFS #518)*

* LENGTH: 8.3 mi, ct

* DIFFICULTY: strenuous

* FEATURES: scenic, balds, nature study

* TRAILHEADS AND DETAILS: The E trailhead of the *South Prong Trail* is at a parking area 0.4 mi W of the Dolly Sods Picnic Area on FR-19. Enter the trail on sections of boardwalks in a wet area for 0.5 mi. On drier treadway reach a rocky ridge line at 1 mi; vistas follow. Forest has spruce, cherry, Canada dogwood, huckleberry, rhododendron, and fly poison. Pass large cairns at 1.5 mi, followed by a rock formation, L, and a scenic campsite, L, at 1.7 mi. At 1.8 mi make a sharp R through a meadow, cross a drain and descend on a steep rocky treadway to FR-70 at 2.7 mi. (To the R on FR-70 it is 1.7 mi to a gate and FR-19, and 0.2 mi R to point of origin for a loop for 4.6 mi. Gated FR-70 is always locked. To the L on FR-70 it is 1.4 mi to the SE terminus of *Boar's Nest Trail*. Beyond, on FR-70, it is 0.7

mi to the end of the road where the 3-mi *Roaring Plains Trail* begins.) Cross FR-70, descend to join an old RR grade, and cross the South Fork of Red Creek at 3.1 mi. Turn a sharp R and begin to parallel the creek. There are remnants of an old cook stove here. The treadway is over conglomerate rocks, and the trees are northern hardwoods. At 4.3 mi leave the RR grade and descend over RR grade switchbacks to cross the creek at 5.1 mi. Follow downstream on old RR grade damaged by floods, and at 5.9 mi reach W terminus of the trail and jct with *Boar's Nest Trail*. To the R, *Boar's Nest Trail* ascends, crosses a woods road in a forest of oak, hemlock, and birch to FR-19 after 0.3 mi. (On FR-19 it is 1.7 mi, R, up the mountain to *South Prong Trail* parking area.) To the L of the trail jct, rock hop the South Fork to follow the *Boar's Nest Trail* and begin a 1240-ft gain in elev on an old logging road. After 0.7 mi leave the road and ascend steeply for another 0.6 mi to dense sections of spruce and arrive on a rocky plateau with huckleberry and mountain laurel. Parts of the treadway are wet. Reach FR-70 at 2.7 mi. To the L it is 1.4 mi to crossing the *South Prong Trail* and another 1.7 mi to FR-19. To the R it is 0.4 mi to the *Roaring Plains Trail*. (*USGS-FS Maps:* The Laneville and Hopeville topos [1969] have a number of incorrect trail routes.)

Flatrock Run Trail (5.1 mi; USFS #519); *Roaring Plains Trail* (3.3 mi; USFS #548)

- LENGTH: 8.4 mi, ct

- DIFFICULTY: strenuous, elev gain 2380 ft

- FEATURES: scenic, geology, isolated

- TRAILHEADS AND DETAILS: From the Red Creek bridge drive W on the paved Laneville Rd (CO-45) for 1.5 mi to the first paved road L, and go 0.8 mi to cross a cement bridge (flooded in high water) over Red Creek to a sign and parking area L. From the W, at the jct of WV-32 and Laneville Rd, drive E for 4.3 mi and, immediately after passing a tan metal building on the R, turn R. It is 0.8 mi farther as described above. (The first trail mi is on private property, but the USFS has a trail-use agreement with the landowner.) Climb over the main gate, if it is locked, and follow a cattle pasture road through a field of grasses and wildflowers such as black-eyed Susan, vipers bugloss, chicory, spotted knapweed (*Centaurea masculosa*), daisy, and common tansy (*Tanacetum vulgare*). Pass through two pasture gates and cross small drains at 1.2 mi and 1.4 mi. Pass an abandoned cabin and enter a forest of hemlock. Turn sharp R on old RR grade at 2 mi, away from Flat Rock Run. At 2.3 mi turn L on the RR grade switchback, but go straight at the next 2 RR grade switchbacks at 2.7 mi and 3 mi. Ferns, black cohosh, and white snakeroot are prominent in the forest of cherry, locust, maple, and birch. Deer, wild turkey, grouse, and owls are often seen in this area. Rock hop cascading and scenic Right Fork of Flat Rock Run at 3.1 mi. A few yds ahead is a large boulder that has walking fern (*Camptosorus*) at eye level. Leave the RR grade, R, at 3.4 mi and ascend steeply for 0.9 mi on a footpath that crosses the old RR grade switchbacks. Reach a R turn at a RR grade at 4.3 mi. The treadway is wet and mossy with patches of ferns. Spruce becomes dominant. At 5.1 mi reach the E terminus of the trail at a jct with *Roaring Plains Trail*, its W terminus.

(To the R the old RR grade, now soggy and overgrown, leads 0.8 mi to Mt Porte Crayon. ATV traffic has made a new, but also muddy, route.) Although there is not any specific trail to Mt Porte Crayon (4770 ft) and its rugged surroundings, it is a significant place. It was dedicated on July 5, 1941, in memory of Gen. David Hunter Strother, artist, author, diplomat, and outdoorsman, who explored the mountains in this area. His pseudonym was "Porte Crayon." The USFS cut a special trail from the A. B. Wolford farm near Harperton for the dedication party of 40 people. Strother's grandson was there and so was the curly-haired, 3-year-old great-grandson, called the "Little General." He was carried to the windswept top on the back of a USFS staff member. Jack Prebble, of *Harper's New Monthly Magazine*, said Strother had "inspired our love of the forest, the streams, and the caverns of his native highlands. Seldom is a man so honored."

Turn L at the jct on *Roaring Plains Trail* and ascend (a spring is R) 0.1 mi to a grassy old RR grade. Turn L and follow the wide clearing through high meadows for 0.5 mi before it narrows to a footpath on a rocky bald (4720 ft). (A stack of rock for a campfire shield is L.) The area has sections of dense grasses, goldenrod, blueberry, mountain ash, and blue gentian *(Gentiana clausa)*. Enter a spruce forest at 1 mi that is intersected with open meadows and dense groves of rhododendron and mountain laurel. Turn sharply L at 2.5 mi, descend slightly to the headwaters of the South Fork of Red Creek. It is 3.4 mi on FR-70 to its locked gate at FR-19, 0.5 mi W of the Dolly Sods Picnic Area. *(USGS-FS Maps:* The Laneville and Hopeville topos [1969] have a number of incorrect trail routes.)

▶SECTION 6: WHITE SULPHUR RANGER DISTRICT

This district is the most southern of the Monongahela National Forest. Its western boundary is the Greenbrier River and its eastern boundary is on the crest of the Allegheny Mtn range, along the West Virginia-Virginia state line. The northern boundary crosses Middle Mtn and Brush Mtn ranges from the E to the Calvin Price State Forest in the W, only a few miles N of the Greenbrier-Pocahontas county line, where it adjoins the Marlinton District. Within the district's 97,928 acres are two recreation areas — beautiful Lake Sherwood on Meadow Creek and Blue Bend on Anthony Creek. In addition to 109.5 mi of hiking trails, the district has 128 mi of forest roads suitable for hiking. The ranger has said that all trails are given maintenance every year or at least every three years. Only the *Civil War Trail* is not maintained. Trail usage is frequent to moderate, with the exception of rare use on the *Laurel Run Trail, Civil War Trail,* and the *Spice Ridge Trail.* Scenic areas with the most outstanding vistas are at the end of Beaver Lick Tower Rd (FR-343) (check with the district office to find out if the road is open), the NW section of *Meadow Creek Mtn Trail,* the *Allegheny Mtn Trail,* and the end of FR-139 from Blue Bend campground to Hopkins Mtn. The Blue Bend Campground is also a good base point for excursions on the *Greenbrier River Trail*, which passes through the community of Anthony (see Chapter 1). The district has more than 97 mi of hiking trails and 18 mi of the *Allegheny Trail*, but some of it is on other trails (see Chapter 11).

• ADDRESS AND ACCESS: District Ranger, White Sulphur Ranger District, PO Box 520, White Sulphur Springs, WV 24986, tel: 304-536-2144. The district office is in the US Post Office Bldg, East Main Street, White Sulphur Springs.

• MAPS: Numbers 29-32

▶ BLUE BEND RECREATION AREA
(Greenbrier County)

There are two campgrounds here: Blue Bend with 22 sites, open year-round, and Blue Meadows with 18 sites, open from Memorial Day through Labor Day during the full recreation season. During the summer season there are flush toilets and water fountains, but in the off-season there are vault toilets and hand water pumps. Neither campground has hookups. Each campsite is provided with a table, grill, waste receptacle, and lantern post. Space is allocated on a first-come, first-served basis, with a maximum of eight people per site and a maximum stay of 14 days.

The area has 25 picnic tables and two large picnic shelters that may be reserved for groups. Swimming is allowed in the cool Anthony Creek and a lifeguard is on duty during the summer months. Near the creek are two bathhouses without baths. For anglers, Anthony Creek is stocked with trout and there are trout and bass in the nearby Greenbrier River. For hikers, the area is ideal for trail variety of day hikes or backpacking trips.

• ACCESS: The eastern access is 3.7 mi W on Little Creek Rd (CO-16) and Big Blue Bend Rd (CO-16/2) from the jct with WV-92 at Alvon. The western access is 8 mi E on Anthony Station Rd (CO-21/2) from US-219 at Frankford.

• SUPPORT FACILITIES: It is 10 mi S on WV-92 to White Sulphur Springs to shopping centers, restaurants, motels, banks, service stations, and a hospital. Green Acres Grocery is 5 mi from the campground on WV-92, 1.3 mi S from the Little Creek Rd jct. It has hunting and fishing licenses also (tel: 304-536-9832). For a campground with hookup facilities, commercial Paradise Campground is 1.2 mi E on Big Blue Bend Rd from the Blue Bend Recreation Area to Big Draft Rd. Open May 1–Sept 15 (tel: 304-536-3223).

Blue Bend Loop Trail (5 mi; USFS #614); *Anthony Creek Trail* (3.8 mi; USFS #618)

• LENGTH: 8.8 mi, ct

• DIFFICULTY: moderate

• FEATURES: scenic river and overlooks

• TRAILHEADS AND DETAILS: From the parking area in the Blue Bend Picnic Area (1944 ft) follow the trail signs across the swinging footbridge over Anthony Creek to the *Blue Bend Loop Trail* (once called *Round Mtn Trail*) to a sign post. From the sign post at the fork turn R and follow downstream through an exceptionally scenic forest of hemlock, ash, poplar, sycamore, beech, basswood, maple, and white pine. Rhododendron and spicebush are in patches. Wildflowers include mandrake, stonecrop, cohosh, wild geranium, and ragwort. At 1.6 mi is a jct with the *Anthony Creek Trail* at the mouth of Big Draft. (*Anthony Creek Trail* goes downstream for 3.8 mi to Anthony Station Rd, CO-21/2.) Turn L here, ascend steeply on four switchbacks to the ridge top at 2.7 mi and to an Adirondack shelter that accommodates eight backpackers. A usually dependable spring is 100 yds from the shelter. Continue ahead on an old road across the top of Round Mtn (2960 ft). Begin ridge descent through an open forest and at 3.6 mi enter a rhododendron thicket. Continue descent to three precipitous overlooks with superb views of the Anthony Creek valley. Trailing arbutus and wintergreen border sections of the trail.

After seven switchbacks complete the descent to the creek side and return to the swinging bridge at 5 mi.

To hike the 3.8 mi *Anthony Creek Trail,* turn at the jct mentioned above, cross the mouth of the Big Draft, and go downstream through a hardwood forest, sometimes following an old tram road. Deer are likely seen on this trail. At 0.5 mi pass L of a rock cribbing and a good fishing hole. Pass other good fishing spots and a number of excellent camping areas. At 2.7 mi cross Laurel Run and at 3.1 mi is a jct L with the *South Boundary Trail.* (The *South Boundary Trail,* described below, ascends 4.8 mi to Jericho Draft Rd, CO-36.) Continue ahead and R to ford the 60-ft-wide Anthony Creek, a stream that may be hazardous to cross at high water times. Wading may be easier upstream at about 200 yds. Rock fanciers will find a wide range of color and variety here. After crossing the creek follow the old road around the base of Gunpowder Ridge, where wild orchids and squirrel cups grow on the road banks. Good campsites are by the Greenbrier River. Exit at the bridge on Anthony Station Rd (CO-21/2). Backtrack for a total of 10.8 mi or have a vehicle shuttle for 4 mi E to the campground. (Across the Greenbrier River bridge is the *Greenbrier River Trail* described in Chapter 6.) (*USGS-FS Map:* Anthony)

South Boundary Trail *(4.8 mi; USFS #615);* Coles Mtn Trail *(1.2 mi; USFS #612)*

- LENGTH: 12 mi, rt, ct

- DIFFICULTY: moderate

- FEATURE: forest succession

- TRAILHEADS AND DETAILS: The easiest access to these trails is to drive E from the campground on Big Blue Bend Rd (CO-21/1) for 1.1 mi to Big Draft Rd (also called Jericho Draft Rd) (CO-36/1) and turn R. Go 3.5 mi on Big Draft Rd to the trailheads and park. (Another access route is from the *Anthony Creek Trail* mentioned above.)

At the trail signs ascend W on the *South Boundary Trail* to a ridge with hardwoods, scattered white pines, rhododendron, mountain laurel, blueberry bushes, and wintergreen. At 0.8 mi cross a forest timber road and follow a jeep trail. At 2.1 mi cross an earthen barrier that prevents vehicular usage of the trail. Follow a private road for 0.4 mi past a hunting cabin, R, to another earthen barrier at the MNF boundary. Cross the barrier in a hardwood forest and reach a knoll (3121 ft) at 3.1 mi. After 1 mi farther begin a steep descent to the jct with *Anthony Creek Trail* at Anthony Creek. Options here are to backtrack, turn R and hike 5.4 mi to the Blue Bend Campground, or ford the creek and go 0.6 mi to the Greenbrier River bridge described above.

At the Big Draft Rd trailheads, across the road from the *South Boundary Trail* is the *Coles Mtn Trail*. Follow E on the logging road through young oaks and white and Virginia pine for 0.5 mi to a slight saddle. Here the road becomes a footpath through mountain laurel and patches of partridge berry to a ridge crest and terminus of the trail at 1.2 mi. Backtrack. (Immediately L of the *Coles Mtn Trail* at Big Draft Rd is an unnamed, unmarked 0.6-mi road-trail that ascends gradually along a small stream to its headwaters. A number of timber side roads provide large segments of mountain laurel, ferns, mosses, wild orchids, and other wildflowers.) (*USGS-FS Maps:* Anthony, White Sulphur Springs)

Beaver's Tale Trail

- LENGTH: 0.3 mi

- DIFFICULTY: easy

- FEATURE: trail for the visually handicapped

- TRAILHEAD AND DETAILS: Across the road from the Blue Meadow Campground in the parking lot, follow the signs on the loop trail with lettered and Braille interpretative signs. In a level area, the visually handicapped can hear and wade in the creek; at other places they can smell plants such as wild phlox, spicebush, and wild roses. The trail is a contribution of the

USFS, the Lewisburg Lion's Club and clubs of District 29-N, and the YCC of 1974–75. It is a *National Recreation Trail*. (*USGS-FS Map:* Anthony)

Camp Wood Trail (USFS #619)

- LENGTH: 1.7 mi
- DIFFICULTY: moderate
- FEATURE: nature study

- TRAILHEADS AND DETAILS: From the Blue Bend Recreation Area drive E on the Big Blue Bend Rd for 2.4 mi and park on the L. (Ahead it is 0.3 mi to road jct at University of West Virginia Camp Wood.) The unmarked and unblazed trailhead is on the R between two locust trees. Ascend an embankment through a young forest for 0.1 mi to a power line and a loop fork. If you turn R, follow a well-graded trail around spur ridges and at 0.3 mi pass a large bed of skunk cabbage, cinnamon ferns, and wildflowers near a hemlock grove. Cross a streambed and ascend on switchbacks to ridge crest. Begin descent at 1 mi. Squaw root and Indian pipe grow here. (*USGS-FS Map:* Alvon)

Civil War Trail (6.3 mi; USFS #686); Slab Camp Trail (5 mi; USFS #617); Peach Orchard Trail (4.1 mi; USFS #616); Laurel Run Trail (5.5 mi; USFS #679); Blue Line Trail (0.7 mi; USFS #680)

- LENGTH: 21.6 mi, ct
- DIFFICULTY: moderate
- FEATURES: historic area, wildlife

- TRAILHEADS AND DETAILS: From the Blue Bend campground drive N on FR-139, up Rocky Run, for 2.4 mi to a fork in the road. Turn L on Laurel Run Rd (FR-298) and go 0.1 mi to trail crossing. (At the R fork on FR-139 the road continues for 1 mi to a radio tower and former site of a lookout tower on Hopkins

Mtn for a superb scenic view.) The trail crossing is almost the midpoint access to the *Civil War Trail*, a trail that connects with, or leads to, all the other trails in this group. At the trail crossing you can hike the *Civil War Trail* E to Little Creek Rd (CO-16 by Dawson Run for 2.6 mi), or W to Auto Road/Slab Camp Rd (CO-11) for 3.7 mi. Either way, the termini are on private property and permission from the 13 property owners should be obtained. (Call the district ranger's office for information.) If acquiring permission is an inconvenience, it is recommended that the *Civil War Trail* be used only to the forest boundary or for connections with other USFS trails.

The *Civil War Trail* received its name from accounts of a troop and pack horse route from Virginia to the Droop Mtn Battlefield area (see Chapter 6). The route is also a legendary Indian path. For these reasons, the USFS has decided to protect the cultural resources by discontinuing maintenance. Nevertheless, the route is open and clear enough to hike and to make connections with other trails and with other forest and hunting roads. Bear, deer, raccoon, squirrel, and wild turkey are hunted in the area. Wildflowers and flowering shrubs are prominent.

If you choose the E route on the *Civil War Trail*, reach a trail jct at 0.5 mi. To the R it is 0.1 mi to the E terminus of the *Peach Orchard Trail* and FR-139. Ahead on the *Civil War Trail* reach the jct with *Slab Camp Trail*, L, at 0.9 mi. Continue R on the *Civil War Trail* and descend on the NE side of Dawson Run to the forest boundary and a stream crossing at 1.9 mi. (It is 0.8 mi farther on the private land to Little Creek Rd.) Backtrack.

The unblazed *Slab Camp Trail* (formerly Slab Camp FR-103, now closed, gated, and maintained for wildlife habitats) is a wide route with comfortable terrain along the Hopkins Mtn ridge in a forest of oak, maple, and dogwood with scattered white pine. Wildlife is likely to be sighted. At 1.8 mi reach Dawson Peak (3250 ft). From here descend to a slight saddle near a Laurel Run tributary watershed and ascend another knob (3105 ft) at 2.8 mi. Descend SW on a ridge, curve N and follow another Laurel Run tributary upstream, and cross the stream at 4.5 mi. At 5 mi reach Auto Road/Slab Camp Mtn Rd

(CO-11) in a curve, the N terminus (3012 ft), almost the same elev as the S terminus. Backtrack or use vehicle shuttle from the campground to Little Creek Rd at Camp Wood and go up Little Creek Rd (CO-16) for 4 mi to Slab Camp Mtn Rd, L. It is another 3 mi on the rough Slab Camp Mtn Rd to the N trailhead.

On the W section of the *Civil War Trail* at FR-298 and FR-797, follow FR-797 W for 0.3 mi to jct L with FR-297, Peach Orchard Rd, also called *Peach Orchard Trail*.

(The *Peach Orchard Trail* is open to vehicular traffic during the deer [gun] season. It is a hardwood forest area on a ridge crest with gentle undulations for 2.5 mi, after which it descends to a jct with FR-296 at 4.1 mi. Vehicle shuttle L is 1.6 mi to Anthony Station Rd [CO-21] and 2.8 mi L to Blue Bend campground.)

Continue ahead on the *Civil War Trail* and FR-797 for another 0.1 mi, where the *Civil War Trail* turns R over a large rock pushed into the road to prevent vehicle access. Descend to a crossing of FR-296 at 0.9 mi from the midpoint origin. Continue descent through a forest of hardwoods in a glen, cross the tributary to Laurel Run at least seven times, and reach the jct with *Laurel Run Trail* and Laurel Run at 2.6 mi in a forest of hemlock, white pine, and rhododendron. If you have private property permission, cross the stream, turn R and follow both trails conjointly for 0.4 mi, where the *Civil War Trail* turns L. After another 0.7 mi reach the terminus of the *Civil War Trail* near a tan house and trail sign by the Auto Road/Slab Camp Mtn Rd (CO-11). To avoid a trespass problem do not cross Laurel Run; instead, hike up the embankment for 100 yds to FR-296 and hike the road, L. After 0.5 mi cross Laurel Creek and rejoin *Laurel Creek Trail*, R. Follow alongside FR-296 for another 0.9 mi to its N terminus on the Auto Road/Slab Camp Rd. Backtrack. If using a shuttle, follow the directions of the *Slab Camp Trail*.

The S terminus of the 5.5 mi *Laurel Run Trail* is also on private property and permission to exit or enter should be obtained from the five owners. The trail follows a stream through a scenic area of hardwoods, conifers, cascades, and wildflowers to a private farm near the Greenbrier River. Three-fourths of the way downstream a forest access point exists; it is the 0.7 mi *Blue Line Trail* off FR-296, 5.7 mi from its jct with Anthony Station Rd (CO-21) and another 2.8 mi E to the Blue Bend campground. (*USGS-FS Maps:* Anthony, Alvon)

Spice Ridge Trail (USFS #621)

- LENGTH: 12.4 mi, rt

- DIFFICULTY: strenuous

- FEATURE: exceptionally remote

- TRAILHEAD AND DETAILS: The trailhead is difficult to reach unless you use a 4WD vehicle on the N end of Little Creek Rd (CO-16) from Camp Wood. (Another difficult route that also needs a 4WD vehicle is from Watogo State Park through Calvin Price State Forest on Beaver Creek Rd, CO-21.) The trailhead is a gated road, but open to the public most of the year. There is no drinking water on the trail. The unmarked and unblazed trail begins by ascending gradually for 0.7 mi to the ridge line. Ahead, the trail undulates, shifting occasionally across the boundary line of the Calvin Price State Forest and the White Sulphur District in a hardwood forest. Elevation change on the trail is approximately 200 ft. At 3 mi cross back into the district and remain on the ridge line for another 1.8 mi. Begin a 1000 ft elev descent at 4.8 mi, where the trail soon becomes a footpath. The trail terminates at the E bank of the Greenbrier River at 6.2 mi. Backtrack. (*USGS-FS Map:* Denmar)

Wild Meadow Trail (USFS #670)

- LENGTH: 6.2 mi, rt

- DIFFICULTY: moderate

- FEATURES: wildlife, scenic

- TRAILHEADS AND DETAILS: On WV-92, 5.3 mi N of White Sulphur Springs and 7.6 mi E and S from the Blue Bend

Recreation Area, is the signed entrance to the trail (2160 ft) at FR-718. Park to the L of the entrace. Hike up a sharp curve on FR-718 for 0.3 mi to an abrupt, unmarked L on a foot trail. Descend to Fleming Run and go upstream. Cross the stream a number of times and reach a good campsite area at 0.5 mi. Vegetation includes white pine, oak, ironwood, Christmas fern, and wild ginger. At 1.3 mi begin the first of four switchbacks on a well-graded trail banked with moss, mountain laurel, and trailing arbutus. At 1.5 mi is a wildlife watering hole, R, and a crossing of FR-718 ahead. Descend to a jct with the end of FR-718 in Whitman's Draft. Turn R and ascend. Exit from the forest on a grassy plateau at 3.1 mi. Backtrack. (Ahead it is 0.1 mi to a private hunting lodge, formerly Weese Farm. Beyond is a jeep road that re-enters the MNF on a ridge and after 0.6 mi crosses into Virginia.) (*USGS-FS Map:* Jerrys Run)

▶ LAKE SHERWOOD RECREATION AREA
(Greenbrier County)

Through cooperative efforts in 1958, the USFS and the West Virginia Department of Natural Resources constructed the Lake Sherwood Recreation Area. Their choice of the Upper Meadow Creek Valley at 2668 ft elev between Meadow Creek Mtn and the Allegheny Mtns has made this beautiful valley one of the Monongahela National Forest's most popular vacation localities. The area is named after the Sherwood Land, Mineral and Timber Company, the former owners.

The appealing 165-acre lake is stocked with largemouth bass, catfish, bluegill, and tiger musky. Deer, turkey, grouse, skunk, red squirrel, fox squirrel, raccoon, and rattlesnakes are in the surrounding forest. (State licenses and USFS stamps are necessary for anglers and hunters.)

There are two sandy beaches, one on the W bank and another on a connecting island. Lifeguards are on duty in the summer months. Boats and canoes are available for rent, and there are three boat launches and docks for public use. Three campgrounds — West Shore Campground, Pine Run Campground, and Meadow Creek Campground — provide 96 camping units, and plans are to add 35 more campsites within the next few years. (Funding for these improvements will depend on Congressional budget allocations.) Most sites will accommodate trailers, but there are no electric or water hookups. During the summer the camping area has rest rooms with electricity and running water. There are no hot water showers. Capacity for each campsite is eight people, and a maximum stay is 14 days. Full-season operation is from Memorial Day through Labor Day. During the off-season 25 campsites are available, with vault rest rooms and hand water pumps. Campsites are not reserved, but reservations may be made for a group of up to 100 campers. Facilities include grates, tables, trash receptacles, and lantern posts. There are 60 picnic sites on the Pine Knoll and Lakeside picnic areas and one large shelter for group or family outings. Reservations are accepted. For hiking enthusiasts, the lake area has eight connecting trails.

- ACCESS: At the jct of WV-92 and Sherwood Lake Rd (CO-14/1) in Neola, drive E on the Sherwood Lake Rd for 10.5 mi.

- SUPPORT FACILITIES: General stores are in Neola. Grocery, camping goods, firewood, and laundry facilities are available at a seasonal country store 1.7 mi from the campground on Sherwood Lake Rd.

Lake Sherwood Trail (3.7 mi); *Virginia Trail* (0.6 mi; USFS #685); *Allegheny Mtn Trail* (11.5 mi; USFS #611); *Dilley Trail* (1 mi; USFS #682); *Snake Valley Trail* (3.6 mi; USFS #684); *Meadow Mtn Trail* (9.7 mi; USFS #610); *(Allegheny Trail)*; *Upper Meadow Trail* (1.2 mi; USFS #672)

- LENGTH: 31.3 mi, ct

- DIFFICULTY: *Lake Sherwood Trail* easy and *Allegheny Mtn Trail* strenuous

- FEATURES: scenic, wildlife, wildflowers

- TRAILHEADS AND DETAILS: Base trailhead is Pine Knoll Picnic

Area in Lake Sherwood Recreation Area for the purpose of this description. These trails are listed together because they all connect, and they will be described individually in the order they are listed with connecting descriptions to follow. For hikers who wish to go farther into the forest with a day pack, or a backpack for overnight camping, these descriptions will offer distance options for loop combinations.

The 3.7 mi *Lake Sherwood Trail* is probably the most hiked trail in the district because of scenic beauty and the concentration of summer campers. From the parking lot at Pine Knoll Picnic Area follow the trail sign through tall white pine, hemlock, and oak to the lake. Turn R. Cattails and witch hazel grow in the coves. Reach the dam at 0.5 mi and cross Meadow Creek below the dam (rock hop if the bridge is washed out). At 0.9 mi is jct with the *Virginia Trail*. (The 0.6 mi *Virginia Trail* ascends to the *Allegheny Mtn Trail*.) At 1.5 mi cross a small stream, and at 2.3 mi cross a footbridge over Meadow Creek to a fork. The *Lake Sherwood Trail* continues L.

(To the R is a 0.2 mi access route to the *Snake Valley Trail*. To reach the trail from here, ascend an embankment to a water fountain at campsite #80. Turn R and follow campground road L of the rest rooms to the Beach Administration sign. Turn R and reach the S terminus of the *Snake Valley Trail* in the traffic circle. The trail goes N to connect with the *Allegheny Mtn Trail* and the *Meadow Mtn Trail* described below.)

Continue on the *Lake Sherwood Trail*, reach a boat access at 2.5 mi in Meadow Creek Campground, and pass another boat access in Pine Run Campground. Follow the trail through the West Shore Campground to the public boat launch and docks, and the swimming area, and return to the Pine Knoll and Lakeside picnic area at 3.7 mi.

The shortest access route to the 11.5 mi *Allegheny Mtn Trail* is on the 0.6 mi *Virginia Trail* mentioned above. Follow the *Sherwood Lake Trail* to the *Virginia Trail* and ascend on an old road under tall trees for 0.3 mi; then ascend on a wide footpath for another 0.3 mi to a saddle on the Allegheny Mtn ridge, the West Virginia-Virginia state line. At this point it is 6 mi R on the

Allegheny Mtn Trail to the S terminus at Rucker Gap and 5.5 mi to the N terminus near High Top.

If you choose a S route on the *Allegheny Mtn Trail*, ascend the old CCC fire road to continue along the ridge in an oak and hickory forest. Serviceberry and filbert patches are scattered along the route. At 0.5 mi there is an excellent view of both Lake Moomaw, E, and Lake Sherwood, W, when the leaves are off the trees. Ascend to a knob (3025 ft) at 1.2 mi and descend to the *Dilley Trail* jct, R, at 1.5 mi.

(The 1 mi *Dilley Trail* descends on a grassy jeep road that encounters a small stream on the L for 0.5 mi to Meadow Creek. It crosses the creek on a footbridge and follows the gated road for another 0.5 mi through oak and white pine, ironwood, sumac, and witch hazel to the Sherwood Lake Rd, 1.4 mi S of Lake Sherwood. To make this route a loop back to the picnic area is a total of 5.4 mi.)

Continue ahead on the *Allegheny Mtn Trail* with views of the Meadow Creek Mtn R (W), Allegheny Mtn ranges with posted Big Lick Farms, Big Lick Draft, Lake Moomaw, and sections of the George Washington National Forest L (E) in Virginia. At 2.6 mi reach the forest boundary line with corner boundary markers on bearing trees. At 3.4 mi is grassy FR-881, R, that descends to Sherwood Lake Rd. Reach Chestnut Knob (3200 ft), a triangle county boundary with Greenbrier in West Virginia and Bath and Allegheny in Virginia at 4.8 mi. There are large oaks here. After another 0.7 mi begin steep descent over numerous "tank traps" (earth mounds) to the S terminus of the trail at 6 mi. On the R at the edge of the woods is the grave site of Pvt 1st Class Adam M. Smith, 29th Div US Army, Dec 28, 1941. Nearby is the parking area, a gated road L, and Rucker Gap (2606 ft). Backtrack for a round-trip of 15 mi or use a vehicle shuttle. From here R, it is 7.1 mi on Rucker Gap Rd. (CO-14) and Sherwood Lake Rd (CO-14/1) to Lake Sherwood. (On the L, in Virginia, the road is SR-781 for 1.9 mi; it connects with SR-661 for 8.7 mi to the town of Callaghan and I-64.)

If you hike the NE section of the *Allegheny Mtn Trail* from the *Virginia Trail* jct, ascend from the saddle along the Allegheny

Mtn ridge through a hardwood forest. Occasional patches of blueberry, buckberry, wintergreen, flame azalea, and pinxter are noticeable. Deer, grouse, and wild turkey are likely to be seen on this trail. At 1 mi the old CCC fire road becomes more of a footpath through rocky sections. At 1.8 mi ascend to a knob (3214 ft) where a faint trail, R, leads down into Meadow Lick Hollow. Here, and at other places, are E overlooks for scenic views of Lake Moomaw and Bolar Mtn. At 3.8 mi jct with the N terminus of *Snake Valley Trail*, L, but it is signed *Meadow Mtn Trail*.

(The 3.6 mi *Snake Valley Trail* goes 0.4 mi through forest to a wildlife opening and jct with FR-815-A. The FR ascends N for 1.5 mi to a jct wtih *Meadow Mtn Trail*. Turn L on the *Snake Valley Trail* and follow Meadow Creek downstream; cross it frequently. Hunting and fishing are popular along this trail. At 1.6 mi cross the Snake Valley tributary. Forest vegetation includes hardwoods, white pines, mountain laurel, rhododendron, and trailing arbutus. For the final crossing of the creek, cross at 3 mi, pass an old beaver dam, a spur trail L to an old man-made dam, and reach the traffic circle at the N edge of the main campground road at 3.6 mi. From here it is 0.7 mi on the main road to the picnic area or take the *Lake Sherwood Trail* as described above for a loop total of 10.9 mi.)

For a longer loop continue N on the *Allegheny Mtn Trail;* it becomes more narrow. At 4 mi the trail passes through exceptionally large beds of wintergreen. Reach the N terminus of the trail at 5.5 mi (3443 ft) at FR-55. A gated road is on the Virginia side, R. Continue ahead for 0.3 mi on the dirt road for a jct (3511 ft), R, with the 0.5 mi road to the former High Top Lookout Tower. A lone red spruce is the only sentinel. Continue ahead on FR-55, pass a scenic view of Lake Sherwood on the L at 5.9 mi, and at 6 mi reach the jct, L, with the 9.7 mi *Meadow Mtn Trail*. A dependable spring is here, N, across the road from a white cement block cottage. Here is also the boundary line between the Marlinton and White Sulphur ranger districts. It is 6 mi N on FR-55 to WV-39.

To hike the *Meadow Mtn Trail*, follow the signs on FR-815 to a wildlife food plot and locked, gated road (except during deer-hunting season) at 0.3 mi. For the next 1.6 mi the grassy fields with elev between 3400 and 3600 ft, the stands of red pine, and the good chance of seeing wildlife make this an extraordinarily pleasant part of the trail. At 1 mi is a jct, L, with FR-815-A (a hunting road that descends 1.5 mi to the N terminus of *Snake Valley Trail*). At 1.4 mi is a foot trail, L, leading to FR-815-A and the *Snake Valley Trail.* Enter the forest and pass a gated timber road, R, at 2.1 mi and another timber road, R, at 2.4 mi. Continue to follow the ridge on what has become a narrow jeep road; ascend and descend the knobs. At 3.8 mi is a superb view of Lake Sherwood. On the R at 4.9 mi the proposed *Allegheny Trail* joins the *Meadow Mtn Trail.* Reach jct, L, with *Upper Meadow Trail* at 5.1 mi.

(The 1.2 mi *Upper Meadow Trail* is a 4WD road, not open to vehicles; it descends to a hollow under tall hardwoods and white pines, and a stream bordered with rhododendron. Pass R of a slate pile at 0.9 mi and R of the amphitheater built by the White Sulphur YCC in 1981 at 1.1 mi. Reach the E terminus, a locked gate across the road from the picnic area at 1.2 mi. For a loop, this is a total of 13.9 mi.)

Continue on the *Meadow Mtn Trail* that runs conjointly with the *Allegheny Trail*, ascend steadily on the ridge line, and descend to a jct with Rider Rd, FR-815-C, formerly *Rider Trail*, at 6.8 mi.

(For another loop, you can hike down Rider Rd for 1.1 mi to Sherwood Lake Rd. Rider Rd follows a power line and crosses Dilley Run to ascend a ridge at 0.7 mi. Parts of this area are on private property. Reach Sherwood Lake Rd in front of a grocery store. It is 2 mi L [N] on Sherwood Lake Rd to the picnic area. This loop is a total of 17.4 mi.)

The *Meadow Mtn Trail* and the *Allegheny Trail* continue ahead, cross Dilly Run, and ascend to the ridge E of a few hunting cottages on private lands. At 8.4 mi *Meadow Mtn Trail* forks L and the proposed *Allegheny Trail* continues ahead on the ridge of Meadow Creek Mtn.

(The proposed route of the *Allegheny Trail* goes approximately 4 mi on the ridge and drops 1000 in elev on switchbacks to cross the Meadow Creek and Sherwood Lake Rd. Here it is

8 mi to Lake Sherwood and 2.5 mi to Neola. The trail continues
S on Laurel Run Rd [FR-375]. See *Little Allegheny Trail* below.)

The *Meadow Mtn Trail* descends to a small stream and rhododendron patches at 8.6 mi, crosses a stream at 9 mi, and passes
two wildlife openings on the L at 9.4 mi. Continue ahead in an
area of young locust, Virginia pine, white pine, and mountain
laurel, and reach the S terminus of the trail at 9.7 mi. Here the
trail is gated in a curve of the Sherwood Lake Rd. It is 3.9 mi
N on the Sherwood Lake Rd to the picnic area. This loop is a
total of 21.1 mi. (*USGS-FS Maps:* Lake Sherwood, Rucker Gap,
Mountain Grove)

Little Allegheny Trail *(USFS #668)*

- LENGTH: 4.2 mi

- DIFFICULTY: strenuous

- FEATURES: wildflowers, scenic, historic

- TRAILHEADS AND DETAILS: From Neola at jct WV-92 take
Sherwood Lake Rd (CO-14/1) for 1.5 mi and park on R at sign.
Begin ascent on gated road to a wildlife opening, R, at 0.1 mi.
Follow the trail on an old road, cross an intermittent drain, and
begin ascent on a well-graded but steep moss-covered trail up
a ravine. Banks of wildflowers and maidenhair fern are prominent. At 0.8 mi on the second of two switchbacks are blueberry
patches, mountain laurel, serviceberry, chestnut, oak, and dogwood. Reach the ridge crest at 1.2 mi for excellent views of
Laurel Run Valley and ski slopes of Warm Springs, Virginia.
Clear-cutting has opened areas for sighting wildlife. Follow the
ridge line with mountain laurel and wild azaleas over knolls for
2.5 mi to FR-309. At 4.2 mi reach gated S terminus of the trail
and jct, R, with Humphreys Draft Rd (FR-309-A) at a grove of
red pine. Options here are to backtrack, hike Humphreys
Draft Rd 3.6 mi down to WV-92, or continue ahead on FR-309
for 1.6 mi to Whites Draft Rd (CO-15/3), which leads 5.2 mi
down the mountain to WV-92. For additional hiking, a loop of
13.3 mi can be made by taking a L on Whites Draft Rd and

descending 0.4 mi to a jct with the proposed N–S *Allegheny Trail* at the West Virginia-Virginia state line. (This is a historic area. During the Civil War the road up Jones Hollow in the SE was used as a supply route across the mountains. See *Civil War Trail* above.) Turn L on the proposed *Allegheny Trail* and follow the foot trail for 4.5 mi to Laurel Run Rd (FR-375). Exit at Sherwood Lake Rd after another 1.6 mi, and take a 1 mi hike L (W) on the road to your point of origin for a total of 13.3 mi. (*USGS-FS Map:* Rucker Gap)

▶ MIDDLE MOUNTAIN AREA
(Greenbrier and Pocahontas Counties)

Middle Mtn Trail (South) *(13.2 mi; USFS #608); (Allegheny Trail); Dock Trail (2 mi; USFS #656); Brushy Mtn Trail (2.1 mi; USFS #655)*

• LENGTH: 17.3 mi, ct

• DIFFICULTY: moderate

• FEATURES: scenic, historic, wildlife

• TRAILHEADS AND DETAILS: In Neola at the post office and jct of WV-92 and North Fork Rd (FR-96), go W on FR-96 for 0.5 mi across the Anthony Creek bridge and ford North Fork to *Middle Mtn Trail,* R. Vehicles must be parked in an area farther up the road. At the S terminus of *Middle Mtn Trail* wade the North Fork, pass through a grassy meadow, and gradually ascend on a foot trail in and out of coves. At 1.2 mi begin the first of four switchbacks and reach the ridge crest at 1.7 mi. A number of signs on the trail mark watersheds of the hollows. For example, Hatfield Hollow at 2.1 mi, Lynch Hollow at 4.3 mi, Coles Run at 4.6 mi, and Sugar Run at 7.2 mi. At 2.3 mi and 2.7 mi are examples of mountain Andromeda (*Pieris floribunda*), a low, white, flowering shrub that blooms in early April. There is a water hole at 3.4 mi; at 4.5 mi the trail becomes a jeep road and is gated at 5 mi with the jct and W end of Coles

Run Rd (FR-875). (It is 3.7 mi on Coles Run Rd to gated entrance at WV-92, 2.4 mi N of Neola.) Continue ahead on a foot trail through an open forest of hardwoods, flame azalea, rose azalea, mountain laurel, white pine, wildflowers such as gold star, and ferns such as the maidenhair. At 7.5 mi reach a low standard forest road, Divide Rd (FR-790). At 8.9 mi pass a wildlife opening. (The proposed route of the *Allegheny Trail* will jct R at 9.5 mi and continue ahead to join the *Dock Trail*.) Reach a jct, L, at 10.8 mi with the *Dock Trail*. Ahead the *Middle Mtn Trail* continues through hardwoods, chiefly an oak and hickory forest, for 2.4 mi to a point where the old FR-790 turned R at the boundary with the Marlinton Ranger District.

(At 0.2 mi ahead reach an intersection with the newly constructed FR-790-B, L. The *Middle Mtn Trail* (N) continues ahead on the ridge, parallels L of the new FR-790-A for a short distance, and gradually descends for 4.6 mi to an exit on WV-39/92, opposite the Laurel Creek picnic area. To the R of the FR-790-B is a new 1.2 mi section of the 3 mi FR-790 that leads down the mountain to a gate at WV-92, 1.4 mi S of the Pocahontas Campground. See Section 5.)

The 2-mi *Dock Trail* is a woods road (FR-310) that is closed to vehicles year-round. It is also the *Allegheny Trail*. From the *Middle Mtn Trail* it descends for 0.6 mi on a spur ridge, S of the headwaters of Douthat Run, before curving L of the ridge and descending to "the Dock" at Douthat Rd (CO-23). The Dock received its name from a timber loading dock used by early timbermen. (To the R on the Douthat Rd it is 7 mi to WV-39/72 in Minnehaha Springs. To the L on the Douthat Rd it is 0.6 mi to gated Beaver Lick Tower Rd [FR-343], a 4.3 mi scenic road open from early October to December 31 and accessible to passenger vehicles. It ascends to a spectacular vista at a dismantled fire tower site [3645 ft]. Here is the highest point in the district and the E trailhead of the *Beaver Trail* in the Marlinton Ranger District.)

Across Douthat Rd at the W terminus of the *Dock Trail* is the *Brushy Mtn Trail*. Follow an old, gated road through a pine plantation to a gate. To the L is a grassy area with beds of mint and violets that is good for campsites. Cross a small drain and reach a fork at 0.4 mi in a meadow of cinquefoil, wild straw-berry, and peppermint. At the fork the *Allegheny Trail* contin-ues L for a 1 mi route to cross the Beaver Lick Tower Rd and join the *Beaver Creek Trail.* To the R the *Brushy Mtn Trail* crosses the drain to ascend gradually W and then N through rhodo-dendron, oak, locust, maple, mountain laurel, sassafras, and Virginia pine to the N terminus at 2.1 mi for a jct with the Beaver Lick Tower Rd. (From here it is 1.1 mi to the disman-tled Beaver Lick Tower mentioned above.) Backtrack. (*USGS-FS Maps:* Alvon, Rucker Gap, Lake Sherwood)

2.

George Washington and Jefferson National Forests

"All walking is discovery. On foot we take the time to see things whole."

— HAL BORLAND

▶ **GEORGE WASHINGTON NATIONAL FOREST**

The George Washington National Forest (GWNF), with its 1,054,922 scenic acres in Virginia (953,866) and West Virginia (101,056), is the largest national forest east of the Mississippi River. It was established by a proclamation from President Herbert Hoover on June 23, 1932. Two of its six districts, Lee and Dry River, are partially in West Virginia. Chiefly on the western slopes of the Shenandoah and Great North mountain ranges in Hardy and Pendleton counties, it is rugged, beautiful, and historic. The West Virginia forest is home for the black bear (the state animal), deer, turkey, grouse, fox, raccoon, squirrel, timber rattlesnake, owl, hawk, and numerous species of songbirds, particularly the warblers. Although a deciduous forest, there are scattered stands of magnificent white pine, Virginia pine, and hemlock. Wildflowers common to the Appalachian region are abundant.

Among its main geological attractions in West Virginia are Lost River sinks, Trout Run sinks, and panoramic ridges of limestone and sandstone cliffs. There are five recreation areas:

Brandywine, Camp Run, Trout Pond, Wolf Gap, and Hawk. All have camping units (no hookups), and Brandywine and Trout Pond have facilities for fishing and swimming. There are more than 90 mi of hiking trails.

• INFORMATION: Contact the district offices or the main office. Dry River Ranger District, 510 N Main St, Bridgewater, VA 22812, tel: 703-828-2591. Lee Ranger District, Windsor Knit Rd, Rte 1, Box 31-A, Edinburg, VA 22824, tel: 703-984-4101. GWNF Hq, Room 210, Federal Bldg (PO Box 233), Harrisonburg, VA 22801, tel: 703-433-2491.

• MAPS: Numbers 33-37

▶ DRY RIVER RANGER DISTRICT

This district has 49,106 acres on the western slopes of the Shenandoah Mtn range where dozens of tributaries flow into the South Branch of the Potomac River. The E-W US-33 passes through the center of the forest at elev 3450 ft on its route between Richmond and Ohio. Two camping areas, Brandywine on US-33 and Camp Run, N of Fort Seybert on Camp Run Rd (CO-3), are in the district. Historic Fort Seybert was the site where pioneers were massacred by the Delaware Indians in 1758. In addition to the district's designated trails, there are more than 85.2 mi of winding forest roads to hike. The district maintains Saw Mill Trail annually, but does not have an established maintenance schedule for the other trails.

▶ BRANDYWINE RECREATION AREA
(Pendleton County)

Nestled in the picturesque cove of Hawes Run, the Brandywine Recreation Area has 60 picnic units, 30 paved camping units (no hookups), a lake for swimming and fishing, drinking water, flush toilets, and two hiking trails. The area is open from May 15 to December 1, and it can be used as a base point to drive to all the other five trails in the district.

• ACCESS: From the town of Brandywine drive E on US-33 for 2.8 mi to entrance on the R. From Harrisonburg, Virginia, drive W on US-33 for 27.2 mi to entrance on the L.

• SUPPORT FACILITIES: A grocery store, motel, restaurant, and service station are in the town of Brandywine. Privately operated Shenandoah Shadow Campground with hookups and open year-round is nearby; tel: 304-249-5184.

Saw Mill Trail (USFS #1035)

• LENGTH: 4.3 mi

• DIFFICULTY: moderate

• FEATURE: wildlife

• TRAILHEAD AND DETAILS: Park in the parking lot, if not camping, and walk 0.4 mi to old logging road with yellow blazes in the second circle of the campground. Pass through opening of wildlife food plot; silverberry is prominent. At 0.3 mi begin first of four crossings of Hawes Run, a small tumbling stream. Pass R of old sawmill site at 1.3 mi in a forest of oaks, white pines, and hemlocks. Ascend the SW slope of a ridge at 2.3 mi, descend, cross another ridge, and descend to a stream in a hemlock grove at 3 mi. Pass through three more wildlife food plots and return to the campground at 4.3 mi. (USGS Map: Brandywine)

High Knob Trail (USFS #1021)

• LENGTH: 5.4 mi, rt

• DIFFICULTY: strenuous, elev gain 2120 ft

• FEATURES: secluded and scenic

• TRAILHEAD AND DETAILS: Park in the parking lot, if not camping, and walk 0.4 mi to a gated wildlife food plot (opposite campsite #28) and go 150 yds along R edge of silverberry border to entrance by a tall white pine. (This trail may be overgrown in sections.) Ascend the steep ridge through a forest of oak, mountain laurel, locust, maple, dogwood, hickory, and white and Virginia pine for the entire ridge length of 2.3 mi. Along the trail are patches of huckleberry, trailing arbutus, and other wildflowers. Near the top of the mountain reach the private road of MacNeff. (It is 0.7 mi L to US-33 at the West Virginia-Virginia state line.) Turn R, go 0.1 mi on the road to a fork, and turn L to High Knob, elev 4080 ft. The lookout tower has been dismantled. Backtrack. (*USGS Map:* Brandywine)

Road Run Trail *(USFS #1023)*

- LENGTH: 2.8 mi, rt

- DIFFICULTY: strenuous, elev gain 1400 ft

- FEATURES: wildlife

- TRAILHEADS AND DETAILS: From Brandywine Recreation Area drive 0.7 mi E on US-33 to jct with West Side Rd (FR-151) on L. Drive 2.7 mi on FR-151 to small parking area on R in sharp curve; trail sign is on R bank before the curve. (Another access is to go 3.1 mi E on US-33 from Brandywine Recreation Area to jct with FR-85 [Hall Spring Hunter Access Rd] on L. This is a rough, narrow but scenic route; you may have to walk it. After 2.6 mi reach the trailhead on L.) From FR-151 trail sign ascend steeply on unblazed path of 0.3 mi to crest of ridge with leaning chestnut oaks. Bear L and ascend on gradual contour in oaks, Virginia pines, and patches of huckleberries. Area is remote. Reach FR-85 at 1.4 mi. Backtrack or use vehicle shuttle. (*USGS Map:* Brandywine)

Bother Ridge Trail (USFS #1026)

- LENGTH: 3.1 mi

- DIFFICULTY: strenuous, elev gain 1820 ft

- FEATURES: scenic views of Reddish Knob and Little Fork Valley

- TRAILHEAD AND DETAILS: From the town of Brandywine jct of US-33 and Sugar Grove Rd (CO-21), drive 9.7 mi S on CO-21 to jct with Moyers Gap Rd (CO-25). Turn L on CO-25 and drive 3.5 mi to narrow dirt road on L for SW trailhead. Park in grassy area of the Transcontinental Cable Route. Trailhead is at the continuing jeep road. For the NE trailhead continue the drive on CO-25, pass FR-61 on R at 0.6 mi, and after 3.4 mi farther reach mountain summit jct with FR-85. (Ahead in Virginia on SR-924, VA-257, and VA-42 it is 21 mi to Harrisonburg. On the R of this jct is FR-85 S and 2.5 mi to panoramic Reddish Knob, 4387 ft.) Turn L on FR-85 N and drive 1.7 mi to fork of FR-85 and FR-85-A. Park here (FR-85-A goes R to Flagpole Knob). Hike L on narrow, rough FR-85 for 0.6 mi to trailhead on L. Descend on yellow-blazed jeep road for 0.7 mi. Turn L off road and follow ridge, which has excellent views. Wild turkey are often seen here. Also, this area is rich in plant life; Fraser's fir *(Abies fraseri)* and red pine are among the conifers near Bother Knob, and fragrant pennyroyal *(Hedeoma pulegioides)* is on the trail. In the middle of October the green-striped-maple leaves turn to brilliant yellows and gold. Views of Reddish Knob, Little Fork Valley, and the US Naval Reservation with huge dishes for radio astronomy and defense purposes are visible from the rock outcrops. At 2.5 mi is a faint red arrow on L. (Ahead for 0.1 mi is yellow blaze for similar direction.) Descend steeply to large walnut tree at jeep road. Turn R, cross small stream, and reach Transcontinental Cable Route parking area at 3.1 mi. (*USGS Maps:* Brandywine, Reddish Knob, Palo Alto)

Sugar Run Trail (USFS #1025)

- LENGTH: 4.5 mi

- DIFFICULTY: strenuous, elev gain 2220 ft

- FEATURES: wildlife and wildflowers

- TRAILHEAD AND DETAILS: From the town of Brandywine drive S on Sugar Grove Rd (CO-21) for 5.5 mi and turn L on Little Fork Rd (CO-24). Drive 2.3 mi on CO-24 (crossing unbridged Little Fork) to FR on L. Park here. (FR may be passable for jeep or 4WD-vehicle.) Begin hike on unblazed trail by crossing Little Fork and reach forest boundary at 0.2 mi. Cross Sugar Run a number of times; excellent campsites are at 1.4 mi. Oaks, white and Virginia pines tower over carpet of ground ivy and bunches of ferns. Take R fork in horseshoe curve of road at 1.8 mi and ascend upstream through tall oaks, maples, ash, and birch. Wildflowers and wildlife are prominent. Reach headwaters in deep cove at 3.8 mi; ascend on old road bordered with mountain laurel to FR-85 at 4.5 mi. Backtrack or use vehicle shuttle. (This trailhead can be reached by following directions to NE trailhead of Bother Knob Trail [see above], but walk 0.1 mi farther on FR-85 to Sugar Run Trail, unsigned but marked with a white blaze on L at entrance.) (USGS Maps: Brandywine, Sugar Grove)

Miller Run Trail (USFS #1022)

- LENGTH: 4.6 mi

- DIFFICULTY: strenuous, elev gain 1880 ft

- FEATURES: mountain streams

- TRAILHEAD AND DETAILS: From the town of Brandywine drive S on Sugar Grove Rd (CO-21) for 2 mi to Miller Run Rd (CO-21/3), turn L and drive 2 mi to gate and posted property of Luther Hoover. Request permission to hike upstream to forest boundary on old road for 2.6 mi along pastoral stream with wildflowers. At the end of the road leave stream L and ascend ridge to switchbacks at 3.5 mi and again at 3.9 mi. At 4.6 mi reach the summit and rough FR-85. (It is 1.6 mi R on FR-85 to *Bother Ridge Trail* trailhead, described above.) Backtrack or use vehicle shuttle. (*USGS Map:* Brandywine)

▶ CAMP RUN RECREATION AREA
(Pendleton County)

This area is tranquil and isolated with nine camping sites, hand pump drinking water, vault toilet, and lake for fishing. The campground is open year-round.

• ACCESS: From the town of Brandywine drive N on US-33 for 3.3 mi to Oak Flat, turn R on Sweedlin Valley Rd (CO-3), and follow it for 9.8 mi to Camp Run Rd (CO-3/1) at Camp Run Store and Swap Shop. Drive 1.5 mi to campground. (Support facilities are the same as for Brandywine Campground described above.)

Buck Lick Run Trail *(USFS #1016)*

• LENGTH: 2.2 mi

• DIFFICULTY: strenuous, elev gain 1802 ft

• FEATURES: wildlife, Cow Knob

• TRAILHEAD AND DETAILS: From the campground go 0.2 mi up Camp Run, turn R on FR-152 (rough, you may have to walk) and go 3 mi to Buck Lick Run. Cross stream; trailhead is on the L. Ascend gradually for 0.9 mi, then ascend steeply to ridge and reach FR-85 at 2.2 mi on the state boundary. (Right, 0.9 mi on FR-85 leads to 4036 ft Cow Knob. If you desire a farther scenic forest loop walk, continue on FR-85 for 2.3 mi to jct with FR-87. Turn R, descend for 4.6 mi to FR-152, R, and hike rough road for 3.7 mi to the origin.) (*USGS Maps:* Cow Knob, Fort Seybert)

▶ LEE RANGER DISTRICT

Three recreational areas — Trout Pond, Wolf Cap, and Hawk — are in the 51,950 acres of this district in West Virginia. Its eastern edge is the crest of the Great North Mountain, the boundary line between the Virginias. Its many tributaries flow into Lost River, which after its 3 mi disappearance into Sandy Ridge becomes Cacapon River, a tributary of the Potomac. Two state highways, 55 in the N between Strasburg, Virginia, and Wardensville, West Virginia, and 259 in the S between Harrisonburg and Wardensville, are the major accesses. The district is noted for its highly folded sedimentary rocks of sandstone and limestone, and for historic communities such as Wardensville, a settlement laid out by George Washington for William Warden. Warden and his family were massacred by the Delaware Indians in 1758. Lost River State Park, another historic area, is near the town of Mathias in the SW corner of the district. Black bear, deer, turkey, and raccoon have a wide range in the predominately oak forest, except for conifer stands on some of the rocky ridges. The district does not have a strict schedule of trail maintenance. However, a priority list of trail needs is followed as funding becomes available. In addition to the district's designated hiking trails, there are 79.2 mi of scenic forest roads.

▶ TROUT POND RECREATION AREA
(Hardy County)

This exceptionally attractive recreational area has 50 campsites for tents or RVs; 29 picnic units, some with shelters; Rock Cliff Lake, a 16-acre reservoir for fishing, boating (no outboards), and swimming; bathhouse, dumping station, hot showers and flush toilets. The season is April 1–December 1. Trout Pond Recreation Area takes its name from the state's only and largest (1.5-acre) natural lake. It is 300 yds upstream from Rock Cliff Lake. USFS operated; tel: 703-984-4101.

Address: Trout Pond Rec Area, Rte 3, Box 40, Lost River, WV 26811, tel: 304-897-6450.

• ACCESS: Drive 6 mi N from town of Mathias or 18 mi S from Wardensville on WV-259 to community of Lost River. Drive 4.5 mi on Mill Gap Rd (CO-16) and turn R on FR-500 for 1.7 mi to the recreation area entrance.

• SUPPORT FACILITIES: A grocery store, restaurant, and service station are on the WV-259 highway between Lost River and Mathias.

Rock Cliff Trail (1 mi; USFS #1010); Chimney Rock Trail (0.8 mi; USFS #1010B); Fishermen's Trail (0.4 mi; USFS #1010A)

• LENGTH: 3.4 mi, ct

• DIFFICULTY: easy

• FEATURES: rare rock outcrops

• TRAILHEADS AND DETAILS: From the fishermen's parking lot at Rock Cliff Lake, follow the sign around the lake perimeter on a well-graded trail. Cross the top of the dam at 0.4 mi to rock formation and jct with *Chimney Rock Trail* on R. *Chimney Rock Trail* descends to a vertical rock outcropping of highly erosion-resistant Oriskany sandstone, crosses Trout Run at 0.4 mi, and ascends for another 0.4 mi to jct with *Trout Pond Trail*. Backtrack. Continue around the lake to jct with blue-blazed *Fishermen's Trail*, R, at 0.7 mi. *Fishermen's Trail* ascends to FR-500 for 0.4 mi. Backtrack and turn R toward bridge across a lake tributary. Complete the combined trails at 3.4 mi. (*USGS Map:* Wolf Gap)

Trout Pond Trail *(2.5 mi; USFS #1008);* ***Long Mountain Trail***
(7.8 mi; USFS #1007)

- LENGTH: 10.3 mi, ct

- DIFFICULTY: moderate

- FEATURES: sinkholes, wildlife

- TRAILHEADS AND DETAILS: *Trout Pond Trail* is a 2.5 mi purple-
blazed trail whose name is derived from the small natural limestone sinkhole pond near the campground. Enter the middle
of the trail between campsites #30 and #31. If going S ascend
for 1.4 mi to gravel Judge Rye Rd (CO-59) and backtrack. (Or
a loop can be made here by ascending Judge Rye Rd for 1.9 mi
to S terminus of yellow-blazed *Long Mtn Trail* on L. Follow *Long
Mtn Trail* on old jeep road for 0.6 mi, then on a foot trail for
another 1.8 mi to jct with *Trout Pond Trail* and *Chimney Rock
Trail.* Turn L on *Trout Pond Trail,* and go 1.1 mi to complete
circle to campground for a total of 6.8 mi.) If going N on the
Trout Pond Trail from campsites #30 and #31, cross creek, pass
L of large sinkhole, and jct with *Long Mtn Trail* at 1.1 mi. (Backtrack, or reverse the loop described above.)

To continue N on the *Long Mtn Trail* (also called *Crack Whip
Furnace Trail*) begin here at jct. Hike along generally even
contour on old road in a hardwood forest with scattered grassy
and brushy areas. At 0.5 mi pass clearing with W view of Ben's
Ridge. At 3.8 mi the road becomes a foot trail for 1.1 mi.
Halfway through the foot trail is a wet area between Cherry
Ridge and Long Mtn. Reach Trout Run Rd (CO-23/10) on the
L side of a private cabin, a few yards W of, and across the road
from, the remains of the Crack Whip Furnace, for a total of 7.8
mi from S terminus on Judge Rye Rd or 6.5 mi from Trout
Pond Campground. Backtrack or use vehicle shuttle. (It is 6.5
mi N on CO-23/10 to the town of Wardensville.) On the S
termini of the *Trout Pond Trail* easy connections can be made
with the N terminus of *North Mtn Trail* (see below).

North Mountain Trail (USFS #1009)

- LENGTH: 6.5 mi

- DIFFICULTY: moderate

- FEATURES: vistas, wildlife

- TRAILHEADS AND DETAILS: To reach the N trailhead drive from Lost City E on WV-59 for 7.8 mi to the state boundary (3005 ft). (*Trout Pond Trail* is 0.8 mi W on *Long Mtn Trail* is 1.2 mi E on this road.) On the Virginia side, drive from Columbia Furnace 9.9 mi (4.5 mi on SR-675, 0.3 mi on SR-789, and 5.1 mi on SR-691). To reach the S trailhead drive from Mathias E 4.8 mi on Upper Cove Rd (CO-20) to Basore jct. Continue 0.3 mi, turn L at poultry house, and ascend for 2.1 mi on steep road to top of the mountain. On the Virginia side, drive from the town of Basye 8.3 mi (3.9 mi on SR-717 and 4.4 mi on SR-720).

  There are no springs on this trail. If beginning at N trailhead follow orange blazes (*Laurel Run Trail* also begins here on L, descending), and reach overlook at 0.8 mi. Purple-blazed *Stack Rock Trail* (also called *Table Rock Trail*) jct is at 2.2 mi, and yellow-blazed *Falls Ridge Trail* is 100 yds farther on the Virginia side. Parts of hardwood forest are lined with huckleberry, mountain laurel, hawthorn, and bear oak *(Quercus ilicifolia)* thickets at 2.3 mi, 3.3 mi, 4.3 mi, and 5 mi. Among the wildflowers are snakeroot, meadow rue, wild geraniums, and woodland sunflowers. Deer, grouse, and turkey may be seen. Large cone-shaped homes of hot-tempered ants are at 3.9 mi and 5.3 mi. Rock outcrops are at 2.7 mi, 3.9 mi, and 4.7 mi. Pass an old homesite at 6 mi. Arrive at gated S terminus at 6.5 mi. (*USGS Maps:* Orkney Springs, Lost City, Wolf Gap)

▶ WOLF GAP RECREATION AREA (Hardy County)

High on the crest of the Virginia-West Virginia state line (2240 ft) is Wolf Gap Recreation Area with ten paved camping units, ten picnic units, a hand pump for drinking water, and vault toilets. It is an excellent base campground open year-round for hikes S to Tibbet Knob and the Trout Pond Recreation Area, and N to Big Schloss and the *Big Blue Trail*. By combining trails and some forest and secondary roadways, scenic and challenging loops can be made in Virginia (described in *Hiking the Old Dominion* published by Sierra Club Books) or in West Virginia. For example, ascend on the scenic *Mill Mtn Trail* and go 6 mi to *Pond Run Trail*. Turn L and go 0.9 mi to jct with *Half Moon Trail*. Follow *Half Moon Trail* for 3.1 mi to Trout Run Rd (CO-32/10). Turn R on paved CO-32/10 and go 1.3 mi to Crack Whip Furnace; turn L on *Long Mtn Trail* (which makes jct with trails into Trout Pond Recreation Area) for 7.8 mi. Reach Virginia Lost City Rd (SR-691), which becomes Judge Rye Rd (CO-59) in West Virginia. Turn L on SR-691 and descend for 2.5 mi to *Tibbet Knob Trail* on L. Ascend on *Tibbet Knob Trail* for 2.4 mi and reach the Wolf Gap Recreation Area for a total of 24 mi.

• ACCESS: From Wardensville in West Virginia drive SE on Trout Run Rd (CO-23/10) for 13.3 mi. From Edinburg, Virginia, follow SR-675 W for 12 mi.

Big Blue Trail

The combined *Big Blue Trail* (144 mi) and the *Tuscarora Trail* (119.7 mi) are an interstate alternate W of the *AT* in Virginia, West Virginia, Maryland, and Pennsylvania. The trails provide three long-distance circuit hikes if the *C&O Canal Towpath* is used; it cuts across the middle of the long, 432-mi loop. The northern loop is 271.1 mi and the southern loop is 264.5 mi. From its southern jct with the *AT* at Matthews Arm Campground in the Shenandoah National Park, the *Big Blue Trail* extends W across the Shenandoah Valley and sections of the GWNF into West Virginia. It joins the *Tuscarora Trail* at Hancock, Maryland, at the Potomac River. (The *Tuscarora Trail's* northern terminus is at Dean's Gap with the *AT* near Donnellytown, Pennsylvania.) Described below is the 19.3 mi West Virginia segment in the GWNF from Hawk Recreation Area near Capron Springs Rd (N) to *Little North Mtn Trail* in Virginia (S). (The Potomac Appalachian Trail Club has published two pocket-size guidebooks, *The Big Blue — North Half* and *South Half* — with maps of the *Big Blue Trail* by Elizabeth Johnston and Lynn Gallagher. For information contact PATC, 1718 N St, NW, Washington, DC 20036, tel: 202-638-5306, weeknights 7–10 P.M. For the *Tuscarora Trail*, contact the Keystone Trails Association, PO Box 251, Cogan Station, PA 17728.)

Mill Mtn Trail (6 mi; USFS #1004); Big Schloss Trail (0.3 mi; USFS #1004A); Big Schloss Cutoff Trail (1.3 mi; USFS #415); Pond Run Trail (Big Blue Trail) (3.9 mi; USFS #1013.2); Peer Trail (3.2 mi; USFS #1002); Half Moon Trail (3.2 mi; USFS #1003); Half Moon Lookout Trail (0.8 mi; USFS #1003A)

- LENGTH: 9.8 mi, ct

- DIFFICULTY: moderate

- FEATURES: panoramic Big Schloss, Half Moon Overlook

- TRAILHEADS AND DETAILS: Begin the hike near campsite #9, ascend on orange-blazed wide jeep road for 0.9 mi to scenic crest of Mill Mtn. Bear L on rocky trail tread and reach jct with white-blazed *Big Schloss Trail* at 1.9 mi. Turn R and ascend sharply for 0.3 mi to massive metamorphosed sandstone rock formation (2964 ft) called the "Castle" by early German settlers. Magnificent views include Trout Run Valley and Long Mtn in the W and Little Schloss Mtn and Little Stony Creek Valley in the E. Return to *Mill Mtn Trail*, turn R on W flank of the Castle to the ridge and reach jct with blue-blazed *Big Schloss Cutoff Trail* at 2.8 mi. (This is a 1.3 mi spur trail that descends E to FR-92, 0.5 mi W from the E terminus of *Little Stony Creek Trail*.) Continue ahead and reach Sandstone Spring in a stand of hemlock and a fern glade at 4.5 mi. (This area is the headwaters of a cascading stream W into the canyon of Deep Gutter Run.) On a straight trail through oaks and mountain laurel ascend to an airway beacon (3293 ft, the area's highest peak) at

5.5 mi. Among the trail's wildflowers are fly poison (*Amianthium muscaetoxicum*) with white petals that turn green with age. Descend gradually through open oak forest and reach jct with *Pond Run Trail* (also called the *Big Blue Trail*) at 6 mi.

(Right, at this jct, the blue-blazed *Pond Run Trail* descends on a jeep road for 0.6 mi to Sugar Knob Gap and a four-way intersection with yellow-blazed *Little Stony Creek Trail* S and nearby Sugar Knob Cabin owned by the PATC; the purple-blazed, 3-mi *Peer Trail*, N, ends on private property of Rex Ferrell in Wilson Cove on Waites Run Rd, 6.7 mi from Wardensville; the continuing E blue-blazed rocky *Three Ponds Trail* [also called the *Big Blue Trail*] goes 3 mi to another *Big Blue Trail*. It is the *Little North Trail* in Virginia where the *Big Blue Trail* continues for 48 miles to the *AT* in the Shenandoah National Park.)

Turn L on the *Pond Run Trail* through large oaks and reach Half Moon Spring, R, at 6.7 mi and jct with *Half Moon Trail* at 6.9 mi. A small, natural wildlife watering hole is here. (Right, the *Pond Run Trail* descends, follows, and crosses the Pond Run stream frequently in hemlock groves for 2.4 mi to Waites Run Rd [CO-5/1], 6 mi from the jct with WV-55/259 in Wardensville.) Continue ahead on the *Half Moon Trail,* and arrive at a jct with the *Half Moon Lookout Trail* R at 7.5 mi. (This 0.8-mi, white-blazed spur trail to the remains of a rock lookout provides superb views of Mill Mtn and Trout Run Valley. Backtrack.) Continue on the *Half Moon Trail;* descend on a well-graded trail carpeted with moss and banked with mountain laurel to Half Moon Run at 8.3 mi. Curve L, cross stream, and follow forest road to gate at Trout Run and CO-32/10 for a total of 10.8 mi. Vehicle shuttle L to Wolf Gap on CR-32/10 is 5.3 mi. (*USGS Maps:* Wolf Gap, Woodstock, Wardensville)

▶ **HAWK RECREATION AREA**
   (Hampshire County)

At a peaceful and remote setting in a hardwood forest, the facilities are 15 campsites (no hookups), a group campground, a ten-unit picnic area, hand pump for drinking water, and vault toilets. The GWNF made this a primitive nonfee campground in 1985; the season is year-round.

• ACCESS: From I-81 in Strasburg, Virginia, follow VA-55 W for 15.3 mi and turn R on FR-502; from Wardensville, West Virginia, go E on VA-55 for 4 mi, turn L on FR-502, turn L on FR-347, and go 0.7 mi to campground entrance on R.

• SUPPORT FACILITIES: A grocery store, restaurant, bank, service station, motel, and laundromat are in Wardensville.

Hawk Trail (Big Blue Trail) (5.2 mi; USFS #1013.4); *County Line Trail (Big Blue Trail)* (8.6 mi; USFS #1013.3); *Vances Cove Trail* (6.3 mi; USFS #400); *Gerhard Trail* (0.6 mi)

• LENGTH: 18.7 mi, ct

• DIFFICULTY: moderate to strenuous

• FEATURES: Great North Mtn, Paddy Run

• TRAILHEADS AND DETAILS: The *Big Blue Trail* system runs through the Hawk Recreation Area. The 5.2 mi *Hawk Trail (Big Blue Trail)* extends NW 1.6 mi to Hawk Run and cascades, and S 3.6 mi from the Hawk campground entrance gate to WV-55. Described here is the S direction. Ascend the blue-blazed trail for 0.7 mi, where it crosses FR-502 and begin a climb of 18 switchbacks to the ridge of the Great North Mtn at 1.8 mi. Bear R, pass two AT&T towers, and reach WV-VA-55 at 3.6 mi. Cross the highway and begin the 8.6 mi *County Line Trail (Big Blue Trail)*, named for the dividing line between counties in the Virginias. Follow an old road. There are a few overlooks, the best at 3.8 mi and 6.8 mi. At 4.3 mi is the Paul Gerhard Memorial Shelter, built by the Terrapin Trail Club of the University of Maryland in honor of the *AT* hiker and climber. (A blue-blazed spur trail with a spring descends here for 0.6 mi to Paddy Run, FR-371.) At 6.7 mi bear R and begin a descent of a 1400-ft drop in elev on a series of switchbacks with numerous rock steps. Reach FR gate at Waites Run Rd

(CO-5/1) at 8.6 mi. Here the *Big Blue Trail* continues S on the *Pond Run Trail* (see description above). (It is 6.3 mi R on Waites Run Rd to Wardensville.)

To hike the 6.3-mi *Vances Cove Trail*, turn L on Waites Run Rd, go 0.9 mi to the beginning of a yellow-blazed FR on the L, and follow Cove Run to its end at 2.1 mi. (A timber sale and road reconstruction with some relocation is planned in the area.) Here the trail continues over a low, flat ridge to follow Paddy Run (a trout-stocked stream) E of FR-371 on an old jeep trail. Reach jct with *Gerhard Trail* at 3.7 mi. Continue downstream, crisscrossing Paddy Run on a frequently overgrown and wet treadway. At 4.7 mi the fisherman's trail is easier to follow than the old jeep road. Vegetation is chiefly hardwood with sparse hemlock, white and Virginia pine. Reach the confluence of Paddy Run and Vances Cove Run. Rock hop to an old campsite and jct with a 4WD-road at 6.3 mi, the N terminus of *Vances Cove Trail*. Access to this point is on FR-93 (suitable for passenger vehicles), 2.7 mi from VA-55 (and 0.8 mi E from the West Virginia-Virginia state line) to a road fork and parking area (R is FR-371). Park here and take a L on the 4WD-road, rock hop the stream, pass under a power line, and at 0.2 mi reach the old campsite and yellow blaze, R. (By using the N access, a round-trip hike of 26.7 mi can be made by turning L on US-55 for 0.8 mi to the jct with the *County Line Trail* and *Hawk Trail*. Turn R on the *Hawk Trail* and return to Hawk Campground.) (*USGS Maps:* Yellow Spring, Wardensville, Mountain Falls)

Squirrel Gap Trail *(2.2 mi; USFS #1006)*; Brushy Hollow Trail *(3 mi; USFS #1019)*

- LENGTH: 6.7 mi, ct

- DIFFICULTY: moderate

- FEATURES: site of old whiskey distillery

- TRAILHEADS AND DETAILS: From Wardensville go S on WV-55/259 for 2.3 mi to the top of the ridge and turn L on Squirrel

Gap Rd (FR-344). Drive 4 mi to post-gated road on R. Park here. Hike the blue-blazed road to fork at 0.4 mi. Turn L through open area that has been timbered. Pass R of old sawdust piles at 0.7 mi and at 1 mi to jct with yellow-blazed *Brushy Hollow Trail*, L. Continue ahead to High Top Ridge at 1.5 mi for a fine view of Lost River valley. Descend steeply to Lost River, rock hop (unless the 125-ft-wide river has high water), and ascend to WV-55/259 at 2.2 mi. A highway pull-off is nearby on R. (From here it is 2.4 mi E on WV-55/259 to a picnic area at Lost River bridge and sinks. West it is 3 mi to jct with WV-29.)

A backtracking hike to *Brushy Hollow Trail* is 1.2 mi; turn R on the 3.0 mi *Brushy Hollow Trail*. Descend on a well-graded foot trail to an old woods road in Ellis Hollow. Pass through a flat area and unseen site of old whisky distillery. At 0.6 mi reach a huge spring gushing from a hole in a rock ledge, 50 yds L of the trail. The spring is on private property. To the R is private property with an old farmhouse and outbuildings. Continue ahead under a forest canopy of tall hardwoods and hemlocks on an old woods road upstream. Mosses, ferns, and liverwort cover sections of the treadway and rocky areas. Cross the stream a number of times and at 2.7 mi leave the low area and ascend from Brushy Holly to Squirrel Gap Road. Backtrack or use vehicle shuttle on Squirrel Gap Rd for 4 mi to point of origin. (*USGS Map:* Baker)

▶ JEFFERSON NATIONAL FOREST

"Of all exercises, walking is the best."
— THOMAS JEFFERSON

The Jefferson National Forest (JNF) has six districts and over 680,000 acres extending in portions from near Kentucky in the W, the Tennessee-North Carolina borders in the SW, and to the James River in the NE. Two of the districts, Blacksburg and New Castle, extend N into the Panhandle of Monroe County, for 18,175 acres.

In Virginia, the Jefferson National Forest has more than 950 mi of hiking and horse trails, the longest of which is the *Appalachian National Scenic Trail* (AT) with 300 mi. In addition to a vast trail system there are 45 recreational areas. It has two outstanding areas of special significance. One is the 154,000-acre Mt Rogers National Recreational Area, designated by Congress in 1966 to provide multiple recreational opportunities. There are more than 200 mi of hiking and horse trails in this magnificent range of Virginia's highest peaks (Mt Rogers, 5729 ft, and White Top Mtn, 5530 ft). The other area is the JNF's only wilderness — the 8703-acre James River Face Wilderness, set aside by the Eastern Wilderness Act of 1975. It is a priceless scenic preserve that borders the James River on the N (across the river from Glasgow and Snowden) and the Blue Ridge Parkway on the S. The *AT* runs through this wilderness and connects with other trails. (Details of the Jefferson National Forest trails are in *Hiking the Old Dominion,* a totebook published by Sierra Club Books.)

The forest boundaries within Monroe County, West Virginia, are the steep Peters Mtn ridge on the edge of the St. Clair thrust fault in the N and the Potts Mtn ridge in the S along the state line. Potts Creek runs NE through the valley between the ridges. The most scenic area in the county is Hanging Rock on Peters Mtn. The districts are chiefly hardwood forests with mixed Virginia and white pine, and hemlock. Rhododendron patches are frequent in the coves and mountain laurel and wild azaleas are on the slopes and ridges. Other vascular plants are haw, alder, blueberry, asters, wild orchids, wintergreen, galax, ferns, phlox, yellow violets, shooting star *(Dodecatheon meadia),* goldenrod, pink corydalis *(Corydalis sempervirens),* and Greek valerian *(Polemonium reptans).* A more infrequent plant, turkey beard *(Xerophyllum asphodelioides),* has been seen on Peters Mtn. Its stalks are considered a delicacy by deer. Grasses and sedges are prominent and varied. Wildlife includes bear, deer, grouse, wild turkey, hawks, owls, squirrels, chipmunks, raccoons, rattlesnakes, and songbirds.

• MAP: Number 38

▶ BLACKSBURG RANGER DISTRICT

The Blacksburg District has 8876 acres in West Virginia, but does not have any maintained forest roads or recreational areas. There are, however, an estimated 20 mi of abandoned woods road, 6 mi of which are on an old RR grade. Adjoining the state line is White Rock Recreation Area with a campground; it is described below. Access to the area is on paved Waiteville Rd (CO-17 and SR-635), a valley road connecting Pearisburg from the SW to Paint Bank in the NE. Running N–S is gravel and partially paved Limestone Hill Rd, also called Gap Mills Rd (CO-15), crooked and steep in sections, which connects Gap Mills in West Virginia to Maggie and VA-42 in Virginia.

Only portions of two trails, the *Allegheny Trail*, which traverses Peters Mtn (4.5 mi), and the *Virginias Nature Trail* (0.3 mi), are in the district. A 4.6-mi segment of the 5.5-mi *Potts Mtn Trail* borders the state line between Monroe and Craig counties. Also under the district's management is a third trail, the *Ground Hog Trail*, on the N side of Peters Mtn and S of the community of Lindside. It is a 1.5 mi access route to the *AT* and the S terminus of the *Allegheny Trail*. The *Virginias Nature Trail* begins in the White Rocks Recreation Area campground, across the road from campsite #9. On a wide and sometimes rocky tread, it goes through a hardwood forest with rhododendron and hemlock in the coves. Ground cedar, wintergreen, and galax are among the ground covers. At 0.6 mi the trail crosses into West Virginia, but returns to Virginia after crossing Stony Creek. The trail loop is complete on the return to campsite #33 and to the point of origin after 1.2 mi. A brochure explains the 22 interpretive nature posts.

From the White Rock Recreation Area it is 11.7 mi to the *Allegheny Trail*. When leaving the campground, turn R on SR-613, go 0.8 mi, turn R on the Waiteville Rd, SR-635, and go 6.1 mi to Gap Mills Rd (CO-15), L. Ascend for 3.9 mi to the top of Peters Mtn and park at a small parking area, L, under a power line. Follow the yellow-blazed *Allegheny Trail* for 1 mi to a spur trail, L, which leads 0.1 mi to Hanging Rock and an observation tower (3812 ft). Here is a spectacular 360° view of the Peters Mtn range and far beyond in both states. From the spur jct the *Allegheny Trail* continues SW for another 3.5 mi in West Virginia and 8.1 mi in Virginia to join the *AT*. (See detailed description in Chapter 11.) (*USGS-FS Maps:* Lindside, Interior, Waiteville, Gap Mills)

In the Virginia part of the district, there are three campgrounds: Walnut Flats, off SR-606, 12 mi NE of Bland; White Pine, off SR-606, also 12 mi NE of Bland; and White Rock, the nearest to West Virginia and described below. Other recreational areas and attractions are the *AT* (and 45 mi on ten other trails); Interior Picnic Area on SR-635, 13 mi NE of Pearisburg; Cascades (70-ft waterfall) on SR-623, 5 mi N of Pembroke; Wind Rock Overlook on the *AT* near White Rock Recreation Area; Minnie Ball Hill, Civil War site, near Wind Rock on SR-613; Mountain Lake Scenic Area and virgin hemlock stand, off SR-613 near Minnie Ball Hill; and Mountain Lake, Virginia's highest natural lake (over 4000 ft) on SR-613 from US-460 at Hoges Chapel.

▶ NEW CASTLE RANGER DISTRICT

The New Castle District has 9299 acres in West Virginia, all in Monroe County, and three forest roads with a total of 10.9 mi and 2.7 mi of rivers and streams. Only Wilson Branch Rd (FR-5031) on the N slope of Potts Mtn range is open. The other forest roads are closed to vehicle traffic. There are no recreation areas or trails, put probably 15 mi of the *Allegheny Trail* will be located in the district, 7 mi of which will be in West Virginia. Access to the area is the same as described above for the Blacksburg District. (*USGS-FS Maps:* Interior, Waiteville, Paint Bank, Craig Springs, Gap Mills)

• SUPPORT FACILITIES: The nearest campground in the Blacksburg and New Castle districts is White Rock Recreation Area. It has 49 campsites, tent pads, tables, grills, drinking water, and rest rooms. Season is April 1–December 1. Access is at the jct of

US-460 and SR-635, 3 mi E from downtown Pearisburg and 3 mi W of Pembroke. Drive 15.7 mi on SR-635 to jct with SR-613. Turn R, go 0.8 mi to campground entrance, and turn L. The nearest general store with groceries and gasoline is near the American Gypsum Plant, 4.1 mi after entering SR-635 from US-460. Pearisburg has motels, restaurants, banks, service stations, a hospital, and shopping centers.

• INFORMATION: Contact the district offices or the main office. Blacksburg Ranger District, Rte 1, Box 404, Blacksburg, VA 24060, tel: 703-552-4641, 1 mi W of Blacksburg on US-460; New Castle Ranger District, PO Box 246, New Castle, VA 24127, tel: 703-864-5195, 2 mi E of New Castle on SR-615; JNF Hq, Forest Supervisor, 210 Franklin Rd, SW, Roanoke, VA 24001, tel: 703-982-6270.

PART TWO

National Park System and Corps of Engineers Trails

Blueberries/Photo by the author

3.

Appalachian National Scenic Trail

"Another mile and the Long Cruise would be over. Almost I wished that the Trail really was endless, that no one could ever hike its length."
— EARL V. SHAFFER

The 2100-mile *Appalachian National Scenic Trail* (AT) weaves, rises, and falls on ridges and valleys of the Appalachian Mountains in 14 eastern states. A continuous scenic corridor from Maine to Georgia, it is a living, changing masterpiece of incredible dreams, design, and dedication. To hike from end to end, the average number of footsteps is 5,240,000 and the average time it would take is between four and five months. More than 1200 hikers are known to have completed the world's most famous trail, and millions of other hikers have been lured by its mystique to walk parts of its path.

Earl Shaffer, a WWII veteran from Pennsylvania, was 29 years old when he began his solitary attempt to become the first to hike the *AT* in one trip. At the time (1948), trail leaders thought such a feat impossible. He started at Mt. Oglethorpe, Georgia, on April 4 and completed the journey on August 5 on Katahdin, Maine. His remarkable adventure is documented in his journal *Walking with Spring*, which was first privately printed in 1981 and later published by the Appalachian Trail Conference in 1984. Shaffer hiked the *AT* in the opposite direction in 1965, the first hiker to complete the *AT* in both directions. He started at Katahdin on July 19, and finished at

Springer Mtn, Georgia, on October 25. (The first person to hike the *AT* in sections was Myron H. Avery, from the 1920s to 1936.)

The first woman to hike the complete distance in one continuous trip was Mrs. Emma Gatewood ("Grandma Gatewood") of Ohio. She started at Mt Oglethorpe on May 3, 1955, and finished at Katahdin on September 25. She followed the same route again in 1957, and by 1964, at the age of 77, completed the third trip she had earlier taken in sections. She was dearly loved by the trail world for many reasons. Among them were her stamina, her love for people, and her great sense of humor. For example, on one occasion she was lost and was reminded of it when found by a forest official. "Not lost," she said, "just misplaced." (The first woman to complete the *AT* in sections was Mary Kilpatrick of Philadelphia. She finished in 1939.)

The name and the concept of this supertrail was solely that of Benton MacKaye, a forester and author from Shirley Center, Massachusetts. He has said that he thought of it in the early 1900s, before the *Long Trail* was begun in Vermont in 1910.

It was that year that James P. Taylor, a Vermont schoolmaster, established the Green Mountain Club and the concept of the *Long Trail* from Canada to Massachusetts. Others who had long trail and connecting trail concepts were Philip W. Ayres, a New Hampshire forester, and Allen Chamberlain, a Boston newspaper columnist and early president of the Appalachian Mountain Club (founded in 1876). They formed the New England Trail Conference in 1916. One of the conference's goals was to connect the New England trails, a linkage that remarkably resembles the later path of the *AT*.

Two other founding fathers were US forester William Hall, who envisioned a link with the southern Appalachians, and Will S. Monroe, professor and seer of the Green Mountain Club. Monroe's concept was to connect the New England trails to trails in New York and New Jersey. In December 1921, Monroe's friend, J. Ashton Allis, proposed connecting the trails as far as the Pennsylvania state line. Two months before Allis's proposal the *Journal of American Institute of Architects* carried MacKaye's article "An Appalachian Trail, A Project in Regional Planning."

The response to a singular name for the trails was immediate, and within a year the Palisades Trail Conference (which later became part of the New York-New Jersey Trail Conference) began construction of a 6-mi section between Lake Tiorati Circle and Arden to connect with another trail in the Palisades Interstate Park. The trail opened on Sunday, October 7, 1923, the first and original section of the *AT*. (The entire *AT* design was initially completed on August 15, 1937, but considerable relocation was to follow.)

The leadership of Arthur Perkins of Hartford, Connecticut, began in 1926 to translate MacKaye's dream and proposal into reality, but it was Myron H. Avery of Lubec, Maine, who probably more than any other leader was instrumental in implementing MacKaye's proposals. He worked and coordinated agreements with government agencies, including the important Civilian Conservation Corps and thousands of volunteers to complete the *AT*. He was the first president of the Potomac Appalachian Trail Club, formed in November 1927, in Washington DC, and served as chairman of the Appalachian Trail Conference from 1930 to 1952.

In 1968 Congress created the National Trails System Act and gave further protection to the *AT* with supplemental amendments in 1970. In 1986, nearly 300 mi of the *AT* remain unprotected. Congressional appropriations to the National Park Service for this purpose will determine additional protective purchases.

The *AT* zigzags along two sections of the West Virginia-Virginia state line for a total of 25.1 mi. The NE section is on the Blue Ridge Mtns between Jefferson County in West Virginia and Loudoun County in Virginia; it is maintained by the Potomac Appalachian Trail Club. The SW section is on Peters Mtn between Monroe County in West Virginia and Giles County in Virginia. It is maintained by the Kanawha Trail Club.

The S entrance to the NE section begins at the corner of Jefferson County in West Virginia and Clarke County in Virginia, 1.3 mi N of Snickers Gap on VA-7 (0.8 mi W of Bluemont). Beginning at the state line it passes the Devil's Racetrack at 2 mi, crosses Wilson Gap Rd at 4.8 mi, and reaches Keys Gap Shelter at 12.1 mi. At 13.1 mi it crosses Keys Gap, VA-9 (6 mi W of Hillsboro, Virginia, and 7 mi E of Charles Town, West Virginia). At 16.6 mi it forks. Here the old *AT* went ahead; the new *AT* goes L into the Harpers Ferry National Historical Park. It descends, passes a R spur to an overlook under a power line, and reaches US-340 at 18 mi. After turning L on the Shenandoah River bridge the trail ascends on the *Cliff Trail* and reaches the Appalachian Trail Conference headquarters at the corner of Jackson and Washington streets at 18.8 mi. From here it turns R on Washington St and turns R again to resume the *Cliff Trail*. Here it turns L on its passage through the lower historic district to the Maryland state line at the Potomac River at 19.4 mi. The *AT* enters Maryland on the B&O RR cantilevered walkway (see Chapter 4).

Access to the state line in the SW section, on Peters Mtn in the Jefferson National Forest, occurs by ascending the *AT* for 4.1 mi from the New River bridge (Senator Shumate Bridge) in N Pearisburg. (There is no water on top of Peters Mtn.) For the next 12.5 mi the trail ascends to knobs and descends to gaps between 3300 ft and 3700 ft elev. It crosses a number of pipeline and power line swaths from which there are scenic views of Little Mtn N in West Virginia and Angels Rest (3500 ft) on Pearis Mtn in Virginia. At 9.5 mi it crosses a hunting road that descends, R, for 2 mi to FR-972 and out to SR-641 on the Virginia side. It enters Symms Gap Meadow, an exceptionally large and scenic area at 11.3 mi. After another 0.7 mi it crosses a jeep road. At 13 mi it jct with the *Ground Hog Trail*, L, a blue-blazed West Virginia access route described below. It passes Dickinson Gap at 14.5 mi, and veers L on the slope of Pine Swamp Knob (3956 ft) at 16.1 mi. At 16.6 mi it leaves the state line and makes a jct with the *Allegheny Trail* (which follows the Peters Mtn ridge NE. See Chapter 11.) The *AT* descends steeply for 1.7 mi, past Pine Swamp Branch Shelter, to an access point on the Waiteville Rd and crosses the road at 20.7 mi. (It is 11.5 mi, R, to US-460 and another 3 mi R on US-460 to Pearisburg.) (*USGS-FS Maps:* Narrows, Peterstown, Lindside, Interior. These regular, photoinspected maps, 1965– 1979, do not have correct *AT* routes.)

The West Virginia access route on the *Ground Hog Trail* to the *AT* is a direct result of the leadership of Bob Tabor, a trail developer activist and a founder of the West Virginia Scenic Trail Association. Tabor, Nick Lozano, Charley Carlson, Bruce Bond, and others shared a dream for a trail route more convenient to West Virginians. They contacted landowners S of Lindside in the 1970s for such a purpose. When the Sugar Camp Farm, a picturesque, 159.1-acre tract owned by Cecil B. McKinney, became available, Tabor and associates persisted in having the Appalachian Trail Conference secure funding from the National Park Service to purchase Sugar Camp. In June 1981, Tabor was appointed chairman of a management committee by the West Virginia Scenic Trails Association, and in 1982 the purchase of Sugar Camp was consummated. For continued development and management purposes, a joint arrangement was made between the WVSTA, the Appalachian Trail Conference, the NPS, and the Blacksburg District of the Jefferson National Forest.

Ground Hog Trail

• LENGTH: 1.8 mi

• DIFFICULTY: easy to strenuous, elev gain 1325 ft

• FEATURES: scenic, wildlife, botanical study

• TRAILHEADS AND DETAILS: From Peterstown jct of US-219 and WV-12 go NE on US-219 for 6.1 mi to Painters Run Rd (CO-219/21), R. (If road sign is missing, notice double blue blazes on a telephone pole, S side of the Full Gospel Assembly church.) Drive 1.2 mi and turn L at jct with Green Valley Rd (CO-219/24). After 0.5 mi arrive at the Sugar Camp parking lot, R. Another entrance route is from Lindside. Turn S on the Spruce Run Rd (CO-219/19, also called Dunkard Church Rd CO-215/15), and drive 0.8 mi. Turn R at Bradley Cemetery sign and continue R for 2.2 mi to Sugar Camp parking lot, L.

Camping is not permitted along *Ground Hog Trail* or on Sugar Camp property.

Begin the hike at the SW corner of the parking lot; pass cairns in the pasture, reach a woods road and turn L, and pass R of a barn at 0.3 mi. Spring water, the only source on the trail, and rest room facilities are available here. Ascend through huge sugar maples and at 0.4 mi pass a large, dead American chestnut *(Castanea dentata)*, unique because it is standing, well preserved, and propped with maples and other trees. Adult trees are now rare. Among the maples are oak, poplar, hickory, locust, and dogwood. Deer are likely to be seen in the area. Cross two spur ridges and at 0.9 mi begin the first of seven major switchbacks to the summit. Pass rock formations that are covered with mosses and lichens, and earth pockets with ferns, alumroot *(Heuchera americana)*, stone crop, sweet chervil, and rattlesnake orchid *(Goodyera pubescens)*. Reach the crest line of Peters Mtn at 1.5 mi and jct with the *AT*. To the L it is 3.9 mi to the temporary jct and S terminus of the *Allegheny Trail*. To the R it is 1 mi to scenic Symms Gap and Meadow, and 12 mi farther to US-460 in Pearisburg.

• INFORMATION: Appalachian Trail Conference, PO Box 807, Harpers Ferry, WV 25425, tel: 304-535-6331; West Virginia Scenic Trail Association, PO Box 4042, Charleston, WV 25304, tel: 304-744-5157; District Ranger, Blacksburg Ranger District, Jefferson National Forest, Rte 1, Box 404, Blacksburg, VA 24060, tel: 703-552-4641.

4.

National Recreation Areas and Historical Parks

"In hiking I find an indescribable sense of belonging to all that has gone before me and all that will follow."

— FRED BIRD

In addition to the *Appalachian National Scenic Trail* mentioned previously, there are two other properties in the state under the jurisdiction of the National Park Service that have foot trails in use or in the developmental stage. They are Harpers Ferry National Historical Park and the New River National Gorge River.

▶ HARPERS FERRY NATIONAL HISTORICAL PARK

In 1773, Peter Stephens, a pioneer trapper and trader, settled at the confluence of the Potomac and Shenandoah rivers. To assist his trade and the emigration of other settlers he established a simple ferry service. The service was expanded in 1747 when Robert Harper, an English emigrant from Oxford, purchased Stephen's log cabin and ferry equipment, and in 1751 obtained a land patent for 125 acres from Lord Fairfax. Harper's success as a millwright and ferry operator led to a small settlement named after him by the Virginia General Assembly. It was originally called "Shenandoah Falls at Mr. Harper's

Ferry." By the 1790s the area had become more industrialized, particularly after Congress established a national armory. Economic development increased in the 1830s when the Chesapeake and Ohio Canal and the Baltimore and Ohio Railroad were constructed along the Potomac. The development of better transportation also made the armory and rifle factory an important location. It was to this location on October 16, 1859, that John Brown, an abolitionist and leader of the Kansas Pottawatomie massacre, led a band of 16 white and 5 black men in an insurrection. His aim was forcibly to liberate the South's slaves and to become Virginia's chief executive in the process. Two days later Colonel Robert E. Lee and Lt. J. E. B. Stuart, with 91 marines, stormed the armory engine house where Brown and his men had taken refuge. Ten of Brown's followers, including two of his sons, and five of Lee's men were killed. Brown was tried by a jury and hanged in nearby Charles Town on December 2 for murder and "treason to the Commonwealth." (Acting as the nation's reporter and artist of the trial for *Harper's* magazine was David Hunter Strother, the famous hiker and outdoorsman, for whom Mt Porte Crayon was named.) Harpers Ferry and John Brown suddenly became national words as the episode further frayed the ties that held the North and South together. Louise McNeill's poem "John Brown," written in 1979, expressed it this way:

"Over the South the rumors ran,
A wild fanatic — his crazy plan —
. . . Over the North the rumors flew,
A Christian soldier — as brave and true — !"

During the Civil War, Harpers Ferry was a strategic objective for both sides, and it changed hands a number of times. One example is that on September 15, 1862, General Stonewall Jackson captured the town and 12,693 Union prisoners. Following the war, Storer College for freed blacks was established; it remained in service until 1955 and is now a training center for the National Park Service personnel. Otherwise the community declined, its buildings abandoned after the devastating floods of the late 19th century. In 1895, a John Brown Fort monument was erected by the B&O Railroad. Fifty years later Congress authorized a national monument of 1500 acres. That area, plus 724 more acres, was designated a National Historical Park in 1963, and restoration began.

Hikers interested in history may wish to spend a couple of days here. There are museums, restored buildings, historic sites, the Appalachian Trail Conference headquarters, and trails that connect the tri-state area. The new cantilevered walkway on the side of the B&O Railroad connects Harpers Ferry with the C&O Canal National Historical Park and the 3.5 mi *Grant Conway Trail* in Maryland Heights. The *AT* has been relocated and now passes through the historic district. Camping is not permitted in the Park. (*USGS Maps:* Harpers Ferry, Charles Town)

• ADDRESS AND ACCESS: Superintendent, Harpers Ferry National Historical Park, Harpers Ferry, WV 25425, tel: 304-535-6371. On US-340 turn onto Shenandoah St on the W end of the Shenandoah River bridge.

• SUPPORT FACILITIES: Camping is allowed at designated sections of the C&O Canal. The nearest campground area from Harpers Ferry is 1.5 mi up the Potomac River on the C&O Canal at Huckleberry Hill Hiker-Biker Overnighter. It has water, wood, and a rest room. A youth hostel is 1.2 mi downstream on the Sandy Hook Rd that parallels the C&O Canal. Also, the Harpers Ferry KOA Campground is 1 mi W of Harpers Ferry on US-340. Its season is April 1–November 1; tel: 304-535-6895. If choosing a hotel, the Cliffside Inn and Conference Center has two restaurants; tel: 304-535-6302. Other places to eat are within walking distance of the lower town. The nearest grocery stores for hikers are High's Dairy Store and Butts Grocery Store, 1.9 mi up Washington St in the town of Bolivar. For additional information contact West Virginia Information Center, Eastern Gateway Travel Council, Box A, Harpers Ferry, WV 25425, tel: 304-535-2482.

Bolivar Heights Trail

- LENGTH: 1.3 mi

- DIFFICULTY: easy

- FEATURES: scenic, history

- TRAILHEAD AND DETAILS: At the US-340 and Washington St jct, turn onto Washington St (at the Eastern Gateway Travel Council bldg) and follow the sign, L, to the Bolivar Heights Battlefield site and parking area. If driving from the Harpers Ferry historic district, drive 2 mi up High St, which becomes Washington St, and turn R to the battlefield site. Follow the scenic loop trail past a series of outdoor exhibits that explain the area's role in the Civil War. Prominent trees are locust, walnut, oak, and hackberry.

Cliff Trail (Jefferson Rock Trail)

- LENGTH: 0.8 mi

- DIFFICULTY: easy

- FEATURES: scenic, history

- TRAILHEADS AND DETAILS: (This trail may also serve as the *AT*.) Park at the visitor center parking area. Near the corner of Shenandoah St and High St, climb the steps that have been cut in the natural rock, pass the restored St Peter's Catholic Church and the ruins of St John's Episcopal Church, and reach the Jefferson Rock at 0.2 mi. The rock is named after Thomas Jefferson, who visited here in 1783 and wrote that where the Potomac and Shenandoah rivers meet "they rush together against the mountain, rend it asunder and pass off to the sea. This scene is worth a voyage across the Atlantic." A balancing rock has been stabilized with stone props. Continue ahead to a spur trail, R, that leads to Robert Harper's grave site. At 0.5 mi reach an access trail that leads 0.2 mi R to the Appalachian Trail Conference headquarters bldg at the corner of Jackson and Washington streets. To the L a 0.1 mi spur trail descends to Shenandoah St. Ahead, follow the ridge slope to the trail's terminus on a steep descent to US-340 at the W end of the Shenandoah River bridge.

Loudoun Heights Trail

- LENGTH: 1.3 mi
- DIFFICULTY: moderate
- FEATURE: scenic
- TRAILHEADS AND DETAILS: The *Loudoun Heights Trail* was formerly a blue-blazed access trail from the Appalachian Trail Conference headquarters to the *AT*. It is now the relocated *AT* except near the ridge where it connects with a scenic overlook. It is maintained by the Potomac Appalachian Trail Club. If parking is difficult on the E end of the Shenandoah Bridge, park at the W end and walk 0.1 mi across the bridge. Climb the highway railing and ascend steeply on a rocky area. At 0.2 mi is a view of the Shenandoah River. Among the plant life are papaw, jewelweed, ferns, wild hydrangea, Solomon's seal, sweet cicely, Indian pipe, and bladdernut *(Staphylea trifolia)*. Polypody and mosses grow on the rocks. For nearly 0.1 mi periwinkle is a dense ground cover. At 0.6 mi cross Chester Hill Rd into a forest of maple, ash, and oak; the trail incline is more moderate. At 0.9 mi is a trail jct. The *AT* relocation is expected to use the L trail by the overlook at the power line at 1.5 mi. The trail ahead once was the access road to the main-line *AT*. The latter route was 1.3 mi. Backtrack.

Virginius Island Trail

- LENGTH: 1 mi
- DIFFICULTY: easy
- FEATURE: history
- TRAILHEADS AND DETAILS: Most of the markers first placed on this trail in 1963 have been washed away by the floods. The

Park Service plans to improve the island's interpretive signs, but a completion date has not been set. A once-used *Virginius Island Trail* pamphlet is useless, according to the Park Service. However, in Dave Gilbert's *Walker's Guide to Harpers Ferry*, there is valuable information about the island.

Begin at the S edge of the visitor center parking area and follow a path up the river. At 0.3 mi cross under a RR grade. Along the way are ruins of an iron foundry, mills and shops, stockhouses, and a rifle factory. The trail loops and returns past two crossovers, the first a bridge over one of the Shenandoah Canal locks at 0.6 mi. Return on the island or on Shenandoah St to the parking area. Plant life includes sycamore, white ash, maple, box elder, sweet gum, spicebush, jewelweed, and asters.

▶ NEW RIVER GORGE NATIONAL RIVER

Congress assigned management responsibility of the New River Gorge National River to the National Park System on November 10, 1978. The purpose was to conserve an "outstanding natural, scenic, and historic" 50-mi section of the New River Gorge and to preserve a free-flowing segment of the New River "for the benefit and enjoyment of present and future generations." An irregular corridor of 62,000 acres was initially planned to extend from Hinton downstream to Ames near the US-19 bridge. But only 17 percent of the total acreage will be owned by the NPS. Other properties include easement acquisitions, state lands, private land donations, and private ownership. River use management is the joint responsibility of the NPS and the state's Department of Natural Resources. Zoning and some of the other management responsibilities are shared by the counties through which the New River flows (Summers, Raleigh, and Fayette).

The park has three management categories. One involves natural zones of undeveloped and more wildernesslike properties to conserve natural resources. Activities that do not adversely affect the environment are classified in this category:

they include hiking, backcountry camping, horseback riding, hunting, and fishing. The historic category protects known cultural resources in the canyon. The third management category of development is the most comprehensive. It includes recreational areas that have picnic units, standard campgrounds, boat ramps, visitor centers, access points and interpretive units, and maintained park roads. In the summer of 1983 the park began visitor service operations with the opening of Canyon Rim Visitor Center (open year-round) at the E end of the US-19 bridge and at the Hinton Visitor Center (open from spring to fall) on WV-3 (the W bank of the river) in Hinton.

At the Canyon Rim Visitor Center there are three short walks that extend to the Canyon Rim for magnificent views of the river gorge. One paved walkway goes L of the center entrance for 92 yds to a view up the river. The other paved walkway goes R of the center entrance, but forks for two different views. The L fork descends on 227 steps (228 if you take the L side at the lower observation deck) to an awesome view of the nation's second highest bridge, 876 ft above the New River. (The nation's highest is at Royal Gorge in Colorado.) The R fork extends to an observation deck with a view of the bridge and highway. Either of these trails is 400 yds round trip.

The geology and hydrology of the New River is remarkably distinctive. It is part of the nation's longest river system that flows north. A descendant of the prehistoric Teays River system, it may also be the oldest river in North America. Its headwaters of two forks begin in Watauga County, North Carolina, and flow through Ashe and Allegheny counties before entering Virginia. There, it meanders through Grayson, Carroll, Wythe, Pulaski, Montgomery, and Giles counties. It cuts its way through the Appalachian Mountains of Virginia to West Virginia's Allegheny Plateau and joins the Gauley River in Fayette County to become the Kanawha River. In this process it drains 6920 sq mi. Its steepest grade, with a drop of 20 ft per mi, is between Thurmond and the Hawks Nest, a popular stretch for white water enthusiasts. Called the "Grand Canyon of the East," its rim is an average of 1000 ft above the river with a complex of rugged ridges, steep drops from massive quartzite conglomeratic sandstone cliffs, and narrow river channels. Most of the rock formations range in age from 340 to 280 million years.

Within the park's boundary are 7.1 million tons of coal reserves that could be strip-mined and some currently active gas wells. It is an area rich in deciduous forest and herbaceous flora, at least 1067 species. Two endemic plants that are endangered in the gorge are Frazer's sedge *(Cartex fraseri)* and mountain mint *(Pyenanthemum torrei)*. It is estimated that the gorge has 40 species of mammals, 80 species of birds, and 58 species of fish (6 of which are endemic).

In 1986 the NPS has not named any foot trails in the river area, but at least 28 mi of hiking trails are in the planning stages. Potential trail development may come from abandoned RR grades, old logging roads, and mining roads. An example is the plan to connect Wolf Creek to Cunard by Kaymoor and from Cunard to Thurmond for approximately 14 mi. Also, there are plans to join the old RR grade from Minden to Thurmond. At Sanstone Falls, an area formerly owned by the state, a 2-mi trail is planned. Other trails to be constructed are to walk-in campgrounds near Chestnut and Glade Creek. Additional short trails will also be developed for visits to coal-mining sites at Kaymoor. It is estimated by the NPS that all the trails — stroller, foot, and horseback riding — will cost $950,000.

Although not called a trail, it has to be one of the more rare hikes when once a year, the second Saturday in October, pedestrians are legally allowed to walk 0.6 mi across an engineering wonder, the world's longest steel-arch bridge (US-19). The walk is part of the Bridge Day Festival, when parachutists jump from the bridge to the river and miles of arts and crafts exhibits and food and antique vendors border the S side of US-19.

The West Virginia Scenic Trails Association is in the process of establishing the *Mary Draper Ingle Trail*, which will eventually run the entire length of the park (see Chapter 10). A scenic, yellow-blazed section, 2 mi long, has been completed from

Wolf Creek to Kaymoor. Access is on WV-82 under the US-19 bridge. The trailhead is at a new footbridge 2.8 mi down from the S rim jct of US-19 and WV-82, and 0.9 mi up the mountain from Fayette Station. (For more information check with the Canyon Rim Visitor Center on the E end of the US-19 bridge.) The staff of Wildwater Expeditions Unlimited, a professional whitewater outfitter in Thurmond (tel: 304-469-2551), is also active in assisting the WVSTA.

• INFORMATION: Superintendent, New River Gorge National River, 137$1/2$ Main St (PO Box V), Oak Hill, WV 25901, tel: 304-465-0508. Travel Director, New River Travel Council, 500 Vermillian St (PO Box J), Athens, WV 24712, tel: 304-384-9453. Fayette Plateau Chamber of Commerce, 214 Main St, Oak Hill, WV 25901, tel: 304-465-5617.

5.

US Army Corps of Engineers Projects

"Heaven is as near by water as by land."
— HENRY W. LONGFELLOW

The US Army Corps of Engineers was formed during the early years of the nation's history as part of the Continental Army. At the time of the Revolution, West Point, a garrison on the Hudson River, was fortified by an act of Congress — an act that authorized a corps of engineers and artillerymen. In 1798 the corps was enlarged and in 1802 Congress made West Point the military academy for the United States. Since then, Congress has authorized a wide range of projects for the Army Corps of Engineers. Among them have been blazing and building roads, clearing waterways and harbors, buildings dams for flood control and hydropower, protecting and restoring shorelines, and providing natural disaster relief, fish and wildlife developments, and multiple recreation opportunities. While emphasizing diversity in recreational usage year-round, it enforces zoning regulations to protect the ecology. To enhance this process the state's Department of Natural Resources has leased project land for additional facilities such as parks and hunting and fishing areas.

The Corps has constructed nine major recreational lake areas. They are R. D. Bailey Lake, Beech Fork Lake, Bloomington Lake, Bluestone Lake, Burnsville Lake, Easy Lynn Lake, Summersville Lake, Sutton Lake, and Tygart Lake. A tenth lake, the Stonewall Jackson Lake near Weston, is under construction. When impounded in 1987 it will have a summer lake surface of 2650 acres. The total federally owned land surrounding all ten projects is 120,000 acres. The total water surface during the summer is 11,300 acres. The Corps's first flood control/recreation project in West Virginia was Tygart Lake on the Tygart River near Grafton, completed in 1938, and the most recent was Bloomington Lake, on the West Virginia-Maryland border near Keyser, completed in 1981. There are other Corps projects with locks and dams, but recreational usage is limited mainly to fishing and boating.

Recreational facilities include campgrounds, usually with hookups, picnic areas with shelters, rest rooms, launching ramps, and marinas. Fishing is a popular sport in all the lakes. Hunting is allowed in specific areas and in accordance with the state game laws. Somewhat less developed are pedestrian, bicycle, horse, snowmobile or ORV trails, some of which are nonexistent. Foot trails identified by the Corps for the purpose of this book are described below.

• INFORMATION: Public Affairs Office, US Army Engineer District, 502 Eighth Street, Huntington, WV 25701, tel: 304-529-5451. Request a directory of "Lakeside Recreation in the Northeast" and brochures on the lakes.

▶ BEECH FORK LAKE
(Wayne and Cabell Counties)

Described as a "little jewel," this 720-acre lake was constructed in 1978 for flood control of Twelvepole Creek, recreational purposes, and fish and wildlife management. The total development includes 12,757 acres with 31 mi of shoreline. The Corps of Engineers has transferred the management of 2100 acres at the upper end of Beech Fork for the Beech Fork State Park (see Chapter 6). Water sports are popular in the summer at the Beech Fork Marina and Boat Launch NE of the dam. Docking facilities, motorboats, canoes, paddleboats, and life jackets are available for visitors at the marina. Picnicking and swimming are allowed at the Stowers Branch area SW of the dam. Here a 4WD-vehicle access road called the Beaver Pond Trail leaves the parking lot near the swimming area for 0.6 mi to Stowers Branch. Backtracking is necessary. The full operational period for the lake is from Memorial Day to Labor Day. (*USGS Map:* Lavalette)

• ADDRESS AND ACCESS: Resource Manager, Beech Fork Lake, USACE, PO Box 600, Lavalette, WV 25535, tel: 304-525-4831. From I-64 in Huntington drive S on WV-152 for 5.5 mi and turn L on Beech Fork Rd (CO-13). Go 3 mi to the lake.

Rock Hollow Trail

• LENGTH: 0.5 mi

• DIFFICULTY: moderate

• FEATURES: scenic, nature study

• TRAILHEAD AND DETAILS: Stop at the resource manager's office for a brochure on the trail. Park near the dam, NE, and follow the trail sign across the road. This interpretive loop trail has 16 posts for shrubs, trees, wildflowers, mosses, lichens, and nature lore on a slope with rock formations. At post #13 is a scenic view of the lake.

▶ BURNSVILLE LAKE
(Braxton County)

The Corps of Engineers began construction of the 970-acre Burnsville Lake in 1972 and it became operational in 1978. Its main purpose was for flood control of the Little Kanawha River, a stream 167 mi long that drains 2320 sq miles in parts or all of seven counties. There are nine recreational and scenic areas; among them are areas for picnicking, camping, water sports, fishing, hunting, and hiking. As in the other Corps projects, the state Department of Natural Resources administers the fish-stocking programs and enforces game and conservation laws. Among the fish in the area are bass, crappie, catfish, bluegill, and sunfish. Game species include deer, rabbit, squirrel, raccoon, grouse, and wild turkey.

The property has approximately 60 mi of fire roads and abandoned access roads that can be used for hiking. These road-trails have names such as *Mud Hole Trail,* Long Run Road, Benny Run Road, *White-tail Trail,* and *Posey Hollow Trail.* Part of the 19th century *Weston and Gauley Bridge Turnpike (Trail)* is being restored between here and the new Stonewall Jackson Lake, now being constructed near Weston on the West Fork River. The road-trails can be used only for day hikes. Also, any road-trail originating in either of the two campgrounds — Riffle Run Camp and Bulltown Camping Area — can be used only by campers for access. The project's two well-graded and maintained trails that are open daily to the public are described below. (*USGS Map:* Orlando)

• ADDRESS AND ACCESS: Resource Manager, Burnsville Lake, USACE, PO Box 347, Burnsville, WV 26335, tel: 304-853-2371 (for lake conditions, 304-853-2398).

Bulltown Battlefield Trail

• LENGTH: 0.3 mi

• DIFFICULTY: easy

• FEATURES: history, scenic

• TRAILHEAD AND DETAILS: From the community of Heaters drive E on US-19/WV-4 to the Bulltown day-use area and turn R (S) to a parking area. The paved loop trail on an open slope with Confederate trenches has an information sign about the Battle of Bulltown, October 13, 1863. Here a small contingent of Confederate forces tried unsuccessfully to control the Weston and Gauley Bridge Turnpike.

Bulltown Historic Overlook Trail

- LENGTH: 1 mi

- DIFFICULTY: easy

- FEATURES: history, scenic

- TRAILHEAD AND DETAILS: On US-19/WV-4 between Bulltown day-use area and Falls Mill, turn N on Millstone Run Rd (CO-19/12) and drive 0.9 mi to the Historical Overlook Area, L. (This is also the route to the Bulltown Camping Area.) From the parking area follow the paved trail to the log St Michaels Catholic Church. Beyond, follow a wood-chip treadway into a forest of walnut, poplar, maple, spicebush, dogwood, and Virginia pine to an overlook and gazebo at 0.4 mi. Wildflowers include ragwort and white snakeroot. Complete the loop and return to the relocated historic village of the Moses Cunningham farm and the Johnson and Fleming houses.

▶ EAST LYNN LAKE
(Wayne County)

The Corps of Engineers constructed the East Lynn Lake for flood control of the Twelvepole Creek. In the process, recreational areas were provided for water sports, camping, picnicking, hunting, fishing, and hiking. Boats, equipment, and dock space can be rented. There are 174 campsites for tents or trailers, many with hookups; laundromat; hot showers; and dumping station. There are also 15 primitive campsites available all year. A foot trail is being developed at the East Fork Campground that will be about 1.2 mi. Full facilities at the lake are open from May 1 to the end of the October. (*USGS Map:* Nestlow)

- ADDRESS AND ACCESS: Resource Manager, East Lynn Lake, USACE, Star Rte, Box 35-C, East Lynn, WV 25512, tel: 304-849-2355. From the community of East Lynn, drive S on WV-

37 for 3 mi to a turn-off R for 1.5 mi to the Lake Side Marina and Picnic Area.

Lakeside Trail

* LENGTH: 1.7 mi

* DIFFICULTY: moderate

* FEATURES: nature study, scenic

* TRAILHEADS AND DETAILS: At the parking lot in the picnic area, follow the trail sign and ascend on a graded yellow-blazed trail in a young hardwood and Virginia pine forest. Ferns and wildflowers are prominent. Reach a knoll at 0.2 mi, turn L and follow the ridge on an old road to a clearing (formerly a cemetery) at 0.6 mi. Continue ahead and turn to the N side of the ridge. The trail picks up another old road leading past an inactive coal mine and descends to the picnic area about 125 yds from the point of beginning at 1.7 mi.

PART THREE

State-Managed Trails

View from Droop Mtn Battlefield State Park/Photo by the author

6.

State Parklands and Historic Sites

"Walking in the woods is a spiritual experience. I am reminded that life has a far greater scope than everyday concerns."
— NANCY BUCKINGHAM

West Virginia has 34 state parks, with a total of 71,440 acres. They are protected by law from commercial exploitation of their natural resources. Some of the parks are vacation areas with resort lodges and completely furnished cabins; others are for day use only. While classified as vacation parks because of their developed facilities, they may also encompass significant natural and historic features as well, preserved for the "benefit and enjoyment of future generations." An example is Blackwater Falls State Park, with the state's highest and largest waterfall. The day-use areas primarily feature facilities for sports-associated activities but have no overnight accommodations. Resort state parks offer overnight accommodations, lodges and cabins, golf courses, complete line of recreational facilities, swimming, tennis, hiking trails, and a year-round recreation and interpretive program. Examples are Grandview State Park and Valley Falls State Park. Historical areas have been established to preserve locations that have historic, archaeological, or scientific significance. These have day-use facilities, but some recreational facilities may also be available. An example is Watters Smith Memorial State Park, which has a swimming pool and hiking trails in addition to its museum.

The vacation state parks are Audra, Babcock, Beech Fork, Blackwater Falls, Cedar Creek, Hawks Nest, Holly River, Lost River, North Bend, Tomlinson Run, and Watoga. The natural areas are Beartown, Cathedral, Pinnacle Rock, and Valley Falls. Day-use areas are Grandview, Greenbrier River Trail, Chief Logan, and Little Beaver. Historical areas include Berkeley Springs, Carnifex Ferry Battlefield, Cass Scenic Railroad, Droop Mountain Battlefield, Fairfax Stone Historical Monument, Point Pleasant Battle Monument, Pricketts Fort, and Watters Smith Memorial. Only the parks that have hiking trails are covered in this guidebook. There are 158 named trails; they cover a total of 285.9 miles.

The state parks system has become one of the state's major tourist attractions. Its development and progress has been outstanding from the beginning when, on July 1, 1937, four parks (Babcock, Cacapon, Lost River, and Watoga) opened for public use. The total attendance for the 1937–38 season was 75,194, and a decade later for the 1947–48 season the attendance had grown to 977,321. When the parks system celebrated its 30th anniversary in 1967, there were 21 parks in operation and 3 others were under construction. Attendance that year passed 3,000,000. In some parks the demands were exceeding the capacity of the facility. In 1984 attendance had risen to the 7,036,790 mark. Out-of-state attendance has always been high. For example, in 1937 it was approximately 40 percent and nearly fifty years later (1984) it was still as high as 29.7 percent.

The history of the state parks system began in 1933 when the state legislature established a Division of State Parks. The bill (Chapter 20 of the West Virginia Code) stated that the purpose of the system was to "promote conservation by preserving and protecting" significant natural, scientific, cultural, historic, and archaeological areas. Another purpose was "to provide outdoor recreational opportunities for the citizens of this state and its visitors." Public hunting, mining, and timber harvesting for commercial purposes would not be permitted. The legislative action was a "direct result of the emphasis placed on conservation" by the United States Emergency Conservation Act approved by President Franklin D. Roosevelt on March 31, 1933.

The first state park, Watoga, was begun in May 1934, under the provisions of the National Park Service. Watoga was a desirable location to begin because in 1925 the state's Game, Fish and Forestry Commission had acquired 4500 acres of timbered hills for a state forest in Pocahontas County. The intention was to create a state wildlife and forest preserve. A lack of state funds delayed development until 1933 when federal funds appropriated by Congress for emergency conservation work became available from the Federal Forestry Service. A Civilian Conservation Corps (CCC) camp was immediately established, and by 1935 the Watoga area had three such camps.

With an increase in public interest in conservation, the state legislature appropriated $70,000 to purchase other lands for park development. With this funding, acreage was doubled at the Watoga State Park area and the acquisition of properties for Babcock, Cacapon, Hawks Nest, and Lost River began. Further advancement of these parks began in the spring of 1934 when the state formed the Conservation Commission, an outgrowth of the old Game, Fish, and Forestry Commission. The new commission began an "ambitious program of recreational development" with manpower and funding from the Civilian Conservation Corps.

During the formative years the division operated successfully by coordinating its administrative, central design, and field personnel branches. The designs and plans of the central design office were submitted to the National Park Service. If approved, the office would inspect the facilities under construction to see that government standards were followed. The actual construction process was administered by the CCC, and the field personnel took care of the day-to-day park operation. These early developments were confined to road building; reforestation; construction of cabins, well and pump houses, hand-dug foot and horse trails, and limited picnic areas. An example of the careful design and grading of a foot trail is the first mile of the Monongaseneka Trail in Watoga State Park.

The Carnifex Ferry Battlefield area was acquired in October 1935, the result of preliminary planning by a special Battlefield Park Commission established by the state in 1931. Although the Division of State Parks assumed administrative responsibility of the Droop Mountain Battlefield in 1937, the park was purchased in 1928 and dedicated as a state historic park on July 4, 1929. This early date has led some historians to call it the "granddaddy" of the state parks system.

Pinnacle Rock in Mercer County was purchased in 1938 and the first of two parcels of land for the Grandview State Park was purchased in 1939. But the main source of funding and manpower through the CCC began to decline in 1940, and on July 2, 1942, Congress passed public law 647, the bill that terminated the CCC. It was the end of a decade of innovative conservation projects to protect natural resources. It was also a change from civilian to military work for thousands of young American men. All the CCC camps were abandoned during WW II. Tomlinson Run CCC camp, completed in 1941, was never occupied, though the camp became a state park in 1939.

After the war, public interest in state parks increased at a time state funding had other priorities. Nevertheless, with the help of the US Army Corps of Engineers, Tygart Lake State Park was established in 1947 and Bluestone State Park in 1955. Purchase of land for Cedar Creek State Park began in 1953 and for the North Bend State Park in 1954. It was during the 1953 session of the state legislature that a major increase in park development was begun through the sale of revenue bonds. In May 1955, the $4,000,000 Revenue Bond Act was signed, and the state park system entered its most progressive period since its early years. Immediate results included the expansion of Blackwater Falls State Park and the opening of Bluestone, Cedar Creek, and North Bend for public use.

On July 1, 1961, a legislative act replaced the Conservation Commission with a Department of Natural Resources and renamed the Division of State Parks the Division of State Parks and Recreation, one of five divisions under the new department. The other four were the divisions of Wildlife, Forestry, Water Resources, and Reclamation, with the later addition of Law Enforcement.

Also in 1961, the Emergency Employment Program (EEP) was created. Its purpose was to improve maintenance, provide recreational renovation and facilities in an expanded program to follow the one-year State Temporary Economic Program (STEP) established in 1960.

Additional assistance to the parks system came in 1963 when the Area Redevelopment Administration (ARA) of the US Department of Commerce allocated approximately $25,000,000 ($16,000,000 of which was a loan) for the future development of six state parks. It was within this year that the land acquisition began for Canaan Valley State Park. Other uses of the ARA funding were: the beginning of land purchases in 1965 for Pipestem State Park; more land for Canaan Valley State Park; land acquisition for Twin Falls State Park in Wyoming County; assistance on the completion of the Cass Scenic Railroad; and additional facilities at Hawks Nest State Park. The purchase of land for Valley Falls State Park began in 1964. In 1967 Pipestem opened, and in 1968, Canaan Valley, Pricketts Fort, and Twin Falls did also. Little Beaver opened in 1972 and the most recent park to begin operation was Beech Fork in 1979. There is only one new park currently in the planning stage; it is the Stonewall Jackson State Park in Lewis County. In 1985, the Division of State Parks and Recreation was transferred from the Department of Natural Resources to the Department of Commerce.

To make your visit to the state parks an enjoyable and successful experience, the following is suggested. First, write or call for information at the state offices listed at the end of this introduction. Make your lodge or cabin reservations far in advance (in some parks, such as Watoga and Blackwater Falls, you may reserve a campsite), and follow the rules and regulations at the parks.

The campground rules state that campers must register; a campsite can be used for a maximum of two weeks; and no more than two vehicles may be at any one campsite. Quiet hours are observed between 10 P.M. and 7 A.M. It is unlawful to damage or remove any of the natural or man-made objects. In many of the parks, alcoholic beverages are not allowed. Campground facilities are provided for the exclusive use of registered campers. Motorbike riding is prohibited, and pets must be restrained on leashes. Hunting or disturbing wildlife is forbidden. In most parks, camping is not allowed along the hiking trails. Where there are exceptions, such as at Lost River and Holly River, permission must be granted by the park superintendent.

• INFORMATION: For highway maps, calendar of events, and tour suggestions, write Travel West Virginia, Department of Commerce, State Capitol, Charleston, WV 25305, tel: 1-800-CALL WVA. They will also provide motel, camping, ski, or golf guidebooks and brochures. For state parks and forests information; hunting and fishing information; camp, cabin, and lodge reservations; and other information on outdoor recreation, write to Travel West Virginia at the address above, tel: 1-800-CALL WVA. The address and telephone number of individual state parks are given with the descriptions of the parks.

▶ **AUDRA STATE PARK**
(Barbour County)

Middle Fork River, which flows through beautiful 355-acre Audra State Park, has a mineral acidity that makes it a clear emerald green. The sculptured rocks within the stream make perfect spots for sun-bathing. The park has 65 campsites (61 suitable for trailers), a laundry, 3 picnic areas, and a concrete slab beach by the river. The park is near enough to Volga for adequate supplies. Open April 15–October 15.

• ADDRESS AND ACCESS: Superintendent, Audra State Park, Rte 4, Box 564, Buchannon, WV 26201, tel: 304-457-1162. From Buchannon go E about 2.5 mi on US-33 to Kesling Mill Rd (CO-3), L, and drive 10 mi to the park entrance, or, from US-119 in Volga, go 6 mi on Audra Park Rd (CO-11) to the park entrance.

Alum Cave Trail

* LENGTH: 2.7 mi

* DIFFICULTY: moderate

* FEATURES: scenic river, Alum Cave

* TRAILHEAD AND DETAILS: From the parking area, S of the bridge, hike downstream on a paved trail and pass the first 4-H campsite, established in 1919. There is a rhododendron border. Leave the paved trail and follow a footpath through tall hardwoods and hemlock. Reach Alum Cave, L, at 0.4 mi; descend to a boardwalk under the large overhang. Continue downstream with excellent views of the river, turn sharp R at 1.3 mi, and ascend on three switchbacks to the ridge crest. At 1.9 mi jct with a spur that leads down the mountain to the cave area. At 2.4 mi pass picnic area, descend to overlook at the river, and backtrack to the parking area. (*USGS Map:* Audra)

▶BABCOCK STATE PARK
(Fayette County)

One of the state's oldest parks, Babcock is another spectacular vacation area with a wide range of recreational conveniences. Half of the 4127 acres are developed and the other half, W of the New River, is wild and scenic where Mann's Creek and Glade Creek have cut canyons through a rock formation with cliff lines. Tall hardwoods and hemlock rise above an understory of mountain laurel, rhododendron, buckberry, ferns, and a wide variety of wildflowers. Ferns, mosses, and wintergreen grow near the purple rhododendron (which blooms in May) and the great laurel (the state's flower, which blooms beginning in mid-June and ending in July). Trout are in the cascading creeks, deer roam the tranquil trails and ridges, and raccoons visit the campground. Added to all this natural beauty is the Glade Creek Grist Mill, a restored water-powered system with parts and materials from a number of other mills, including the original Cooper's Mill once located near the current park headquarters. Cornmeal and buckwheat flour are ground and sold here.

Facilities include: 26 cabins; 50 campsites, laundry, and hot showers; dumping station; restaurant; commissary and souvenir shop; swimming pool; boat rentals (nonmotorized); picnic units; game courts; tennis; and nearly 20 mi of hiking trails. Season is May 1–October 15. (*USGS Maps:* Thurmond, Fayetteville, Winona, Danese)

• ADDRESS AND ACCESS: Superintendent, Babcock State Park, Clifftop, WV 25822, tel: 304-438-6205. From Beckley it is 32 mi N on WV-41, and 3.8 mi S on WV-41 from US-60 near Clifftop.

Skyline Trail (2 mi); Rocky Trail (1 mi); Fisherman's Trail (2 mi)

• LENGTH: 5 mi, rt, ct

• DIFFICULTY: easy to moderate

• FEATURES: sandstone cliffs, nature study

• TRAILHEADS AND DETAILS: Follow the red-blazed *Skyline Trail* from the overlook at Mann's Creek Picnic Area. At 0.5 mi jct with the blue-blazed *Rocky Trail*, R. For a loop, turn R, descend steeply, cross a stream, turn L on an old RR grade and reach the jct with the *Fisherman's Trail* at 1 mi. (The *Fisherman's Trail* is a rocky trail used primarily by fishermen up and down the river for about 2 mi.) Cross the wood footbridge over Glade Creek and follow an old RR grade R to a gravel road, L, at 1.6 mi. Hike on the road to a paved area and cottage #13 at 2.5 mi. At 2.8 mi turn L near cottage #7 through a dense rhododendron patch to a swinging footbridge. After crossing the bridge follow the trail between cottages #4 and #5 to ascend steeply. Cross a small bridge over a ravine at 3.1 mi. Wildflowers are prominent in the spring and summer. Scenic views of Glade Creek canyon are at 3.8 mi. Reach jct with *Rocky Trail* at 4.5 mi and return to the point of origin at 5 mi.

Island in the Sky Trail (0.4 mi); *Wilderness Trail* (2 mi)

* LENGTH: 4.8 mi, rt, ct

* DIFFICULTY: moderate

* FEATURES: overlooks, wildlife

* TRAILHEADS AND DETAILS: From the parking area of the administration bldg, pass the Grist Mill and ascend on an asphalt trail for 150 yds to a jct with the *Wilderness Trail.* Turn R onto a rocky area, climb a wood scaffold and ascend to a ridge and an overlook at 0.3 mi. Follow a spur trail to the road, W, and parking area at 0.4 mi. Turn R on the green-blazed *Wilderness Trail* on a serene wilderness road with hardwoods, ferns, and flowering shrubs. Wildflowers include pink lady's slipper and wood betony. Deer are frequently seen on the old road. At 2.2 mi cross a wood bridge; the blaze ends and the trail direction becomes faint at 2.4 mi. Backtrack.

Lake View Trail

* LENGTH: 1.2 mi

* DIFFICULTY: easy

* FEATURE: wildflowers

* TRAILHEAD AND DETAILS: From the park office drive W on Sugar Camp Run Rd to the Boat Dock, L, at Boley Lake. Begin the hike, R, through young forest of oaks, sassafras, and maple. Along the way are huckleberry, dogwood, pinxter, asters, and wood betony. Cross a branch through mature trees and over some rocky edges. Reach the dam, 1.1 mi. Complete the loop at 1.2 mi. The lake is named for James C. Boley, who gave 42 yrs of service to the state parks.

(There are two short trails near the entrance of the park and the beginning of the Mann's Creek Cabin and Picnic Area Rd. *The Natural Arch Trail* ascends E through oaks, poplar, and dogwood to a natural arch and backtracks for 255 yds. Across the road W is a 0.3 mi loop *Nature Trail* with 30 interpretive posts about wildflowers, trees, and shrubs. Trailing arbutus and wintergreen are natural ground covers.)

▶ BEARTOWN STATE PARK
(Pocahontas and Greenbrier Counties)

This day-use educational park of 110 acres is named from a local legend that tells of families of black bear inhabiting a labyrinth of deep crevasses in a sandstone mountainside. The 0.4 mi loop *Beartown Boardwalk Trail* is an easy journey into a massive natural wonder of sculptured stone. Some of the pitted surfaces are from leaching, often caused by rock cap ferns. Trees in the channels are mainly yellow birch and hemlock. Interpretive signs are at the entrance and along the boardwalk. (*USGS Map:* Droop)

• ADDRESS AND ACCESS: Caretaker, Beartown State Park, Droop, WV 24933, tel: 304-653-4254. From the Droop post office on US-219, drive S for 2 mi and turn L on Beartown Rd (CO-219/11) at a log church, and drive 1.6 mi to the park entrance.

▶ BEECH FORK STATE PARK
(Wayne and Cabell Counties)

Under continuing development, this 3981-acre park has an exceptionally large campground — 276 campsites, many with full-service sites for any size RV. There is a large visitor center, country store, playground and games area, and a boat launching ramp. The major sports activities are fishing, boating, and hiking. The lake is part of the Beech Fork Dam, constructed by the US Army Corps of Engineers (see Chapter 5). Future plans for the park include a total resort-style park with golf course, swimming pool, lodge, and vacation cabins. (*USGS Map:* Winslow)

• ADDRESS AND ACCESS: Superintendent, Beech Fork State Park, Rte 2, Box 333, Barboursville, WV 25504, tel: 803-522-0303. From I-64 jct with WV-10, drive S on WV-10 for 1.7 mi to Hughes Branch Rd (CO-43), and follow CO-43 for 7.3 mi to park entrance, R.

Hiking Trail (1.1 mi); Overlook Trail (1.5 mi)

• LENGTH: 2.6 mi, rt, ct

• DIFFICULTY: moderate

• FEATURES: overlooks, nature study

• TRAILHEADS AND DETAILS: From a parking area across from camping sites #82 and #83, climb the embankment to cross the campground road. Follow the yellow-blazed trail up a steep hill, pass L of a cemetery, and reach a trail fork at 0.2 mi. Turn R, pass through a hollow, and exit at the children's playground and bathhouse near campsite #48. Turn L on the main road, pass a bog with swamp rose, L, and at 0.7 mi re-enter the forest. Pass R of a log cabin, L of an overlook, and return to the trail jct. Backtrack to the point of origin at 1.1 mi. The *Overlook Trail* is E on the main road between this point and the visitor center. Follow the signs and cross a footbridge in a grassy area. Ascend a steep hill and bear R at the trail jct. At 0.3 mi is a rock overlook of the campground. Follow the ridge for 0.4 mi and then bear L on a N slope of open hardwoods. Descend to a ravine, cross another footbridge, and complete the loop at 1.3 mi. Return to the road at 1.5 mi. Often seen in this meadow and at the edge of the woods are bluebirds and fritillary butterflies.

Lost Trail

- LENGTH: 2.7 mi

- DIFFICULTY: moderate

- FEATURES: wildlife, wildflowers

- TRAILHEAD AND DETAILS: Between campsites #34 and #35 follow the blue-blazed loop trail over a footbridge. The area has black walnut, redbud, ash, and buckeye. At 0.4 mi is jct R near a grove of ash and swamp rose. Quail, songbirds, and deer are often seen here. Pass through a stand of poplar with scattered spicebush, mandrake, and bloodroot. At 1 mi curve L, ascend to a ridge away from the lake, and enter a more mature forest. Lake views are excellent here when the leaves are off the trees. Descend by cliffs at 1.5 mi and return to the first loop at 1.8 mi. Turn R, follow on an old road, and ascend on mossy patches to the hilltop. At 2.3 mi turn L, downhill, pass a papaw patch, and jct with the first trail. Return to the campground at 2.7 mi.

▶ BLACKWATER FALLS STATE PARK
(Tucker County)

This 1688-acre resort park is a year-round tourist attraction. It is near the state's highest town, Davis, at 3101 ft elevation. The town was founded in 1883 by Senator Henry G. Davis, who established America's first night train in 1848. The park is named for the falls of the Blackwater River, a river that begins in Canaan Valley and whose waters are ambered from the tannin of high-country conifers. The 63-ft Blackwater Falls opens a canyon from the E side of the park that divides the park with a N and S rim. Canyon rim overlooks are at Pendleton Point on the N side, and a number of overviews are along the S side of lodge and cabin area. From the parking area at the Trading Post are stairways and boardwalks that allow visitors a descent to the base of Blackwater Falls. This is an enchanting view any season of the year.

Facilities include: 55 rooms, 25 completely furnished (bring only food and clothes) cabins, 65 tent and trailer campsites (some of which can be reserved), hot showers and laundromat at the campground (but no hookups at campsites), outdoor swimming area, nature and recreation center, restaurant with additional facilities for a private banquet, paddleboating on Pendleton Lake, horseback riding at the stables, cross-country ski trails, sledding, picnic areas, concessions, playground and naturalist programs, and hiking trails (including sections of the *Allegheny Trail*). (*USGS-FS Maps:* Blackwater Falls, Mozark Mtn)

• ADDRESS AND ACCESS: Superintendent, Blackwater Falls State Park, PO Box 490, Davis, WV 26260, tel: 304-259-5216. In Davis on WV-32, turn off at sign on Blackwater Falls Rd (CO-29) to park entrance.

Gentle Trail (100 yds); Hemlock Trail (0.5 mi)

• TOTAL LENGTH: 0.6 mi

• DIFFICULTY: easy

• FEATURES: geology, scenic

• TRAILHEADS AND DETAILS: After entry into the park take the Lodge and Cabin Rd, cross the Blackwater River bridge, and park at the first parking area, R. Follow the *Gentle Trail* for a few yds and pass the entrance of the *Hemlock Trail*, R. The *Gentle Trail* is a level, wide, asphalt trail, 100 yds long, constructed for easy access for the physically handicapped. Nine companies and the Women's Club of Thomas made the trail possible and had native plants selected to decorate the trail border. At the observation deck is a sign that reads "So that all may equally enjoy the wonder of God's handiwork." At the lookout is an extraordinary view of the Blackwater Falls and the Blackwater Gorge. The green-blazed *Hemlock Trail* descends into a stand of large red spruce and hemlock with a rhododendron and mountain laurel understory. Reach the Blackwater River edge and loop back to the *Gentle Trail* over a rocky section. Red squirrels are frequently seen on the trails.

Falls View Trail

- LENGTH: 1.5 mi
- DIFFICULTY: easy
- FEATURE: nature study

• TRAILHEADS AND DETAILS: A few yds before arriving at the *Gentle Trail* parking area is a park service and maintenance road, L. At the road entry, R, the dark-green-blazed *Falls View Trail* begins. Follow the trail through a mixture of hardwoods and conifers, cross Falls Run and Engine Run, and reach a crossing of the Stables Rd and the *Allegheny Trail* at 0.7 mi. (To the L, at the stables, the *Allegheny Trail,* formerly the *Davis Trail,* continues S for 2.8 mi to FR-13. The *Red Spruce Trail* begins at the stables and is used by both equestrians and cross-country skiers.) Continue on the *Falls View Trail,* which parallels the Lodge and Cabin Rd, cross Tank Run, and reach the road across from the lodge after another 0.8 mi for a total distance of 1.5 mi.

Elakala Trail

- LENGTH: 0.4 mi
- DIFFICULTY: easy
- FEATURE: Elakala Falls

• TRAILHEADS AND DETAILS: From the parking area of the lodge, SW, follow the red-blazed trail and descend for 0.1 mi to a footbridge over the Upper Elakala Falls on Shay Run. Continue on the trail through an area of huge boulders and a hemlock forest to exit at the Lodge and Cabin Rd. Across the road is the entrance, N, to the *Balanced Rock Trail.* Backtrack or return on the paved road to the lodge.

Balanced Rock Trail (1 mi); Rhododendron Trail (0.4 mi);
Cherry Lane Trail (0.8 mi)

• TOTAL LENGTH: 2.2 mi

• DIFFICULTY: easy

• FEATURES: Balanced Rock, nature study

• TRAILHEADS AND DETAILS: The *Balanced Rock Trail* and the
Rhododendron Trail directly connect, and the *Cherry Lane Trail's*
N terminus is only 0.3 mi N of the *Rhododendron Trail* on the
Cabin Rd. The *Balanced Rock Trail* may be entered from the
main Lodge and Cabin Rd, across the road from the *Elakala
Trail* (0.5 mi W of the lodge), or it can be entered by cabin #13
on the Cabin Rd. If entering from the cabin, follow the orange-
blazed trail for 0.2 mi to jct with the *Rhododendron Trail.* Continue R in a forest of hemlock, rhododendron, birch, and cinnamon fern. Cross Shay Run and go R on the trail that leads to
the observation deck on Balanced Rock at 0.4 mi. Backtrack to
the jct, continue ahead for 0.6 mi to reach *Elakala Trail,* or turn
L at the jct and return on the white-blazed *Rhododendron Trail,*
which exits between cabins #9 and #11. The yellow/white-
blazed *Cherry Lane Trail* begins on the Cabin Rd 0.3 mi from
cabin #9 and below cabin #1. Follow the *Cherry Lane Trail*
through beech, yellow birch, maple, cherry, and scattered
hemlock to a loop that goes in front of cabin #25 to a cul-de-sac
and beyond to a loop jct and point of origin at 0.8 mi.

▶ **BLUESTONE STATE PARK**
(Summers County)

At the confluence of the Bluestone River and the New River
in the southeast corner of the state is 2146-acre Bluestone State
Park. Rugged, forested mountains surround the park, but
views of the state's second largest lake — the 1800-acre Bluestone Lake — are superb. Facilities include 25 deluxe cabins,
87 tent-trailer campsites with hot showers, swimming pool,
restaurant, and dumping station. Rental canoes, boats, water

skiing equipment, game courts, and a playground are available. Also, there are areas for picnicking, fishing (for bluegill, largemouth and smallmouth bass, crappie, and catfish), and hiking. Nearby is Pipestem State Resort Park and the Bluestone Public Hunting and Fishing Area. (*USGS Map:* Pipestem)

• ADDRESS AND ACCESS: Superintendent, Bluestone State Park, Box 3, Athens Star Route, Hinton, WV 25951, tel: 304-466-1922. From Princeton on WV-20, NE, go 28 mi. From Hinton go SW on WV-20 for 5 mi.

Rhododendron Trail

• LENGTH: 0.8 mi

• DIFFICULTY: easy

• FEATURE: cascading stream

• TRAILHEADS AND DETAILS: From the activities bldg follow the red-blazed foot trail through the forest and descend, cross park road, and continue descent on the R side of Surveyors Branch (a stream with cascades unless the summer is dry) to the boat launching ramp. Backtrack or have a vehicle shuttle.

Big Pine Trail *(1.7 mi)*; Riverview Trail *(1.6 mi)*

• LENGTH: 3.3 mi, ct

• DIFFICULTY: moderate

• FEATURES: scenic, wildlife

• TRAILHEADS AND DETAILS: To begin the *Big Pine Trail,* drive past the swimming pool to the launching ramp area. Trail is R. Ascend steeply through oak and locust forest on a gradual elevation with borders of ferns and mosses. Occasional green blazes remind you of the trail. At 0.9 mi pass the ruins of a log cabin. Spicebush grows nearby. Reach a jct, R, with the *Riverview Trail* at 1 mi. (The *Riverview Trail* descends for 0.5 mi to the swimming area.) Continue ahead and reach a jct, L, with the *Boundary Trail* at 1.1 mi. (The *Boundary Trail* is described separately below.) Continue ahead and ascend a narrow ridge, pass under a power line with excellent views at 1.3 mi, and descend slightly. The lake can easily be seen in this area in the wintertime. At 1.5 mi is a trail jct. The *Big Pine Trail* descends L 0.2 mi to a sharp curve in the access road for its terminus at 1.7 mi. (The R trail descends 0.2 mi to Meadow Camping Area. (Ahead for 0.2 mi is a spur trail to a rocky area that has an outstanding view of the Bluestone River and the New River convergence. Backtrack to the jct.)

Across the road from the E terminus of the *Big Pine Trail,* begin the E trailhead of the *Riverview Trail.* Cross the road guardrails and follow the blue-blazed trail downstream. At 0.2 mi is a waterfall and in a few yds is a jct with a spur trail, R, that ascends to the access road. Ahead, a section of the trail may be under water or overgrown. If so, continue on the access road. Pass the campground and reach an old road W of the swimming pool at 1.1 mi. Here the trail ascends for 0.5 mi to a jct with the *Big Pine Trail.* Or hike 0.2 mi on the access road, L, to the point of origin.

Boundary Trail

• LENGTH: 1.9 mi

• DIFFICULTY: moderate

• FEATURES: wildlife, scenic

• TRAILHEADS AND DETAILS: In the cabin area, walk in at cabin #17 entrance but follow the trail sign, R, around the cabin and ascend the ridge. At 0.3 mi pass an open area with a view of the Gib Lilly canyon. Descend on two switchbacks to a stream (which may be dry in the summer) and the park boundary at 0.6 mi. Area has filbert, locust, ash, maple, poplar, ragwort, squirrel cups, and wild rose. At 1.2 mi ascend on a ridge before turning L to flank a deep, open forest cove. Descend on two switchbacks and reach a jct with *Big Pine Trail* at 1.9 mi. One exit option is to turn L on the *Big Pine Trail* and follow it E for

0.6 mi to the main access road, 0.2 mi SW of the park head-quarters.

▶ **CACAPON RESORT STATE PARK**
   (Morgan County)

Cacapon Resort State Park (Ka-KAY-pun) is among the old-est of the state's parks; it opened on July 1, 1937. Its 6115 acres are mainly on the E side of Cacapon Mtn, stretching from the Virginia state line to within sight of the Potomac River and the state of Maryland. At the widest point are rolling hills and a valley between the communities of Omps and Ridge W of US-522. Although the park has retained its old and rustic charm with facilities constructed of native stone and timber in the Old Inn, it also has the most modern of conveniences in its 50-room lodge overlooking the 18-hole championship golf course. Other facilities are 30 cabins; restaurant (suitable for a banquet); snack bar and gift shop; a lake for swimming, boat rentals, and a sandy beach; picnic areas; game courts for ten-nis, volleyball, and basketball; children's playground; club-house; and riding stables. Fishing is allowed in the lakes. There are five color-coded hiking trails, some of which overlap to form loops and have multiple-color blazes. Hikers may not camp in the park, but hikers who wish to rent a horse and arrange a guide from the stable master may camp overnight on the ridge top of Cacapon Mtn. (*USGS Maps:* Ridge, Great Caca-pon)

• ADDRESS AND ACCESS: Superintendent, Cacapon Resort State Park, Berkeley Springs, WV 25411, tel: 304-258-1022. From Berkeley Springs S it is 8.5 mi, R, on US-522, and from Ridge N it is 2.8 mi, L, on US-522.

Ziler Trail (2.3 mi)

* CONNECTING TRAILS:
  Laurel Trail (1.8 mi)
  Central Trail (5 mi)
  Ziler Loop Trail (5.1 mi)

* TOTAL LENGTH: 14.2 mi

* DIFFICULTY: moderate to strenuous

* FEATURES: wildlife, wildflowers, scenic rock outcroppings

* TRAILHEADS AND DETAILS: The *Ziler Trail* is the park's main through-trail from its lowest area to its highest area on the ridge line of Cacapon Mtn. The three connecting trails form succession loops, each providing a distinctive and scenic view of the park's terrain. All the trails have large patches of blueberries and mountain laurel. The forest is mainly hardwoods with scattered Virginia pine. Wildflowers include bird's-foot violet, wild senna, pink lady's slipper, and pipsissewa. Deer and grouse are frequently seen.

To begin the *Ziler Trail* after entering the park, drive 0.7 mi to pass L of the golf course and L again at the fork with the picnic and tennis court signs to a parking area, L. Park near the tennis court. Cross the road to the orange-blazed *Ziler Trail*, the park's only trail that does not loop, and the green-blazed *Laurel Trail*, a jointly running trail for the first 0.9 mi. Pass cabin #24 at 0.1 mi, cross a dirt road at 0.2 mi and horse trails soon thereafter. Ascend and veer R at 0.5 mi to arrive at a rock outcropping. Pass through a stand of mountain laurel and reach a jct with the red-blazed *Central Trail* at 0.9 mi.

(The *Central Trail* goes R and L to form a scenic loop on the mountainside. If taking the L, go down a slope, cross the cabin road, and after 0.8 mi cross Middle Fork Indian Run. At 1 mi reach a jct with the blue-blazed *Ziler Loop Trail*, R. Ahead it is 0.1 mi past the Batt Picnic Area and a park road that leads L for 1.3 mi back to the tennis court. After joining the *Ziler Loop Trail* ascend 0.2 mi before turning R. Go through an open forest of hardwoods, thick patches of blueberries, and mossy rock formations for another 0.9 mi to a spur trail, R, which descends to cabin #1. Continue ahead, pass a rock formation, cross the *Ziler Trail* at a resting bench at 2.1 mi, and pass another spur trail, R, which descends to cabin #10. At 3.1 mi the joint trails part. The *Central Trail* bears R and the *Ziler Loop Trail* ascends L. The *Central Trail* follows a horse trail for 0.3 mi before turning R to later cross the cabin road and the North Fork Indian Run. At 4.7 mi arrive at a jct with the *Laurel Trail*. A turn L on the *Laurel Trail* is 0.3 mi to cabin #22 where another 0.3 mi on the road to the tennis court provides a circuit of 5.3 mi. A turn R on the *Laurel Trail* ascends for 0.3 mi for a return to the *Ziler Trail* and a completion of the *Central Trail* loop at 5 mi.)

The *Ziler Trail* follows a partial ridge of Piney Ridge on a wide trail before beginning a steep ascent. The trail is a pioneer route over the Cacapon Mtn. Reach a jct with the *Central* and *Ziler Loop Trails* at 1.3 mi. Continue ahead and ascend steeply to the ridge top of Cacapon Mtn and jct again at 2.3 mi with the *Ziler Loop Trail*. Backtrack or take a longer route, R or L, as described below for the *Ziler Loop Trail*.

(The blue-blazed *Ziler Loop Trail*, partially described above with the *Central Trail*, leaves the *Central Trail* 0.8 mi N of the *Ziler Trail*, ascends steeply W on a horse trail, and climbs steadily SW to the Cacapon Mtn ridge top with switchbacks and a vista bench along the way. On the ridge top turn S and pass a horse stable, R. Reach a jct with the *Ziler Trail*, L, at 2.3 mi. Descend gradually, pass a rock formation at 3.1 mi and jct with the *Central Trail* at 3.6 mi. Turn L and reach the spur trail to cabin #1 at 4.7 mi, and return to the mountainside jct with the *Ziler Trail* for a loop of 5.1 mi.)

Ridge Trail

- LENGTH: 0.9 mi

- DIFFICULTY: easy

- FEATURE: rock formations

- TRAILHEAD AND DETAILS: From the playground parking lot near the tennis court go across a small stream toward the snack bar and turn R on the yellow-blazed *Ridge Trail.* Go upstream for 0.2 mi before turning L to ascend a moss-covered rocky area with oak and witch hazel. Reach the ridge top of Warm Spring Ridge at 0.4 mi, curve L, pass viewing areas, descend to the bathhouse, turn L, and return to the snack bar to complete the loop at 0.9 mi.

▶ CANAAN VALLEY RESORT STATE PARK
(Tucker County)

"A land flowing with milk and honey" (Joshua 5:6). "A wholesome family-type resort in a superb natural setting" *(New York Times).* The first statement refers to the Land of Canaan, between the Jordan River and the Mediterranean Sea, and the second quote refers to Canaan (Ka-NAN) Valley Resort State Park, in West Virginia. Both are about a "promised land." The West Virginia "Land of Canaan" is a magnificent 6015-acre highland plateau with facilities for year-round recreation.

Its altitude is ideal for winter sports. A main chair lift extends to a 4280-ft summit on Cabin Mountain where 21 slopes provide an 850-ft drop in elevation for skiing. Night skiing is scheduled from Tuesday through Saturday. There is an outdoor ice rink for day and night skating as well as trails for cross-country skiing. Among the summer sports are fishing, swimming, hiking, camping in the 34 full-service campsites, tennis, and golf on an 18-hole course (frequently visited by deer and Canada geese). The 250-room luxury lodge has a restaurant and conference rooms. There are also 15 deluxe cabins. These and other facilities and services make it one of the state's most popular parks. The park is only four hours from Richmond, Baltimore, Charleston, or Washington, DC; only three hours from Pittsburgh; and half a day from Philadelphia or Cleveland. Near the park are Blackwater Falls State Park and the scenic Dolly Sods Wilderness Area in the MNF. (*USGS-FS Maps:* Blackwater Falls, Laneville)

• ADDRESS AND ACCESS: Superintendent, Canaan Valley Resort State Park, Rte 1, Box 39, Davis, WV 26260, tel: 304-866-4121. From Davis go S on WV-32 for 12 mi, or from Harmon go N on WV-32 for 9 mi.

Blackwater River Trail

• LENGTH: 0.8 mi

• DIFFICULTY: easy

• FEATURE: wildlife

• TRAILHEAD AND DETAILS: From the parking lot at the golf-course parking area follow the trail sign W through a young forest of hawthorn, then an open forest of maple and cherry to an old RR grade. At 0.4 mi skirt Blackwater River, where beavers are active. Unique rock formations are here. Deer are likely to be seen.

Middle Ridge Trail (2.3 mi); Canaan Mtn Trail (1.2 mi); (Allegheny Trail); Railroad Grade Trail (1.6 mi); Chimney Rock Trail (1.4 mi); Club Run Trail (1.3 mi); Ridge Top Trail (0.1 mi)

• TOTAL LENGTH: 7.9 mi

• DIFFICULTY: moderate to strenuous

• FEATURES: wildlife, beaver bogs, scenic

• TRAILHEADS AND DETAILS: Some of these trails are excellent cross-country skiing trails, and all of them connect or overlap. The description below is an option on how to make a long loop for 4.5 mi on three of them. The mileage is increased if the trails are completely looped or hiked separately with a backtrack. After entrance into the park follow the main road to a parking overlook (Balsam Swamp Overlook) W of the lodge. Follow the yellow-blazed *Middle Ridge Trail* for 0.2 mi to a trail loop jct. Turn R through a beautiful forest of hemlock, cherry, black and yellow birch, and maple on an old tram road. At 1.1 mi are open bogs and another trail jct. The *Middle Ridge Trail* turns L here and makes a loop back to the point of origin for a total of 2.3 mi. Continue ahead, cross Club Run, and pass through a meadow of wildflowers and ferns. Cross Enoch Run and at 1.5 mi jct with the yellow-blazed *Allegheny Trail,* R and L, and the blue-blazed *Railroad Grade Trail,* L. (It is 6.3 mi R on the scenic *Allegheny Trail* and Blackwater-Canaan Mtn Cross-Country Ski Trail, which run jointly, to Blackwater Falls State Park.) Turn L on the jointly running *Allegheny Trail* and the *Railroad Grade Trail* through a deep forest and over small drains to a jct with the green-blazed *Chimney Rock Trail* at 3.1 mi. (The *Railroad Grade Trail* ends here, and W half of the *Chimney Rock Trail* begins here. It ascends R for 0.7 mi to Chimney Rock (4081 ft) for an outstanding view of Canaan Valley.) Continue L on the *Chimney Rock Trail* and the *Allegheny Trail* for 0.2 mi to the headwaters of Club Run and a field where the *Allegheny Trail* turns R and the *Chimney Rock Trail* turns L. (The *Allegheny Trail* leaves the park after 0.4 mi on its way to the Jenningston/Lanesville Rd [CO-45] and Red Creek.) Follow the *Chimney Rock Trail* to its terminus in the cul-de-sac near the cabin area at 3.6 mi. Follow the paved road 100 yds and turn L on the red-blazed *Club Run Trail.* At 3.9 mi the *Club Run Trail* forks for a loop of 1 mi. If not taking the loop, turn R and go 0.1 mi to a jct with the white-blazed *Ridge Top Trail,* a connecting trail to *Middle Ridge Trail.* Rejoin the *Middle Ridge Trail* at 4.1 mi, turn R, descend, turn R again, and return to the Balsam Swamp Overlook at 4.5 mi.

Weiss Knob Trail *(1.1 mi)*; Bald Knob Trail *(1.2 mi)*

- LENGTH: 2.3 mi, rt, ct

- DIFFICULTY: strenuous (950 ft elev change)

- FEATURE: Bald Knob

- TRAILHEADS AND DETAILS: Drive to the parking lot at the ski area. Ride the ski lift to the top of Cabin Mtn and begin the *Weiss Knob Trail* into a forest of spruce N of Weiss Knob. Descend on a rocky trail for 0.3 mi to a gas pipeline swath. (Although the park lists this trail as terminating here, I have extended it another 0.8 mi to connect with the *Bald Knob Trail.*) Turn L and follow an open area to a wet saddle of ferns and wildflowers. Ascend to panoramic Bald Knob (4308 ft) for views of Canaan Valley at 1.1 mi. In mid-August the mountain is blue with blueberries. Return to the parking lot by descending W on the steep but scenic *Bald Knob Trail* for a round-trip hike of 2.3 mi.

Deer Run Trail

- LENGTH: 1.3 mi

- DIFFICULTY: easy

- FEATURE: nature study

- TRAILHEADS AND DETAILS: After entrance into the park, turn R at the first road and park at the park headquarters. You will see woodchucks on the wide, manicured road borders. Walk W across the campground entrance road and follow the sign into a lush forest. The orange-blazed interpretive trail has red spruce, hemlock, birch, beech, oak, rhododendron, club mosses, maple, oak, black locust, white ash, yellow iris *(Iris pseudacorus),* and ferns. Cross a boardwalk on Abe Run and, after meandering through low areas and over other boardwalks, arrive at the swimming pool at 1.3 mi.

▶ CARNIFEX FERRY BATTLEFIELD STATE PARK
(Nicholas County)

This historic site of 156 acres has areas mainly for picnicking, hiking, and the study of the Civil War. Scenic, peaceful, and manicured, it even has deer grazing on its pastures. It was at this mountain top, Camp Gauley, that on September 10, 1861, troops led by Union Brig. Gen. W. S. Rosecrans engaged the Confederate troops and forced them to evacuate their entrenched positions. The Confederate commander, Brig. Gen. John B. Floyd, retreated with his 2000-man force across the Gauley River and E to Meadow Bluff. In the skirmish, the Patteson House, now a museum, was in the line of artillery and musket fire. (*USGS Map:* Summersville Dam)

- ADDRESS AND ACCESS: Superintendent, Carnifex Ferry Battlefield State Park, Keslers Cross Lanes, WV 26675, tel: 304-872-3773. For an E entrance from the jct of US-19 and WV-129 (S of Summersville), go 5.1 mi on WV-129, and turn L on Carnifex Ferry Rd (CO-23) for 0.8 mi. For a W entrance turn on WV-129 from US-33 in Drennen for 5.9 mi.

Carnifex Ferry Trail (1.2 mi); Patteson Trail (1.7 mi); Nature Trail (0.3 mi); Pierson Hollow Trail (0.8 mi); Laurel Trail (0.2 mi); Fishermen's Trail (0.6 mi)

- TOTAL LENGTH: 7.3 mi, rt, ct

- DIFFICULTY: moderate to strenuous

- FEATURES: history, scenic overlooks, and forests.

- TRAILHEADS AND DETAILS: All the trails connect and the *Nature Trail* overlaps. The description below is one of a number of beginning or ending points. At the main parking area near the historic marker and picnic shelter, begin the hike on the old Ferry Rd, the *Carnifex Ferry Trail* by picnic shelter #3. The trail is wide and frequently traveled. At 0.2 mi pass a jct with *Patteson Trail*, R. Rhododendron, hemlock, mountain laurel, holly, and hardwoods are prevalent. Descend gradually on the route that Confederate Gen. Floyd used for his troops to slip away from Rosecrans's forces after midnight and during the early morning hours of September 11, 1861. At 0.9 mi pass a large rock formation, which echoes the sounds of the Gauley River Canyon, and at 1.2 mi reach the river banks where Gen. Floyd crossed to the mouth of the Meadow River. It was here the Confederate general destroyed the footbridge and flatboats behind him. Thanks to this retreat the Kanawha Valley was free and the statehood movement was enhanced.

Backtrack to the *Patteson Trail*, L, and after 0.3 mi jct with the *Nature Trail*. (The *Nature Trail* is 0.3 mi across a number of footbridges and up the hillside to the rest rooms and parking area.) Continue ahead, pass a spring, ascend to and cross a gravel road at 0.5 mi. Here is another *Nature Trail* sign. At 0.8 mi enter a field and reach the Patteson House. Cross the paved road, descend in a field to the forest, and reach a jct with the *Pierson Hollow Trail*, L, at 1 mi. (The *Pierson Hollow Trail* descends into a superb forest of tall, virgin hemlock. Rhododendron and rock formations flank the gorge. Pass *Laurel Trail*, R, at 0.3 mi. The *Laurel Trail* is a 0.2 mi spur to rejoin the *Patteson Trail*. Descend steeply on the *Pierson Hollow Trail* through rhododendron and rock formations to the Gauley River at 0.8 mi. Backtrack to the *Laurel Trail* or to the *Patteson Trail*.)

On the *Patteson Trail* reach a scenic spur at 1.2 mi, a hemlock grove and *Fishermen's Trail* at 1.5 mi. (The *Fishermen's Trail* is an exceptionally steep and rocky descent to the Gauley River Canyon for 0.6 mi. Backtrack.) Continue on the *Patteson Trail* to its jct with the *Carniflex Ferry Trail* at 1.7 mi. If you have hiked all these trails at this point, counting the backtracks, you have hiked at least 7.3 mi.

▶ **CATHEDRAL STATE PARK**
(Preston County)

One mile E of the historic town of Aurora (1787) is the only large stand of mixed virgin timber left in the state. The stands of hemlock are estimated to be 350 yrs old, many over 100 ft high and towering like cathedral spires. The largest hemlock in the state (123 ft high, 21.6 ft in circumference, and 66 ft in limb spread) is behind the park headquarters bldg. Purchased by the state in 1942 from Brandon Haas, who had protected the virgin woods, the 133-acre preserve was entered into the National Registry of National Historic Landmarks in 1976. In 1983, the Society of American Foresters recognized the park in the National Areas Program. Among the park slogans are "dedicated to scientific and educational purposes . . . a better understanding of man's environment." Facilities include picnicking, with grates and shelters; camping is not allowed. (*USGS Map:* Aurora)

• ADDRESS AND ACCESS: Superintendent, Cathedral State Park, Aurora, WV 26705, tel: 304-735-3771. From the jct of WV-24 and US-50, go W on US-50 for 0.5 mi and from Aurora on US-50 go E 1 mi.

Cathedral Trail (1.3 mi); Giant Hemlock Trail (0.2 mi); Partridge Berry Trail (0.2 mi); Trillium Trail (0.1 mi); Wood Thrush Trail (0.5 mi)

• LENGTH: 2.3 mi, rt, ct

• DIFFICULTY: easy

• FEATURES: virgin forest, Rhine Creek

• TRAILHEADS AND DETAILS: (It is suggested that you take time to linger on these trails.) From the parking area follow the trail signs, first on the *Cathedral Trail,* which makes two loops in the forest, and on any of the other trails for connections and loops. The 0.1 mi *Trillium Trail* is usually backtracked. Over 175 species of vascular plants have been identified, including 9 fern and 50 wildflower species. Rhododendron is common along Rhine Creek. The *Wood Thrush Trail* loops across US-50 on its return to the parking area.

▶ CEDAR CREEK STATE PARK
(Gilmer County)

In one of the Cedar Creek bends is a 2443-acre park with fine recreational facilities, shale outcrops, tributaries flowing through forested glens, and a tranquil environment. It is Cedar Creek State Park, with facilities that include 46 campsites (some with water and electrical hookups), laundromat, swimming pool, tennis courts, picnic area with shelters, bathhouses, and playground. Fishing (bass and muskellunge) and hiking are other recreational activities. (*USGS Maps:* Glenville, Cedarville)

• ADDRESS AND ACCESS: Superintendent, Cedar Creek State Park, Rte 1, Box 9, Glenville, WV 26351, tel: 803-462-7158. From Glenville drive S on US-119/33 for 3.1 mi and turn L on Cedar Creek Rd (CO-17) for 3 mi. From Cedarville drive NW on Cedar Creek Rd (CO-17) for 7 mi.

Stone Trough Trail (2.5 mi); Two Run Trail (2.2 mi); North Boundary Trail (1 mi)

• LENGTH: 6.5 mi, rt, ct

• DIFFICULTY: moderate

• FEATURES: history, wildlife

• TRAILHEADS AND DETAILS: After crossing the Cedar Creek Bridge turn R at the fork and drive to the parking area nearest campsites #7 and #8. Follow the red-blazed *Stone Trough Trail* upstream along Long Lick Run in a hardwood forest. Papaw, redbud, and dogwood are part of the understory. At 0.8 mi reach a jct with the white-blazed *Two Run Trail*, R. Bear L, pass ruins of old farmhouse (an old cream separator is a historic reminder), ascend steeply, and reach a unique hand-chiseled stone watering trough at 1 mi. Piped water constantly runs in the trough. Reach the ridge crest at 1.2 mi, veer R at 1.4 mi, and begin a descent. After switchbacks in a rocky area, return to the campground road, turn L, and return to the point of origin at 2.5 mi.

The *Two Run Trail* also begins at the Long Lick Run but branches R and parallels the campground road for 0.2 mi before curving around the ridge to Two Run. Follow upstream to a jct with *North Boundary Trail*, R, at 0.7 mi. Ragwort and other spring flowers are prominent. Deer are likely to be seen. (*North Boundary Trail* ascends to the park boundary in a rocky area, curves L, and descends to rejoin the *Two Run Trail* after 1 mi.) Continue upstream on the N side of the ridge and reach a jct with *North Boundary Trail* at 1.3 mi. Turn L, ascend to the ridge top on an old woods road in an oak forest. Descend to the jct with the *Stone Trough Trail* at 2.2 mi. Deer, grouse, and chipmunk are often seen on this trail. Turn L and follow the *Stone Trough Trail* downstream to the campground for a total of 3 mi, or 3.5 mi if the *North Boundary Trail* is included.

Park View Trail (1.7 mi); Fishermen's Trail (0.9 mi)

- LENGTH: 2.6 mi, rt, ct
- DIFFICULTY: moderate
- FEATURES: overlook, Cedar Creek

- TRAILHEADS AND DETAILS: Park at the athletic field and hike E at the curve of Cedar Creek Rd. Ascend steeply in a hardwood forest to an overlook of the park and the Cedar Creek area at 0.3 mi. After a long rugged L curve over the ridge with a number of good views, descend to Cedar Creek Rd at 1.7 mi. Cross the road and hike upstream on *Fishermen's Trail* to the athletic field and point of beginning at 2.6 mi.

▶ CHIEF LOGAN STATE PARK
(Logan County)

Before development, the park area was an abandoned coal field and camp. Now it is a popular day-use park of 3305 acres.

It is mainly known for the summer outdoor drama of "The Aracoma Story," the tragic love story of Princess Aracoma, daughter of Indian Chief Cornstalk and an English scout, Boling Baker. It is also a popular park because of its large activities building with a dining hall able to provide superb cuisine for parties, proms, and public events. Other facilities are a 280,000-gallon swimming pool and bathhouse, 75 acres of large picnic areas with shelters, field archery area, miniature golf course, game courts, amphitheater, tennis courts, physical fitness course, and trails for nature study. A proposed campground will be constructed W of the swimming pool area along Buffalo Creek. The old coal mine sites, tipple chute, and silo will likely be incorporated into a *Coal Mine Interpretive Trail* after the campground is completed in 1987–88. Currently under construction is the *Guyandotte Beauty Trail*. It will connect two hollows that have abundant wildlife and wildflowers, including the rare Guyandotte Beauty *(Synandra hipudula)*. (The 1.7-mi trail will pass an abandoned coal mine fan hole used for ventilation in the mines and will start at the head of Mud Lick Hollow, which is the first paved road to the L in the main picnic ground, and will end at picnic shelter #4.) Near the restaurant is an old steam locomotive, a gift from the C&O Railway Company as a monument to coal mining and railroads. (For information on "The Aracoma Story," write PO Box 2016, Logan, WV 25601, tel: 304-752-0253.) (*USGS Maps:* Henlawson, Chapmanville)

• ADDRESS AND ACCESS: Superintendent, Chief Logan State Park, Logan, WV 25601, tel: 304-752-8558. For entrance to the park drive 3 mi N of Logan on WV-10 along the Guyandotte River to the park, L.

Lake Shore Trail (0.8 mi); Backbone Trail (2.2 mi); Cliffside Trail (0.6 mi); Buffalo Trail (1.4 mi); Nature Trail (1 mi)

- LENGTH: 6 mi, ct

- DIFFICULTY: easy to strenuous

- FEATURES: wildlife, nature study

- TRAILHEADS AND DETAILS: After entering the park go 0.9 mi, turn R at the activities building, and go N for 1 mi, R, to a parking area near the dam of a small lake. The *Lake Shore Trail* begins L of the Wolfpen Hollow stream and the *Nature Trail* begins on the R. If taking the *Lake Shore Trail,* follow the service road, pass the lake, cross a meadow L of a gas well, and enter a hardwood forest of large beech, oak, and maple. Circle the hollow on a foot trail and reach a jct with the *Nature Trail,* R, and the *Backbone Trail,* ascend steeply on a graded treadway of the N slope with seven switchbacks for 1 mi to the ridge top. At the crest are large oaks and hickories. Along the way, in a deciduous forest, are banks of Christmas fern and numerous species of wildflowers. Descend from the ridge on the S side, pass under a power line and reach a jct, R, with the *Cliffside Trail* on the mountain slope, cross under a power line, pass R of a cave and rock overhang, and reach a jct, R, with the *Buffalo Trail* at 3.6 mi. (An access point is L to a picnic and parking area on the main road.) Ascend on the wide *Buffalo Trail* among poplar, oak, and beech. Reach a jct with the *Nature Trail* and the end of the *Buffalo Trail* at 5 mi. (A spur trail goes 0.1 mi L to the point of beginning.) Follow the *Nature Trail* for 0.5 mi by the lake to the point of beginning for a loop of 6 mi. All of these trails have many wildflowers. Among them are putty-root *(Aplectrum hyemale),* sweet cicely *(Osmorhiza longistylis),* Greek valerian *(Polemonium reptans),* wood betony, asters, and jewelweed.

Woodpecker Trail *(1.5 mi)*; Chief Logan Fitness Trail *(1.0 mi)*

- LENGTH: 2.5 mi, ct

- DIFFICULTY: easy

- FEATURES: nature study, physical fitness

- TRAILHEADS AND DETAILS: From the park entrance drive 0.7 mi to a parking area, R, and the sign of the *Woodpecker Trail*, L. Hike across Buffalo Creek on a footbridge, turn R, and go upstream. The forest has yellow buckeye, beech, sycamore, oak, birch, poplar, place locust, elm, and papaw. Cross six small drains (often dry in the summer and fall), parallel an old RR grade part of the way, and reach the trail terminus at 1.5 mi. Backtrack or turn R, then L, to cross Buffalo Creek on an old RR grade trestle. Cross the picnic field to the paved road, turn R, and follow the paved road back to the point of origin for a loop of 2.5 mi. Another choice after crossing the creek is to follow the Vita-Course fitness trail. It is an easy treadway of 15 exercise posts that form a loop; it has its beginning across the road from the C&O steam locomotive.

▶ DROOP MOUNTAIN BATTLEFIELD STATE PARK (Pocahontas County)

On November 6, 1863, Union troops commanded by Gen. W. W. Averell defeated Confederate forces under Gen. John Echols on Droop Mountain, a high plateau on a ridge W of Greenbrier River. It was the state's largest battle engagement of the Civil War. In 1929 the area was made a park; it now has 287 acres with picnic areas, a museum with Civil War artifacts, a playground, a lookout tower, and hiking trails. It is a day-use facility and camping is not allowed.

- ADDRESS AND ACCESS: Superintendent, Droop Mountain Battlefield State Park, Droop, WV 24933, tel: 304-653-4254. On US-219, 27 mi N of Lewisburg and 15 mi S from Marlinton, enter the main gate, W.

Cranberry Trail (0.7 mi); *Old Musket Trail (0.5 mi)*; *Horse Haven Trail (0.3 mi)*; *Overlook Trail (0.4 mi)*; *Minnie Ball Trail (0.2 mi)*

- LENGTH: 2.1 mi, ct

- DIFFICULTY: easy

- FEATURES: history, battlefield, scenic overlooks

- TRAILHEADS AND DETAILS: After entering the park, follow the main road to the park headquarters and parking lot. Follow the trail sign across the road to the *Cranberry Trail*. After a few yds the *Old Musket Trail* goes L for 0.4 mi to a gravel road. Turn R at a stone shed and rejoin the *Cranberry Trail* at 0.5 mi. (It is 0.2 mi, R, back to the parking area.) Pass near a cranberry bog in a forest of hardwoods, white pine, mountain laurel, and patches of wintergreen. Cross the main road to the *Horse Haven Trail*, where there are overlooks. Return to the main road, but turn L after 0.1 mi on the *Overlook Trail*. Here are exceptional views of the Hills Creek Valley, Briery Knob (4518 ft), Jacox Knob, and Hock Knob. Continue ahead and pass Civil War entrenchments to Caesars Mtn Rd. Turn R on the road and return to the parking area. From here, E, downhill and parallel to the gravel road, is the short *Minnie Ball Trail*.

▶ GRANDVIEW STATE PARK
(Raleigh County)

Established in 1939 by the Civilian Conservation Corps, this extraordinarily beautiful park of 891 acres has breathtaking overlooks (1400 ft down) into the New River Gorge. Geological formations here of sandstone, shale and limestone all add to the grandeur of the canyon rim. During the summer there is an outdoor musical theater in the Cliffside Amphitheater. Reservations are recommended. A moderately priced theater dinner is served from 4:45 to 7 P.M. Reservations are required. For more information write Theater West Virginia, PO Box 1205, Beckley, WV 25801, tel: 304-253-8313 (June, July, and

August call toll-free, 1-800-642-2766). Other facilities are picnic areas, game courts, a playground, and hiking trails. (*USGS Map:* Prince)

• ADDRESS AND ACCESS: Superintendent, Grandview State Park, Rte 9, Beaver, WV 25813, tel: 304-763-3145. From Beckley go S on US-19/WV-3 for 3 mi to jct with WV-304. Go 4 mi on WV-304 to Grandview Rd (CO-9), turn L, and go another 5.9 mi.

Caves and Tunnel Trail (0.6 mi); *Castle Rock Trail* (0.7 mi); *Canyon Rim Trail* (1.6 mi)

• LENGTH: 2.9 mi, rt, ct

• DIFFICULTY: easy to moderate

• FEATURES: vistas, rock formations

• TRAILHEADS AND DETAILS: From the parking area near the amphitheater, follow the signs to the main overlook for spectacular views. Turn R and descend on a unique trail to caves and through tunnels for a round-trip of 0.6 mi. Back at the main overlook descend to the *Castle Rock Trail*, N, and follow the base of the cliffs of sandstone, alum, and coal veins. Reach the jct with the *Canyon Rim Trail* at 0.7 mi. Turn R and follow the *Canyon Rim Trail* to a paved road, turn R and follow the road for 0.1 mi. Enter the forest again, return to the road, and, finally, after a number of road contacts, reach post #42 at 1.2 mi from the main overlook. Backtrack to complete the S end of the *Canyon Rim Trail* to a jct with *Castle Rock Trail*. Follow the numbered posts that designate species of trees, shrubs, and flowers. Among them are flame azalea, Indian cucumber root, oak, birch, teaberry, maple, orchids, beech, and fringe tree (*Chionanthus virginica*). Reach the north overlook, pass L of a water fountain, and return to the main overlook at 1.1 mi — a round-trip total of 2.3 mi. (The *Turkey Spur Overlook Trail* is a short climb to the top of huge boulders for an outstanding view of the New River. This overlook is reached by driving the Rim Rd from the amphitheater to Turkey Run Overlook.)

Big Buck Trail (0.8 mi); *Bridge Trail* (0.6 mi)

- LENGTH: 1.4 mi, rt, ct

- DIFFICULTY: easy

- FEATURE: wildlife

- TRAILHEADS AND DETAILS: Drive to the picnic area and park near shelters #2 and #3. Beyond shelter #2 follow a wide road-trail under tall hardwoods. The understory is striped maple, sassafras, arrowwood, and ferns. Loop to a valley and return to the shelter at 0.8 mi. At the parking lot follow the *Bridge Trail* loop for 0.6 mi through a hardwood forest with mountain laurel and buckberry *(Vaccinium stamineum)*.

▶ GREENBRIER RIVER TRAIL
(Greenbrier and Pocahontas Counties)

The 950-acre *Greenbrier River Trail* is part of the state's park system, though supervised and maintained by the state's Division of Forestry. Often referred to as the "nation's longest state park," it is a narrow (generally 100 ft wide), 75-mi corridor that was formerly the Chesapeake and Ohio RR from North Caldwell to Cass. Consistently winding with the banks of the Greenbrier River, it crosses more than 35 bridges, some of which are historically significant, and twice tunnels the mountains to avoid long horseshoe-shaped curves. It passes tranquil rural communities, pastureland, groves of flowering plants, and often hugs the slate and sandstone canyon walls. Wildlife are frequently seen on its pathway and along the riverside. Its elev change is approximately 10 ft for each mile.

Motorized traffic is not allowed. In a continuous process of development, the park is used for hiking and backpacking, bicycling, and cross-country skiing. It is also used by bird-watchers and by fishermen as an access route to the river. The November 4, 1985, flood damaged trail sections for nearly 30 mi. Although foot travel is possible without difficulty, through-

bicyclists or skiers should contact the Greenbrier State Forest office for current trail conditions.

Camping is allowed at designated sites as indicated in the trail description below, but for through-hikers staying overnight, camping is permitted within 50 ft of center of the trail on either side. Campsites must be off the trail and out of sight of road crossings. Care should be used to not park or hike on adjoining private property. At each jct there is a trail marker with printed rules and regulations for trail use. Because clean water is rare, hikers should purify all drinking water. Lotions or proper clothing should be used to prevent sunburn on the exposed long sections of the trail. (*USGS-FS Maps:* Lewisburg, White Sulphur Springs, Anthony, Droop, Denmar, Hillsboro, Marlinton, Edray, Clover Lick, Cass)

• INFORMATION: Superintendent, Greenbrier River Trail, Star Rte, Box 125, Caldwell, WV 24925, tel: 304-536-1944. Greenbrier River Hike, Bike, and Ski Trail, Inc., PO Box 828, Lewisburg, WV 24901, tel: 304-572-3771.

Greenbrier River Trail

• LENGTH: 75.2 mi

• DIFFICULTY: easy to moderate

• FEATURES: RR history, scenic, wildlife, botanical study, remote

• TRAILHEADS AND DETAILS: The following list of mile points, access points, points of interest, and other descriptions is to assist hikers in making plans for short or long treks. The usual highway map may be of sufficient use for some hikers. Otherwise, a county map provides complete details for the roads, houses, and landmarks. Topo map names are listed above. Some of the C&O mileposts are missing, and others are inconsistently placed. The S terminus of the trail begins at approximately 3.6 mi from the main line in Whitcomb, thus the first C&O mile post, #6, is 2.4 mi on the trail mile point. Access points explain exits to major highways and what facilities are available in the vicinity.

Greenbrier River Trail

MILE POINT		LOCATION AND DESCRIPTION
From S	From N	
		From North Caldwell to Hooper (2.4 mi)
0.0	75.2	On Stone House Rd (CO-38), 1.4 mi from US-60 in North Caldwell. *First entrance:* C&O RR crossing
0.1	75.1	*Second entrance:* Stone House Rd
0.3	74.9	*Third entrance:* Camp Allegheny Rd (CO-38/1) extends E across the Greenbrier River. Trail banks have ferns, ragwort, wild geranium, pinxter, and bloodroot
1.1	74.1	S end of islands
1.4	73.8	N end of islands
1.9	73.3	Cottages W and small stream
		From Hooper to Keister (5.3 mi)
2.4	72.8	*Access Point:* Hooper community, cottages W. C&O milepost #6. Harper Rd (CO-30/3), 4.8 mi out to US-219
2.8	72.4	Cottage E, on island. Trail banks have trillium, twayblade, soapwort, yellow buckeye, stone crop.
3.7	71.5	C&O milepost #7
4.3	70.9	Cottages W, cross bridge over small stream
4.7	70.5	C&O milepost #8, waterfall W
5.4	69.8	Private road crossing
5.7	69.5	C&O milepost #9; spring W; river islands, and sycamore, maple, birch, and poplar near river edge
5.8	69.4	Cottages E, close to the river
6.0	69.2	Private road crossing to cottages. Border of red bud on the trail. *Trillium grandiflorum*, wild ginger, columbine on the rocky banks

6.7	68.5	C&O milepost #10
7.0	68.2	Private gazebo E
7.2	68.0	Log house E. Telephone Pioneers of America have installed bluebird houses. High slope W
7.5	67.7	Road crossing to private home E, pastures W

From Keister to Anthony (3.2 mi)

7.7	67.5	*Access Point:* Keister, houses E and W. C&O milepost #11. Road crossing, Keister Rd (CO-30), 2.2 mi out to Alum Springs, and 3.1 mi farther on Benedict Lane (C0-219/19) to US-219 near the Greenbrier Valley Airport.
8.5	66.7	N end of houses E
8.6	66.6	Cross bridge over small stream
9.2	66.0	River is wide; small cascades W; large beds of wild pink on embankment W
9.5	65.7	C&O milepost #13
9.6	65.6	Private campground
10.2	65.0	C&O milepost #14
10.4	64.8	Cross bridge over small stream
10.7	64.5	Houses W and E, cross private road

From Anthony to Spring Creek (7.4 mi)

10.9	64.3	*Access Point:* Community of Anthony. Anthony Station Rd (CO-21/2), E, is over bridge of the Greenbrier River and to White Sulphur District of the MNF, where camping is allowed by the river on Anthony Creek Trail. West is 4 mi to US-219 in town of Frankford, West on Anthony Station Rd for 0.3 mi is Anthony General Store, groceries, camping, and fishing supplies, tel: 304-497-2508. Post office
11.2	64.0	Old bridge foundation. Telephone Pioneers of America have installed bluebird houses
11.3	63.9	Rhododendron grove
11.6	63.6	C&O milepost #15

11.9	63.3	Views of Greenbrier Youth Camp and river islands. Steep slope W.
12.7	62.5	C&O milepost #16
12.8	62.4	Community of Woodman, cottages E
12.9	62.3	Remnants of old railroad trestle
13.4	61.8	Spring W, near old logging road
14.0	61.2	Old path W
14.1	61.1	Flat area of river bend, potential camping in 0.2 mi of MNF, White Sulphur District, E
14.4	60.8	South edge of horseshoe bend in the river. High peak E
14.8	60.4	Rock formations W
15.9	59.3	Cross two small bridges
16.5	58.7	North edge of horseshoe bend in the river. High peak E.

From Spring Creek to Renick (3.3 mi)

18.3	56.9	*Access Point:* Community of Spring Creek and Spring Creek Station Rd (CO-13); W goes 2 mi out to US-219 and N 3.1 mi to US-219 in Falling Spring.
18.4	56.8	Cross steel bridge (built by Bethlehem Steel Co. in 1929) over Spring Creek
18.7	56.5	Large grassy meadows E to river
19.5	55.7	Meadows E and W, grassy hillsides W
20.7	54.5	Small limestone cave W
20.9	54.3	Geological survey marker

From Renick/Falling Spring to Horrock (4.8 mi)

21.6	53.6	*Access Point:* Community of Falling Spring (Renick PO), old RR station. Cross Auto Rd (CO-11), W is 0.4 mi to US-219 and grocery store, gasoline, telephone. East goes across the Greenbrier River to Peach Orchard Rd (FR-296) in the White Sulphur District of the MNF.
22.3	52.9	Road crossing

23.0	52.2	Railroad grade is close to the river. Islands E. Civil War route for supplies to Droop Mtn from Virginia through Alvon on WV-92.
24.3	50.9	Cross bridge over small stream
24.8	50.4	Wide lowland E
26.0	49.2	Islands in the river

From Horrock to Denmar (9.4 mi)

26.4	48.8	*Access Point:* Community of Horrock, cross bridge over small stream. Rorer Rd (CO-7/2) is W for 0.4 mi to jct with Julia Rd (CO-7/1), L to Brownstone Rd (CO-7), R for 1.4 mi to US-219
27.4	47.8	Old house W; cross bridge over small stream. Rorer community E
27.6	47.6	South entrance of 430 ft Droop Mtn Tunnel; creosote boards on S entrance; some falling rocks. N entrance has C&O milepost #31.
28.7	46.5	C&O milepost #32
29.7	45.5	C&O milepost #33
30.6	44.6	C&O milepost #34, low river rapids nearby
31.6	43.6	C&O milepost #35
32.1	43.1	Boundary of Greenbrier (S) and Pocahontas (N) counties. Unmarked ford of river to remote *Spice Ridge Trail* in White Sulphur District, MNF (see Chapter 1).
32.6	42.6	C&O milepost #36
33.6	41.6	C&O milepost #37, W banks have array of wild bleeding heart.
34.2	41.0	Steel and wood bridge over Locust Creek. Deer frequently seen here
34.6	40.6	C&O milepost #38, W banks filled with trillium
34.8	40.4	Meadows, farm, private swinging bridge over the river
35.1	40.1	*Access Point:* House, W; Beard Post Office Rd (CO-31/8) crossing. West for 0.3 mi to Den-

mar Rd (CO-31), R for 4.9 mi on CO-31 to Hillsboro on US-219.

From Denmar to Seebert (6.4 mi)

35.8	39.4	*Access Point:* Denmar. Access W on Denmar Station Rd (CO-31/7) through Denmar State Hospital grounds for 0.3 mi to Denmar Rd (CO-31). Right for 4.3 mi to Hillsboro on US-219. At the hospital are first aid, telephone, drinking water, and soft drinks. Camping allowed between the trail and the river for through-hikers only. East is the fording of the river for connection to the mouth of Laurel Run, the dividing line between the Calvin Price State Forest (S) and the Watoga State Park (N)
37.4	37.8	Cross bridge over Mill Run, rows of river birch and purple-flowering raspberry
38.1	37.1	Cross bridge over stream at Burnsides, flat area across the river
38.6	36.6	Excellent view NE of the Lookout Tower in Watoga State Park
39.3	35.9	Cross road of farm entrance
39.4	35.8	C&O milepost #43
40.1	35.1	Watoga State Park Campground on the other side of the river
40.4	34.8	C&O milepost #44. At low water, the river can be waded here to the campground for fee campsites, showers, rest room, laundry.
41.3	33.9	C&O milepost #45
41.6	33.6	Private homes in Seebert W and E

From Seebert to Buckeye (6 mi)

42.2	33.0	*Access Point:* Seebert River Rd (CO-27/3). Right, across the bridge is Watoga State Park. Numerous facilities (see below). Left in Seebert are groceries, gasoline, camping and fishing supplies. West on Seebert Rd it is 2 mi

		to US-219, between Hillsboro and Mill Point.
42.3	32.9	C&O milepost #46, grove of yellow buckeye
42.6	32.6	Cross Stamping Creek bridge
43.2	32.0	Cross bridge over Stevens Hole Run and Seebert Rd (CO-27); C&O milepost #47
43.3	31.9	Locked gate to exclude motorized vehicles
44.0	31.2	Scenic Watoga Bridge crossing of the Greenbrier River. Some of the material made in 1899, constructed in 1925. C&O milepost #48
44.3	30.9	Whistle point
45.1	30.1	C&O milepost #49
45.4	29.8	Cross Beaver Creek bridge in Violet. Islands W.
46.1	29.1	C&O milepost #50; white cedar, yellow buckeye, and ninebark
46.3	28.9	Cross bridge over Griffin Run/Improvement Lick Run
47.0	28.2	C&O milepost #51; viper's bugloss, New Jersey tea (*Ceanothus americanus*), St John's wort
48.0	27.2	Gated to exclude motorized vehicles; farms E

From Buckeye to Marlinton (3.7 mi)

48.2	27.0	*Access Point:* Buckeye Station Rd (CO-219/15) 0.5 mi W across the river on a bridge to community of Buckeye and US-219 for groceries, gasoline, motel
48.9	26.3	C&O milepost #53. Canada geese frequently seen on islands.
49.9	25.3	C&O milepost #54. MNF property, R, across the road to Stillhouse Rd (CO-39/2), L, into Marlinton. Right is to FR-1002 for possible camping sites near Sunday Lick
50.9	24.3	C&O milepost #55. Cross Stillhouse Run
51.0	24.2	Marlinton City Park, W, camping allowed for hikers only

51.4	23.8	Water treatment plant W
51.5	23.7	Cross Knapp Creek on steel bridge built in 1924
51.8	23.4	To Ninth St and post office

From Marlinton to Clover Lick (14.4 mi)

51.9	23.3	*Access Point:* Marlinton, county seat of Pocahontas County. Restaurants, hotel, motel, grocery stores, service stations, hospital, restored railroad depot, Marlinton Ranger District of MNF (tel: 304-799-4334), Pocahontas County Historical Museum (tel: 304-799-4973), Pioneer Days Festival, second weekend in July (tel: 304-799-4315)
53.3	21.9	Old RR water tower. Large stacks of RR rails, ties, cables. Trail gated to prevent motorized vehicles
53.7	21.5	C&O milepost #58
54.6	20.6	C&O milepost #59. South edge of MNF boundary
56.4	18.8	Cross two bridges, the most N is Halfway Run. Campsites here.
56.5	18.7	Cross Thorny Creek bridge at base of Thorny Creek Mtn
57.5	17.7	C&O milepost #62
58.2	17.0	North edge of MNF boundary. Cross Thorny Creek Mtn Rd (CO-11/2), a road usually in poor condition
58.5	16.7	C&O milepost #63
59.4	15.8	C&O milepost #64
60.4	14.8	C&O milepost #65
60.7	14.5	South edge of scenic Sharp's Trestle and Tunnel (510 ft). Cuts through a mountain ridge with a sharp horseshoe curve by the river. Most of area in MNF; camping allowed near the river S of bridge.
60.9	14.3	North edge of Sharp's Trestle and Tunnel
61.3	13.9	C&O milepost #66; long straight stretch

62.1	13.1	Big Run jeep road W
62.3	12.9	C&O milepost #67; cross Big Run bridge
63.3	11.9	Across the river is Seneca State Forest
64.1	11.1	C&O milepost #69; MNF, L, and curves around Rabbit Knob
66.1	9.1	C&O milepost #71

From Clover Lick to Stony Bottom (3.6 mi)

66.3	8.9	*Access Point:* Clover Lick community. East is old bridge (washed away in 1985, but being rebuilt) over the river on Laurel Creek Rd (CO-1/4) for 4.1 mi to WV-28, and 2.6 mi S of Dunmore. West is 10.7 mi on Back Mtn Rd (CO-1) to US-219 in Edray, 3.6 mi N of Marlinton.
66.5	8.7	Cross bridge over Clover Creek
67.1	8.1	C&O milepost #72; islands in the river, trail alongside River Rd (CO-1/19)
69.7	5.5	Cross bridge over Elklich Run

From Stony Bottom to Sitlington (1.8 mi)

| 69.9 | 5.3 | *Access Point:* Stony Bottom with motel, grocery store (tel: 304-456-4721); W on Back Mtn Rd (CO-1) it is 5 mi N to Cass |
| 71.0 | 4.2 | C&O milepost #73 |

From Sitlington to Cass (3.5 mi)

| 71.7 | 3.5 | *Access Point:* Sitlington Crossing. Cross Sitlington Rd (CO-12) and jct with the *Allegheny Trail*, N and E. East over the river it is 3.1 mi to WV-28 in Dunmore. (The Greenbrier River bridge, damaged by the 1985 flood, is being restored.) (The *Allegheny Trail* follows Sitlington Rd for 1.1 mi before turning S on its ascent to Thomas Mtn in the Seneca State Forest.) |
| 71.9 | 3.3 | C&O milepost #74 |

72.8	2.4	C&O milepost #75. South end of original RR with ties and rails remaining
72.9	2.3	Cross bridge over Moses Spring Creek, N boundary of Seneca State Forest
73.7	1.5	South edge of Greenbrier Ranger District, MNF, across the river
74.0	1.2	Islands in the stream
74.2	1.0	*Access Point:* Deer Creek Rd (CO-1/13) N 1 mi to Cass
75.2	0.0	*Access Point:* Cass, and Cass Scenic Railroad State Park. North terminus of the *Greenbrier River Trail* (but the *Allegheny Trail* continues across the bridge and N to Little Mtn). East on WV-7 across the bridge it is 5.5 mi to WV-28. West through Cass to US-219 in Linwood it is 1.6 mi on Back Mtn Rd (CO-1) to Thorny Flat Rd (CO-1/3) for 7.4 mi and Linwood Rd (CO-9) for 2.4 mi. Cass has Whittaker Camping Area with hot showers and RV hookups (tel: 304-456-3218), groceries, service station, cafe, and other facilities in season (Memorial Day to Labor Day). Cass Scenic Railroad, Box 75, Cass, WV 24927, tel: 304-456-4300

▶ **HAWKS NEST STATE PARK**
(Fayette County)

There are many superlatives for the grandeur of this 276-acre park on the New River Gorge — "The Grand Canyon of the East." It has been said that Chief Justice John Marshall admired the views from here more than anywhere else in western Virginia in 1812. The year-round park has a 31-room lodge and restaurant built on the canyon rim. Other facilities are a swimming pool, tennis courts, picnic units, playground, museum with Indian and pioneer artifacts, tramway, and marina for boating and fishing. The tramway descends 446 ft in elev over the Mill Creek Canyon to the marina. The aerial descent is spectacular in itself; to see a C&O train gliding over the Hawks Nest Lake enhances the visual display. (*USGS Maps:* Ansted, Fayetteville, Beckwith)

• ADDRESS AND ACCESS: Superintendent, Hawks Nest State Park, Ansted, WV 25812, tel: 304-658-5212. US-60, between US-19 jct E and WV-39 W, passes through the park.

• SUPPORT FACILITIES: There are a number of private campgrounds in the area. One nearby is the Patty Hill Campground on US-60 E of Ansted, with full service. Open May 15–September 30. Address: Victor, WV 25938, tel: 304-658-4784.

Hawks Nest Trail

• LENGTH: 0.5 mi

• DIFFICULTY: easy

• FEATURE: nature study

• TRAILHEAD AND DETAILS: Park at the picnic area. Ascend to and pass the picnic shelter into an oak and hickory forest with scattered hemlock. Large patches of mandrake and Solomon's seal are in the rich, damp cove. Complete the loop after 0.5 mi.

▶ HOLLY RIVER STATE PARK
(Webster County)

For many centuries this incomparable land of natural splendor was home for the Shawnee Indians. According to legend, Tecumseh's brother Tenskwatawa was born here. Relics of their history (including red hematite, which they used for facial decorations, found in the Laurel Fork Valley) are on display in the park office. In recognition of these famous Indian leaders, two of the park's four major waterfalls have been named after them. If they returned today they would find the 8292 acres much as they left them — rich forested mountains with deer and turkey and bobcat; trout darting in the crystal streams; a wide range of songbirds such as the indigo bunting, wood thrush, bluebird, and scarlet tanager; and an incredible paradise of vascular plants. What has been changed is the construction of nine rock and log cabins in a "island of rhododendron." There are 88 campsites (65 with electric hookups), a laundromat, swimming pool, picnic areas, game courts, tennis courts, playground, commissary, and restaurant (open from Memorial Day to Labor Day). Cabins are available from the last weekend in April to the fourth Monday in October. Hiking and fishing are additional attractions. There is also a primitive campground for overnight backpackers. The park has two short trails: *Red Spruce Trail* is a 0.2 mi nature trail near campsite #86 and across a sphagnum moss bog with cinnamon ferns to a stand of red spruce at Laurel Fork. The other trail, *Nature's Rock Garden Trail*, is a beautiful, 0.5-mi, 25-post, self-guided interpretive trail through rocks, trees, and wildflowers. Among them are papaw, witch hazel, blue cohosh, pink lady's slipper, wild lily-of-the valley, yellow birch, beech, and hemlock. Some of the ferns are the wood fern, Christmas fern, and lady fern. (*USGS Maps:* Hacker Valley, Goshen)

• ADDRESS AND ACCESS: Superintendent, Holly River State Park, Hacker Valley, WV 26222, tel: 304-493-6353. Access is 2.0 mi N from the post office in Hacker Valley and 6.3 mi S of Cleveland on WV-20.

Tramontane Trail *(2.3 mi);* **Salt Lick Trail** *(1.2 mi);* **High Rock Trail** *(1.3);* **Oak Ridge Trail** *(1.8 mi);* **Wilderness Trail** *(4.0 mi);* **Railroad Grade Trail** *(1.3 mi);* **Reverie Trail** *(2.5 mi)*

• LENGTH: 14.4 mi, rt, ct

• DIFFICULTY: easy to strenuous

• FEATURES: wildlife, wildflowers, history, waterfalls

• TRAILHEADS AND DETAILS: These connecting trails are described so as to offer a number of loop options from 2.7 mi to 9.1 mi. If you are backpacking overnight at a primitive campsite, plans and permission must be arranged with the park superintendent. A central base point is at the picnic parking area near (W) the park office. Hike across the footbridge of Laurel Fork in a tall hemlock stand on the red-blazed *Tramontane Trail* for 125 yds to a jct with the *Salt Lick Trail*, which goes R for 0.4 mi to the campground entrance, and L for 0.8 mi to a jct with the crescent-shaped *Tramontane Trail*.

A turn L would be the shortest loop of combined trails. Follow the scenic *Salt Lick Trail* to the *Tramontane Trail*, turn L, cross the road at cabin #9, cross Laurel Fork again, and pass R of the tennis courts. Cross Pickens Rd to *High Rock Trail*, join the *Reverie Trail* near its terminus at the main park road, cross the road to the campground road, follow the campground road across Laurel Fork to the *Salt Lick Trail*, turn L, and return to the point of origin for a loop of 2.7 mi. For the second loop, continue on the *Tramontane Trail*, ascend in a deep hardwood forest with thick patches of white snakeroot, ragwort, and ground pine. At 0.9 mi arrive at a jct with the white-blazed *Oak Ridge Trail*, R. (The *Oak Ridge Trail* follows Oak Ridge to an overlook and then descends steeply in sections to the S end of the campground for 1.8 mi.) Turn L, follow a grassy woods road to a fork at 1.2 mi, bear R, cross under a power line, pass ruins of an old homesite, a cinnamon fern patch, wildlife food plot #9, and at 1.8 mi reach a jct with the blue-blazed *Wilderness Trail*. To the L, with the *Salt Lick Trail*, pass cabin #9, and follow the same directions given above for the 2.7 mi route, except this is a circuit of 4.1 mi.

To hike a third circuit, continue R on the *Wilderness Trail* at the jct with the *Tramontane Trail*, pass through a forest of chestnut tree skeletons and a rusty tub and bed frame from an old homesite. At 2.2 mi are huge boulders of sculptured sandstone; ascend, cross the ridge, descend, and at 2.4 mi jct with a spur trail, R. (It leads 0.5 mi to a view of Tenskwatawa Falls and a gated park fire road. This has been an old route of the red-blazed *Potato Knob Trail*, but there is an easier and more desirable route described below.) At 2.7 mi the *Wilderness Trail* forks. The third and fourth loops go L and the fifth option goes R. (The R fork of the *Wilderness Trail* goes 1.2 mi to its terminus at a former fire tower site and gated forest fire road. On its route it crosses Crooked Fork and makes an immediate jct with the *Railroad Grade Trail*, L. The *Wilderness Trail* must be backtracked.) To the L at the *Wilderness Trail* fork, follow down Crooked Fork by caves and cascades to make a sharp R near huge cliffs at 3.3 mi. Moss and wood sorrel patches are under tall hemlocks. Squeeze through rocks at 3.5 mi. Cross a footbridge over Laurel Fork in a scenic area of cascades and pools bordered with rhododendron at 3.7 mi. At 3.8 mi the *Wilderness Trail* turns L at a jct with the *Reverie Trail*. The *Wilderness Trail* follows Laurel Fork downstream to the park cabin #1 at 4.6 mi. From here a turn L on the *Tramontane Trail* and a R on the *Salt Lick Trail* take you back to the picnic area for a loop of 5.7 mi.

The fourth loop occurs by taking the yellow-blazed *Reverie Trail* at the jct described above. Ascend, cross Park Rd (also called Pickens Rd) at 3.9 mi, ascend steeply, and reach a primitive campsite at 4.4 mi. From the natural spring begin a steep climb, cross two ridges, and pass under a power line. At 5.1 mi pass under picturesque Tecumseh Falls. Descend steeply, reach Dreamer's Meadow, jct with *High Rock Trail,* and reach the park's main road at 6.3 mi. Cross the road to the campground road entrance and pass the check-in station. Turn L, cross Laurel Fork, and immediately turn L on the *Salt Lick Trail* to return to the point of beginning for a round trip of 7 mi.

The fifth loop can be arranged by taking the R fork of the *Wilderness Trail* described above and turning off L on the *Railroad Grade Trail* for 1.3 mi to a gated fire road at the jct with the gravel Park Rd (CO-10). (At this road jct and confluence of the R, middle, and L forks of the Laurel Fork, the park map may show a much larger loop of the *Railroad Grade Trail.* Hikers interested in this extension should inquire about its condition before attempting the circuit.) Turn L at the jct on the Park Rd and descend for 2.0 mi to a jct with the *Reverie Trail,* R. Follow the *Reverie Trail* as described above for a return to the point of beginning and a round trip of 9.1 mi.

Potato Knob Trail

- LENGTH: 2.2 mi, rt

- DIFFICULTY: strenuous

- FEATURES: scenic, waterfalls

- TRAILHEAD AND DETAILS: From the park entrance drive S on WV-20 for 1.3 mi to the Holly River Rd (CO-3, also called Pickens Rd and Pickens Grade Rd). Drive upstream for 4.2 mi to a Falls sign. Parking space is difficult on the main road; depending to the weather, a 4WD-vehicle may be necessary to descend to the Left Fork of the Holly River. Walk down the spur road for 0.1 mi to a sign that indicates the Upper Fall is to the L. To the R for 0.3 mi is "the Chute" and the beginning of the climb to Potato Knob. There are three spurs to the Chute, all less than 75 ft from the jeep road. There is a legend that the facial image in the river rocks at the middle spur is that of a Shawnee Indian hunter who drowned in the rapids. The red-blazed *Potato Knob Trail* ascends steeply 640 ft in elev on a rocky and sometimes slippery ridge. Large rock outcroppings on the cone-shaped knob allow for spectacular views of the Holly River canyon. Rhododendron, mountain laurel, oaks, and pines cling to the precipitous slopes. Ferns and mosses mottle the rocks. Reach the summit at 0.7 mi from the base. Backtrack.

▶ LOST RIVER STATE PARK
(Hardy County)

This 3712-acre historic forest park with an abundance of wildlife, wildflowers, and scenic overlooks is named for the Lost River that disappears for three miles under Sandy Ridge near Wardensville. Formerly owned by the Lee Family of Virginia, the restored cottage of Gen. "Light-Horse Harry" Lee is now a museum. The area was a CCC camp in the 1930s. Facilities include 9 deluxe and 15 standard cabins; restaurant; grocery and souvenir store; swimming pool; horse and hiking trails; game and tennis courts; playground and recreation building; and picnic areas. It is open from April 1 to December 15. A private campground adjoins the park on Dove Hollow Rd (CO-14) near the stables. (*USGS Map:* Lost River State Park)

• ADDRESS AND ACCESS: Superintendent, Lost River State Park, Mathias, WV 26812, tel: 304-897-5372. In Mathias turn off WV-259 on Howards Lick Run Rd (CO-12) and drive 3.8 mi to the park.

> *Razor Ridge Trail (1 mi); Laurel Trail (0.5 mi); East Ridge Trail (2.5 mi); Howards Lick Run Trail (1.2 mi); Arbutus Trail (0.7 mi); Loblolly Trail (0.8 mi); Staghorn Trail (1 mi); Wood Thrush Trail (0.4 mi); Red Fox Trail (0.3 mi); Light Horse Harry Lee Trail (1.3 mi); Covey Cove Trail (0.5 mi); Copse Cove Trail (1.8 mi); Lee Trail (0.5)*

• LENGTH: 12.5 mi, ct

• DIFFICULTY: easy to moderate

• FEATURES: vistas, Lee's Sulphur Spring

• TRAILHEADS AND DETAILS: A variety of short and long loops can be made of these well-graded, color-coded trails. Below is described a combination of trails that loop the ridges around the Cabin Run Rd for 4.5 mi. From cabin #3, at the swimming pool parking lot, begin this loop at the fork of *Razor Ridge Trail* and *Howards Lick Run Trail*. Ascend on the orange-blazed *Razor Ridge Trail* through an oak forest with an understory of buckberry and a floor of moss. At 0.6 mi is jct R with *Laurel Trail*. (It goes R for 0.5 mi to the Cabin Run Rd.) An open shelter is at 0.9 mi; scenic view is NE. Junction with red-blazed *East Ridge Trail* at 1 mi. (Here a loop can be made by taking the *East Ridge Trail* L and descending to the blue-blazed *Howards Lick Run Trail* to follow it back to the swimming pool for a total of 3.3 mi.) Continue R on the *East Ridge Trail*. At 1.3 mi is a jct with the yellow-blazed *Arbutus Trail*. (It goes R for 0.7 mi to *Loblolly Trail*, a horse trail, and to a road at the employee dorm and storage area off Cabin Run Rd.) At 1.5 mi pass the blue-blazed

Staghorn Trail R. (It descends for 1 mi to Cabin Run Rd near cabin #17.) On the L, at 1.7 mi, are huge ant hills; a few yds farther is a vista from an open shelter. At 2.1 mi is a jct with the green-blazed *Wood Thrush Trail.* (It descends 0.3 mi to *Staghorn Trail* with an exit out to Cabin Run Rd on the *Staghorn Trail.*) At 2.4 mi is a jct with the *Red Fox Trail,* L, and the *Copse Cove Trail* ahead. The *East Ridge Trail* ends here. (The *Red Fox Trail,* a horse trail, ascends for 0.3 mi to Piney Ridge Rd.) After 0.1 mi on the *Copse Cove Trail,* turn L on the green-blazed *Covey Cove Trail* to the Piney Ridge Rd. At 2.8 mi there is a shelter on the L; turn R on the forest road through chestnut oak and scattered Virginia pine. Turn R off the road at 3 mi and after a few yds join the yellow-blazed *Copse Cove Trail.* (To the R it joins the *Light Horse Harry Lee Trail,* a horse trail, which follows the slope downstream to the recreation building.) Continue ahead on the *Copse Cove Trail,* descend to a jct with the orange-blazed *Lee Trail* at 3.4 mi. (The *Lee Trail* is a 0.5 mi spur jct with the *Light Horse Harry Lee Trail* and the *Copse Cove Trail* to Cabin Run Rd and cabin #8.) At 4.1 mi pass another spur, R, which leads to Cabin Run Rd, and continue ahead through a grove of hemlocks to Lee's Sulphur Spring and shelter at 4.3 mi. (Across the stream is the Lee Cabin Museum.) Follow a side trail past cabin #1 to the point of origin at the swimming pool parking lot at 4.5 mi.

White Oak Trail *(1.8 mi);* **Miller's Rock Trail** *(3.7 mi);* **Big Ridge Trail** *(2 mi);* **Shingle Mill Lake Trail** *(1 mi)*

- LENGTH: 8.5 mi, rt, ct
- DIFFICULTY: moderate to strenuous
- FEATURES: Cranny Crow Lookout, fire tower
- TRAILHEADS AND DETAILS: Backpacking and camping are allowed on these trails with permission from the park superintendent. Begin on orange-blazed *White Oak Trail,* a horse trail, at the stables on Dove Hollow Rd. Ascend 0.6 mi to the Fire-tower Truck Rd. (This road is gated at the bridge on Howards

Lick Run Rd, but it is accessible for hiking to connect with all of the above trails.) Cross the road and continue ascent to an open shelter at 1 mi. Huckleberries, pennyroyal, goldenrod, and snakeroot are plentiful. At 1.8 mi reach a jct with *Miller's Rock Trail*. Turn R to view the park from the vista at Cranny Crow Lookout (3250 ft). Allegheny sand myrtle *(Leiophyllum buxifolium)*, sundrops *(Oenothera tetragona)*, and catnip *(Nepeta cataria)* grow here. (An orange-blazed section of *Miller's Rock Trail* follows the ridge out to Cheeks Rock, S of Cranny Crow.) Backtrack past *White Oak Trail* jct and reach the Firetower Truck Rd at 2.2 mi. Follow the road R and curve L of the picnic area to restored Mtn Farm Cabin, built in 1840 by William Tusing. Continue ahead to enter the Game Refuge Area. At 3 mi reach the 80-step fire tower for views of Cove Mtn and the Shenandoah Mtn in the GWNF. From here it is 0.7 mi ahead to Miller's Rock and more scenic views. Backtrack to the picnic area, enter the yellow-blazed *Big Ridge Trail*, a horse trail, near a large walnut tree R of the picnic area. After a descent of 2 mi reach the Truck Rd, turn R, ascend to *White Oak Trail*, turn L, and return to the stables for a round trip of 8.2 mi. Another horse trail, *Shingle Mill Lake Trail*, goes 1 mi from the stables to cross Cove Hollow Rd and leads to a picnic area on the main road.

▶ NORTH BEND STATE PARK
(Ritchie County)

In this tranquil resort-type park is a trail for the handicapped called "The Extra Mile," but a vacation at this 1405-acre Eden proves the staff goes an extra mile for everyone. Deluxe vacation cabins; a lodge and restaurant; two campgrounds; a swimming pool; picnic areas; tennis and game courts; playgrounds; and hiking trails are among its facilities. Through the center of this peaceful place flows the North Fork of the Hughes River with its scenic horseshoe bend. Deer roam freely in the park. *(USGS Map:* Harrisville)

• ADDRESS AND ACCESS: Superintendent, North Bend State Park, Cairo WV 26337, tel: 304-643-2931. From the W on US-50 take WV-31 near Nutter Farm (20 mi E of Parkersburg) to Cairo. Turn L on Low Gap Run Rd (CO-14) and go 3.3 mi. From the E on US-50 take WV-16 at Ellenboro S to Harrisville. Go W on North Bend State Park Rd (CO-5) for 3.6 mi.

River Trail (1 mi); Nature Trail (3 mi); Gibbons Nature Trail (0.4 mi); Castle Rock Trail (0.2 mi); Giant Tree Trail (0.2 mi); Lonesome Pine Trail (0.1 mi)

• LENGTH: 5.9 mi, rt, ct

• DIFFICULTY: easy to moderate

• FEATURES: wildlife, forest, river views

• TRAILHEADS AND DETAILS: From the camping and picnic area (near the swimming pool) follow the *River Trail* downstream under big trees of beech, poplar, and oak. Blue cohosh, maidenhair fern, ground ivy, and spicebush are part of a lush ground cover. Moss covers the damp rocks. Leave the river at 0.5 mi, ascend, reach a picnic area at 0.8 mi, and descend toward the river. Wood mint, bee balm, ironweed, and soapwort border the trail. At 1 mi the trail becomes the *Nature Trail*. Pass under a power line, ascend, cross the ridge and reach a gravel road at 1.6 mi. Turn L for 75 ft and re-enter the woods, R. Pass caves and cliffs (to explore, go L and rejoin the trail after 0.1 mi). Turn L on the ridge at 2.3 mi and follow an old woods road. Reach the paved main road and cable gate at 3 mi. Turn L, follow the road for 0.2 mi, and turn R up the steps. Reach another paved road at 3.4 mi, turn R, go down the road for 100 ft, and turn L before the road sign. Cross a footbridge, descend to a rocky area, and at 4 mi reach the point of beginning.

From here a trek can be made to the swimming pool parking area to hike the 0.4 mi *Gibbons Nature Trail*. Among the trees, wildflowers, and ferns is white walnut (*Joglans cinerea*). Two other short trails are the *Lonesome Pine Trail*, which loops at the playground, and the *Giant Tree Trail*, which connects the recreation area with the main picnic area. Another short trail, the scenic *Castle Rock Trail,* is accessible from either of the campgrounds. If you hike from the lower campground, follow the old RR grade upstream to a paved road for 0.5 mi. Cross (usually you can wade) a cement bridge over Hughes River by the waterfalls and circle the rock formations. Backtrack.

Overhanging Rock Trail *(0.5 mi);* **Woodland Trail** *("Extra Mile Trail") (0.6 mi)*

- LENGTH: 1.7 mi, rt, ct

- DIFFICULTY: easy

- FEATURES: nature study, special population service

- TRAILHEADS AND DETAILS: From the lower camping area, cross the bridge over the river to the sign and ascend on the *Overhanging Rock Trail* (built in 1975 by the YCC). Descend to a ravine in a glen of ferns — silver spleenwort, marginal wood fern, Christmas fern, walking fern — and reach a maintenance shed at 0.5 mi. Exit here at the playground for the handicapped. Turn R on an old RR grade, the paved *Woodland Trail* for special populations. Both English and Braille are used on 21 information posts. Reach the end of the pavement at 0.3 mi and the trail terminus at 0.6 mi near the river and the ruins of an old oil well. Backtrack. (A physical fitness trail is planned in the park to be constructed by the Governor's Youth Summer Work Program.)

▶ PINNACLE ROCK STATE PARK
(Mercer County)

The state's most southern park, this 245-acre day-use facility has picnicking, hiking, and fishing. Pinnacle Lake is stocked with trout. Bass, bluegill, and channel catfish are also in the lake. A fishermen's footpath circles the 15-acre lake. Access to the lake is on Pinnacle Rock Rd (CO-52/4), 1 mi E of Bramwell on US-52. Electric motors only are allowed on the boats. Camping is prohibited. On US-52 there is a parking area for picnicking and a 0.1 mi *Pinnacle Rock Trail* that ascends on stone steps to a towering ridge of quartzite sandstone (2700 ft), as well as scenic views. (*USGS Map:* Bramwell)

• ADDRESS AND ACCESS: Superintendent, Pinnacle Rock State Park, Box 342, Bramwell, WV 27415, tel: 703-945-9150. Drive 5 mi NW from Bluefield on US-52 to the park, L, or 1 mi E from Bramwell on US-52.

▶ **PIPESTEM RESORT STATE PARK**
   (Mercer and Summers Counties)

It is difficult to find the equal of this magnificent resort park in any state park system. Since the park's opening on Memorial Day 1970, it has become one of the state's most popular vacation resorts. In its 4023 acres is a wide range of recreational facilities and accommodations that provide exceptional opportunities for enjoyment. All the natural beauty of the Bluestone River Canyon, the rugged mountains, and the waterfalls has been retained in the construction of 2 luxury lodges (143 rooms); 25 deluxe cottages; 3 restaurants; 18-hole championship and 9-hole par golf courses; indoor-outdoor Olympic swimming pools; convention center facilities; and lighted tennis courts. The campground is complete with water, electrical and sewage hookups, hot showers, and a laundromat. Additionally, there is a stable for horseback riding and camping, trails for hiking, a nature center, sled run, lake for fishing, cross-country ski trails, and a crafts and gift shop. A 3600-ft-long aerial tramway provides access to the Mountain Creek Lodge at the base of the Bluestone River Canyon for a 1000-ft elev drop. The park's name is from a local pink and white flowering plant *(Spirea alba),* a close relative of bridal wreath, used by Indians and early settlers to clean their pipestems. Open season is year-round. (*USGS Map:* Pipestem)

- ADDRESS AND ACCESS: Superintendent, Pipestem Resort State Park, Pipestem, WV 25979, tel: 304-466-1800. From Princeton take WV-20, NE, for 16 mi to the park entrance, L. From the Blue Stone Lake take WV-20, SW, for 8 mi.

Pipestem Knob Tower Trail

- LENGTH: 0.6 mi, rt

- DIFFICULTY: easy

- FEATURE: panoramic vista

- TRAILHEAD AND DETAILS: After the park entrance stop at the Pipestem Knob parking area. Follow the paved trail up to the observation tower through a forest of maple, oak, hickory, dogwood, sumac, ferns, and wildflowers. From the Knob (3000 ft) are scenic views of Little Mtn and Peter's Mtn, E, and the Allegheny Plateau, W.

Lick Hollow Trail (1.1 mi); Canyon Rim Trail (0.7 mi); River Trail (6.5 mi); Farley Ridge Trail (0.7 mi)

- LENGTH: 16.9 mi, rt, ct

- DIFFICULTY: moderate to strenuous

- FEATURES: Heritage Point, Bluestone Canyon, wildlife, history

- TRAILHEADS AND DETAILS: Except for the first trail in this group, all the others must be backtracked, thus doubling the walking distance and requiring adequate time allowance. Park at the visitor center and enter the Lick Hollow Trail at the NW corner of the parking area. Pass large silverberry bushes, follow a grassy path for 0.1 mi, and turn R on a narrow trail in a young forest. Descend into a forest of mature hardwoods and fern beds. Ascend to a spur trail for a view of the Bluestone Canyon and the horseback riding camp at 0.4 mi. Turn L at 0.6 mi where old chestnut railings may be seen. Descend in a shagbark hickory stand and complete the loop back to the parking area at 1.1 mi.

From the visitor center follow the sign at the NE corner on the blue-blazed *Canyon Rim Trail*. Descend and cross the *River Trail* at 0.4 mi. Reach the end of the trail at scenic Heritage Point overlook (2280 ft) at 0.7 mi. Backtrack to the *River Trail*. Here, ascend to the parking area or take the *River Trail* E or W. If E, follow an old road (used for cross-country skiing) for 1.1 mi to the main road at Pipestem Lodge. If W, follow the old road under the tramway, cross a cascading stream, and pass through a forest of ash, oak, walnut, poplar, maple, and hemlock. Deer are frequent. At 0.8 mi reach a jct with the N terminus of the *County Line* (horse) *Trail*. The *River Trail* becomes a horse/hiking trail and descends R to the Bluestone River for another 1.1 mi. Rock hop or wade. Follow downstream for another 0.9 mi to the Mountain Creek Lodge (1542 ft). Junction here with the 0.7 mi white-blazed *Farley Ridge Trail*, a footpath that ascends steeply to the overnight horseback camp. Continue downstream for another 1.2 mi and curve away from the river to ascend and cross Bearwallow Ridge. Arrive at the overnight horseback camp and log cabin (2240 ft) at 5.4 mi from the jct with the *Canyon Rim Trail* or 6.5 mi from the Pipestem Lodge. Backtrack.

County Line Trail

- LENGTH: 4.2 mi, rt

- DIFFICULTY: moderate

- FEATURE: Indian Branch Falls

- TRAILHEADS AND DETAILS: From the parking lot at the nature center follow the red-blazed horse trail on a jeep road and descend for 1.4 mi to scenic Indian Branch waterfalls and cliffsides on the L. Ahead are indications of a former homestead with old chestnut rail fences and tree rows. Some parts of the trail are rocky. Large trees border the road before its jct with the *River Trail* at 2.1 mi. Deer are likely to be seen on this trail. Backtrack or use the *River Trail* described above.

Northside Nature Trail

- LENGTH: 0.7 mi
- DIFFICULTY: easy
- FEATURE: Braille/English text
- TRAILHEAD AND DETAILS: Park at the parking area behind the park office. Follow the trail signs on this self-interpretive trail built by the YCC in 1979 for the visually handicapped through a forest of tall trees, shrubs, and flowers. At one post is a large sugar maple. The sugar maple is the state tree of West Virginia, as well as that of Vermont and Michigan. Other trees are hickory, oak, poplar, beech, dogwood, and black cherry. Large (15 inch circumference) striped maple *(Acer pensylvanicum)* is part of the understory. Complete the circle and return to the parking lot.

Long Branch Nature Trail *(0.4 mi)*; Cottage Loop Trail *(0.6 mi)*; Southside Loop Trail *(1.3 mi)*; Lake Shore Trail *(2.3 mi)*; Lakeview Trail *(0.8 mi)*

- LENGTH: 7.3 mi, rt, ct
- DIFFICULTY: moderate
- FEATURES: Long Branch Lake, wildlife
- TRAILHEADS AND DETAILS: Described below is an example of how these connecting trails may be made into shorter or longer loops. Total mileage includes both loops and backtracking routes. Park at the Long Branch Lake parking area near Pipestem Lodge. Walk W on the paved road for 0.1 mi, turn L at the trail signs and gated road. Descend on the orange-blazed *Long Branch Trail* in a hardwood forest with scattered white pine and rhododendron. Reach the *Lake Shore Trail* at 0.4 mi, turn R, and jct with the *Cottage Loop Trail,* R, at 0.9 mi. (Green-blazed *Cottage Loop Trail* ascends 0.2 mi to cottages #1–#9 and

the park road. It is 0.4 mi from here, R, to the *Long Branch Trail*.) Continue ahead to the jct with the *Southside Loop Trail* at 1.3 mi. (The yellow-blazed *Southside Loop Trail* goes through a hardwood forest with a ground cover of running cedar to the main road near the park office.) Curve L on the road and re-enter the forest for a loop of 1.2 mi for rejoining the *Lake Shore Trail*. Continue on the *Lake Shore Trail*, cross a stream, pass a bee tree in a large white oak on the L at 1.5 mi. Hike through an open area. At 1.6 mi jct with the *Lake View Trail*. (This red-blazed trail ascends on an old road for 0.8 mi to the main road, across the road from the nature center.) Continue ahead on the *Lake View Trail* with views of the lake on the L; more club moss is on this section. Reach an open space below the dam at 2.6 mi; jct with a ski trail on the R. Turn L, ascend, reach the top of the dam, turn L off the paved road, and follow the lake to the jct with the *Long Branch Nature Trail* at 2.9 mi. Return to the gated road and the point of beginning at 3.1 mi.

▶ TOMLINSON RUN STATE PARK
(Hancock County)

The state's most northern park at the top of the panhandle (NW of Pittsburgh) has 1401 acres of meadows, lakes, steep hills, and overhanging sandstone cliffs. In the park's center is a 29-acre lake from which Tomlinson Run flows through a gorge to drop into the Ohio River. The park has 100 species of birds and among the animals are deer, wild turkey, raccoon, beaver, squirrel, and fox. Facilities include a swimming pool; 100-acre picnic area, two tent/RV campgrounds with hot showers and laundromat (no hookups); group camp; four bass fishing ponds; row boat and paddleboat marina; tennis courts; dumping station; nearby grocery store, and hiking trails. The season is April 15–October 15. (*USGS Map:* East Liverpool South)

• ADDRESS AND ACCESS: Superintendent, Tomlinson Run State Park, Box 97, New Manchester, WV 26056, tel: 304-564-3651.

From the jct of WV-2 and WV-8 in New Cumberland, take WV-8 for 4 mi to the park entrance, L.

Big Foot Trail *(1.2 mi)*; Fern Trail *(0.5 mi)*

- LENGTH: 3.2 mi, rt, ct

- DIFFICULTY: easy

- FEATURES: beaver dam, wildflowers

- TRAILHEADS AND DETAILS: Begin 100 yds W of the picnic area gate and ascend on the red-blazed *Big Foot Trail* in a young forest of cherry, locust, and maple. Reach the lakeside at 0.3 mi where goldenrod, asters, Devil's paintbrush *(Hieracium aurantiacum)*, Solomon's seal, monarda, filberts, and sensitive fern grow. At 1 mi are signs of active beavers. Cross a swampy area and reach the park road, Shepard Valley Rd (CO-12), at 1.2 mi. Turn L and hike on the road for 1.3 mi to the boat rental building. Ascend the steps on the R of the road and begin the orange-blazed *Fern Trail.* This is a beautiful trail of young white and Virginia pine, club moss, hay-scented fern, and violets. At the jct with a spur trail, turn L, and reach the picnic road at 0.5 mi. Turn R of the lake and return to the point of origin at the picnic area at 3.2 mi.

Laurel Trail *(2.5 mi)*; Beech Trail *(1.1 mi)*

- LENGTH: 3.6 mi, rt, ct

- DIFFICULTY: moderate

- FEATURES: sandstone cliffs, gorge vistas

- TRAILHEADS AND DETAILS: From the group camp drive W to the road jct Washington Rd (CO-3) and park near the bridge. Hike R (N) 0.1 mi and enter the forest on a blue-blazed trail. Follow the rim of the gorge on the *Laurel Trail* for scenic views for 1 mi. (The white-blazed trail ahead is *White Oak Trail,* which is not maintained.) Turn L, descend to the river, and go downstream to the Boy Scouts Camp. Wild hydrangea, witch hazel, and spicebush grow at the base of the cliffs. Wade the creek (or ascend to the original trail). Continue downstream to the road and bridge at 2.5 mi. Begin the yellow-blazed *Beech Trail* at the parking area on the S side of the bridge; ascend in an open forest of cherry and maple. Reach the crest of the ridge at 0.3 mi, go up the road past the cliffs on the L, turn L, and take the lower fork. Cross Tomlinson Creek at 0.7 mi. (Wading is necessary, or cross on slippery sycamore.) Ascend to the paved road at 0.8 mi and turn L for a return to the parking area at the bridge for a 1.1 mi loop.

▶ TWIN FALLS RESORT STATE PARK
(Wyoming County)

Another of the state's resort-type parks, these 3776 acres in the southern highlands are outstanding for their natural and created beauty. Open year-round, the park is an oasis for recreational activities, luxury accommodations, and historic preservation. Facilities include 13 deluxe cabins; 20-room lodge and restaurant; 50 full-service campsites with hot showers, laundromat, and country store; picnic areas and swimming pool; nature center; tennis courts; playground; historic sites; expansive golf courses; and hiking trails. Additionally, an early 1800s pioneer homestead has been restored on Bower's Ridge, and a museum of county historic relics is near the White Horse Knob Observation Tower, elev 2330 ft. Wildlife frequently seen in the park are deer, raccoon, wild turkey, and grouse. (*USGS Map:* McCrawe)

• ADDRESS AND ACCESS: Superintendent, Twin Falls Resort State Park, PO Box 1023, Mullens, WV 25882, tel: 304-294-4000. From Pineville drive 6 mi E on WV-97.

***Cliffside Trail** (2.8 mi);* ***Hemlock Trail** (1.2 mi);* ***Falls Trail** (0.7 mi);* ***Nature Trail** (1.2 mi)*

- LENGTH: 7.8 mi, rt, ct

- DIFFICULTY: moderate

- FEATURES: Twin Falls, nature study

- TRAILHEADS AND DETAILS: To enter the *Cliffside Trail* in the campground, go to the Fox Hunter's Point and park between the rest room and campsite #24. Follow the trail sign through a hardwood forest on a ridge; bear R at the Bear Wallow spur trail at 0.5 mi. Turn L at the next jct. The trail becomes narrow; descend and reach a scenic cliff edge at 1.4 mi. Hemlock, rhododendron, and mountain laurel add to the natural beauty. Backtrack to the campground and begin the *Hemlock Trail* behind the contact center. Descend on an old road through a magnificent forest of hardwoods, hemlock, ferns, mandrake, ragwort, and banks of club mosses. At 1.2 mi jct with the *Falls Trail;* turn L, cross the Black Fork stream and jct with the *Nature Trail* at 1.3 mi, R. (The *Nature Trail* makes a loop of 1.2 mi with ascent to the park's main road and return to the *Falls Trail.*) Continue downstream; bear L for 0.1 mi to the Black Fork Falls. Continue downstream for another 0.5 mi to the Cabin Creek Falls. (These two falls give the park its name.) Backtrack. (There is a shorter entrance to the falls on a park service road near the park's entrance.) Total mileage for backtracking or making a loop on all four trails is 7.8 mi.

Huckleberry Trail

- LENGTH: 1.4 mi

- DIFFICULTY: easy

- FEATURE: Pioneer Farm

- TRAILHEADS AND DETAILS: Drive SW from the campground to the parking area at the Pioneer Farm. This is a loop trail and you can descend from here along the farm fence to the forest or cross the road and ascend E into a young pine and dogwood forest. Either way, the trail will cross the road at the top of the ridge near a grassy field. Along the way are sumac, locust, blackberry, huckleberry, club moss, and wildflowers. Deer are likely to be seen.

Two other trails are in the park. One is the 0.5 mi *Cemetery Trail* (which requires a backtrack) at the N end of the golf course. It ascends on a cemetery road, passes one cemetery on a hillside, and terminates at the road's end. Names such as Cox, Phillips, Clay, and Owens are on the stones. Another trail is the *Twin Oaks Braille Trail*, a loop of 0.3 mi developed by the Mullens Lions Club. It is on the park's main road, 1.3 mi from the entrance. The park has approximately 8 mi of fire and horse trails.

▶ TYGART LAKE STATE PARK
(Taylor County)

The headwaters of the Tygart Valley River begin at 4000 ft elev in the Cheat Mountains. Turbulent, cascading, and sometimes still in pools and valleys, it flows N to Elkins and to Philippi before it becomes a lake S of the historic town of Grafton. (Grafton is known for its International Mother's Day shrine, the Andrews Methodist Church, where Anna Reeves Jarvis was a member. It was she who observed her first "Mother's Day" on the second anniversary of her mother's death on May 12, 1907. The following year the first organized Mother's Day for all mothers was observed on May 10, 1908. The church at 11 E Main Street is open weekdays and Saturday afternoons, May–October. For information call 304-265-1589.)

The lake area is also historic as a result of other events. It was in Grafton that the first Union soldier, T. Bailey Brown, was killed in the Civil War. He is buried in the state's only national cemetery, a 3.2-acre plot at 431 Walnut Street. South of Grafton in Philippi, the first land battle of the Civil War (without casualties) was fought on June 3, 1861. For historic and recreational information on this area contact the Grafton Area

Development Council, 131 East Main St, Grafton, WV 26354, tel: 304-265-1183. For information on the West Virginia Railway Heritage Festival, held annually the second weekend in September, call 304-265-1957.

The Tygart was impounded by the Corps of Engineers in the 1930s for flood control. It is at the dam that the 13-mi lake has become part of a 2134-acre state park. Its waters also extend SW to the Pleasant Creek Public Hunting Area. The state park is outstanding for its beauty, as well as its sport facilities for fishing, boating, water skiing, and swimming. Added to these sports facilities are a marina; a 20-room lodge with a restaurant; 40-unit campground; picnic units; playground; game courts; and 10 deluxe cabins. The completely furnished cabins are constructed of native wood and have native stone fireplaces. Although named trails are few, "fishermen's trails" are numerous. (*USGS Maps:* Grafton, Thornton)

• ADDRESS AND ACCESS: Superintendent, Tygart Lake State Park, Rte 1, Box 260, Grafton, WV 26354, tel: 304-265-3383. In Grafton take Park Rd (CO-44) S to Scab Hollow Rd (CO-9/7) to the park entrance.

Ridge Trail (1 mi); Lake Trail (0.4 mi)

• LENGTH: 2.3 mi, rt, ct

• DIFFICULTY: easy

• FEATURE: nature study

• TRAILHEADS AND DETAILS: Park at the park office parking lot and cross the main road to begin the red-blazed *Ridge Trail*. Ascend in a forest of beech, oak, sycamore, and birch. Ferns and wildflowers, such as bloodroot (*Sanguinaria canadensis*) used by the Indians for dyes and insect repellent, border the trail. Descend to picnic area #1 after 1 mi. Turn L and walk back on the paved road for 0.5 mi to the parking area. The white-blazed *Lake Trail* descends from the park office through picnic area #3 to a cove at the lake for 0.4 mi. Backtrack.

▶ VALLEY FALLS STATE PARK
(Marion and Taylor Counties)

Valley Falls was called the "Evil Spirit Falls" by the Cherokee Indians, and white explorers called it "Hard around Falls" in the early eighteenth century because of the two-tier 30-ft drop. It was also called "Falls of the Big Muddy," an appropriate title 150 yrs later when the floods washed away a thriving community of over 125 houses and business establishments. By the 1750s it was called "Tygart Falls" after David Tygart, a pioneer who had settled near the stream N of Elkins. The Falls changed owners a number of times and on each occasion the deeds referred to the "great falls of the Tygart Valley" as part of the land grant. An example was in 1784 when Governor Patrick Henry of Virginia granted 1000 acres to David Gray and Samuel Hanway. In 1852 the Baltimore and Ohio Railroad completed a branch through the canyon. From then until the great floods of 1884 and 1888, and the disastrous fire of 1886, it was a "boom town" with a post office, hotel, mills, factories, a Wells-Fargo office, B&O depot, school, and church. In the early 1960s the state wisely purchased 1145 acres for a state park. It opened in 1964 as a day-use facility for picnicking, history study, and sightseeing. There are plans for a campground and other facilities as funds become available.

Hiking trails are also planned. The 0.2 mi *Tygart Valley River Trail* begins near the Falls and parallels the B&O RR and the river, downstream. It is a scenic path among oak, beech, locust, maple, and ash. Other trails under construction or planned are the *Red Fox Trail* (0.7 mi), *Deer Overlook Trail* (3 mi), *Rocky Trail* (1.5 mi), *Twenty-Seven Falls Trail* (3 mi), and *White Oak Trail* (1.5 mi). (*USGS Maps:* Fairmont E, Grafton)

• ADDRESS AND ACCESS: Superintendent, Valley Falls State Park, Rte 6, Box 244, Fairmont, WV 26554, tel: 304-363-3319. In Fairmont at I-79 exit 137, take WV-310, S, for 7.7 mi to Valley Falls Rd (CO-31/14). Turn R and go 2.8 mi to Valley Falls.

• SUPPORT FACILITIES: The nearest campground is 13 mi farther on WV-310 to US-50 in Grafton and S on US-119 to Park Rd (CO-44) and to Tygart Lake State Park.

▶ **WATOGA STATE PARK**
  (Pocahontas County)

The state's largest (10,106 acres) and oldest (begun in 1934) park is bordered on the W by the Greenbrier River. It is "the river of islands," according to the Cherokee Indians who called the area *watauga*. Historic as an old CCC camp, vast and varied in scenic beauty in the Appalachian highlands, and modern in facilities, the N half has a wide range of recreational facilities and its S half is roadless and wild. The S boundary is with the Monongahela National Forest and the Calvin Price State Forest, an area from Rock Run to Laurel Run that is a sanctuary for wildlife. Its chief facility is the Laurel Run Primitive Campground. The state's longest trail, the Allegheny Scenic Trail, passes through the NE corner of the park. It is likely that wildlife will be seen on the trails or even on the roads. Among them are deer, grouse, wild turkey, quail, raccoon, woodchuck, squirrel, and chipmunk. Watoga is an excellent base camp for hiking excursions in the Monongahela National Forest, the Greenbrier River Trail, Droop Mtn State Park, and Beartown State Park.

Facilities are 4 cabin areas with a total of 33 cabins; 88 campsites (38 at Beaver Creek campground and 50 at Riverside), some with electric hookups; hot showers, laundry, dumping station, restaurant (open Memorial Day to Labor Day), commissary, swimming pool, game courts, playground, picnic units, arboretum, stables for horse rentals, boat rentals, a lake for fishing, cross-country skiing areas, and trails for hiking. Additionally, there is a naturalist on duty in the summer. The season is April 1–December 10; open campground dates may differ. (*USGS Maps:* Denmar, Lake Sherwood)

• ADDRESS AND ACCESS: Superintendent, Watoga State Park, Star Rte 1, Box 252, Marlinton, WV 24954, tel: 304-799-4087. From the W take Seebert Rd (CO-27) at jct with US-219 between Mill Point and Hillsboro. From the E take Beaver Creek Rd (CO-21) S from Huntersville.

• SUPPORT FACILITIES: Fishing bait and equipment, groceries, and a service station are across the Greenbrier River in the community of Seebert. A restaurant and other stores are in the town of Hillsboro, 3 mi W from Seebert.

Laurel Ridge Trail (1.3 mi); *Allegheny Trail* (4.5 mi); *Jacobs Well Trail* (1.3 mi); *Honeymoon Trail* (3.5 mi); *Ten-Acre Trail* (0.2 mi)

• LENGTH: 6.3 mi, ct

• DIFFICULTY: moderate to strenuous

• FEATURES: wildlife

• TRAILHEADS AND DETAILS: These trails have exits at other trails or park roads, but they also connect for loop arrangements. The 5 mi length is the shortest loop. At the picnic shelter go E on the orange-blazed *Laurel Ridge Trail* for 0.5 mi to the road jct of Pyles Rd (CO-21/3) and Pyles Mtn Rd (CO-21/4), 0.7 mi from the park's E entrance. The *Allegheny Trail* crosses here and runs conjointly S with the *Laurel Ridge Trail*. Follow both through hardwood and hemlock forest with dense buckberry and mountain laurel stands to the red-blazed *Jacobs Well Trail*, L, at 1.2 mi. (The *Jacobs Well Trail* descends 1.3 mi to the park's Beaver Creek Campground, S. There are plans to reroute the *Allegheny Trail* to run conjointly with the *Jacobs Well Trail*.) Continue ahead to join the white-blazed *Honeymoon Trail* at 1.3 mi. (The *Honeymoon Trail* has its origin, R, 0.1 mi from the parking area for cabin #34.) Continue ahead on the *Allegheny Trail* and *Honeymoon Trail* to 2.8 mi where the *Allegheny Trail* continues on the ridge and the *Honeymoon Trail* bears R. (The *Allegheny Trail* descends to Beaver Creek Rd [CO-21] at 4.5 mi, crosses into Calvin Price State Forest, and joins *Beaver Creek Trail* at 6.4 mi. Here you could turn L, go 0.7 mi to the S area of Beaver Creek Campground, and follow *Jacobs Well Trail* back to the point of origin for a total loop of 9.1 mi.) Continue ahead on the *Honeymoon Trail* along the Pyle Mtn ridge to the blue-blazed *Ten-Acre Trail*. (The *Ten-Acre Trail* descends steeply 0.2 mi in a grove of white pine to the T.M. Cheek Rd. Left at the road it is 1 mi S to the superintendent's residence and the S entrance to the park on Beaver Creek Rd.) Continue on the *Honeymoon Trail* to a number of parallel points with the T.M. Cheek Rd. Pass R of the Ann Bailey Lookout Rd at 3.7 mi (2036 ft). (Ann Bailey is known as the famous "White Squaw of the Kanawha," a scout and message-carrier in the late 18th century.) Pass R of the T.M. Cheek Memorial at 4.1 mi and reach cabin #21 in the cabin area at 4.7 mi. Turn L to return to the Picnic Shelter at 5 mi or R to cabin #34 and rejoin the *Allegheny Trail*, L, for a loop of 5.7 mi.

Lake Trail *(1.1 mi)*; Beaver Bog Trail *(0.3 mi)*

- LENGTH: 1.4 mi, ct
- DIFFICULTY: easy
- FEATURE: Killbuck Lake

- TRAILHEADS AND DETAILS: Park at the park office. Cross the road to the lake and follow the orange-blazed trail R from the boat dock. (If fishing, four trout are the maximum.) Cross the footbridge at 0.4 mi and again at 0.9 mi at the spillway. Excellent view of the lake from the N side. *Beaver Bog Trail* is short — a loop below the dam. The name of the trail is not contingent on seeing either a beaver or a bog. Return on the road to point of origin.

*Honeybee Trail (4.7 mi); Buckhorn Trail (0.8 mi); Dragon
Draft Trail (1.4 mi)*

- LENGTH: 6.9 mi, ct

- DIFFICULTY: moderate

- FEATURE: nature study

- TRAILHEADS AND DETAILS: Park at the Brooks Memorial Arboretum on the park's main road, 1.5 mi E from the Greenbrier River entrance. Follow the loop signs, cross footbridge, turn R on the red-blazed *Honeybee Trail*, and ascend steeply to the crest of the ridge. An open hardwood forest of oak, maple, and sourwood remains consistent on the trail. Reach the ridge top at 1 mi, begin descent E of the ridge to a jct with the *Buckhorn Trail* at 1.1 mi, L. (*Buckhorn Trail* descends 0.4 mi to the spring and the central *Dragon Draft Trail* in the loop.) At 1.7 mi at the shelter and spring is a jct with the *Dragon Draft Trail*. (The *Dragon Draft Trail* follows Two-Mile Run for 1.4 mi back to the parking area.) Continue ahead on the *Honeybee Trail* through numerous dead trees, victims of fierce ice storms. At 3.2 mi is jct with the *Buckhorn Trail* that descends L for 0.4 mi to the *Dragon Draft Trail*. Pass L of the rocky overhangs and descend to the *Dragon Draft Trail* and the footbridge at 4.5 mi and then 4.7 mi to the parking area.

*Jesse's Cove Trail (2.4 mi); Arrowhead Trail (1 mi); Turkey
Spur Trail (0.4 mi)*

- LENGTH: 5.1 mi, ct

- DIFFICULTY: strenuous

- FEATURES: wildlife, Ann Bailey Tower

- TRAILHEADS AND DETAILS: Begin at the S edge of the Riverside Campground and follow the yellow-blazed *Jesse's Cove Trail* downriver for 0.4 mi to where it leaves an old road bed and ascends. Railings are along the cliff passages. Cross the stream at 0.7 mi and parallel L of the cascading Rock Cove Run through tall hardwoods, hemlocks, ferns, and copious wild-flowers. Reach the Ann Bailey Lookout Rd at 2.4 mi. Turn L and follow the ridge road to the Ann Bailey log tower at 3.9 mi. Here are magnificent views of the Greenbrier River, the *Greenbrier River Trail* (formerly the C&O Railway), and Droop Mtn. Cleared area has patches of huckleberry and wild phlox. To return to the campground, descend steeply on an old road, the *Arrowhead Trail*. After 0.8 mi reach a jct with the *Turkey Spur Trail*, L. (The yellow-blazed *Arrowhead Trail* goes R for 0.2 mi to cabin #3 and the main park road.) Follow the *Turkey Spur Trail* on an old road for another 0.4 mi back to the campground at site #6 for a loop of 5.1 mi.

Monongaseneka Trail

- LENGTH: 8 mi

- DIFFICULTY: strenuous

- FEATURES: wildlife, rock outcrops

- TRAILHEADS AND DETAILS: Monongaseneka means "place of the big stone." At the W entrance of the park at the Greenbrier River, drive 0.6 mi to a small parking area on the R. The trail is on the L. Ascend gradually on the W slope of the mountain. Pass rock overhangs at 0.4 mi. Wild pinks are on the banks. At 1.1 mi leave the original trail made by the CCC and descend to a cove, cross a small stream, begin a steep ascent, and reach the ridge crest at 1.5 mi. (A 0.5-mi loop to the L goes to a potential view of the Greenbrier River.) Turn R and follow the trail to a jct with the *Buck and Doe Horse Trail* at 4 mi.) Backtrack.

▶ WATTERS SMITH MEMORIAL STATE PARK
(Harrison County)

This 532-acre park has a surprising trail system filled with wildlife. A day-use park, its main publicized attraction is the pioneer homestead restoration in honor of the Watters Smith family. A large swimming pool is on top of a hill and there are meeting rooms, a museum and souvenir shop, picnic areas, a playground, horseback riding stable, and hiking trails. The park also has 12 gas wells. It is open from Memorial Day to Labor Day. (*USGS Map:* West Milford)

• ADDRESS AND ACCESS: Superintendent, Watters Smith Memorial State Park, Box 296, Lost Creek, WV 26385. On US-19 in West Milford, drive S on Duck Creek Rd (CO-25/6) for 1.7 mi. From Lost Creek drive W on West Milford Rd (CO-27) for 4 mi to Duck Creek Rd as described above.

White Oak Trail (2 mi); Dogwood Trail (0.8 mi)

• LENGTH: 2.8 mi, ct

• DIFFICULTY: moderate

• FEATURES: scenic, historic, wildlife

• TRAILHEADS AND DETAILS: From the picnic area follow the sign of the white-blazed *White Oak Trail* beside the fence line, pass a huge white oak at 0.2 mi, turn R on an old road, then L by a walnut tree. Other trees on the trail are beech, dogwood, cherry, redbud, and a variety of oak species. Reach the ridge top at 0.4 mi and the high point at 0.6 mi. Wildlife that may be seen are deer, wild turkey, grouse, red, gray, and flying squirrels, and rabbit. Pennyroyal and white snakeroot are on the seeded road. Pass a grazing field and begin a descent at 1.3 mi. Wild senna (*Cassia hebecarpa*) grows on the dry rocky area with locust, sycamore, and Virginia pine. Views are here of the strip mines. Cross an old mining road and jct with the *Dogwood Trail* at 1.7 mi. Turn R, wind around a drain, and reach the activity center at 2 mi. (The *Dogwood Trail* exits L on the activity center road.) To return to the point of beginning, turn R, follow an old road by a lake full of bluegill, and reach the parking area at the swimming pool at 2.3 mi. (It is 0.4 mi more on an old road behind the swimming pool to the picnic area and parking lot.)

7.

West Virginia State Forests

"I hike to study wildlife, rare flowers, and for exercise in the quietude of Nature."
— CHARLES CARLSON

Seven of the state's nine forests are in mountainous counties adjoining Virginia, Kentucky, or Pennsylvania. The other two are slightly more central, Kanawha in Kanawha County, and Kumbrabow in Randolph County. Only one county, Pocahontas, has two state forests, Seneca and Calvin Price. Their total acreage is 79,307. Coopers Rock State Forest, part of which is leased to the West Virginia University Department of Forests, is the largest (12,698 acres) and Greenbrier State Forest is the smallest (5130 acres). Total trails: 48; total mileage: 84.7 mi.

The primary use of the forests is for the management of commercial timber sales. In the early 1970s all the state forest lands were inventoried for their potential in timber harvesting. During the development of forest management plans for individual forests, the public reaction was mixed, but Charles Carlson, Howard and Dorothy Guest, and other conservation and environmental leaders in the Charleston area opposed timber harvesting in the Kanawha State Forest. The result was a legislative victory to preserve Kanawha's natural beauty. In many ways it now resembles a state park.

The state has long been recognized for its remarkable deciduous forests. There are at least 50 indigenous species of trees. Northern hardwoods are dominant in four of the state forests

283

— Coopers Rock, Calvin Price, Kumbrabow, and Seneca. These common species are in a varied upland and cove mixture, depending on the loamy soil and the annual rainfall. Among the species are American beech *(Fagus grandifolia)*, red maple *(Acer rubrum)*, sugar maple *(Acer saccharum)*, yellow birch *(Betula alleghaniensis)*, Northern red oak *(Quercus rubra)*, black cherry *(Prunus serotina)*, and white ash *(Fraxinus americana)*. Eastern hemlock *(Tsuga canadensis)* and Eastern white pine *(Pinus stobus)* are the major conifers.

Central hardwoods flourish in the other five forests. These species include the hickories: bitternut *(Carya cordiformis)*; mockernut *(Carya tomentosa)*; shagbark *(Carya ovata)*; and pignut *(Carya glabra)*. Other trees are the American elm *(Ulmus americana)*; slippery elm *(Ulmus rubra)*; black gum *(Nyssa sylvatica)*; black locust *(Robinia pseudoacacia)*; sassafras *(Sassafras albidum)*; and the white, red, scarlet, and black oaks. Prominent among the pines are pitch *(Pinus rigida)*, Virginia *(Pinus virginiana)*, table mountain *(Pinus pungens)*, and short leaf *(Pinus echinata)*.

The management of the state forests is split to accommodate the multiple-use concept. Forest resources are managed by the Division of Forestry in the Department of Agriculture; recreational facilities and activities are managed by the Parks and Recreation Division of the Department of Commerce. The Division of Wildlife of the Department of Natural Resources is responsible for wildlife protection, hunting, trapping, and fishing regulations.

Historically, the state forest system runs concurrently with the state parks system. During the 1930s designated forests were established as Civilian Conservation Corps (CCC) camps. Among these were Cabwaylingo, Coopers Rock, Greenbrier, Kanawha, Kumbrabow, and Watoga (which later became the first state park). The CCC crews assisted in the building of roads, cabins, fire towers, picnic areas, trails, reforestation, and other conservation work. When the CCC was phased out in 1942, the state purchased land in Pocahontas County as a game preserve and for the management of forest resources. The area was Seneca State Forest, the state's first designated forest.

All the state forests, except Calvin Price, have either campgrounds or cottages, or both. Many of their facilities are similar to state parks, and the same 22 rules and regulations governing public use of the parks are also used for the forests and for the state hunting and fishing areas. The list of rules is posted at all campgrounds, offices, and other conspicuous places on the public lands. They were carefully created to provide safety and security for visitors, protection of wildlife and plant life, and preservation of the natural environment.

Hikers may find the trails in the state forests to be less crowded than some of the better known or more popular national forest trails. When the many miles of state forest jeep, fire, and timber roads are included with the designated trails, the opportunity for study of animal and plant life, geology, and natural scenic beauty may be as much or more rewarding than other public properties. All the forests except Calvin Price have designated trails, but the *Allegheny Trail* runs through the extreme NE panhandle. The 9482-acre preserve is generally undeveloped. A primitive campground provides a base for hunters and for exploratory hikers. The forest is not described in detail elsewhere in this book; information may be obtained by writing the Superintendent, Calvin Price State Forest, Dunmore, WV 24934, tel: 304-799-6213.

• INFORMATION: Division of Forestry, Department of Agriculture, State Capitol Bldg, Charleston, WV 25305, tel: 304-348-2201; Wildlife Resources Division, Department of Natural Resources, 1800 Washington St E, Charleston, WV 25305, tel: 304-348-2771; Division of Parks and Recreation, Department of Commerce, 1900 Washington St E, Charleston, WV 25305, tel: 304-348-2764.

▶ **CABWAYLINGO STATE FOREST**
(Wayne County)

Although this 8125-acre forest is in Wayne County (bordering the Kentucky state line), its name is a combination of Cabell, Wayne, Lincoln, and Mingo counties. Wild, rugged, and remote, the numerous coves have fresh mountain streams that drain into the area's main channel, Twelvepole Creek, a stream stocked with trout. Old lumber and hunting roads wind into the valleys and up to the ridges where deer and turkey are prominent, and the more than 25 commercial oil wells remind the hiker that the forest provides more than lumber, venison, and pan-fried rainbow trout. Facilities include picnic areas with tables, grills, firewood, drinking water, and rest rooms; the campground area has similar facilities and hot showers. A fire tower at the campground provides a panoramic view of the forest and a 1 mi *"Indian Trail"* descends from the campground through hardwoods, hemlock, and pine to connect the S edge of the group camp. There are 13 vacation cabins, completely furnished. Other facilities are a children's playground and a swimming pool with a bathhouse. The season is May 1–October 15. (*USGS Maps:* Kiahsville, Wilsondale)

• ADDRESS AND ACCESS: Superintendent, Cabwaylingo State Forest, Rte 1, Dunlow, WV 25511, tel: 304-385-4255. From Dunlow go 2.5 mi S on WV-152 to jct with Twelvepole Creek Rd (CO-35) and turn L on CO-35, near Missouri Branch.

• SUPPORT FACILITIES: Groceries and a service station are nearby on WV-152.

Ash Branch Trail

• LENGTH: 2.3 mi

• DIFFICULTY: moderate

• FEATURE: nature study

• TRAILHEAD AND DETAILS: After entry into the forest follow upstream and park near cabins #8 and #9. Enter the trail at the sign; after 90 yds begin ascent in a hardwood forest with scattered hemlock and wildflowers. At 0.2 mi are wide beds of crested dwarf iris (*Iris cristata*). Cross a footbridge and follow switchbacks to a ridge crossing. Descend, pass a large rock overhang in a damp area; ferns and stonecrop *(Sedum ternatum)* are here. Enter a hemlock grove, descend on a steep area to a service road, and turn L downstream on Long Branch. Cross stream at 1.4 mi and twice more before reaching the picnic shelter near stone-crafted trail. Reach children's playground at 1.6 mi; turn L, cross bridge to picnic area, go up steps, and follow upstream to bridge for a return to point of origin at 2.3 mi.

Long Branch Trail

• LENGTH: 1.9 mi

• DIFFICULTY: easy

• FEATURE: oil wells

• TRAILHEAD AND DETAILS: Park at the Long Branch Picnic Area (downstream from where Long Branch and Twelvepole Creek meet). Ascend on switchbacks near rocks on L side of hollow. Reach ridge crest at 0.4 mi and bear R at white oak tree. After another 0.2 mi make a sharp L at a white oak and shag-bark hickory. Descend, cross a dirt-bike trail, enter a hemlock grove, cross a stream near a metal gate, and reach Sweetwater Branch and paved road at 1.3 mi. Green pipe for oil well is here. Hike down the road to Hank Hollow Picnic Area and cabin #13 at the main road at 1.9 mi. Turn L and reach the point of origin for a length of 2.1 mi.

Martin Ridge Trail *(1.6 mi)*; Sleepy Hollow Trail *(1 mi)*

• LENGTH: 3.8 mi, rt, ct

• DIFFICULTY: moderate

• FEATURES: caves, ferns

• TRAILHEADS AND DETAILS: At the end of the picnic area at the swimming area on the main road, ascend N on an old wagon road in a hardwood forest. Pass a rock overhang on the L and R. Curve R at 0.4 mi in a mountain laurel section, then L up the ridge to a logging road at 0.7 mi. (A number of logging roads and seeded roads may confuse you in this area.) At 1.6 mi jct with *Sleepy Hollow Trail;* turn R beside a large white oak and a hickory tree, and descend on the *Sleepy Hollow Trail.* Pass a gas pipe, descend to a huge rock formation with caves and overhangs, and in the summer notice the numerous fern and lichen species here. Cross a footbridge, enter a hemlock grove, follow a stream, and reach Sweetwater Branch Rd at 2.6 mi. Turn R, walk to the main road and turn R, and follow downstream to the point of origin for a total loop of 3.8 mi.

Spruce Creek Trail

- LENGTH: 2.8 mi, rt

- DIFFICULTY: moderate

- FEATURE: nature study

• TRAILHEAD AND DETAILS: Drive up the main road and park at the Right Fork Picnic Area (across the road from cabins #11 and #12). Follow the trail sign, ascend through a forest of large hemlock and beech on the L side of the stream to Spruce Fork. Reach the Tick Ridge road (CO-35/5) at 1.4 mi. Backtrack. (CO-35/5 leads R [NW] to the campground with spur roads off the ridge. This road and other hunting roads are excellent for hiking but are not recommended for use during the hunting season. Check with the superintendent for exploratory routes in the forest.)

▶ CAMP CREEK STATE FOREST
(Mercer County)

Primarily a day-use recreational area, the 6000-acre Camp Creek State Forest has facilities for picnicking (with shelters), hiking, hunting, and fishing. There is a rustic tent campground that has fireplaces and firewood, tables, drinking water, and vault toilets. Camp Creek is stocked with trout, and deer roam the forest. Many miles of fire trails exist, but permission from the forest superintendent should be granted to hike into an unknown primitive area. (*USGS Map:* Odd)

• ADDRESS AND ACCESS: Superintendent, Camp Creek State Forest, Star Rte, Box 310, Camp Creek, WV 25820, tel: 304-425-9481. From US-19 and I-77, exit at Camp Creek (16 mi N of Princeton), follow the signs, and go 1.8 mi on Camp Creek Rd (CO-19/5).

Farley Branch Trail

• LENGTH: 2.3 mi, rt

• DIFFICULTY: moderate

• FEATURES: waterfalls, wildlife

• TRAILHEADS AND DETAILS: Pass the service bldg and park near the picnic area on the L. Enter the forest on the L side of Farley Branch and follow through a mature forest of hardwoods and sparse conifers. Reach a small waterfall at 0.5 mi. (A spur trail goes R across the branch for 0.8 mi to the Blue Jay Camping Area at site #1.) Curve L and reach the ridge top at 0.9 mi (fire trail goes R). Continue ahead on the slope of the ridge in an oak forest and descend to a scenic waterfall on Mash Fork at 1.7 mi. Turn L on the forest road and return to the point of origin at 2.3 mi.

▶ COOPERS ROCK STATE FOREST
(Monongalia and Preston Counties)

The state's largest forest, 12,698 acres, is also large in the dimension of its services and facilities. Purchased in 1936, it serves a concentrated population in Morgantown, Fairmont, and West Virginia University. A multiple-use area, the emphasis is on timber, wildlife, soil and water management; recreational facilities; and preservation of natural beauty and historic sites. Outstanding features are overlooks to the Cheat

River Canyon, a virgin hemlock grove, and an old iron ore furnace. Facilities include cross-country skiing, skating, botanical research, hunting, fishing, picnicking, camping, and hiking. There are 24 campsites (none with hookups, but hot showers are available), a playground, and a concession-gift stand.

In the early part of the nineteenth century, this area was bought by iron companies to mine ore and limestone, and produce charcoal. By the turn of the century the Kendall Lumber Company had purchased large holdings for extensive lumbering. In 1959 approximately 7500 acres of the forest were leased on a long-term basis to West Virginia University's Division of Forestry. It uses the forest for forest management field programs, research, recreation, and nature study.

The forest is named for a cooper, a maker of barrel staves who, according to legend, was an escaped convict making his hideout in the forest. The area has an endangered species — the flat-spired, three-toothed snail *(Triodopsis platysayoides)*. *(USGS Maps:* Bruceton Mills, Lake Lynn)

- ADDRESS AND ACCESS: Superintendent, Coopers Rock State Forest, Rte 1, Box 270, Bruceton Mills, WV 26525, tel: 304-594-1561. Drive 10.5 mi E of Morgantown from the jct of US-48 and WV-7 on US-48, or 8 mi W of Bruceton Mills at exit #15.

Raven Rock Trail *(3.6 mi); Clay Run Furnace Trail (3.6 mi); Scott Run Trail (1.6 mi)*

- LENGTH: 8.8 mi, rt, ct

- DIFFICULTY: moderate

- FEATURES: Raven Rock, Clay Iron Furnace

- TRAILHEADS AND DETAILS: In the McCullum Campground, R of the bathhouse at the trail sign, ascend to the ridge, then E on slope of the ridge to another ridge. At 0.6 mi cross a fire road, turn L on a jeep road at 0.7 mi, and continue ahead at road jct at 1 mi. Area has hickory, poplar, oak, cherry, rhododendron, and copious banks of hay-scented fern. At 1.7 mi reach a ridge crest and the Raven Rock overlook at 1.8 mi. Superb view of Cheat River. (Molten cement and insulation of power line is from lightning in 1984.) Backtrack.

To hike the *Clay Run Furnace Trail,* cross the paved road at the entrance to the campground and descend to Clay Run. Follow downstream for 1.8 mi to the Henry Clay Iron Furnace, built between 1834 and 1836 by Leonard Lamb for Tassey and Bissell. The furnace produced four tons of pig iron each 24 hours, employed 200 workers, and lasted until 1847. (It is 0.5 mi N on a sled road to a parking area for a shorter hike, but a 3.9 mi drive from the campground is necessary. Also, at the furnace it is 1 mi S, ascending on a trail to Rock City at the picnic area, and a 2 mi hike downstream, W, along Clay Run to its mouth with the Cheat River Dam at Mont Chateau and the West Virginia Geological and Economic Survey Headquarters.) Backtrack to the campground.

Scott Run Trail begins at McCullum campground gate. Descend on an old logging road to a damp tributary area of Scott Run. Cross a footbridge at 0.4 mi and curve around a dry ridge to Scott Run at 0.8 mi. Bobcats, deer, timber rattlesnakes, and wild orchids have been seen on this trail. Backtrack.

Rock City Trail *(1.2 mi)*; Clay Furnace Hiking Trail *(2 mi)*

- LENGTH: 3.2 mi, rt, ct

- DIFFICULTY: easy

- FEATURES: rock formations, Clay Iron Furnace

- TRAILHEADS AND DETAILS: Drive to the farthest loop of the picnic area and park near the trail signs at shelter #3. Follow the *Rock City Trail* sign on a wide trail among tall trees of cherry, poplar, and oak. Pass two wildlife food plots; reach a picnic shelter at 0.4 mi and a sign for cross-country skiers. Explore rock crevices and outcrops at 0.6 mi. Backtrack. In the curve of the parking lot road is the *Clay Furnace Hiking Trail.* It is orange-blazed on a woods road and descends for 1 mi to the Clay Run and the Clay Iron Furnace. Along the way are chestnut oak, mountain laurel, hemlock, maple, rhododendron, and wintergreen. Backtrack.

▶ GREENBRIER STATE FOREST
(Greenbrier County)

One of the marvels of the Mountain State is that a resort complex with the international reputation of the 650-room Greenbrier Hotel and a pristine forest of 5130 acres with vacation log cabins can be only 3.5 miles apart. Serving their constituencies with equal professional skill, they share in the history and charm of White Sulphur Springs, settled in 1750. Such diversity has its advantages; a hiker on the *Black Bear Trail* by day can enjoy continental cuisine and social elegance by night.

Facilities at the state forest include a number of picnic units; swimming pool with bathhouse; 16 campsites (more planned); and foot trails. Hunting is allowed at designated forest areas with proper licenses and permits. Fishing is convenient in the nearby Greenbrier River. The forest staff presents a Show-Me-Hike the last Saturday in April, beginning at picnic shelter #1 at 10 A.M. Information is also available on such flora as Kates Mountain clover *(Trifolium virginicum)* and box huckleberry *(Gaylussacia brachycera)*, neither of which are as rare as once thought. The latter is used locally for "juniper berry" pies. The Greenbrier State Forest staff also administers the *Greenbrier River Trail* (see Chapter 6). *(USGS Maps:* White Sulphur Springs, Glace)

• ADDRESS AND ACCESS: Superintendent, Greenbrier River State Forest, Caldwell, WV 24925, tel: 304-536-1944. Drive 2 mi W of White Sulphur Springs on I-64 or US-60 to Harts Run exit and follow Harts Run Rd (CO-60/14) 1.3 mi to entrance.

Young's Nature Trail (1.7 mi); *Black Bear Trail* (2.4 mi); *Old Road Trail* (1.5 mi); *Rocky Ridge Trail* (2 mi)

- LENGTH: 7.6 mi, ct

- DIFFICULTY: moderate

- FEATURES: wildflowers, Kate's Mtn Overlook

- TRAILHEADS AND DETAILS: From the main picnic area, ascend through a forest of tall oaks, white pine, and hemlock on *Young's Nature Trail* to a jct with the *Black Bear Trail*, L, at 0.4 mi. *Young's Nature Trail* continues ahead, ascends R of a usually dry streambed, and reaches Kate's Mtn Rd at 1.7 mi. Backtrack. (A 0.3 mi turn L on the Kate's Mtn Rd leads to a picnic area with a shelter.) On the *Black Bear Trail,* reach a ridge crest at 0.8 mi. On the trail banks are wild pink, bird's-foot violet, trailing arbutus, flame azalea, and squirrel cup *(Hepatica americana)*. Yellow lady's slipper and other wild orchids also grow in this area. Descend on the ridge edge at 1.6 mi and jct with the *Old Road Trail* at 1.7 mi. (A less used extension of the *Old Road Trail* goes R and then curves L down to the swimming pool for another 1.5 mi.) Descend on an old road, pass sections of a fitness trail on the R, and reach the main road at 2.4 mi near the cabin area. Turn L and walk up the road to the beginning point at 2.8 mi.

Another hiking trail, the less used 2 mi *Rocky Ridge Trail,* is accessible on the *Old Road Trail,* 0.2 mi from the swimming pool. It ascends the mountainside to its E terminus at Kate's Mtn Rd (CO-60/34). A turn L on the road is 0.4 mi to the spectacular Kate's Mtn Overlook (2700 ft). Access to this point for vehicular traffic is 4.8 mi from White Sulphur Springs (near the Greenbrier Hotel) on Kate's Mtn Rd (CO-60/34). The road is paved as it begins, but becomes rough as it climbs the mountain. Another access is to drive S from the campground area on Hart's Run Rd (CO-60/14) to its jct L with the Kate's Mtn Rd for a total of 5.1 mi.

▶ KANAWHA STATE FOREST
(Kanawha County)

Within 8 miles of the capital city, Charleston, this forest paradise of 9431 acres is an example of the wisdom of state government and individual citizens, such as Charles Carlson, to preserve some of the state's priceless natural history and beauty. Although it has magnificent hiking opportunities, it also has an excellent 4-unit campground with full service; a swimming pool; numerous picnic areas; a playground and a game area. Hunting and fishing are allowed in specified areas with appropriate licenses and permits. Among the wildlife are bear, deer, gray squirrel, grouse, turkey, bobcat, scores of songbird species, and four species of woodpeckers. There are 1046 species of flora that have been identified, including 23 species of wild orchids — probably more than in any of the other state forests or parks. The gated hunting and fire roads provide additional miles for the exploring hiker, who may pass as many as 23 natural gas wells, a reminder that natural resources can be used in conjunction with the protection of other resources. The forest is popular for outings by the Kanawha Trail Club, whose lodge on Middlelick Branch is on adjoining property. (*USGS Maps:* Charleston W, Racine)

A 0.5-mi-loop *Interpretive Trail* for the physically handicapped is under construction, with assistance from the Greater Kanawha Valley Foundation, Cross Lanes Junior Woman's Club, the Boy Scouts, White Lincoln-Mercury, Inc., and the Telephone Pioneers of America. The entrance will be across the main road from the old stables, and the trail will skirt both sides of Davis Creek.

• ADDRESS AND ACCESS: Superintendent, Kanawha State Forest, Rte 2, Box 285, Charleston, WV 25314, tel: 304-346-5654. From the jct of I-64 and US-119 (exit 58-A) in Charleston, drive S on Oakwood Rd (US-119) for 1.2 mi. Turn L on Oakwood Rd (CO-13/10), which becomes State Forest Connell Rd (CO-23), and go 6.5 mi S through Laudendale to the forest entrance. (Also, look for forest route signs.)

Hiking Trail (2.4 mi); Pigeon Roost Trail (2.2 mi)

- LENGTH: 5.7 mi, ct

- DIFFICULTY: moderate

- FEATURE: nature study

- TRAILHEADS AND DETAILS: From the Davis Creek Campground begin the *Hiking Trail* near campsite #14. On the steep ascent are spicebush and black cohosh among the hardwoods. Reach the ridge crest at 0.3 mi. (To the L, by a large *P* sign, is the N terminus of the *Pigeon Roost Trail.*) Turn R, by a large *D* sign, and follow the ridge line to a fork. Either route descends to a gated road. Turn R. At 1.3 mi reach a ball field and picnic area. Turn R at a service road jct and follow upstream through a forest of maple, oak, cucumber, birch, and beech to the campground at 1.7 mi, and to the point of beginning for a loop of 2.4 mi. To make a loop of the *Pigeon Roost Trail,* walk out to the main road, turn R, pass the picnic area, enter the gated gravel walk and reach another picnic area, R, at 0.8 mi. Here is the S terminus of *Pigeon Roost Trail.* For 0.7 mi follow a wide white-blazed trail on an old road, cross a ravine and pipeline, turn L off the old road, climb steeply in an eroded area, and reach a hunting road. Turn R on a vehicular road with road banks of huckleberries. At 2.1 mi turn R at a road jct and follow the ridge road that makes first a slight decline and then an ascent to a curve at 2.8 mi. Turn R on a foot trail and jct with the *Hiking Trail* at 3 mi; turn R, descend, and return to campsite #14 for a loop of 3.3 mi.

Johnson Hollow Trail

- LENGTH: 1.6 mi, rt

- DIFFICULTY: moderate

- FEATURE: wildflowers

- TRAILHEADS AND DETAILS: From the Johnson Hollow Picnic Area parking lot on the main road, ascend to picnic shelter #7.

Enter a rich, damp forest; first travel upstream, then R in an ascent on a ridge slope. Prominent among the wildflowers are wild hydrangea, mandrake, black cohosh, jewelweed, and meadow rue. Pass the stream again before final ascent to the gated Middle Ridge Rd at 0.8 mi. Backtrack.

Bowers Trail *(2.1 mi); Lookout Trail (0.8 mi)*

- LENGTH: 2.9 mi, rt, ct
- DIFFICULTY: moderate
- FEATURES: scenic, wildflowers
- TRAILHEAD AND DETAILS: From the swimming pool area, drive upstream on the main road for 0.5 mi to a picnic and parking area, L. On the L side of the road walk up the road for 230 yds to the trail entrance, L. Cross Davis Creek on a footbridge. Ascend on a white-blazed trail and cross under a power line at 0.5 mi. The forest has huge hardwoods and displays of wildflowers such as crested dwarf iris and trillium. Fern patches include maidenhair fern. Cliffs, caves, and sandstone formations add to the trail's scenic attractiveness. Reach an old road at 0.8 mi; turn R. After another 0.3 mi turn L onto a foot trail for a steep descent to the main road at the Dunlop Hollow play area. Turn R, follow the paved road for 130 yds, turn R off the road, cross a footbridge, and enter an open area (may be weedy in the summer). Turn L at a footbridge and cross Davis Creek at 1.9 mi. Reach the point of beginning for a loop of 2.1 mi. Across the road, but N of the stables, is the *Lookout Trail*. It is a steep trail that ascends 0.2 mi to a forest road where a R turn for another 0.2 mi leads to a scenic overlook of Davis Creek Valley. Backtrack.

Beech Glen Nature Trail

- LENGTH: 3.2 mi, rt

- DIFFICULTY: easy

- FEATURE: natural history

- TRAILHEAD AND DETAILS: Park at the Polly Hollow Picnic Area. (According to legend, Polly was a courageous girl who crusaded for a schoolhouse in the valley.) (At the Polly Hollow Picnic Area is the SE terminus of the unmarked, 30 mi *Wyatt Trail*, a Boy Scout trail that goes W–NW to St. Albans. It was created in honor of Bill Wyatt of Troup 146. See "Boy Scouts of America" (Chapter 10) for information on permission and guides to hike this trail.) At the gated road, follow it upstream. Some of the trees are ash, hickory, black birch, oak, Virginia pine, and hemlock. At 0.8 mi turn L off the road at a sign. (The *Wyatt Trail* continues ahead on the forest road. Dead-end roads are on the R and L in its climb to the ridge crest and forest boundary line after 0.5 mi. A sharp turn R leads to a jct with Bee Mountain Rd [CO-15, also called Middle Fork Rd]. Here it turns L, leaves the Kanawha State Forest, and descends to Brier Creek and the community of Olcott after 2.5 mi.) Cross Polly Hollow stream at 1 mi, near an old coalmine, and ascend. Bluebead lily, wild sweet potato *(Dioscorea villosa)*, coreopsis, and bedstraw grow here. Reach a rock formation of sandstone and iron ore segments and moss-covered cliffs at 1.6 mi. (A faint trail ahead for 130 yds leads to a ridge where a R turn up the ridge leads to the forest boundary road. A turn R on the boundary road connects with the Polly Hollow Rd, which leads, R, down the mountain to rejoin the *Beech Glen Nature Trail* after a loop of 2.1 mi.) Backtrack, but at the road jct bear R on an old RR grade with an excellent treadway that parallels the road to reach the point of origin.

Lake Trail

- LENGTH: 1.3 mi

- DIFFICULTY: easy

- FEATURE: nature study

- TRAILHEAD AND DETAILS: From the main entrance to the forest, drive 0.2 mi to the picnic and lake parking lot, L. Cross Davis Creek and follow the trail by the lake, turn L, and ascend to a jct with Middleridge Rd at 0.4 mi. Backtrack to the lake, turn L upstream, and reach the forest office at 0.9 mi. Turn R on the main road and walk back to the point of origin for 1.3 mi. Wildflowers include wild orchids, trillium, and twayblade.

Alligator Rock Trail (0.6 mi); Lindy Trail (0.6 mi); Ballard Trail (0.7 mi); Martin Trail (0.3 mi); Critz Trail (0.6 mi)

- LENGTH: 3.2 mi, ct

- DIFFICULTY: moderate to strenuous

- FEATURES: geology, nature study

- TRAILHEADS AND DETAILS: From the swimming pool parking area, walk E, cross Shrewsbury Hollow stream, ascend to a gated gravel forest road and turn R. After 0.3 mi, turn L at a large A sign on the white-blazed *Alligator Rock Trail*. Pass a rock formation, descend to a streambed, follow upstream, and reach a forest road, Middle Ridge Road, at 0.9 mi. (Across the road is *Lindy Trail,* which descends steeply 0.6 mi to Middlelick Branch and the Kanawha Trail Club Lodge. From here it is 1 mi N, downstream, to the main forest entrance, L.) A turn L on the road also descends to Middlelick Branch. Turn R and follow the road for 0.5 mi to a jct with the *Ballard Trail,* L. (The 0.7 mi *Ballard Trail* is another steep access trail to Middlelick Branch Rd, upstream from the Kanawha Trail Club Lodge.) Continue ahead on the road for another 0.3 mi to *Martin Trail,* L. (The *Martin Trail* descends steeply 0.3 mi to the gated Hoffman Hollow forest road that leads L to a jct with the Middlelick

Branch Rd.) On the R is an unnamed, faint forest trail that descends into a hollow. It crosses ravines, follows a S slope, passes rock formations, crisscrosses a stream, and exits at the Shrewsbury Hollow Rd after 0.6 mi. (I have called it the *David Critz Trail* because he guided me on this route. Another route, 1.3 mi, which brings the hiker to this exit, is to follow the Middle Ridge Rd S to the first R turn, the Shrewsbury Hollow Rd.) Turn R on the Shrewsbury Hollow Rd, pass the *Alligator Rock Trail* jct at 3 mi, and return to the parking lot for a loop of 3.3 mi.

Rock Camp Trail *(1.1 mi)*; North-South Trail *(0.7 mi)*; District Line Trail *(1.5 mi)*; Left Fork Trail *(0.7 mi)*; Bays Fork Trail *(2.1 mi)*

- LENGTH: 6.2 mi, ct
- DIFFICULTY: moderate
- FEATURE: natural history
- TRAILHEADS AND DETAILS: In the NW section of the forest there are a number of access points to gated forest roads and jeep trails. Two of these access points are described below. One is the Rock Camp Branch access, S of Ruth, and the other is the Bays Fork access, S of the Ivydale community. If approaching the Rock Camp Branch area from the main forest entrance, drive 6.7 mi NW, downstream by Davis Creek, to the community of Davis Creek at the jct with US-119. (It is 3.5 mi E on US-119 to Charleston and I-64.) Turn L on US-119 (or WV-214 if US-119 is under construction), travel 2.6 mi to Ruth and jct with Trace Fork Rd (CO-11/2). Drive upstream for 1.7 mi on Trace Fork Rd to a fork. (A burgundy-colored house is in the fork across the bridge.) Turn L and park at the first jeep road, R. Hike across Rock Camp Branch and follow the jeep road in a forest of tall poplar, ironwood, oak, and beech. (One tree bears the carved message "Susan loves Doug.") Caves are on the L. At 0.6 mi the jeep road turns R and becomes the *North-South Trail*, which ascends and connects with a hunting

road. The *Rock Camp Trail* continues ahead but becomes a foot trail. Ascend in a young forest and reach the trail's terminus at *District Line Trail* on the ridge crest at 1.1 mi. (To the L the *District Line Trail* goes 0.8 mi on a jeep road to private property at Long Branch.) Continue R on the *District Line Trail* for 0.7 mi to its S terminus and jct with the *Left Fork Trail* and a hunting road on a perpendicular ridge line. Make a sharp L and descend on the 0.7 mi *Left Fork Trail* to its terminus and jct with the *Bays Fork Trail*. (Downstream, the *Bays Fork Trail* goes 1.3 mi to Middle Creek and Bee Mtn Road (CO-15), the other access route mentioned above.) Turn R on the *Bays Fork Trail*, cross the stream, and ascend to the headwaters in a deep hollow. Reach the ridge crest after 0.8 mi and jct with a hunting road. Here, you may backtrack to the point of origin for a total of 6.6 mi. Or, turn R on the jeep road and follow it for 0.9 mi to the *District Line Trail* jct, R, for a return mileage of 6 mi. (Another option is to continue W on the hunting road to a more established road and after 0.7 mi take the first R, the *North-South Trail*. This partial return loop is 6.2 mi.)

The other vehicular access point is through the community of Ivydale. From Davis Creek community and jct of US-119 and Davis Creek Rd (CO-20), drive 0.5 mi on Davis Creek Rd to the W. J. Watters Bldg and turn R across the bridge onto Bee Mtn Rd (CO-15, also called Middle Fork Rd). (It is 6.2 mi upstream on Davis Creek Rd to the main entrance of the forest.) Follow upstream for 3.6 mi beside Middle Fork, pass through Ivydale, and reach the jct with the Bays Fork and *Bays Fork Trail*, R. After Ivydale, the road becomes a streambed, easily flooded, and the road beyond this point is narrow, often rough; a 4WD-vehicle may be necessary. The *Bays Fork Trail* begins first as a jeep road, but becomes more of a footpath after passing under the power line at 0.6 mi. At 1.3 mi it connects with the *Left Fork Trail* as described above.

There are other road-trails beyond the Bays Fork. For example, to continue 0.7 mi upstream by Middle Fork is a jct with gated Rattlesnake Run hunting road, L. It goes 1.7 mi E, crosses a ridge, and descends through the forest service area for a connection to the forest main road, 0.5 mi N of the swimming pool. (For another 4.5 mi CO-15 continues upstream, ascends a mountain ridge to the forest boundary, and descends to the community of Olcott.) The forest has numerous unnamed hunting roads and jeep trails, many that dead-end at gas wells. Hikers unfamiliar with the forest should have directions from the superintendent before taking long exploratory hikes.

▶ **KUMBRABOW STATE FOREST**
  (Randolph County)

Between Holly River State Park (W) and the Monongahela National Forest (E) are 9431 acres of absolute pristine delight. You can choose a sequestered vacation in one of the 5 pioneer cabins within the sound of Mill Creek Falls or at the 12 primitive campsites by a trout stream. More wildlife than people visit these sanctuaries. The forest is named for three prominent families — Kump, Brady, and Bowers — who influenced the forest purchase. Highest of all the state forests, its lowest elev is 2500 ft and its highest elev is 3734. With 20 wildlife food plots and swift, pure streams, a hiker has a good chance to see and photograph bear, deer, turkey, grouse, or owls. Once among the state's best forest for hemlock and spruce, the forest now has large stands of second-growth cherry, ash, maple, and yellow and black birch. Rainfall is high, approximately 70 inches annually, and substantiates the state's slogan that West Virginia is wild, wet, and wonderful. Recreation activities include fishing, hunting, picnicking, and hiking. (*USGS Maps:* Valley Head, Adolph, Pickens)

• ADDRESS AND ACCESS: Superintendent, Kumbrabow State Forest, PO Box 65, Huttonsville, WV 26273, tel: 304-335-2219. East entrance is halfway between the towns of Huttonsville and Valley Head on US-219 and WV-50 to Kumbrabow Forest Road (CO-219/16). Ascend 3.8 mi to forest entrance. West entrance from Pickens is on Haker Valley Road (CO-47) and Turkey Bone Rd (CO-45) for 8 mi.

• SUPPORT FACILITIES: Huttonsville/Mill Creek has groceries, a service station, bank, hardware store, motel, restaurant, and other services.

Raven Rocks Trail (1.2 mi); Rich Mountain Fire Trail (3.1 mi); Meatbox Run Trail (1.4 mi); Potato Hole Run Trail (1.5 mi)

• LENGTH: 7.2 mi

• DIFFICULTY: moderate to strenuous

• FEATURES: Raven Rocks, woodlore, wildlife

• TRAILHEADS AND DETAILS: From the campground go 0.5 mi W on the main road and park. Ascend steeply to a superb view of Mill Creek Valley and the campground from Raven Rocks at 0.2 mi. Turn L on a wide ridge trail and at 1.2 mi reach a jct with the *Rich Mtn Fire Trail* (sign is marked 4 mi to Pickens-Monterville Rd; it should read 3.1 mi to Turkey Bone Rd). Bear L on a grassy road bordered with a lush array of ferns. Reach a road jct. L at 2.3 mi. (*Meatbox Run Trail* begins 100 yds L on this dead-end road. Descend on the footpath along Meatbox Run and reach the Mill Creek Rd at the picnic area at 3.7 mi. Turn L and walk back to the point of beginning for 4 mi loop.) (Another loop can be made by continuing on the dead-end road mentioned above. After 0.5 mi reach a cul-de-sac. On the S side begin a descent on the *Potato Hole Run Trail* into a damp and deep forest of hemlock and rhododendron to the confluence of a stream with Potato Hole Run at 3.5 mi. Reach the forest office at 4.3 mi. Turn L on the Mill Creek Rd and walk back to the point of beginning at 6.2 mi.) To continue on the *Rich Mtn Fire Trail,* disregard numerous spur roads, R or L, pass R of Buck Knob at 2.8 mi and R of Whitman Knob to reach Turkey Bone Rd (CO-45) at 4.3 mi. Backtrack to point of beginning for 8.6 mi or use a vehicle shuttle.

▶ PANTHER STATE FOREST
(McDowell County)

There is a legend in parts of this valley that Tommy Lester, a pre-Civil War inhabitant, met a panther face-to-face. When Lester's gun failed, he had to fight the beast with a knife and help from his dogs. It is assumed he won the fight. As a result the post office, community, creek, and the 7810-acre forest are named Panther. This once exceptionally wild and rugged hill country near the corners of Virginia, Kentucky, and West Virginia has numerous streams named after animals — deerskin, crane, fox, cub, and, of course, panther.

Facilities are six campsites; a vault toilet; a playground; a group camp with men's and women's barracks, kitchen, and dining areas; picnic areas; swimming pool; and trails. Hunting and fishing (in rainbow-stocked stream) allowed with appropriate licenses and permits. Season is April to November. (*USGS Maps:* Panther, Iaeger)

• ADDRESS AND ACCESS: Superintendent, Panther State Forest, PO Box 287, Panther, WV 24872, tel: 304-938-2252. At the jct of Greenbrier Mtn Rd (CO-3) and Johnny Cake Rd (CO-1) in Panther, go S for 0.4 mi on the Greenbrier Mtn Rd, turn L on Trap Fork Rd (CO-3/1), which becomes Panther Creek Rd (CO-3/2), for a total of 5 mi.

• SUPPORT FACILITIES: The nearest food and other supplies are in Iaeger, 12 mi E on US-52.

Drift Branch Trail *(1.3 mi)*; Twin Rocks Trail *(0.6 mi)*

• LENGTH: 3.2 mi, rt, ct

• DIFFICULTY: strenuous

• FEATURE: panoramic views

• TRAILHEADS AND DETAILS: Park at the Cowshead Picnic Area. Cross footbridge at the sign and follow up the stream of Drift Branch. Among the wildflowers are trillium, foamflower, black

cohosh, bloodroot, and rhododendron. At 0.2 mi jct with the
0.6 mi spur trail, *Twin Rocks Trail*, R, that goes to the group
camp. Continue ahead through an oak forest, pass remains of
an old log cabin, and ascend under a power line to a jct with an
old fire road at 1.3 mi. Here is a 45-ft high fire tower established in 1940 at an elev of 2065 ft. Views of hills and forests
are panoramic. Backtrack.

Crane Branch Nature Trail

- LENGTH: 1.3 mi

- DIFFICULTY: moderate

- FEATURE: overlook

- TRAILHEADS AND DETAILS: From the camping area cross the
road and begin an interpretive trail with 29 markers of trees,
shrubs, and wildflowers. Cross Crane Branch, ascend on
switchbacks, and reach scenic Buzzard Roost Overlook at 0.6
mi. Return on a N direction of the trail and descend to
George's Fork Picnic Area at 1.3 mi. Turn L on the road and
walk back to the campground at 1.5 mi.

▶ SENECA STATE FOREST
(Pocahontas County)

The state's oldest (1942) forest is named for the Seneca Indians, a tribe of the Iroquois family, who made peace with the US
in 1815. Across the nation there are rivers, lakes, counties,
creeks, mountains, and rock formations with the name of Seneca. A few hundred of the Seneca descendants are in a reservation in New York state.

A forest of 11,684 acres, the Seneca is bordered on the W by
the historic Greenbrier River and on the E by Michael Mtn.
The Greenbrier Ranger District of the MNF adjoins on the N.
Only a few miles N are Cass Scenic RR State Park and the
National Radio Astronomy Observatory. Fishing (bass, trout,

pike), hunting (deer, grouse, wild turkey) and picnicking are its main recreation activities. Also available are seven rustic, isolated cabins and ten campsites (without hookups). The *Allegheny Trail* passes through the forest; other trails and old forest roads provide good hiking. (*USGS Map:* Clover Lick)

• ADDRESS AND ACCESS: Superintendent, Seneca State Forest, Dunmore, WV 24934, tel: 304-799-6213. From the town of Dunmore go 5.3 mi S on WV-28, and from Huntersville go N on WV-28 for 10 mi.

Crestline Trail

• LENGTH: 5.4 mi, rt

• DIFFICULTY: moderate

• FEATURE: rock outcrops

• TRAILHEAD AND DETAILS: From the picnic area of WV-28, drive (or hike) the steep gravel road for 2.1 mi to a small parking area on Michael Mtn. Begin the hike at the trail sign and follow a narrow, rocky treadway. Hemlock, white pine, and chestnut oak are dominant. Fragrant trailing arbutus, huckleberry, and mosses are between the rocks and on the open banks. Follow the ridge crest over rough ledges and cliffs to the highest point on the trail (3650 ft) at 1.5 mi. There is an orange blaze from 1.8 mi to the trail end at 2.7 mi. Backtrack.

Hill Top Trail (1.5 mi); Scarlet Oak Trail (1 mi); Horseshoe Trail (1.1 mi)

• LENGTH: 4.5 mi, ct

• DIFFICULTY: moderate

• FEATURE: nature study

• TRAILHEADS AND DETAILS: In the campground, from site #8 follow the trail through an area of rhododendron, white pine, and ferns. Pass the *Horseshoe Trail,* R. Cross Seven Mile Run and ascend to the ridge crest at 0.5 mi. At 0.6 mi is a jct with the *Hill Top Trail* (R is to Lake Rd). Turn L on the *Hill Top Trail* and descend along the ridge. Turn R at 1 mi; descend steeply, go through a stand of white pine, and reach the forest office and parking area at 1.5 mi. Turn R on Lake Rd through a deep forest. At 1.7 mi jct with *Little Mtn Trail*, L. At 1.8 mi turn R on *Scarlet Oak Trail*, ascend steeply, and reach a jct with the Loop Rd at 2.4 mi (L is the Lake Rd and spur trail to the lake). Turn R, and return to the *Hill Top Trail* at 2.8 mi. Reach the *Horseshoe Trail* jct L, at 3.4 mi near the campground. Turn L, ascend on the *Horseshoe Trail* to a ridge and a young forest with wintergreen and mosses. Descend to the campground for a loop of 4.5 mi.

Black Oak Trail

- LENGTH: 1.2 mi

- DIFFICULTY: easy

- FEATURE: nature study

- TRAILHEADS AND DETAILS: From the forest office drive the Lake Rd for 2.4 mi to the fire tower crossroads and park. (The yellow-blazed *Allegheny Trail* crosses here, N–S.) Hike R on the Firetower Rd and *Allegheny Trail* for 0.2 mi to the *Black Oak Trail*, L. (It is another 0.2 mi up the road to the fire tower and panoramic views from 3458 ft elev.) Descend on a footpath through a mature forest, wildflowers, and Indian pipe *(Monotropa uniflora)*. Reach a forest road at 1.2 mi, turn L, and walk up the road to the crossroads and beginning point at 2.2 mi.

Thorny Creek Trail *(3.9 mi);* *Little Mountain Trail* *(0.6 mi)*

* LENGTH: 4.5 mi, ct

* DIFFICULTY: moderate

* FEATURES: scenic, wildlife

* TRAILHEADS AND DETAILS: After parking at the dam, follow the sign downstream through hemlock, rhododendron, and mountain laurel to a meadow of elderberry and sumac. At 0.7 mi cross Thorny Creek on a footbridge near the ruins of an old cabin. Club moss and wintergreen are prominent. At 1.8 mi is a cow pasture on the R. Deer and grouse are often seen in this area. Ascend L of a fence to a ridge, then climb another ridge to a jeep road at 2.3 mi. Follow the jeep road and reach the top of Little Mtn at 2.7 mi. Jct with the *Little Mtn Trail* at 3.2 mi. (The *Little Mtn Trail* is 0.6 mi R to the forest office.) Continue ahead; reach the jct of the Lake and Loop rds at 3.9 mi. Turn L on the Lake Rd and return to the dam parking area at 4.4 mi.

8.

State Public Hunting and Fishing Areas

"I'm for protecting the wildlife; their future depends on us."
— BERNARD GIBSON

West Virginia has 45 public hunting and fishing areas (PHFAs) with a total of 247,505 acres. Campgrounds are on 17 acres, with 5 primitive (undeveloped, may have drinking water); 10 rustic (vault toilet, well water, and cleared campsites); and 2 standard (grill, tent pad, picnic table, hot showers, flush toilets, and spigot water). The latter two are Laurel Lake PHFA at Lenore and Moncove Lake PHFA at Gap Mills. Like the state park and forest campgrounds there is a nominal fee. Camping is permitted only at designated areas to protect the natural environment. The campgrounds are usually open year-round, depending on the weather. It is wise to check in advance if dates are other than Memorial Day to Labor Day. Although hunting and fishing are the primary activities, the hunting roads and jeep trails provide an incredible network of mileage for hikers. There is space for all types of outdoor activists and nature lovers, and those who do not hunt should choose a time other than the game hunting seasons. Some of the PHFAs have named and marked trail systems (Lewis Wetzel PHFA is an example), others have only numbered footpaths (Short Mountain PHFA is an example), and others have pathways named on paper but not on sign posts (Sleepy Creek PHFA is an example). The PHFAs described below are the ones that listed named and marked trails in a PHFA survey. Nevertheless, for hikers who wish a remote and natural area to walk, all PHFAs have something to offer. For the protection of wildlife during the breeding seasons, many hunting roads may be locked. An advance check with the Wildlife Resources Division is recommended. Described below are 59.6 mi on 27 trails.

•INFORMATION: For information on PHFAs with camping facilities, contact Travel West Virginia, Dept of Commerce, State Capitol, Charleston, WV 25305, tel: 1-800-CALL-WVA. For information on hunting, trapping, and fishing contact the same office.

▶ ELK RIVER PHFA
(Braxton County)

Located at the geographic center of the state, this exceptionally attractive preserve is the state's oldest public hunting and fishing area. It has a vast area (17,184 acres — 6949 state-owned and 10,235 leased from the Corps of Engineers) for hunting, fishing, boating, water skiing, hiking, and nature study. For management purposes, the area is divided into two sections: the Holly on the N side of Sutton Lake, and the Elk on the S side. Because the S side has named trails, it is described below. Approximately 30 mi of "hunting trails" are in the forest, and some of these road-trails lead to coves with virgin trees 3 to 5 ft in diameter. Camping is not permitted in the PHFA, but is allowed at three campgrounds on the adjoining Lake Sutton, a US Army Corps of Engineers project. Game species include deer, squirrel, wild turkey, grouse, and raccoon. Anglers can expect bass, walleyes, channel catfish, bluegill, and crappie. Trout are stocked below Sutton Dam. The forest is popular in early April for its morels (genus *Morchella*). Bird-watchers will also find this forest, with its wildlife food plots and water holes, ideal. It is open year-round. (*USGS Maps:* Sutton, Newville, Little Bush)

• ADDRESS AND ACCESS: From downtown Sutton, cross the bridge on Old Turnpike Road (CO-19/40) and go S for 3.8 mi to a jct with Wolf Creek-Centralia Rd (CO-17). Turn L on CO-17, go 4.1 mi and bear L at the Spruce Lick Methodist Church; drive 2.7 mi farther and turn L on Stony Creek Rd (CO-17/9). Go another 2.5 mi to Elk River PHFA headquarters.

Hickory Flats Trail (4.8 mi); Dynamite Trail (1.0 mi); Tower Falls Trail (0.8 mi); Woodell Trail (2.2 mi); Canoe River Trail (3.6 mi); Gibson Trail (0.9 mi); Billy Linger Trail (4.4 mi)

• LENGTH: 17.7 mi, rt, ct

• DIFFICULTY: easy to strenuous

• FEATURES: wildlife, plant life, scenic

• TRAILHEADS AND DETAILS: The named and signed grassy road-trails form loops, overlaps, and dead-ends. They are well maintained and wide enough for hiking, horseback riding, or 4WD-vehicles. In the description below, the main ridge trail is emphasized with the side or spur trails in parentheses. Individual mileage is for round-trip, but a wide range of combination mileages can occur.

Some of the trees, shrubs, and wildflowers are pignut hickory, white pine, poplar, red and sugar maple, basswood, cucumber tree, hemlock, locust, papaw, yellow root, redbud, jack-in-the-pulpit, mountain laurel, and rhododendron.

Begin from the headquarters parking lot and follow the main road N for 0.2 mi to a locked gate. Pass the gate, slightly descend, and reach the *Dynamite Trail* at 0.5 mi. (The *Dynamite Trail* goes 0.5 mi toward the headwaters of Oldlick Run. Backtrack.) Continue ahead and reach the *Tower Falls Trail*, R, at 0.7 mi. (The *Tower Falls Trail* goes through a wildlife plot and after 0.5 mi dead-ends. Backtrack or connect with the *Woodell Trail*.) At 1 mi jct with the *Woodell Trail*, R. (The *Woodell Trail* makes a loop and has a spur among a number of wildlife food plots. Mileage potential is 2.2.) On the main route, *Hickory Flats Trail*, reach a jct with *Canoe Trail*, R, at 1.2 mi. The Hickory Flats

Shelter is L. (The *Canoe Trail* adjoins the *Woodell Trail*, but soon turns L and descends to Canoe Run. There it crosses the stream and extends toward Sutton Lake. Backtrack for a total of 3.6 mi.) At 2.4 mi the *Hickory Flats Trail* becomes the *Billy Linger Trail*. To the R is the *Gibson Trail*. (The *Gibson Trail* descends and passes a wildlife food plot and water hole for a loop of 0.9 mi.) Continue ahead on the *Billy Linger Trail* through a gate, pass R of a cabin at 2.6 mi, and reach scenic views of Lake Sutton at 3 mi and 3.3 mi. Ahead, curve L on the ridge peninsula and descend toward the lake for another 1.3 mi. Excellent views when the leaves are off the trees. Backtrack.

There are other trails in the area. For example, at the entrance to the area the *Stony Creek Hunting Trail* and the *Cherry Tree Hunting Trail* go W. The *Stony Creek Hunting Trail* is approximately 2.5 mi to Mortons Rd (CO-17/3), where a L turn exits to Wolf Creek Rd (CO-17). (A spur trail goes 0.8 mi downstream on Stony Creek to the lake.) The trail has wildlife food plots. The Cherry Tree area extends 1.7 mi to a variety of food plots W of the PHFA office.

▶ LEWIS WETZEL PHFA
(Wetzel County)

For hikers who desire nearly 35 mi of old woods roads and hunter's trails on steep ridges of 1500 ft elev, deep and damp hollows, and meadows with trout-stocked streams, this 9125-acre wildlife area is the place to be. That is, during the hunting off-season, because these hills and valleys have the state's highest ruffed grouse *(Bonasa umbellus)* population. Other managed game species are deer, gray squirrel, raccoon, wild turkey, fox, muskrat, mink, and rabbit. Rattlesnakes are among the reptiles and spring peeper among the amphibians. Some of the streams are stocked with rainbow trout. Vegetation consists of central hardwoods such as oaks, hickories, sycamore, black locust, black walnut, buckeye, and beech. There is also cherry, papaw, and white pine. Among the wildflowers are black-eyed Susan, bee balm, milkweed, and goldenseal. The Wildlife Division has planted birds-foot trefoil, ladino clover, and autumn olive (silverberry) for numerous wildlife food plots.

This wildlife management area, and the county, received their names from the famous Indian fighter Lewis Wetzel. He was from a courageous pioneer family of explorers and settlers. Lewis, with his brother Jacob, was captured by the Indians in 1777. One of his other three brothers was killed. After his escape Wetzel became a marksman with vengeance on his mind. He was also an expert game hunter and country dance fiddler.

Facilities in the area are 20 primitive campsites at the campground, hand pump well, and vault toilet. Permission must be granted by the superintendent for overnight camping outside the campground. Hunting roads usually need 4WD-vehicles. Open year-round. (*USGS Maps:* Big Run, Center Point, Pine Grove)

• ADDRESS AND ACCESS: Superintendent, Lewis Wetzel PHFA, Rte 1, Jacksonburg, WV 26377, tel: 304-889-2233. In Jacksonburg at the jct of WV-20 and Buffalo Run Rd (CO-82) follow the Buffalo Run Rd for 3.2 mi to the forest office and another 1.2 mi to the campground.

• SUPPORT FACILITIES: Groceries and basic supplies are in Jacksonburg, but accommodations and other stores are 23 mi NW on WV-20 to New Martinsville.

Horse Run Trail (0.9 mi); *High Knob Trail* (3.3 mi); *Lesin Run Trail* (1.1 mi); *Hart Ridge Trail* (1 mi); *Nettle Run Trail* (1.4 mi); *Huss Pen Trail* (0.9 mi); *Hiles Run Trail* (0.7 mi)

- LENGTH: 9.3 mi, ct

- DIFFICULTY: moderate to strenuous

- FEATURES: wildlife, history

- TRAILHEADS AND DETAILS: These connecting trails are all E of Buffalo Run and are used by hunters and hikers. West of the stream are mainly jeep trails, some of which have rough sections and are used by hunters. From the superintendent's office it is 1.2 mi upstream by Buffalo Run to the campground. Here is a base for a combined circuit of the above trails. From the campground, walk out to the entrance road to the *Horse Run Trail,* R. Walk around the locked gate and follow upstream. There are plenty of wildflowers, such as black-eyed Susans, bellflowers, and daisies. Walnut, cherry, and buckeye are also prominent. At 0.3 mi keep R and at 0.4 mi begin ascent, cross the stream and reach the crest of the ridge at 0.9 mi to jct with the *High Knob Trail,* L. Follow the *High Knob Trail* L (N) and jct with the *Lesin Run Trail* after 1.1 mi (2 mi from the campground). (The *Lesin Run Trail* descends, L, for 1.1 mi to the Buffalo Run Rd. A 0.2 mi L turn on the road back to the campground is a loop of 3.3 mi.) Continue ahead and at 2.3 mi reach a jct with the *Hart Ridge Trail,* L. (The *Hart Ridge Trail* follows the ridge line before making a steep descent to the gate at Buffalo Run Rd at 1 mi. A 0.3 mi L turn on the road back to the campground is a loop of 3.6 mi.) Continue on the ridge and jct with the *Nettle Run Trail* at 2.7 mi. (The *Nettle Run Trail* descends for 1.4 mi to the forest office. Along the way it follows an old road, passes under a gas pipeline swath to the headwaters of Nettle Run in a dark, damp hollow, reaches a gate and gravel road, and exits R of the office to Buffalo Run Rd. A L turn up the road for 1.2 mi to the campground is a loop of 5.3 mi.) Continue on the *High Knob Trail* on a grassy hunter's road. At 3.1 mi is a sign, R, to Ashcamp Run. Skirt the E slope of the ridge and reach a road jct at 3.3 mi. *High Knob Trail* forks L and the road continues on the R to connect with *Huss Pen Trail* and *Hiles Run Trail* described below. Follow the *High Knob Trail* on a spur ridge line to a pipeline swath and wildlife food plot, and begin an exceptionally steep descent at 3.7 mi. Reach the Buffalo Run Rd on the N side of Nettles Run by the forest office. A turn L and walk up the road to the campground is a loop of 5.4 mi. Along the main ridge from the *High Knob Trail* fork go 0.2 mi to a jct with the *Huss Pen Trail*, L. (The *Huss Pen Trail* descends steeply in sections and L of a streambed to exit after 0.9 mi at Buffalo Run Rd and a gas pipeline. From here it is 1.9 mi L to the campground for a loop of 6.3 mi.) A final trail from the ridge is another 0.7 mi to a jct with *Hiles Run Trail*. (Descend on the *Hiles Run Trail*, L, steeply in sections, for 0.7 mi to a cove and on the L of an abandoned oil well before reaching Buffalo Run Rd. From here, L, it is 2.3 mi back to the campground for a loop of 7.2 mi.)

▶ MONCOVE LAKE PHFA
(Monroe County)

Referred to as an "outdoorsmen's delight," this 895-acre tract in peaceful Sweet Springs Valley has a 144-acre lake filled with largemouth bass, bluegill, and channel catfish. Built on Devil's Creek in 1959, the lake is 2503 ft in elev. Game hunting is for deer, wild turkey, quail, and woodcock. The campground has 48 tent or trailer campsites with drinking water, picnic tables, grills, rest rooms, and hot showers. Swimming is allowed at designated spots. Other activities are boating, hiking, and picnicking. The camping season is almost year-round, but recreation facilities are open from Memorial Day to Labor Day. (*USGS Map:* Paint Bank)

• ADDRESS AND ACCESS: Superintendent, Moncove Lake PHFA, Gap Mills, WV 24941, tel: 304-772-3450. From Gap Mills go NE on Devil's Hollow Rd (CO-8) for 5.3 mi.

Moncove Lake Trail

• LENGTH: 1.2 mi

• DIFFICULTY: easy

• FEATURES: wildlife, nature study

• TRAILHEADS AND DETAILS: The foot trail begins between campsites #39 and #40 in a white pine forest and reaches an old woods road. At 0.6 mi turn L at an old woods crossroads and enter a swamp area. Care should be used here in crossing an old beaver dam on logs. At another woods road, turn L and cross a small drain at 1 mi. Turn sharply L off the woods road, cross the stream, and return to the campground at site #42 for a loop of 1.2 mi.

▶ SLEEPY CREEK PHFA
(Morgan and Berkeley Counties)

Thirty years of management by the state's Conservation Commission and the Department of Natural Resources have made an outstanding transformation in this 23,000-acre double mountain range. By 1835 all the deer had disappeared and by 1915 all the wild turkey had been killed. By 1910 all the timber had been ravished, and by 1942 a devastating forest fire further diminished forest life on the ridges and in the Meadow Branch valley.

In 1950 the state began purchasing the property from the Farmers Bank of Pittsburgh for only $152 an acre. Until 1954 it was managed as a state forest. Now the forest is growing with oak, Virginia and white pine, hickory, hemlock, beech, and maple. Deer roam the forest, wild turkey are back, and the grouse, quail, squirrel, and raccoon population is increasing. There are 42 wildlife food plots.

The forest gets its name from the three-pronged Sleepy Creek in Morgan County. The county line of Morgan and Berkeley runs along the ridge of Sleepy Creek Mtn, but most of the preserve is in Berkeley County. The E mountain ridge is

Third Hill Mtn, and in the lower half of the area the two ridges are joined with a crossbeam ridge called Locks-of-the-Mountain. Nearby is the preserve's highest peak, Shanghai Beacon (2172 ft).

In the center of the forest is a 205-acre lake, opened in 1964, where anglers may catch stocked largemouth bass, bluegill, crappie, northern pike, and channel catfish. In keeping with the tranquility of the forest, only paddleboats and boats with electric motors are permitted. Primitive campgrounds with 75 units are near the lake or at designated places. Well water and vault toilets are available.

There are more than 50 mi of 12 seasonal access hunting roads and 16 mi of 12 foot trails that have names, but are not signed or marked. A designated foot trail, the longest, is 20.8 mi of the *Big Blue Trail*. It parallels the Little Brush Run in the S, the Meadow Branch in the middle, and the Sleepy Creek Mtn ridge line in the N. It overlaps or connects with a number of other footpaths and hunting roads on its route through Sleepy Creek PHFA. Its route through Virginia and other areas of West Virginia is described in Chapter 11.

Big Blue Trail

• LENGTH: 20.8 mi

• DIFFICULTY: easy to moderate

• FEATURES: wildlife, scenic, remote

• TRAILHEADS AND DETAILS: To enter from the S, drive 2.5 mi W of Glengary on WV-45 to a parking area. Follow the blue blazes on a dirt road and at 0.6 mi turn R to enter the Sleepy Creek PHFA. After 1.5 mi reach wildlife food plot #38 and a jct, R, with the *Big Run Trail*. (The 0.7 mi *Big Run Trail* is an unsigned foot trail that goes to another food plot and the E boundary of the forest.) At 2.5 mi reach a jct with *High Rock Trail*, L, and food plot #34. (The 0.6 mi *High Rock Trail* crosses Brush Creek and ascends to High Rock for jct with the Sleepy Creek Mtn jeep trail.) Reach a jct with the Sleepy Creek Mtn jeep road, L, at 4.5 mi. Continue ahead to a jct, R, with the Pee Wee Point jeep road, ahead to a camping registration board at 4.8 mi, and the jct with the Locks-of-the-Mountain on Hampshire Grade Rd (CO-7/13). Follow the road for 0.8 mi to a jct with an old jeep road, R, the *High Knob Trail*. (The *High Knob Trail* is an unsigned trail that ascends to the Shanghai Beacon for 1 mi.) Ahead, after 0.1 mi on the Hampshire Grade Rd, turn L on the Old Still Rd. It descends and follows a ridge past more wildlife food plots. At 8.4 mi reach the Dead Mule jeep trail that goes R and up the slope to gated Third Hill Mtn Rd. Continue ahead between Roaring Run and Meadow Branch, but cross Roaring Run at 9.6 mi. (To the R is a footpath, the 1 mi *Roaring Run Trail*, which goes up Roaring Run to Third Hill Mtn Rd.)

Arrive at the gravel lake road at 10 mi and pass Upper Campground at 10.9 mi. Pass Myers Place Campground at 11.2 mi and reach a road fork at 11.3 mi. (To the R it is 3.9 mi on the road to the superintendent's office and another 2.3 mi to Back Creek Rd [CO-7] and Jones Springs.) To the L at the fork, continue on the *Big Blue Trail* and pass Piney Point Campground and Lower Campground. At 13 mi leave the lakeside road, cross two small streams, and at 13.8 mi turn L at a fork. (The R fork is *Meadow Branch Trail,* which passes under a power line and turns E to jct with the Third Mtn Trail Rd.) At 14 mi cross Meadow Creek, pass under a power line, and begin an ascent. Reach White's Gap and Sleepy Creek Mtn jeep road at 16 mi. (To the R is the unsigned *White's Gap Trail,* a footpath that descends 1 mi to the crossing of Meadow Branch and a fork. The R fork is the 0.5 mi *White's Knob Trail* and the L fork is *Dug Road Trail.* Both jct with the Third Hill Mtn jeep road.) Continue on the *Big Blue Trail* from White's Gap by ascending to the ridge top and follow the ridge for 4 mi of undulating treadway. Here, as elsewhere in the forest, are mountain laurel, wild azaleas, and dogwood among the oaks. At 20 mi reach a jct with the *Devil's Nose Trail,* R. (The 1.5 mi *Devil's Nose Trail* is an unsigned route that descends to and rises from Meadow Creek, but runs along the proboscis-shaped curve of Meadow Creek before ascending to Paines Knob on

Short Mtn. There it joins a fire trail, other unsigned foot trails, and the 1 mi *Morgan Trail* in the Hedges Mtn area. (There is a vehicular access route to the Hedges Mtn area on part public and part private lands. For information on this access, contact the superintendent.)

Continue ahead on the *Big Blue Trail* and reach the Devil's Nose Knob (1540 ft) at 20.5 mi. Descend steeply and at 20.8 mi leave the Sleepy Creek PHFA to enter private property. Continue the descent, cross Meadow Creek, and reach Spruce Pine Roadside Park by WV-9 at 22 mi, 8.3 mi E of Berkeley Springs.

· ADDRESS AND ACCESS: Superintendent, Sleepy Creek PHFA, Rte 2, Box 109-F, Hedgeville, WV 25427, tel: 304-754-3855. From the jct of WV-9 and Back Creek Rd (CO-7), 1.8 mi W of Hedgeville, turn on Back Creek Rd and drive 6.3 mi to Jones Springs. From here continue S for 0.6 mi to Meadow Branch Rd (CO-7/9) and turn R. It is 2.3 mi to the superintendent's office and another 3.9 mi to the Sleepy Creek Lake. From the jct of WV-45 and Back Creek Rd (CO-7) in Glengary, go N for 8.3 mi to Meadow Branch Rd (CO-7/9) and follow directions as above. (An access road that crosses into Morgan County is Hampshire Grade Rd [CO-7/13], which begins in Shanghai on CO-7, 4.7 mi N of Glengary.)

PART FOUR

Municipal and County Trails

Monarch butterfly/Photo by the author

9.

Municipal and County Parks and Recreation Areas

"The swiftest traveler is he who goes afoot."
— HENRY DAVID THOREAU

There are 32 towns and cities and 21 counties in the state that have parks and recreation boards, commissions, or departments. They operate on separate public administrative units, but occasionally combine their resources; an example is the city of Grafton and Taylor County. Their recreation areas vary in size, facilities, and scope from simple day-use picnic areas to lighted sports fields and courts to elaborate sports centers. Kanawha County Parks and Recreation has one of the most comprehensive park systems with four localities: Shawnee Regional Park at Institute; Coonskin Park near Charleston; Geary Park in Clendenin; and Big Bend Golf Course at Tornado. In addition, the commission supervises rural recreation programs at four county high schools. Among the city parks, Oglesby Park in Wheeling is a remarkable example. Its facilities and trails are described in more detail below. A few parks have designated and signed foot trails; they are covered in this chapter, but other parks have unnamed trails and popular walking paths. Examples are Ritter Park in Huntington and Little Creek Park in South Charleston. Others, such as Princeton City Park, have physical fitness trails.

- INFORMATION: For a list of county parks and recreation areas contact Community Development, Office of Community and

Industrial Development, Bldg 6, Rm B-522, Capitol Complex, Charleston, WV 25305, tel: 304-348-4010.

▶ COONSKIN PARK
(Kanawha County)

This scenic 947-acre park on a bend by the Elk River is one of three parks and two golf courses operated by the Kanawha County Parks and Recreation Commission. Only Coonskin Park has a foot trail. The park has an Olympic-sized heated swimming pool and clubhouse; 9 lighted tennis courts at the Ivor F. Boiarsky Tennis Center; 18-hole, par 3 golf course; skeet range; fishing area; 19 picnic areas with shelters; restaurant that can accommodate 275; 18 exercise stations on a Parcourse; snow-skiing slope; ball field; and nature trail. In the summer a floral display designed in the shape of the state is opposite the tennis courts. The park is open year-round. (*USGS Map:* Big Chimney)

• ADDRESS AND ACCESS: Director, Coonskin Park, Coonskin Drive, Charleston, WV 25311, tel: 304-345-8000. At the jct of I-77 and WV-114 near the state capitol in downtown Charleston, take WV-114 and drive 2.6 mi to Coonskin Dr (CO-51), L. After 0.8 mi arrive at Coonskin Park entrance.

Coonskin Nature Trail

• LENGTH: 1 mi

• DIFFICULTY: moderate

• FEATURE: natural science

• TRAILHEAD AND DETAILS: After 0.5 mi from the entrance, park on the R at the picnic area gate and follow the sign. Descend into a cove with tall poplar, maple, beech, and hemlock. At a fork, keep L, upstream and pass under a unique rock ledge. At 0.3 mi climb steps to a rock overhang. Cross a footbridge and begin a return of the loop; walk under a small waterfall at 0.7 mi. Among the flora are foamflower, wild ginger, papaw, sourwood, arrowwood, and Solomon's Seal. Complete the loop and return to the point of beginning at 1 mi.

▶ GRAND VUE PARK
(Marshall County)

The 600-acre Grand Vue Park that overlooks the Ohio River Valley is called "heaven on a hill" and is operated by the Marshall County Parks and Recreation Dept. It is open year-round. Its summer facilities include an 18-hole golf course; a lighted driving range; a mini-golf course; Olympic-sized swimming pool; eight grass-tex tennis courts; fully equipped picnic shelters; outdoor theater and children's "Red Barn" play area; and a nature trail. Winter activities are chiefly cross-country skiing and sledding. Deluxe vacation cabins are available any season; banquet rooms with professional catering services are also available. The park adjoins Moundsville, an internationally known area for glassware (Fostoria, for example) and for the nation's largest prehistoric Indian (Adena) burial mound (Grave Creek Mound, 79 ft high), on Jefferson Ave. The Delf Norona Museum and Cultural Center is nearby. (*USGS Map:* Moundsville)

• ADDRESS AND ACCESS: Manager, Grand Vue Park, PO Box 523, Moundsville, WV 26041, tel: 304-845-9810. In Moundsville on US-250 and WV-88 go E to the Fostoria Glass Co., turn on Fostoria Ave to Oak Ave and to Grandview Rd for park entrance.

Cabin Trail

- LENGTH: 1.8 mi

- DIFFICULTY: easy

- FEATURE: nature study

- TRAILHEAD AND DETAILS: Between picnic shelter #1 and the driving range on the E side of the road is a hiking trail sign. Follow the sign on a mowed field for 0.2 mi to a young forest of ash, cherry, apple, and elderberry. In the summer, large patches of milkweed are frequented by monarch butterflies. Enter another field and another woods and descend to a glen at 1.1 mi. Turn L, ascend, return to the main trail and loop back for 1.8 mi.

▶ MOUNTWOOD PARK
(Wood County)

The 2600-acre park has a 50-acre lake for boating (canoes, pedal boats, and rowboats), fishing (stocked with trout and bass five months annually), and swimming. Other facilities are tennis courts, ball fields, and a nature study trail. The park has 81 full-service RV campsites, 16 of which have sewer hookups; group and family cottages; and 18 tent campsites. The White Oak Village Lodge complex has facilities for year-round conferences, banquets, dinners, and lodging.

- ADDRESS AND ACCESS: Manager, Mountwood Park, Rte 2, Box 56, Waverly, WV 26184, tel: 304-679-3611 or 304-422-7121. From the jct of US-50 and I-77 in Parkersburg, go E on US-50 for 12 mi to Volcano Rd (CO-5), R. Continue E on US-50 for 0.7 mi to the campground, L, on Boreland Spring Rd (CO-20).

Mountwood Lake Trail

- LENGTH: 2.2 mi

- DIFFICULTY: moderate

- FEATURES: geology, scenic

- TRAILHEADS AND DETAILS: Begin at Loeb's Boat Dock and follow the paved road for 0.3 mi. Turn L and ascend on a treadway of wood chips. Forest is cherry, Virginia pine, maple, oak, and hickory. Pass Wright's Overlook at 0.5 mi and Wilson's Overlook at 0.8 mi. Maidenhair ferns and spicebush are in the forest and crown vetch is at the dam area. Cross the spillway at 1.2 mi and take a 0.1 mi spur trail to the Devil's Tea Table, a unique rock formation at 1.3 mi. Continue around the lake, pass another overlook at 1.9 mi, and reach the beach parking area at 2.2 mi. It is 0.8 mi from here to the Loeb's Boat Dock.

▶ OGLEBAY PARK
(Wheeling)

One of America's outstanding municipal resort parks, Oglebay is West Virginia's finest for recreational, cultural, and educational activities. The 1460-acre park was originally Waddington Farm, the country estate of Col. Earl W. Oglebay, who was born and grew up in the area, but was better known as a Cleveland industrialist and philanthropist. On his death, in 1926, he gave the estate to the City of Wheeling for "as long as the people shall operate it for purposes of public recreation and education," with the stipulation that a quarter of the land remain undeveloped. In 1928 it officially became a park, to be operated by the Wheeling Park Commission.

Of particular interest is the Brooks Nature Center, named in honor of Alonzo B. Brooks, a famed forester, author, and park naturalist whose efforts on behalf of Oglebay's natural beauty were outstanding. When he retired, in 1942, the report was made that "he lives in every tree, every flower, every bird, and every scampering furry creature at Oglebay Park." (He was the uncle of another famous naturalist and author, Maurice Brooks, professor emeritus of wildlife management at West Virginia University, and reverently named "Dr. Appalachia" by Roger Tory Peterson of the Peterson Guides. Uncle and nephew are members of a prominent family from French Creek in Upshur County.) The center is open year-round, and nature walks begin here. In the center is the Oglebay Institute Nature Education Department, which offers courses in ecology and environmental education, as well as a nature camp program at its mountain retreat near Terra Alta. Backpacking courses include studies in vascular plants, mushrooms, herpetology, and wild foods.

Oglebay offers an exceptional range of activities. A partial list includes the Speidel Championship Golf Course (and two others) with associated services; indoor and outdoor swimming pools; 11 lighted tennis courts; horseback riding at the riding academy, forest, and arena; skiing (ski shop and rental equipment); boating and fishing in Schenk Lake; picnicking; and nature study. Among the facilities are the Wilson Lodge with 202 guest rooms, executive conference suites, and dining rooms that can accommodate up to 700 persons, spa, and lounges; garden center and greenhouses; 65-acre Good Children's Zoo with Benedum Nature Science Theater and Planetarium; Mansion Museum (this was the summer home of Oglebay) with Burton Galleries; Speidel Observatory; Wigginton Arboretum; Burton Wildlife Sanctuary; and outdoor theater. Additionally, there are festivals, concerts, lecture series, celebrations, tournaments, and exhibitions year-round. (*USGS Map:* Wheeling)

• ADDRESS AND ACCESS: Visitors Services, Oglebay Park, Wheeling, WV 26003, tel: 304-242-3000. At the jct of I-70 and US-40, exit 2A and Oglebay Park signs, go E on US-40 0.2 mi, turn L on WV-88, and go 2.4 mi to park entrance.

Bowles Hemlock Trail *(0.4 mi);* ***Thoreau Trail*** *(0.8 mi);* ***Brooks Trail*** *(0.4 mi);* ***Beech Trail*** *(0.7 mi)*

- LENGTH: 3.9 mi, rt, ct

- DIFFICULTY: easy to moderate

- FEATURES: scenic, nature study

- TRAILHEADS AND DETAILS: Park in front of, and begin hikes behind, the Brooks Nature Center. These trails form three loops; to hike them all, backtracking will be required on some sections. Start at post #1 of 14 posts for the *Bowles Hemlock Trail*. Descend to an old watering trough (used by Colonel Oglebay's horses). Go across Schenk Run, slightly ascend, and turn L (at jct with *Beech Trail,* ahead). Descend and cross a footbridge. Ascend to an overlook of cascades and at post #11 (near a large white oak) turn L at 0.3 mi. Here is a jct, R, with the *Thoreau Trail.* Return to the center along a wood fence for another 0.1 mi. Vegetation includes coltsfoot, stonecrop, jewelweed, swamp buttercup, bluets, asters, wild ginger, ferns, hemlock, locust, cherry, and oaks.

A second loop is to follow the *Thoreau Trail* at the jct mentioned above. Cross Falls Rd and enter a wide trail with red spruce and large hardwoods S of the cabins. After 0.4 mi curve R in patches of meadow parsnip, cross a stream, and at 0.5 mi cross Falls Rd bridge. Follow downstream, cross the stream here and again above the waterfall, and jct with the *Brooks Trail,* L. Ahead, upstream on the Schenk Run, return in the gorge to join *Bowles Hemlock Trail* and reach the center at 1 mi.

For a longer loop, follow the *Brooks Trail* up a steep embankment and take a narrow path on the hillside in a forest of large cherry, ash, oak, maple, and beech to a connector trail, R, at 0.3 mi. Ahead, pass a crescent bench and go 0.1 mi to the end of the trail at a shale rock formation and cascades on Brooks Trail Run. Backtrack to the connecting trail, turn L, ascend for 0.2 mi, and reach *Beech Trail.* (It is 0.1 mi L to a dead-end at the zoo.) Turn R on the scenic and wide *Beech Trail* at a large white oak, pass below the cabins, and return to the *Bowles Hemlock*

Trail. Reach the Nature Center for a complete loop, including the backtracks, of 2.5 mi.

Arboretum Trail

- LENGTH: 2.8 mi, rt
- DIFFICULTY: easy to moderate
- FEATURES: scenic, botanical study

- TRAILHEADS AND DETAILS: The 8-ft wide asphalt trail can be hiked in short or long loops by using a variety of interconnecting trails and can be entered near the Speidel Observatory (across the road from the Brooks Nature Center), at the garden center (near the park's main office), at Schenk Lake, or at the Good Zoo. From any point there are outstanding views of flowering shrubs, red and white pine and hemlock groves, manicured hillside lawns and landscaped hardwood sections. If choosing a 1.4 loop around the perimeter from the Brooks Nature Center, parallel the Falls Rd by Wilson Lodge. After 0.7 mi pass through a pine grove to the garden center and greenhouses. From a stone and wood arbor there is a magnificent view of the lakes and hillsides. Go between the greenhouses and the outdoor theater to an overlook and descend to a road jct at Good Zoo at 1.1 mi. Turn L, descend to Schenk Lake at 1.2 mi, and follow the road past the Children's Center to Brooks Nature Center for another 0.2 mi.

▶ RIDENOUR PARK
(Nitro)

This city park has a 24-acre lake for fishing, picnic shelters, playground areas, outdoor amphitheater, rest rooms, and a nature trail. It is open year-round, daily, 9 A.M.–9 P.M.

- ADDRESS AND ACCESS: Director, Nitro Parks and Recreation Dept, City Hall, Nitro, WV 25143, tel: 304-755-0701. From exit 45 on I-64 in Nitro, go 2.1 mi on WV-25 to 21st St and turn L to the park entrance.

Ridenour Lake Trail

- LENGTH: 1 mi, rt
- DIFFICULTY: easy
- FEATURE: nature study

- TRAILHEADS AND DETAILS: From the parking area on the S side of the lake, hike on a wide gravel trail around the lake through a forest of buckeye, beech, maple, hickory, oak, and arrowwood *(Viburnum acerifolium)*. Elephant's foot *(Elephantopus carolinianus)* grows on the slope and ironweed grows near the lake edge. Descend on 33 steps at 0.3 mi, cross a small bridge, and reach a paved road at Lakeview Estates at 0.5 mi. It is another 0.2 mi on the road to the picnic area or backtrack.

▶ SAINT ALBANS CITY PARK
(Saint Albans)

The park has a lighted baseball field, petting farm, miniature golf, playgrounds, picnic area with shelters, physical fitness course with 20 stations, and hiking trails. It is open daily from mid-April through October, and is operated by the city's Parks and Recreation Dept.

- ADDRESS AND ACCESS: Director, St Albans Parks and Recreation Dept, 500 Washington St, St Albans, WV 25177, tel: 304-727-2101. In St Albans on US-60, turn onto Walnut St and go 0.6 mi to Kanawha Terrace. Turn R and go 0.1 mi to Vine St and turn L. Go 0.2 mi to Monmouth Ave and turn R. After 0.4 mi reach the park entrance.

Saint Albans Nature Trail

- LENGTH: 0.5 mi

- DIFFICULTY: easy

- FEATURES: covered bridge, plant life

- TRAILHEAD AND DETAILS: After entrance in the park there is a parking area and display board on the R. Follow the paved *Nature Trail* that is suitable for the physically handicapped. After 250 yds cross a small covered bridge, then take a dirt footpath. Descend and weave through a forest of maple, poplar, oak, and ash. Among the wildflowers are jewelweed, celandine poppy, comfrey *(Symphytum officinale)*, blue-eyed Mary, asters, and trout lily *(Erythronium americanum)*. Complete the loop by ascending to the parking area.

▶ WINE CELLAR PARK
(Dunbar)

The 314-acre Wine Cellar Park was dedicated in 1982 by the city of Dunbar and financed by the city and the Land and Water Conservation Fund. It has a lighted picnic shelter with fireplace, picnic tables, playground, rest rooms, and drinking water on the W side of the park. Plans are to construct hiking trails in this area. On the E side are the three restored wine cellars built in the early 1860s, a paved nature trail, and a lake for fishing.

- ADDRESS AND ACCESS: Park Manager, Wine Cellar Park, City of Dunbar, Dunbar, WV 25604, tel: 304-766-0223. Turn off I-64 at exit 53 and go 1.7 mi on Dutch Hollow Road (CO-25/5).

Wine Cellar Nature Trail

- LENGTH: 0.6 mi

- DIFFICULTY: easy

- FEATURES: botany, wine cellars

- TRAILHEAD AND DETAILS: Begin at the roadside sign and follow a paved trail suitable for the physically handicapped. Pass through ash, oak, maple, birch, sycamore, and poplar. Among the wildflowers are jewelweed, tall bellflower, sweet cicely, and asters. Ferns are prominent. The trail crisscrosses the stream on footbridges. At the concave is a spur trail up an embankment to the lake. Complete the loop at the wine cellars.

PART FIVE

Private, College, and Special Property Trails

Country road in Harrison County/Photo by the author

10.

Private Trails and College Trails

"There is our honey tree
Out in the woodland's deep
Down where the fog-trails meet,
Octaves of gold."

— LOUISE MCNEILL PEASE

Of the 106 known private trails in West Virginia that have names, only 46 are covered in this chapter because some private land and home owners do not wish public traffic on their trails and resort owners require trail users to be registered guests. Examples of the latter are such luxurious resorts as Greenbrier in White Sulphur Springs and Glade Springs in Daniels. The same applies to rustic localities such as private Smoke Hole Lodge (accessible by 4WD-vehicles) near Petersburg. Some of the state's private garden trails receive immaculate maintenance. Some woods trails are being developed on abandoned farms. A few trails are on ranches or in large private timber or mining industry lands. Other trails are on Nature Conservancy properties, and a large number of trails are in private camps. In the limestone region there are 14 known cave trails, but at the request of the owners only two are described below. Hikers are requested to respect private boundaries and to announce their presence to their hosts. A few trails are on both public and private lands, such as the *Allegheny Trail* and the *Big Blue Trail*. Four MNF trails, the

Seneca Creek Trail, the *Blackbird Knob Trail,* the *Civil War Trail,* and the *Red Creek Trail,* may be traversed in their entirety only by permission from the private land owners.

Trails on the grounds of educational institutions are rare; only West Virginia University cited its forestry trails and arboretum trails. Because it is a state university, all the trails are open to the public; its restrictions are described below. Some trails on private property are rarely hiked. An example is the spectacular annual October hike guided by Joseph R. Gregory, PO Box 26, Hendricks, WV 26271.

▶ BOY SCOUTS OF AMERICA

West Virginia has eight Boy Scout Councils with 12 camps or reservations that comprise a total of 6053 acres (5150 in state and 903 outside the state). There are also four other councils outside the state that serve West Virginia counties. Hiking, backpacking, and camping have long been a significant part of scouts' outdoor experiences, and their outdoor code is a model for all hikers. Some excerpts are: "As an American I will do my best to treat the outdoors as a heritage to be improved for our greater enjoyment. . . . I will be careful with fire. . . . I will treat private and public property with respect. I will remember that use of the outdoors is a privilege I can lose by abuse... and I will learn how to practice good conservation of soil, forests, minerals, grasslands, and wildlife. . . ."

Although they hike on their own private trails, they also take long hikes on public and semi-public trails in and out of the state, such as the *Appalachian Trail, Chesapeake and Ohio Trail, Warrior Trail, Anthony Wayne Trail, Buckeye Trail,* and the *Big Blue Trail.* Numerous trails in the Monongahela National Forest are also used. Medals, patches, and pins are awarded the scouts when hiking "accredited scouting trails."

The Tri-State Council, Boy Scouts of America (BSA), has two major private trails open to the public, in Cabell, Mason, and Putnam counties. Permission and advance notice are required to hike the *Adahi Trail* (19.5 mi) and the *Kanawha Trace* (31.7 mi). Both are accessible from Camp Arrowhead. The *Adahi Trail* has its S terminus here and the *Kanawha Trace* passes through on its E–W route. Access to Camp Arrowhead is on Blue Sulphur Rd (CO-17), N from the community of Blue Sulphur (W of Ona on US-60), and Boy Scout Rd (CO-17/4). The *Adahi Trail* runs jointly for 1.5 mi with the *Kanawha Trace* before its N route to the Ohio River. It has a number of historic sites, with an emphasis on pioneer life, Civil War skirmishes, and the Albert Gallatin Jenkins Historical Marker.

The *Kanawha Trace* is actually a combination of trails — the *Midland Trail*, the *James and Kanawha River Turnpike*, and the *Hannan Trace*. The W trailhead of the *Kanawha Trace* is at the Woody Williams Bridge, jct of Merrick Creek Rd (CO-19) and Mud River Rd (CO-21), at the N edge of Barboursville. It reaches Camp Arrowhead at 5.3 mi and Williams Shelter at 5.5 mi, then runs jointly with the *Adahi Trail* from 9.2 mi to 10.7 mi. At 14.6 mi, on Dry Ridge Rd (CO-11), is Meadows Grocery and at 19.9 mi is Blackjack School Camp (use of building requires advance registration). The E trailhead (31.7 mi) is at Fraziers Bottom on US-35 near the Kanawha River at Sider's Country Store.

• INFORMATION: Tri-State Council, BSA, 733 7th Ave, Huntington, WV 25701, tel: 304-523-3408. The council has published a *Guidebook to Hiking the Kanawha Trace*, by Charles Dundas and John Gibson. The guidebook has mileposts, elevation points, descriptions, and topo map routes. Charles Dundas's address is PO Box 169, Lesage, WV 25537, tel: 304-523-3082.

A semi-private trail is the 30-mi *Wyatt Trail* in Kanawha County between St Albans and Kanawha State Forest. Created in honor of Bill Wyatt of Troop 146 of the Buckskin Area Council, the trail emphasizes biological life, old RR grades, mining areas, and scenic countryside. Permission, a guide, and advance notice are required. (See Kanawha State Forest, Chapter 7.)

• INFORMATION: Roger Rassmussen, Troop 146, 2519 Winter St, St Albans, WV 25177, tel: 304-727-8492; or Buckskin Council, BSA, 2829 Kanawha Blvd, E. Charleston, WV 25311, tel: 304-925-0319.

Other Boy Scout council addresses are: Appalachian Council, BSA, PO Box 1498, Bluefield, WV 24701, tel: 703-326-3303; Central WV Council, BSA, 227 S, 3rd St, Clarksburg, WV 26301, tel: 304-623-3379; Chief Cornstalk Council, BSA, PO Box 1710, Logan, WV 25601, tel: 304-752-4428; Kootaga Council, BSA, 1340 Juliana St, Parkersburg, WV 26101, tel: 304-277-4507; Mountaineer Council, BSA, PO Box 388, Fairmont, WV 26555, tel: 304-366-3940; and National Trail Council, BSA, PO Box 6186, Wheeling, WV 26003, tel: 304-277-2660.

Councils outside the state are Fort Steuben Council, BSA, 135 N 4th St, Steubenville, Ohio 43952, tel: 614-282-3669, which includes Brooke and Hancock counties; Potomac Council, BSA, PO Box 212, Cumberland, MD 21502, tel: 301-729-1300, which includes Grant, Hampshire, Hardy, and Mineral counties; Shenandoah Council, BSA, PO Box 3207, Winchester, VA 22601, tel: 703-622-2551, which includes Berkeley, Jefferson, and Morgan counties; and Stonewall Jackson Council, BSA, PO Box 813, Waynesboro, VA 22980, tel: 703-943-6675, which includes Pendleton County.

Although no Girl Scout Councils listed trails open to the public, interested hikers may contact the Girl Scouts of America, National Office, 830 Third Ave, New York, NY 10022, tel: 212-940-7500.

▶ COOLFONT RESORT
(Berkeley Springs)

Coolfont is a private, family-owned resort in a scenic valley between Cacapon Mtn and Warm Springs Ridge near historic Berkeley Springs. Open to the public all year, it is a 1200-acre retreat described as "Re+Creation" for recreation and a center for renewing and restoring the human "mind and senses." The resort has a conference center, the famous Treetop House Restaurant, a lodge, chalets, cabins, deluxe mountain homes, a health spa, and health workshops (including one on stress management). Recreational activities include hiking, fishing (no license required), horseback riding, boating, tennis, biking, summer day camps, summer swimming (and indoor pool), winter cross-country skiing, and ice skating. Cultural events are chamber music, a film series, and an artist-in-residence. Its campground has 103 units, 33 that have full service. There are central rest rooms and hot showers. There is also a laundry and wood supply. The campground is open Easter through Thanksgiving, and the facility is 6 mi NW of Cacapon State Park (which does not have a campground). (*USGS Map:* Great Cacapon)

• ADDRESS AND ACCESS: Manager, Coolfont, PO Box 613, Berkeley Springs, WV 25411, tel: 304-258-4500. At the jct of US-522 and WV-9 in Berkeley Springs take WV-9 W for 0.7 mi; turn L on Coolfont Rd and go 3.7 mi. From Cacapon State Park, go N on US-522 for 3.6 mi, turn L on Quarry Rd and go 2.4 mi.

White Trail (1.8 mi); *Green-Orange Trail* (1.3 mi); *Green Trail* (2.5 mi); *Blue-Orange Trail* (0.8 mi); *Blue-Red Trail* (0.6 mi); *Blue Trail* (1 mi)

• LENGTH: 8 mi, ct

• DIFFICULTY: moderate to strenuous

• FEATURES: wildlife, scenic

• TRAILHEADS AND DETAILS: No camping is allowed on the trails. At the jct of the Cold Run Valley Rd and the Manor House Rd, turn on the Manor House Rd. To the R begin the *White Trail* and the *Green-Orange Trail*. Follow the bridle trail briefly and then begin ascending on the *White Trail*. (Some sections are exceptionally steep.) Chestnut oak, sassafras, scrub pine, beech, and basswood are in the forest. Jct with *Green Trail*, R, at 0.8 mi. (The 2.5 mi *Green Trail* goes W and gradually ascends the mountain to the scenic Prospect Rock. Along the way it jct with the *Green-Orange Trail,* R, at 0.6 mi.) Continue on the *White Trail,* pass a rocky area and jct with *Blue-Orange Trail* at 1.6 mi. (The *Blue-Orange Trail* goes R to Prospect Rock.) The *White Trail* goes L for 0.2 mi to its terminus at the beginning of the *Blue-Red Trail,* L, and the *Blue Trail,* R. (The *Blue-Red Trail* ascends steeply to the ridge line and drops acutely to its terminus at Rock Slab, a spectacular view of Coolfont and the valley.) The *Blue Trail* also ascends steeply but veers R at the Cacapon Mtn ridge line to Prospect Rock (1500 ft). From here are views of West Virginia, Virginia, Maryland, and Pennsylvania. Also, there are views of the Cacapon River, Potomac River, and the town of Great Cacapon. Return on either the *Blue-Orange Trail* (descent of 2.4 mi to highway) or on the *Green Trail* (descent of 3.3 mi to highway). Wildflowers on these trails are mandrake, starry champion, sweet cicely, spearmint, and tall bellflower. Deer, grouse, squirrel, and wild turkey are the most frequently seen animals.

Yellow Trail (2.1 mi); Yellow-Red Trail (1.1 mi); Yellow-Orange Trail (1.1 mi)

- LENGTH: 4.3 mi, ct

- DIFFICULTY: easy to moderate

- FEATURES: history, scenic

- TRAILHEADS AND DETAILS: No camping is allowed on the trails. These trails begin or connect from the campground in a hardwood forest. The *Yellow Trail* begins behind the Treetop House Restaurant, between Lake Lisa (smaller of the two) and Lake Siri at the picnic grove. Cross the footbridge and ascend into the campground area. Cross a campground road between sites #17 and #21 and jct with the *Yellow-Red Trail* at 0.4 mi. Join the *Yellow-Red Trail* for a few yds and then turn R to curve and ascend to Warm Springs Ridge. Turn R on the ridge and descend to the Bobcat Section of the campground. Cross the *Yellow-Red Trail* and reach the trail's end at a road intersection in the Crow Section of the campground after 2.1 mi.

At the E end of the road in the Crow Section of the campground, begin the *Yellow-Red Trail.* It ascends, turns W, crosses the *Yellow Trail,* and joins the *Yellow Trail* ahead on the slope. It soon separates to end where the *Yellow-Orange Trail* begins. The *Yellow-Orange Trail* circles a ridge knob of Warm Springs Ridge, passes the Old Lime Furnace, and returns to connect with the *Yellow-Red Trail,* or take a R and descend to the Cold Run Valley highway.

▶ FOX FIRE RESORT
(Cabell County)

A private campground "designed with the family in mind," the Fox Fire Resort has 122 full-service campsites and standard facilities. The resort also has some special features. For example, the second weekend in May is the Bluegrass Music and Hot Air Balloon Festival. Other facilities are the Slippery Creek Water Slide, picnic areas, swimming and fishing lakes, sport fields, and tent campground. If you just wish to hike the trail, request a visitor pass. (*USGS Map:* Milton)

• ADDRESS AND ACCESS: Manager, Fox Fire Resort, Rte 2, Box 291-C, Milton, WV 25541, tel: 304-743-5622. From the town of Milton go W on US-60 for 2 mi and turn R.

Fox Fire Nature Trail

• LENGTH: 1.1 mi

• DIFFICULTY: easy

• FEATURE: nature study

• TRAILHEADS AND DETAILS: Park at the old barn in the campground, ascend on a paved road to the top of the hill and to an observation tower at 0.2 mi. Bear L, descend in a forest of locust, poplar, oak, and pine at 0.5 mi. Reach the resort main road, turn L, and return to the point of beginning.

▶ HUNTINGTON GALLERIES
(Huntington)

Huntington Galleries is the state's largest professionally accredited art museum; it is also a preserve with an arboreal display and a network of nature trails in its 52 acres. In its cultural complex are elegant exhibits of paintings, silver, artifacts, and glass; an observatory; an art library and studios; and an auditorium for film and performing arts. It is open year-round, Tues–Sat, 10 A.M.–5 P.M. and Sun 12–5 P.M. There is an admission charge in the galleries, but the trails are open to the public free of charge. Volunteer assistance on the trails includes the Jr. League of Garden Clubs, Women's Club of Huntington, and Tri-State Community. (*USGS Map:* Huntington)

- ADDRESS AND ACCESS: Nature Coordinator, Huntington Galleries, Park Hills, Huntington, WV 25701, tel: 304-529-2701. From the jct of I-64 and WV-527 (exit 8) drive 0.1 mi on WV-527 to Miller Rd; turn R. Drive 1 mi and turn L on McCullough Rd and go 0.6 mi.

Tulip Tree Trail (1 mi); Sculpture Trail (0.2 mi); Spicebush Trail (0.3 mi)

- LENGTH: 1.5 mi, ct

- DIFFICULTY: moderate

- FEATURE: nature study

- TRAILHEADS AND DETAILS: From the parking area walk to the R of the building to the trailhead for the *Tulip Tree Trail.* Descend on a well-graded trail, pass R of the *Sculpture Trail,* curve E and N and then SW to jct with the *Spicebush Trail* (loop) at 0.4 mi. Among the tall hardwoods are sugar maple, red and white oaks, yellow poplar (tulip tree), beech, black locust, ash, and hickory. Wildflowers include sweet cicely, May apple, and trillium. Spicebush, ferns, and mosses are prominent. Gray squirrels and chipmunks are likely to be seen on the trails.

Ascend, steeply in sections, and jct with the *Sculpture Trail*, L, at 0.8 mi. Return on either trail for a total route of 1.5 mi.

▶ MARY INGLES TRAIL

The Mary Ingles Chapter of the West Virginia Scenic Trails Association was formed in 1983 by Bob Tabor and associates. The purpose was to organize groups for planning and developing a 500-mi trail to commemorate the heroic journey of Mary Draper Ingles. At the age of 23 she was captured by a Shawnee Indian war party in a massacre at Draper's Meadow (now the area of VPI and State University in Blacksburg, Virginia). Several months after her capture, she escaped near Big Bone Lick (now a state park) in Boone County, Kentucky, and found her way home by following the Ohio, Kanawha, and New rivers. Her successful escape, survival, and journey for approximately 500 mi are described by a grandson, John P. Hale, in *Trans Allegheny Pioneers*. Other historic information has been available from a descendant, Mrs. Roberta Ingles Steele, of Radford, Virginia. Retracing Ingles' route, researching land rights, acquiring easements from private owners (on whose property most of the route lies), trail construction, securing volunteers, and funding are the goals of the WVSTA chapter.

The first 2 mi are yellow-blazed from the footbridge at Wolf Creek to Kaymoor mine. Access is on WV-82, 2.8 mi from US-19, W of the bridge, and 0.9 mi up the mountain from Fayette Station. The scenic trail is an old mining road among hemlocks, oaks, maple, beech, ferns, wildflowers, mountain laurel, and rhododendron along the New River Gorge National River.

• INFORMATION: Mary Ingles Chapter, West Virginia Scenic Trails Association, PO Box 813, Fayetteville, WV 25840, tel: 304-574-0225 or 304-743-3968.

▶ PINE HILL CAMPGROUND
(Preston County)

In the NE corner of the state there is a quiet 110-acre scenic nature preserve that has the ideal campground. It reminds you of Roy Lee Harmon's "West Virginia June" with "hallowed hills" and where "plain old troubles just melt away." Franklin and Norma Sparber have designed this retreat with generous care for 30 years, and the care for campers is equally generous. Facilities include 60 campsites (all with water and electric hookups, and some with sewage hookups); picnic areas; playground; tent sites; flush toilets and hot showers; and nature trails. The campground is within 30 minutes of the Cheat Lake Resort and the Deep Creek Lake Resort. (*USGS Map:* Brandonville)

• ADDRESS AND ACCESS: Pine Hill Campground, Rte 3, Bruceton Mill, WV 26523, tel: 304-379-4612 (or 216-466-1451). From exit 29 on US-48 in Hazelton drive S on CO-5/18 (look for campground signs) for 3 mi to jct. Turn R on Cherry Grove Mountaindale Rd (CO-5/14) and go 1.3 mi to the entrance, R.

Blackberry Trail; Lone Pine Trail; Red Pine Trail; Overlook Trail

• LENGTH: 1 mi, rt, ct

• DIFFICULTY: easy

• FEATURE: nature study

• TRAILHEADS AND DETAILS: Because the manicured trails overlap and interloop with each other, they are measured as a unit. Follow the trail signs from the parking area through a network of walkways that may take you on side trails in spruce and pine to an overlook toward Kelly's Knob. The Sparbers may change the trail designs and the names; thus, each visit is a new nature study. The trails are open to the public without charge, but the owners request you notify them if you are on the grounds.

▶ PONDEROSA POND PARK
(Morgantown)

Kennedy's Ponderosa Pond, Inc., has 225 acres of a private forest for hiking and camping. Other facilities are for fishing (ponds stocked weekly), hunting, and swimming. The campground has electrical and water hookups as well as hot showers. Open March 15–November 15. The *Ponderosa Pond Trail* begins at a sign in the campground. Go across the creek to a woods road for a nondirectional hike on any of the spur paths. The forest has cherry, maple, beech, and locust with flowering mountain laurel and rhododendron. (*USGS Map:* Morgantown South)

• ADDRESS AND ACCESS: M.F. Kennedy, Rte 10, Box 158, Morgantown, WV 26505, tel: 304-292-9174. From US-48 and WV-7 (exit 4), go N on WV-7 for 1.4 mi and turn L at the traffic light onto CO-857. After 2.1 mi turn L at the 4-way stop on Old Kingwood Pike (CO-81) and drive 2.1 mi to sign on L. Drive on a steep road down to a meadow for another 0.6 mi.

▶ THE RIVERMEN CAMPGROUND
(Fayetteville)

The Rivermen are white water rafting specialists with a campground only 2 mi from the New River Gorge Bridge. Their chief guided raft trips are on the New River, Gauley River, and the Big South Fork. Their base camp has a motel, restaurant, lounge, and campground with hot showers, picnic shelters, and hookups. A foot trail forms a crescent at the campground. (*USGS Map:* Fayetteville)

• ADDRESS AND ACCESS: The Rivermen, PO Box 360, Fayetteville, WV 25850, tel: 304-574-0515. On US-19 in Fayetteville, turn W on Laurel Creek Rd and take the first R.

Laurel Trail

- LENGTH: 0.7 mi

- DIFFICULTY: easy

- FEATURE: nature study

- TRAILHEADS AND DETAILS: From the meeting center walk up-hill to a group camping area in a grassy field. Cross the field and follow the trail through a forest of dogwood, black gum, oak, and Virginia pine. Curve around the campground and cross a footbridge at 0.5 mi. Pass through a section of rhodo-dendron, Christmas fern, and Indian Pipe to return to the parking area.

▶ SPELEOLOGY TRAILS

In the eastern Appalachians of the state are large limestone belts estimated to be 395 million years old. In them are thou-sands of caves, fissures, subterranean waters, and sinks. The most geologically significant caves have become commercial. They are Organ Cave, one of the longest in the world (40 mi), near Ronceverte; Lost World Cave, a registered national land-mark near Lewisburg; Seneca Caverns, noted for their flow-stone colors; and Smoke Hole Cavern, which has the world's longest ribbon stalactite, near Petersburg. These and other less known caves, also on private property, are protected by West Virginia state law, code WV-20/7A. Part of these regulations are: "It is illegal to write, mark, break, or deface, or remove any natural material, or to dump refuse, or to disturb, or harm the bats, or other living creatures, or to disturb any artifacts, or bones." Underground hiking can be dangerous, and inexperi-enced hikers should have both a guide and proper equipment.

- INFORMATION: West Virginia Speleological Survey, PO Box 200, Barrackville, WV 26559. West Virginia Geological and Economic Survey, PO Box 879, Morgantown, WV 26507, tel: 304-594-2331. For guided cave explorations contact Venture

Underground, PO Box 6C, Ronceverte, WV 24970 tel: 304-645-6984.

Saltpeter Cave Trail

* LENGTH: 0.6 mi

* DIFFICULTY: moderate

* FEATURES: history, geology, zoology

•TRAILHEADS AND DETAILS: The *Saltpeter Cave Trail* is in the Saltpeter Caves of Monroe County. There are two essential preparations for this hike. First, call or write the owners and request permission. You may also do so on your arrival. The owners are Byron and Thelma Rudell, Box 59, Greenville, WV 24945, tel: 304-832-6210. The other preparation is to select a guide; otherwise, do not go alone. Wear a hard hat, hiking boots or work shoes, warm clothing, and take a 6-volt, heavy-duty lantern (for example: Ray-O-Vac sportsman lantern or Dacor; an extra flashlight is advisable).

From the jct of US-219 and WV-122 at Raines Corner (1.8 mi N of Rock Camp), drive W on WV-122 for 4.6 mi to jct of Laurel Creek Rd (CO-23/4). (Entrance from the W to Greenville on WV-122 at jct with WV-12, Forest Hill, is 7 mi.) A state marker on the caves is at the Laurel Creek Rd jct. (Ahead in Greenville it is 0.4 mi to the center of the community; the property owners live in the fourth house, R, the general store.) At the marker, take Laurel Creek Rd N and descend for 0.4 mi to a little red barn, R, and a fence gate, L. Park off the road, cross the locked gate, and follow a cow path in the meadow for 0.2 mi to the large mouth of the water cave entrance, downstream. Enter with caution, rock hop the stream for 100 yds, and ascend on the embankment, R. A white arrow offers some assistance in direction. The treadway is rocky or sandy. There are high-vaulted ceilings with colonies of bats and huge boulders along the route. (There is a R spur route that leads into the other side trails and requires backbending to reach the saltpeter cave mines and another access on the W side of the

mountain, where Jacob and John Mann manufactured saltpeter for several years.) Stalagmites on the floor and stalactites
on the ceiling are not prominent. Exit on the S side of the ridge
at 0.6 mi. Backtrack or turn R and walk up the valley past a
barn and saltpeter cave entrance (fenced) and return to the
point of entry for 0.8 mi. (*USGS-FS Map:* Greenville)

Sinks of Gandy Trail

* LENGTH: 0.6 mi

* DIFFICULTY: moderate

* FEATURES: geology, zoology

* TRAILHEADS AND DETAILS: The Sinks of Gandy are on private
property in Randolph County. As described above, there are
some necessary preparations for underground trails. First,
write or notify the owner on arrival (Max D. Teter, Rte 2, Box
10, Glady, WV 26268) of your identity and the others with you.
(There are no telephones in this area.) Other preparations are
to wear a hard hat and take a heavy-duty, preferably waterproof, 6-volt hand lantern or flashlight (also, an extra flashlight is advisable). Because you will get wet and muddy, wear
warm clothes and shoes you can use for this purpose only. *Note:*
Do not enter the Gandy Creek cave when there is danger of a
flash flood, and do not wade in still deep water or enter water
where there is danger of underground suction.

For access, drive 10.3 mi from Whitmer on the Whitmer Rd
(CO-29) to a jct with FR-1 (Spruce Knob Area). Turn R and
continue on Whitmer Rd for 0.5 mi to jct with Dry Fork Rd
(CO-40), R. Keep L, make a sharp curve after 0.7 mi, and after
another 0.8 mi reach the mail box and entrance gate L to the
Teter farm ranch. (From here it is 4.1 mi ahead to Laurel Fork
Campground and Wilderness Area. Be sure to close the gates
between here and the Teter house.) Park in the meadow (0.3
mi from Dry Fork Rd) near the mouth of Gandy Creek cave
(3500 ft elev.) Barn swallows (*Hirundo rustica*) have built nests at
the cave entrance, and you may see cave salamanders (*Eurycea*

lucifuga) on some of the mud flats in the dark tunnel. There are some difficult passages in the stream, and footholds are deep in the sticky and slick clay. At 0.5 mi an embankment on the R of still water has a hole, which is the only passage out to a large dry area of high vaults. Exit is on the hillside, R of the stream. (Jim Tingler owns the property on this side of the cave.) A return can be over the hill and through the pastures. (This area is scenic in any season, particularly the open slopes of Yokum Knob [4270 ft] to the NW, the red spruce groves near the sinks, and a profuse variety of wildflowers in the pastures.) (*USGS-FS Map:* Sinks of Gandy)

▶ **SUNRISE MUSEUMS**
  (Charleston)

Sunrise Museums is a 16-acre cultural and educational complex with two historic mansions, a museum, children's museum and planetarium, gardens, nature center, and nature trails. The privately supported nonprofit Sunrise Foundation, Inc., is funded primarily by membership dues and private contributions. The children's museum is the former home of William A. MacCorkle, ninth governor of West Virginia. It was built by him in 1905 and named after his family home in Virginia. On the grounds of the children's museum is an analemmic sundial, the largest in the state. Visiting hours are Tues–Sat, 10 A.M.–5 P.M. and Sun 2–5 P.M. Guided tours arranged by appointment.

• ADDRESS AND ACCESS: Sunrise Museums, 746 Myrtle Rd, Charleston, WV 25314, tel: 304-344-8035. From the jct of Bridge Rd and Virginia St downtown, take Bridge Rd across the river, ascend, and turn R on Myrtle Rd to parking area. Another access is at the jct of MacCorkle Ave (US-119 and WV-61) and Thayer St, near the Amtrak station.

Garden Trail of the Five Senses (86 yds); *Sunrise Carriage Trail* (0.7 mi)

- LENGTH: 1.5 mi, rt, ct

- DIFFICULTY: easy to moderate

- FEATURES: Braille signs, scenic, historic

- TRAILHEAD AND DETAILS: From the parking area walk to the L of the children's museum through a rose and herb garden to the old carriage road. Here is the *Garden Trail of the Five Senses*, created chiefly for the visually handicapped by the Kanawha Garden Council Patrons. Descend on the carriage road. There are scenic views of the city and resting benches along the trail. Natural vegetation includes papaw, hemlock, buckeye, poplar, oak, and rhododendron. At 0.7 mi the carriage road ends at its former entrance near MacCorkle Ave and Bridge Rd. Backtrack.

▶ WARRIOR TRAIL ASSOCIATION

The 67-mile *Warrior Trail* has 45.5 mi in Pennsylvania and 22 mi in Marshall County, West Virginia. It has been developed by the 145-member Warrior Trail Association of Waynesburg, Pennsylvania. Originally the trail had aluminum strip blazes, but now it has yellow paint blazes. It crosses the 27-mi *Catawba Trail* in Greene County, Pennsylvania, S of Kirby, between US-29 and I-79. The *Catawba Trail* is another trail developed by the association. In recent years the West Virginia section of the *Warrior Trail*, which is on private lands, has not been maintained, though the association has continued to invite West Virginia assistance. The trail enters the state E of Cameron, crosses Woodruff Rd (CO-98) and US-250 one mi S of Cameron, and traverses the main E/W ridgeline to Woodlands at WV-2 and the Ohio River. Hikers interested in the West Virginia section of the *Warrior Trail* should seek information from one of the sources below before attempting a through hike.

• INFORMATION: Warrior Trail Association, 313 County Office Bldg, Waynesburg, PA 15370 (Attn: Bert Waychoff), tel: 412-627-5030 (office), 412-627-5039 (home). A set of maps of the Pennsylvania section is available for $3 from James Hennen, 519 4th Ave, Waynesburg, PA 15370, tel: 412-527-5255.

▶ WEST VIRGINIA UNIVERSITY
(Morgantown)

West Virginia University, founded in 1867, has over 22,500 students and is the largest educational institution in the state. It is located in Morgantown, a city known for having more hand-made-glass factories than any other American city and for its computer-controlled rapid transit system. Settled in 1772, the city received its name from Zackquill Morgan, son of Morgan Morgan, who became the state's first permanent settler in 1731, when he settled in what is now Berkeley County. Although the university is the focal point of the city, the federal government has a number of research centers here, among them the Forest Sciences Laboratory, a Bureau of Mines research center, and the Appalachian Laboratory for Occupational Respiratory Diseases. The university has two major areas of interest to hikers: the Core Arboretum and the University Forest.

▶ THE CORE ARBORETUM

This 75-acre arboretum was established in 1948 on a forest slope between Monongahela Blvd and the Monongahela River by the Department of Biology. It was originally designed as an outdoor biology laboratory for study and research and for public educational purposes. In 1954 it was officially dedicated and opened to the public as the West Virginia University Arboretum under the leadership and direction of Earl L. Core, professor of biology at the university. On July 1, 1975, the arboretum was named the Core Arboretum in his honor (Dr.

Core and Dr. P.D. Strausbaugh are the authors of a definitive, 1075-page work titled *Flora of West Virginia*, first published in 1952.)

- ADDRESS AND ACCESS: Curator, The Core Arboretum, Department of Biology, Brooks Hall, West Virginia University, Morgantown, WV 26506, tel: 304-293-5201. From exit 155 on I-79, turn E on US-19/WV-7 (Monongahela Blvd), pass the coliseum, and park R at the arboretum sign.

Circular Trail, Strausbaugh Trail, Sheldon Trail, Nuttall Trail, Granville Island Trail, Rumsey Trail, Taylor Trail, Brown Trail

- LENGTH: 2.8 mi, rt, ct
- DIFFICULTY: easy to moderate
- FEATURE: botanical study

- TRAILHEAD AND DETAILS: These trails all connect in a pattern suitable for short loops (such as the 0.2-mi *Circular Trail*) or extended loops, with some unmarked spurs in between. Elev change is 240 ft. The longest circuit, 1.6 mi, is described below. Begin on the *Circular Trail*, R, and descend on the *Strausbaugh Trail* (named in honor of Dr. P.D. Strausbaugh, former chairman of the university's Department of Biology). Some trees seen on this trail are black cherry, hackberry, sweet birch, black and sugar maples, and oak. Wildflowers include black cohosh, trillium, twinleaf, Celandine poppy *(Stylophorum diphyllum)*, and starry campion *(Silene stellata)*. Pass the *Sheldon Trail*, L (named in honor of Dr. John L. Sheldon, former professor of botany at the university). This trail is noted for its springtime display of wildflowers, particularly Virginia bluebells *(Mertensia virginica)*.

Cross the B&O RR at 0.5 mi and pass the *Nuttall Trail*, L (it parallels the RR in a low area near the lagoon and has a number of aquatic plants). The chinquapin oak near the jct with the *Sheldon Trail* is thought to be the second largest in the state. Parallel the Monongahela River on the *Granville Island Trail*, R of the lagoon, at 0.6 mi. Silver maple, black willow, jewelweed, and ground ivy are prominent. Curve L to the east jct of the *Nuttall Trail* (named for Lawrence W. Nuttall, a distinguished amateur botanist from Fayette County). Cross the B&O RR again at 0.9 mi and at 1 mi jct with the *Rumsey Trail,* R (it is named in honor of William E. Rumsey, a former state entomologist). Follow the *Rumsey Trail* through a hollow where oak, walnut, and maple tower over natural beds of wildflowers. Ascend, and at 1.3 mi reach a trail jct with the Melvin *Brown Trail,* L, and the *Taylor Trail,* R. Among the trees in this area are elm, white ash, shagbark hickory, and red oak. The trail is named for Leland H. Taylor, a former professor of zoology at the University. At 1.6 mi return to the *Circular Trail,* where a wide range of native trees and shrubs has been planted.

▶ **WEST VIRGINIA UNIVERSITY FOREST**
 (Monongalia and Preston Counties)

In 1959 the West Virginia University Division of Forestry joined in a long-term lease arrangement with the state's Department of Natural Resources for 7500 acres in Coopers Rock State Forest (see Chapter 7). Conveniently located within 12 mi of the University, the forest is used for outdoor classwork, field trips, research and forest management, and recreational activities. School groups and organizations interested in a field trip may contact the forest manager for arrangements. The day-use only forest is open to the public for licensed fishing and hunting, cross-country skiing, and hiking. The forest headquarters is open weekdays, 8 A.M.–5 P.M. (*USGS Maps:* Lake Lynn, Bruceton Mills)

• ADDRESS AND ACCESS: Forest Manager, WVU Forest, Rte 1, Box 269, Bruceton Mills, WV 26526, tel: 304-292-6003. Drive 10.5 mi E of Morgantown from the jct of US-48 and WV-7 on expressway US-48, or 8 mi W of Bruceton Mills, exit #15. Go N on Chestnut Ridge Rd (CO-73/1, also called Sand Springs Rd) for 2 mi to WVU Forest headquarters on the L.

Virgin Hemlock Trail

- LENGTH: 1.2 mi

- DIFFICULTY: easy

- FEATURE: virgin hemlock grove

- TRAILHEAD AND DETAILS: From Coopers Rock State Forest headquarters (at US-48, exit 15, N) drive E on CO-73/73 for 2.4 mi and park near a culvert and trail sign. Follow a white-blazed trail into a rocky area with trillium, rhododendron, and wood sorrel. Cross a footbridge over Lick Run, turn L at 0.2 mi, follow old tram road through mountain laurel and rhodo-dendron thickets and groves of tall virgin eastern hemlock (*Tsuga canadensis*). Reach a jct with *Tryon's Trail* at 0.6 mi. (*Tryon's Trail* leads upstream for 0.7 mi to connect with *Ken's Run Trail*.) Cross Little Laurel Run, ascend to an old road, but turn R after 140 ft at 0.7 mi. Descend on a slope through hardwoods with spots of wintergreen and trailing arbutus. Cross Little Creek, rejoin the trail, and return to the parking area at 1.2 mi. (The state champion hemlock is in Cathedral State Park.)

Ken's Run Trail

- LENGTH: 6.3 mi, rt

- DIFFICULTY: moderate

- FEATURE: forest study

- TRAILHEADS AND DETAILS: From the WVU Forest headquar-ters drive 0.2 mi N on the Chestnut Ridge Rd (also called Sand Springs Rd) and turn R to the old Archery Range parking area. Follow the trail sign and descend on an old road through a verdant forest of red spruce and pine, oak, maple, poplar, and hickory to the S side of Little Laurel Run. Cross a gas pipeline at 1.2 mi. Continue downstream on an old RR grade for an-other 0.6 mi to a Little Laurel Run tributary, L, and *Tryon's Trail*, R. (*Tryon's Trail* is a 0.6 mi connector trail downstream to the *Virgin Hemlock Trail*.) Follow the trail L upstream, parallel with Ken's Run to an old logging and hunting road at 2.8 mi. Turn L on the road, pass under a power line at 4.1 mi and pass R of the WVU-TV tower to Chestnut Ridge Rd at 4.6 mi. (On the road, L, is an access road for 0.3 mi to Sand Springs fire tower, partially dismantled.) A hike S on the road for 1.7 mi makes a loop back to the parking area at 6.3 mi.

Ryan Nature Trail

- LENGTH: 1.7 mi
- DIFFICULTY: easy
- FEATURE: nature study
- TRAILHEAD AND DETAILS: From the old Archery Range parking area (described above) follow the trail signs through white pine, Norway spruce, red pine plantations, and among hardwoods such as aspen, black cherry, birch, black walnut, hickory, poplar, and maple. Ferns and wildflowers, past land use, forest succession, old iron pits, and wildlife fields are part of the interpretive trail. (This trail is under reconstruction.)

Glade Run Trail (1.4 mi); Lick Run Trail (1.7 mi)

- LENGTH: 3.1 mi, ct
- DIFFICULTY: moderate
- FEATURE: black cherry plantation
- TRAILHEADS AND DETAILS: From the jct of Chestnut Ridge Rd and CO-73/73 0.5 mi E from the Coopers Rock State Forest headquarters, drive 1.1 mi N on Chestnut Ridge Rd. *Glade Run Trail* is on the L and *Lick Run Trail* is on the R. (A loop can be made by walking 1.5 mi on CO-73/73 to connect the trails for a combined total of 4.8 mi.) On the beautiful *Glade Run Trail* gradually descend, pass through a black cherry plantation, and at 0.7 mi cross Glade Run. Under a canopy of deciduous trees are rhododendron, mountain laurel, spicebush, and numerous wildflowers such as downy false foxglove *(Aureolaria virginica)*

and wild indigo *(Baptisia tinctoria)*. Reach Coopers Rock Lake (Trout Pond) at 1.4 mi. Backtrack or walk 0.2 mi around the lake to CO-73/73 (Old 73). It is 2.2 mi L on the Old 73 Rd and Chestnut Ridge Rd to the point of origin for a loop of 3.8 mi.

On the *Lick Run Trail* descend on an old woods road through a forest of tall poplar, cherry, oak, and hickory in a moist treadway to CO-73/73 (Old 73) at 1.7 mi. Backtrack or walk the CO-73/73 R and the Chestnut Ridge Rd to the point of origin for a loop of 3.2 mi.

Goodspeed's Highway Trail *(2.7 mi)*; Johnson Hollow Trail *(3.5 mi)*; Darnell Hollow Trail *(2.4 mi)*

- LENGTH: 10.6 mi, rt, ct

- DIFFICULTY: moderate to strenuous

- FEATURES: wildlife, forest study

- TRAILHEADS AND DETAILS: With a combination of old tram roads, jeep roads, and state secondary roads, these trails can form two pleasurable loops from the SW corner of the forest. The first and shortest loop combines part of *Goodspeed's Highway Trail* and all of *Johnson Hollow Trail* for 5.5 mi. The second and longest loop combines all of *Goodspeed's Highway Trail*, all of *Darnell Hollow Trail*, an old jeep road, and part of *Johnson Hollow Trail* for 8.9 mi.

Begin at the parking area at the W end of CO-73/73 (2.4 mi from Cooper's Rock State Forest headquarters at exit 15 of US-48). Hike 0.3 mi up Quarry Run Rd (CO-69/5) to joint trailheads of *Goodspeed's Highway Trail* and *Johnson Hollow Trail*. Go R on *Goodspeed's Highway Trail*, the old "Glade Ridge Road," and ascend on a ridge. In the forest are maple, oak, poplar, hickory, cherry, and mountain laurel. Pass under a power line at 0.3 mi and reach the ridge crest N of Quarry Run, and at 2 mi jct with *Johnson Hollow Trail*, L. (The *Goodspeed's Highway Trail* continues R and is described below.)

Take the *Johnson Hollow Trail* and descend steeply for 0.9 mi to a stream crossing; follow downstream on a slope, R of Johnson Hollow Run, for another 0.7 mi. Cross Johnson Hollow Run and jct with a jeep road, R. Curve L on the *Johnson Hollow Trail* around a ridge and at 4.9 mi cross Birch Hollow Run. Pass under a power line at 5.0 mi and reach the point of beginning at 5.5 mi.

For the longer loop, take the first 2.0 mi of the *Goodspeed's Highway Trail* and pass by the *Johnson Hollow Trail*. After another 0.7 mi arrive at the paved Chestnut Ridge Camp Rd (CO-69/2), W of Harris Lake. (To the R it is 0.4 mi to the jct with Sand Springs Rd and the WVU Forest headquarters.) Turn L on the Chestnut Ridge Camp Rd, pass the restored Cheat Mtn School House (1932–1940), and reach a parking area and the E trailhead of the *Darnell Hollow Trail* after 0.4 mi on the road. Descend steeply on a jeep road. The forest is mainly red and white oaks, maple, locust, hickory, ash, cherry, and sassafras. Pines, hemlock, rhododendron, dogwood, and mountain laurel are among the other trees and shrubs. Patches of ferns and wintergreen are prominent. Wildlife includes deer, grouse, wild turkey, raccoon, chipmunk, and red squirrel. At 0.5 mi parallel Darnell Hollow Run, pass a field and an abandoned ski slope. Cross the run and remain on the S slope of the canyon for the remainder of the distance. Pass rocky sections and reach a jct with the Johnson Hollow Rd (CO-69/18), L. (Ahead it is 0.2 mi to Calvary Church and jct with paved Fairchance Rd [CO-857].) Turn L on the Johnson Hollow Rd and go 0.8 mi to where the road becomes a jeep road. Pass under a power line, cross Johnson Hollow Run, and join the *Johnson Hollow Trail* after another 0.8 mi. Turn R on the *Johnson Hollow Trail* and follow it for 1.8 mi to the point of beginning for a circuit of 8.9 mi.

11.

The Allegheny Trail and the Big Blue Trail

The two longest trans-state trails in West Virginia have many characteristics in common. They are N–S trails that begin in Virginia and reach Pennsylvania on a traverse of national forest, state properties, and private properties. They overlap some other named trails in the process. They both have sponsoring organizations that had their roots in parent organizations for direction and security, and the organizations have used similar techniques in approaching land easements and using volunteers for trail maintenance. Parts of both trails are on public roads. Both had guidebooks published about them in 1983–84 by conservationist-hikers who hiked and measured the trails to write from personal experiences. And they both have options for extension: the *Allegheny Trail* to the proposed *Trans-Virginia Trail* or other S routes and to the *Laurel Highlands Trail* in Pennsylvania; and the *Big Blue Trail* to join the *Allegheny Trail* on the *Great North Mountain Trail* in Virginia. They also have their contrasts. The *Allegheny Trail* is unfinished; it has all the excitement of completion dates, section by section. It will also be 150 mi longer than the *Big Blue Trail*. The topography, ecosystems, and types of forest flora and fauna are of greater variety on the *Allegheny Trail*. Each has special points of interest unduplicated by the other.

▶ ALLEGHENY TRAIL

"The ultimate outdoor experience for many of us is building and maintaining trails."
— BOB TABOR

In October 1971, at the close of an Izaak Walton League of America meeting in Charleston, two trail leaders and dreamers, Bob Tabor and Nick Lozano, discussed a "long trail" through West Virginia. Later they shared their thoughts with other trail-oriented leaders and environmentalists, and within a year the concept and initial strategy for both the *Allegheny Trail* and the West Virginia Scenic Trails Association had begun. Since then, 150 mi of the *Allegheny Trail* have been completed in a proposed route of 300 mi from Monroe County in the S through Preston County in the N.

Tabor has said that the development of the *Allegheny Trail* has been modeled on that of the *Appalachian Trail (AT)*, with the West Virginia Scenic Trails Association administratively similar to the Appalachian Trail Conference. "Working all day painting blazes, cutting brush, and moving rocks on the trail makes me feel good about myself," said WVSTA board member Shirley Schweizer, "I feel very fortunate to live in West Virginia and be a part of the Allegheny Trail."

The trail is divided into four long sections with a trail coordinator for each. Section I is from the Pennsylvania-West Virginia state line to Blackwater Falls State Park for approximately 88 mi; Section II is from Blackwater Falls State Park to Cass for 88.9 mi; Section III includes the area from Cass to Meadow Creek near Neola for 63.5 mi; and Section IV is from Meadow Creek/Lake Sherwood Rd to the *Appalachian Trail* at Pine Swamp Branch near the Virginia-West Virginia state line for approximately 55 mi. It is with Section IV that the following S–N trail description begins.

Section IV: Appalachian Trail to Lake Sherwood Road

There are three access routes, all from the *Appalachian Trail*, to the S terminus of the *Allegheny Trail*. One is 1.7 mi, another is 5.7 mi, and the longest is 16.9 mi. To approach the 1.7-mi access route, drive 0.3 mi E from Pearisburg, Virginia, on US-460, and turn L at the White Rocks Recreation Area sign on SR-635. Drive 10 mi to a small parking area, L, near a bridge over Stony Creek. Hike 40 yds on a spur access to the *AT*, turn L, ascend, pass R of the stone Pine Swamp Branch shelter at 0.4 mi, and continue to ascend on a steep rocky footpath. Cross Pine Swamp Branch, which may be running underneath the boulders, depending on the season. Reach a leveling-out area, arbored with rhododendron. On the L are huge hemlocks and on the R is the jct with the *Allegheny Trail* at 1.7 mi. (A short relocation of the *AT* is being considered here.)

To use the 5.7-mi access, take the blue-blazed *Ground Hog Trail*, a side trail that ascends the N side of Peters Mtn in Monroe County, West Virginia. It is accessible from the jct of US-219 and Painters Run Rd (CO-219/21), 2.4 mi SW of Lindside on US-219. After 1.2 mi on Painters Run Rd turn L at jct with Green Valley Rd (CO-219/24) and go 0.5 mi to the parking area on the R. Ascend the *Ground Hog Trail* for 1.8 mi to a jct with the *AT*. Turn L on the *AT* for 3.9 mi to the jct with the *Allegheny Trail* as described above. (See Chapters 2 and 3 for more information on the *Ground Hog Trail*.) The longest route, 16.9 mi, follows the *AT* from the Senator Shumate Bridge in N Pearisburg N to the jct with the *Allegheny Trail*.

Follow the *Allegheny Trail* for 0.3 mi on a slight ascent to the Peters Mtn ridge crest and turn R on the ridge. In an open forest of oak, hickory, maple, and cherry follow a wide footpath that becomes a 4WD forest road at 0.7 mi. At 0.8 mi is an old hunter's cabin with twin springs that may be dry in the summer or fall. Continue on the winding road, which is sometimes muddy and rutted by 4WD vehicles; leave the road for a short distance at 2.6 mi. At 3.6 mi FR-945 goes R, down the mountain. Turn L and after 0.2 mi reach a level area with a private cottage, L, and a hunter's road that descends into West Virginia. Turn R at a large buckeye tree. Follow this road for 0.5 mi and reach a foot trail at 4.3 mi. To the L is a private grassy field with apple trees and deer blinds. A pioneer area with remnants of a heating stove and barrel hoops is at 4.8 mi.

Nearby is an intermittent drain. Large hunting fields are on the L slope. Pass R of another private hunting area at 5.4 mi. From a wide gap ascend to a scenic rock formation at 5.6 mi; leave the foot trail at 6.3 mi. Follow an old forest road through a forest of hickory, chestnut oak, striped maple, white snakeroot, fern beds, and mountain laurel. Wildlife likely to be seen are wild turkey, grouse, and deer. At 7.5 mi reach a jct with a vehicle-use road, L, that descends into the West Virginia side. At 8.1 mi enter Monroe County, West Virginia. Reach the top of a ridge at 8.2 mi, leave the foot trail, enter an old road at 8.4 mi, and reach the top of another ridge at 9.3 mi. Begin gradual descent on a scenic road to a damp area with mountain laurel and a locked gate at 10.1 mi. To the R is a spring on a vehicle-use road. At 10.2 mi is a water hole; at 10.7 mi pass through a grazing field. Cross the center of the field and follow an old logging road with blueberry bushes and running cedar in an area of saplings. The road becomes a foot trail at 10.9 mi. Creasy salad, mullein, wintergreen, galax, and shooting star are seen throughout this area. Leave the leeward side of the ridge and cross to a rocky area at 11.5 mi. At 11.7 mi, R, is an unmarked spur trail for 0.1 mi to a scenic rock formation and Hanging Rock Raptor Migration Observatory (3812 ft). Formerly a fire tower, the observatory has a railed deck constructed around a glassed enclosure for full 360-degree viewing. It is maintained by the John W. Handlan Chapter of the A.B. Brooks Bird Club from St Albans.

Back on the main trail, continue on the foot trail to the N side of a gap and 4WD entrance from the L at 12.1 mi. To the R is private property and a posted sign. Continue on the N side of the ridge on a rocky treadway; pass under a power line and descend from the ridge to a gap and Mill Gap Rd (CO-15), also called Limestone Hill Rd, at 12.6 mi. Parking space for 5 vehicles is available in a field under the power line. The *Allegheny Trail* temporarily ends here. (*USGS-FS Maps:* Lindside, Interior, Waiteville, Gap Mills)

It is 3.8 mi R (S) on CO-15 to Waiteville Rd (CO-17), and another 6.9 mi to FR-613, L, to White Rock Campground. It is another 6 mi on the paved road (which becomes SR-635) to the

AT access at Pine Swamp Branch. To return to Sugar Camp, follow the L (N) side of CO-15; it is 1.8 mi to Zenith Rd (CO-29), L. After 9.1 mi the road forks. The R fork goes 10.8 mi to Sugar Camp, for a total of 21.7 mi. If taking the L fork on the Zenith Rd, follow Back Valley Rd (CO-29/2) — the road is narrow — and keep L at all other road jcts to arrive at Sugar Camp with a total of 17.3 mi.

The proposed continuation of the *Allegheny Trail*, N, is on FR-5057, a 4.5-mi stretch on the S side of Peters Mtn to Crowder Rd (CO-20), a rough road from Gap Mills over the mountain to Laurel Branch and Waiteville Rd (CO-17). Its present gated access point on CO-15 is 0.9 mi down the S side of the mountain in the second major curve. From the Crowder Rd the trail would enter Craig County, Virginia, about 2.5 mi farther on. After 8 mi in Craig County the trail would leave the New Castle District of the Jefferson National Forest and enter the James River District of the George Washington National Forest in Alleghany County, Virginia. After another 16 mi in the GWNF it would cross I-64 at Jerry's Run. From here it would ascend approximately 6 mi to Greenbrier County, West Virginia, and to the end of Section IV along Laurel Run Rd (FR-375) at Meadow Creek and Lake Sherwood Rd. (It is 7.7 mi N on Lake Sherwood Rd to Lake Sherwood Recreation Area. See Chapter I, Section 6.) (*USGS-FS Maps:* Paint Bank, Potts Creek, Allegheny, Jerry's Run, Rucker Gap)

Section III: Lake Sherwood Road to Cass

The current trail route is L on Lake Sherwood Rd (CO-14) for 2.6 mi to Neola and the jct with WV-92. (Groceries, gasoline, PO, and phone are here.) Cross WV-92, go W on FR-96 for 0.5 mi across the Anthony Creek bridge, and ford the N fork of the Anthony Creek (once on the graveled road and again on the *Middle Mountain Trail*). After 13.2 mi on the *Middle Mountain Trail*, turn L on the *Dock Trail* for 2 mi as described below. (From Lake Sherwood Rd there is a 14.8-mi proposed trail route. It would cross Meadow Creek, ascend Meadow Creek Mtn, descend to and cross WV-92, and follow

Middle Mtn [total distance: 6.5 mi] to turn L on the *Dock Trail* for 2 mi. From here it would ascend W to *Middle Mountain Trail* and follow it N for about 1 mi to turn L on the *Dock Trail* for 2 mi. The W terminus of the *Dock Trail* is at Douthat Rd [CO-23], 7 mi SW of Minnehaha Springs.) From here the *Allegheny Trail* is completed and open for 137.6 mi, 48.7 mi of Section III and 89.9 mi of Section II. References to and partial descriptions of the trail are made elsewhere in this book because it crosses or runs jointly with other trails. An examination of the Index will indicate the page numbers. These sections have also been described and mapped in more detail in the *Hiking Guide to the Allegheny Trail* printed by the West Virginia Scenic Trails Association and edited by Fred Bird and Doug Wood. (Descriptive brevity is warranted in this book because my research and measurements are similar to theirs. A difference is that I hiked the trail from S to N.)

From the Douthat Rd jct follow the *Allegheny Trail* and *Brushy Mtn Trail* jointly on a gated forest road through a pine plantation. After 0.4 mi fork L, ascend and cross Beaver Lick Mtn into the Marlinton District of the MNF, and at 3 mi jct with the blue-blazed *Beaver Creek Trail*. (The *Beaver Creek Trail* turns R and goes 0.7 mi to the Beaver Creek Campground of Watoga State Park. Hot showers and a laundry are available from Memorial Day to Labor Day.) Pass through the Calvin Price State Forest, and at 9.1 mi reach a jct with Pyles Mtn Rd, the main road W to Watoga State Park's multiple facilities. (There are plans to relocate the *Allegheny Trail* onto *Jacobs Well Trail* in the park.) After the park, descend to Beaver Creek and ascend to follow the old *Buckley Mountain Trail* in a deciduous forest, mainly oaks, that has understory sections of mountain laurel and buckberry. Descend to Gilden Hollow and reach Beaver Creek Rd (CO-21) at 22.6 mi. Turn L and reach Huntersville after 1 mi. (Here are limited groceries, PO, and phone.) Turn L on WV-39, but after 0.8 mi turn R on WV-28. After another 0.5 mi turn L and ascend steeply to Marlin Mtn range. Follow the ridgeline and reach an Adirondack shelter at 28 mi. Continue on the ridge, reach Marlin Mtn peak (3326 ft) at 30.2 mi. Turn E, cross the Marlin Lick Run headwaters, and return to

WV-28 at 33.4 mi. Turn L and after 0.5 mi turn L to ascend Thorny Creek Mtn; enter a jeep road in Seneca State Forest. At 38.5 mi cross the forest's main road (it is 2.4 mi E to forest headquarters and WV-28), pass a lookout tower, and follow the Loop Rd to the forest boundary at 39.7 mi. Descend to Laurel Run Rd (CO-1/4), turn L, and after 0.3 mi turn R and begin ascent of Thomas Mtn. Descend on a jeep road to Sitlington Rd (CO-12) at 44.1 mi (it is 2.2 mi R to WV-28 and Dunmore). Turn L, cross the Greenbrier River, and join the *Greenbrier River Trail* at 45.2 mi. (Because of flood damage in this area, the trail may have been relocated.) Turn R and reach Cass at 48.7 mi, the N terminus of Section III. (Facilities here include groceries, gasoline, PO, phone, campground [tel: 304-456-3218], and other facilities from Memorial Day to Labor Day.) (*USGS-FS Maps:* Rucker Gap, Lake Sherwood, Marlinton, Minnehaha Springs, Clover Lick, Cass)

Section II: Cass to Blackwater Falls State Park

To begin Section II, cross the Greenbrier River bridge, turn L and follow a private road for 1.5 mi to the Greenbrier Ranger District of the MNF. Cross a stream, ascend by another stream, and reach the crest of Little Mtn at 4 mi. The forest is deciduous, with scattered hemlock, Virginia pine, wild azaleas, mountain laurel, and witchhazel. Deer, wild turkey, and grouse are commonplace and bear have been sighted. Outstanding views of the National Radio Astronomy Observatory are along the ridgeline. At 7.2 mi begin to follow the old blue-blazed *Little Mtn Trail* and follow it in parts for 6.5 mi. At 8.1 mi is a side trail, L, for 0.2 mi to Little Mtn Knob (3417 ft). Cross Laurel Fork at 9.2 mi and follow up the W side for nearly 1 mi before ascending to another ridge line of scenic Little Mtn. Cross Brush Run at 14.2 mi, Spillman Run at 16.3 mi, ascend to a saddle in Sandy Ridge, and descend to Durbin at 18.3 mi. (Durbin has laundry, groceries, hardware, phone, gasoline, PO, restaurant, and pharmacy. It is 2.5 mi E on US-250 to the Greenbrier Ranger District in Bartow.)

Follow US-250 W for 2.7 mi and turn R into the MNF.

Descend to and cross Fill Run, ascend to and cross Simmons Rd (CO-250/1), and continue ascent, steep in places, to Shavers Mtn at 25.4 mi. To the L is a 0.2-mi access from Gaudineer Knob Rd (FR-27). Turn R and for the next 20 mi follow the high scenic ridge line, formerly the blue-blazed *Shavers Mtn Trail* (also called the *North-South Trail*). Elevation averages 4000 ft; red spruce and hemlock groves are among the deciduous hardwoods of oak, cherry, and maple. Wildlife includes bear, deer, red squirrel, grouse, wild turkey, and plenty of chipmunks. At 26.9 mi enter the Gaudineer Scenic Area and reach FR-27 at 27.1 mi. Immediately turn R and reenter the forest. Pass through marshy area at 29.2 mi and reach the Johns Camp Run shelter at 30.5 mi. (The 0.8-mi *Johns Camp Run Trail* is an access route to FR-317.) Water is plentiful here. Wildlife visits frequently. Arrive at the Wildell Shelter at 37.7 mi. At 38.8 mi jct with *High Falls Trail.* (It is 1 mi R [E] to Little River Rd [FR-44] and 1.5 mi L [W] to the High Falls on Shavers Fork.) Reach Elliots Ridge Rd (CO-22) at 43.4 mi. Turn R and go 0.3 mi on the paved road to a crossroads in Glady. (A few yds to the R is Shifflett's general store with gasoline, limited supply of groceries, PO, and phone; store hours are irregular, usually from 11 A.M. to 3 P.M.) For the next 1.8 mi follow paved Glady Fork Rd (CO-27), turn R into the forest, descend, and ford Glady Fork at 46.4 mi. (If high water prevents crossing, backtrack to the Glady Fork Rd and go 7.5 mi N on the paved road to Alpena and US-33.) Follow sections of old RR grade, and jct with *McCray Creek Trail* at 49.5 mi. Follow sections of an old RR grade, cross a number of tributaries, and reach US-33 in the community of Evenwood at 54.4 mi. (It is 1.5 mi, R [E] up the mountain on US-33 to Wymer, with a general store of groceries, gasoline, PO, and phone — regular opening hours. It is 1.3 mi L [W] to Alpine Lodge and Restaurant [tel: 304-636-1470], and 10 mi to Elkins.)

Cross US-33, pass through an old farm for 0.3 mi and cross a secondary road. Pass a farm area and enter the Cheat Ranger District of the MNF to follow old RR grades, forest roads, and foot trails on an exceptionally scenic route for 17 mi along Glady Fork. (Parts of the trail were damaged by the November

1985 flood and are in the process of repair.) Water sources and excellent campsites are plentiful. Reach FR-240 at 60.4 mi and leave the road at 63 mi on Gladwin Rd (CO-12). Turn L, follow the Gladwin Rd for 0.2 mi to cross Glady Fork and jct with the *Mylius Trail* at 63.4 mi. From here follow gated FR-162 for the next 8.5 mi to Richford Rd (CO-26), cross a low water bridge over the Glady Fork, and reach a paved road at 72 mi in Gladwin. Follow the Gladwin Rd (CO-35/15) along Dry Fork for 3.2 mi and cross the Jenningston Bridge. Turn R and follow Laneville Rd (CO-45) to Red Creek community and WV-72. Turn L, go 0.1 mi on WV-72 and turn R on Laneville Rd (CO-45). After 1.5 mi on the gravel road, turn L to enter Canaan Valley State Park at 80.4 mi. At 80.8 mi jct with *Chimney Rock Trail*. The *Allegheny Trail* turns L. (A R turn is 0.7 mi to the lodge and restaurant and multiple facilities. Open year round.) The trail runs jointly with the *Railroad Grade Trail* for 1.4 mi, then begins an ascent to Canaan Mtn in the MNF at 83.7 mi in a scenic area of hardwoods and conifers. Reach the Canaan Loop Rd (FR-13) at 84.9 mi; turn R, go 1.2 mi on the gravel road, and make a L turn on what was formerly the *Davis Trail*. The area is chiefly rocky and has red spruce groves and large patches of ferns and mountain laurel. This is also a cross-country ski trail, the only one in the state that connects two major state park lodges. Cross *Plantation Trail* at 87.3 mi and pass R of the Canaan Mtn Shelter and spring. Reach the Blackwater Falls State Park stables parking area at 88.9 mi. (From here it is 0.8 mi L to the lodge and restaurant. To the R is the campground and other facilities. It is 2.3 mi from this point to Davis for motels, restaurants, groceries, gasoline, pharmacy, hardware, PO, and phone.) (*USGS-FS Maps:* Cass, Green Bank, Durbin, Wildell, Beverly East, Glady, Bowden, Harman, Mozark Mtn, Blackwater Falls)

Section I: Blackwater Falls State Park to Pennsylvania State Line

The 88-mi Section I begins at the Blackwater Falls State Park stables parking area. It is mainly on secondary roads, with scenic areas through Tucker and Preston counties, and it is in the process of development for off-road locations and additional campsites. (Roads washed away in the November 1985 flood have been reconstructed.)

Follow the *Allegheny Trail* blazes on the paved road across the park, past the campground, to the parking area of the Pendleton Lake Swimming Area. Enter the forest, N, and reach Douglas Rd (CO-27) at 4.4 mi. Turn L, cross the bridge over the N Fork of the Blackwater River, and follow the scenic Canyon Rim Rd (FR-18) for 8.5 mi in the MNF to US-219. Turn R, go 2.1 mi on US-219, and turn L on paved Sugar Lands Rd (CO-25). (It is 4 mi ahead on US-219 to Thomas.)

Follow Sugar Lands Rd for 0.4 mi before a R turn on graveled Close Mtn Rd (CO-16). Descend the W slope of Backbone Mtn to a ridge with pastureland, and after 3.1 mi enter the MNF and descend 1000 ft for 1.3 mi on an exceptionally steep roadway to Horseshoe Run Rd (CO-7). (To the L it is 0.6 mi to the Horseshoe Rec Area in the Cheat Ranger District. See Chapter 1, Section 1.) Turn R on the paved road and go 0.8 mi to the community of Lead Mine. (A general store with groceries and gasoline is here.) Total trail distance from Blackwater Falls State Park is 20.6 mi.

Continue on Horseshoe Run Rd upstream, pass through the community of Shafer, and at 3.1 mi cross Twelve Mile Run. Turn L, go upstream for 0.8 mi, and reach the Preston County line in the MNF. (Campsites are in this area.) Here the road changes name and number to Twelve Mile Rd (CO-112/1). Follow upstream in a hollow to the headwaters and ascend to a ridge. Follow the ridge past a few private homes to a jct with Stemple Ridge Rd (CO-112) in the community of Sell, 3 mi from the county line and a total of 27.5 mi from Blackwater Falls State Park.

Cross Stemple Ridge Rd to Snake Rd (CO-110) and descend

through a remote area for 4 mi to Hardesty and US-50. Turn L. (To the R on US-50 it is 5.4 mi to Aurora and another 1 mi to Cathedral State Park.) Pass a motel, restaurant, grocery store, and Cheat River Campground, and after 1.8 mi on US-50 turn R on Madison Rd (CO-84). Follow Madison Rd for 4.1 mi, turn L on Manheim Rd (CO-80, also called Lantz Ridge Rd), and go 3.9 mi to Rowlesburg. (Here are restaurants, grocery stores, service station, laundromat, phone, and PO.) The total mileage from Blackwater Falls State Park is 41.3 mi.

After crossing the B&O RR tracks, go N on Shaver M&K Rd (CO-80/2) and Calver Shaver Rd (CO-80/1) for 5.6 mi to Huffman Rd (CO-80/6), immediately after crossing Stamping Ground Run. Turn R on Huffman Rd and go 1.4 mi to Fitchett-Ambersburg Rd (CO-86), L. Ascend and descend on Caddell Mtn and, after 5.6 mi on CO-86, jct with WV-7 for a total of 53.9 mi.

Turn R on WV-7 and go 2.4 mi to old Terra Alta Pike (CO-45/3), L, at the edge of Terra Alta. (Restaurants, laundromat, motel, PO, groceries, service station, phone, and other stores are here.) After 2 mi and six stream crossings, turn L on Laughry Hollow Rd (CO-7/33); go 1.9 mi, pass through two gates to Crane School West End Rd (CO-3/12), and turn L. Proceed for 1.5 mi to Crane School East End Rd (CO-45/1) and turn L. Reach St Joe/Albright after another 2.3 mi, for a total of 64.2 mi from Blackwater Falls State Park. (Albright has a grocery store, service station, PO, and phone.) (This area was severely damaged by the November 1985 flood.)

The trail goes through Albright for 0.7 mi to jct with WV-26 and N for 1.3 mi on WV-26 to Beech Run Rd (CO-26/23), L. After 6.3 mi through the countryside, turn L on Harmony Grove Rd (CO-14/5) and go 2.9 mi to Mt Nebo, where CO-14/5 becomes Rockville-Mt Nebo Rd (CO-14). The trail is now 74.9 mi from Blackwater Falls State Park.

Go N on CO-14, cross the Big Sandy Creek bridge, and after 2.2 mi turn L on George Walls Rd (CO-14/1). Go 1.9 mi and turn R on Laurel Run Rd (CO-73/5) for 0.6 mi. Pass under US-48 and jct with old US-48 (CO-73-73). (To the R it is 4.9 mi to Bruceton Mills for groceries, service station, PO, phone, restaurant, and general stores. To the L it is 2.5 mi to Coopers Rock State Forest.) Cross the road to a gravel road that goes through a farm, and after 2.6 mi turn R on Dickie Hill Rd (CO-2/5). Go 0.7 mi to join Bensons Rd (CO-2/2, also called Lake O'Woods Rd). Turn L on Hileman Rd (CO-73/9) and go 1.9 mi; turn L on Bryte Rd (CO-6/2) and go 1 mi. Turn R on Mt Grove Rd (CO-4/1) at a church cemetery. Proceed for 1.2 mi and turn L on Clifton Mills Rd (CO-4, also known as State Line Rd) for 0.6 mi to the Pennsylvania state line (The Mason-Dixon Line) for a total of 88.2 mi from Blackwater Falls State Park. (*USGS-FS Maps:* Blackwater Falls, Mozark Mtn, Lead Mine, Aurora, Terra Alta, Kingwood, Valley Point, Bruceton Mills)

• INFORMATION: For more information on the sections, write or call the following: (Section I) George Rosier, 633 West Virginia Ave, Morgantown, WV 26505, tel: 304-296-5158; (Section II) Fred Bird, 236 Terrace Ave, Elkins, WV 26241, tel: 304-636-7478; (Section III) Anita Tracy, Box 37, Parsons, WV 26287, tel: 304-478-2318 or 478-4555; (Section IV) Doug Wood, 401 Fourth St N, St Albans, WV 25177, tel: 304-727-8463 or 348-5929. For information on the *Hiking Guide to the Allegheny Trail,* write or call WVSTA, PO Box 4042, Charleston, WV 25304, tel: 304-744-6157.

▶ BIG BLUE TRAIL

"I worked on the Big Blue Trail because we need a legacy of Nature for future generations." — ELIZABETH JOHNSTON

Twenty-five years ago there was concern among Appalachian Trail Conference leaders that the continuous route of the *AT* was jeopardized on private lands in northern Virginia. The 144 mi *Big Blue Trail* is a product of that concern. It was designed, constructed, and is maintained by the Potomac Appalachian Trail Club. Among the early leaders are James Denton, Woody Kennedy, and Fred Blackburn, who had 54 mi of the Big Blue finished by 1970. Notable in the history of trail building and securing private land easements is Tom Floyd; he constructed the final 66 mi. On October 11, 1981, the final mile was finished near the West Virginia-Virginia state line at the Great North Mtn range. The joining of the *Big Blue Trail* with the 110-mi *Tuscarora Trail* created an *AT* alternate that runs from Matthews Arm in the Shenandoah National Park to rejoin the *AT* in Dean's Gap, Pennsylvania.

The *Big Blue Trail* has 11 sections, numbered from the Potomac River to the Shenandoah National Park. Sections 1, 2, 5, 6, and parts of 3, 4, and 7 are in West Virginia for a total of 65.9 mi. Only the West Virginia mileage is emphasized in this book and is described S to N. The first 19.3 mi, from S to N, is in the George Washington National Forest. That part is in Sections 7 and 6, and is described with its joint trail routes from *Little North Mountain Trail* at the West Virginia-Virginia state line to Hawk Campground in Chapter 2.

To reach Hawk Campground by vehicle, go 4 mi E from Wardensville on WV-55 and turn L on FR-502. (It is 1 mi E on WV-55 to the Virginia state line and another 15.3 mi to I-81 in Strasburg, Virginia.) Drive 3 mi on FR-502, turn L on FR-347, and go 0.7 mi to the rustic Hawk Campground entrance, R. Hike the blue-blazed *Big Blue Trail* NW for 1.6 mi in the GWNF to Hawk Run. Cross Hawk Run three times, ascend to ridge, follow woods roads, and cross Capon Spring Road (CO-16) and bridge at 3.8 mi. Pass near a private home, cross Middle Ridge and Dry Run, and pass historic grave site of Jemima Farmer at 5.7 mi. At 6.6 mi pass under a power line and follow woods and jeep roads to cross Milk Rd (CO-23/11) at 7.5 mi. After passage through rural settings of woods and fields, reach branch of Kump Rd (CO-23/9) at 8.1 mi and pass a deserted schoolhouse. Return to the gravel Kump Rd (CO-23/10) and go E along Lohman branch to a parking area at the asphalt road at 11.3 mi. This is the end of Section 5, S of Lehew. (It is 0.8 mi N on Back Creek Rd [CO-23/3] to Lehew and WV-259.)

Section 4 begins here and goes 1.8 mi in West Virginia before it enters Virginia again for 11.7 mi to its end in the community of Gore. Follow Back Creek Rd, R, cross bridge at 0.5 mi, turn

L on Gore Rd (CO-23/11) (SR-704 in Frederick County, Virginia), but turn off road after 0.1 mi onto a jeep road. At 1.9 mi leave the jeep road and enter Lucas Woods, the site of a dedication ceremony of the *Big Blue Trail* completion in 1981. Camping is allowed. Ascend on switchbacks (approx 1000 ft elev change) to the scenic ridge line of Great North Mtn at 3.2 mi. Vegetation on the mountain includes mountain laurel, wild azaleas, blueberry, sassafras, Virginia pine, oak, hickory, maple, dogwood, trailing arbutus, wintergreen, and pink lady's slipper. Animal life is mainly deer, wild turkey, grouse, gray squirrel, and chipmunk. At 5.6 mi and at 6.2 mi jct with the historic orange-blazed *Frye Path Trail.* Reach Pinnacle Rocks and the Devil's Backbone area at 5.8 mi. Descend on switchbacks and enter a gorge at 6.8 mi. Pass through a rocky area for the next 2.3 mi and join a jeep road at 10 mi. At 12.9 mi arrive at a dirt road that becomes paved after 0.1 mi. This is SR-853. Cross Back Creek bridge and Winchester RR tracks into Gore at 13.5 mi. Section 4 ends here. (Gore has a grocery store, phone, gasoline, and post office.)

Begin Section 3 at the jct of SR-853 and SR-751, turn R on SR-751 and walk out to US-50. Follow US-50 for 0.9 mi and turn L on SR-688. Go 3.3 mi through a farming area and reach jct, R, on SR-684 in the community of Gainsboro. Turn L on SR-600, cross US-522, and follow SR-600 to Isaacs Creek. Turn L on SR-689 at 7 mi. Pass through meadows, farming areas, and woods to a jct with *Fishing Pond Trail* at 9 mi. Pass the Dresel Wayside campsites (a private campground available to through hikers), and continue through farmland and tranquil woodland of oak and pine. At 10.8 mi, cross SR-600, and again at 12 mi. (Artesian water is 40 yds L on SR-600, S of Siler jct.) Follow the trail to road jct with SR-681, which becomes WV-45 at 15.1 mi, the state line. Follow WV-45 for 1.4 mi to the end of Section 3 at 16.5 mi. Section 2 begins here (2.6 mi W of Glengary on WV-45).

Section 2 begins at a parking area and dirt road. Follow the road for 0.7 mi and turn R into Sleepy Creek PHFA. It ends at the Spruce Pine Roadside Park at 22 mi. This section is described in detail in Chapter 8 because 20.8 of its mileage is in the Sleepy Creek PHFA. After it leaves the Sleepy Creek PHFA it enters private property and an area near Meadow Branch where a resident painted the blue blazes brown. According to Tom Floyd, manager of the *Big Blue Trail*, the PATC has purchased two pieces of land in the vicinity to have a clear right-of-way. He stated that it will be a scenic relocation down Sleepy Creek Mtn and to WV-9. The relocation will also include a backpacking campground and will be relocated through Spruce Pine Roadside Park in a 65-acre wilderness area known as the General Adam Stevens Park, a property of the Sons of the American Revolution.

At the Spruce Pine Roadside Park (or the new location) enter Section 1 on the paved road across WV-9 (0.3 mi E of the Sleepy Creek bridge) and make an immediate L turn on a footpath. At 0.8 mi turn L on Burnt Mill Rd (CO-1/3) and cross Sleepy Creek bridge at 1.9 mi. Reach jct of paved Potomac River Rd (CO-8) at 2.2 mi, turn R and, after 0.2 mi at jct with Jim West Rd (CO-6), enter a footpath between the roads. Pass through farms and rolling hills, cross Dugan Hollow stream at 5.6 mi, and enter a forest owned by PATC where camping is allowed. Leave the PATC area after 1 mi, cross a stream, enter pastureland and at 6.6 mi join Culp Rd (CO-1/1). Turn L and immediately R to cross Culp Rd into a meadow. Arrive at the River Rd (CO-1) at 7.2 mi, turn L and reach US-522 at 9.5 mi. Cross the Potomac River bridge into Hancock, Maryland, take a sharp L, go under the bridge and across the RR yard to the *C&O Canal Towpath*. Here is the end of Section 1 at 10.2 mi. (It is 0.2 mi L to a town park and exit to Hancock, and 8 mi E on the *C&O Canal Towpath* to the jct with the *Tuscarora Trail.*)

For more detail, the *Big Blue Trail Guide*, written by Elizabeth Johnston and published by the PATC, is recommended. The trail guide is in two pocket-size books with maps and photography. Contact PATC, 1718 N St, NW, Washington DC 20036, tel: 202-638-5306, weeknights 7–10 P.M.)

Appendix: Resources

Kanawha Trail Club

The Kanawha Trail Club began as the Charleston Daily Mail Hiking Club in July 1942. Sol Padlibsky of the *Charleston Daily Mail* collaborated with H. M. F. Kinsey, a Boy Scouts executive, in organizing group hiking. In September 1944, the group reorganized with 54 charter members and changed the club name to the Kanawha Trail Club. Three years later the club was incorporated and a charter obtained. Plans followed for a rustic lodge on the Middle Lick Fork of Davis Creek, 7 mi from Charleston, and the lodge that was built has been in use since October 1948. The club maintains 20.7 mi of the *AT*, from the New River north to the Stony Creek Valley on the Waiteville Rd. About 80 percent of the club's outings are in the 9052-acre Kanawha State Forest, an area adjoining the club's lodge. In 1978 several club members, including Charley Carlson and Howard and Dorothy Guest, were active in lobbying for a state bill that prohibits commercial timber cutting in this forest. The club has 150 members, and membership is open to all ages.

• INFORMATION: Kanawha Trail Club, PO Box 4474, Charleston, WV 25364, tel: 304-744-6575.

Potomac Appalachian Trail Club

The Potomac Appalachian Trail Club is the largest trail-oriented club in the south with over 3500 members. It was established in 1927 with seven members who built 19 mi of the *AT*. By 1936 it had completed 250 mi of the *AT* from the Susquehanna River in Pennsylvania to Rockfish Gap in Virginia. Today it maintains 235 mi of the *AT* in which the route into Harpers Ferry and short sections into Jefferson County are included. In addition, the club maintains approximately 600 mi of other foot trails in the area, including Pennsylvania, Maryland, the District of Columbia, northern Virginia, and such trails as the *Big Blue Trail* in West Virginia.

Exceptionally active, the club maintains 15 primitive cabins and 22 shelters for *AT* hikers, as well as several trail work centers, provides roving *AT* patrols to help hikers in the peak seasons, and supervises the hut system for long-distance hikers in the Shenandoah National Park. The club also publishes detailed guidebooks, maps, brochures, and other informational materials on such topics as land acquisition for protecting the *AT* and other trails, and government policies and agencies affecting the trails.

• INFORMATION: Contact the main office at 1718 N St NW, Washington, DC 20036. This office is open to the public from 7 A.M. to 10 P.M., Monday through Friday, tel: 202-638-5306.

The Nature Conservancy

The Nature Conservancy is a national nonprofit organization whose objective is to protect, preserve, and conserve the biological diversity of the nation's natural areas. It cooperates and works with other private and public conservation agencies to attain its objectives. Currently it manages a national system of over 800 nature sanctuaries with nearly 2 million acres in all 50 states, Canada, and the Caribbean. The conservancy acquires funding from individual contributors, foundation grants, corporate gifts, and investments. Organized in 1950, it had over 205,000 members in 1985. It publishes *The Nature Conservancy News*.

The West Virginia chapter, formed in 1963, protects nearly 30,000 acres in 13 private preserves, some of which provide limited hiking opportunities. Two of the preserves have short designated trails. One is Brush Creek, a scenic area in Mercer County near Pipestem State Park. Its 123 acres encompass a section of Brush Creek canyon and the Bluestone River area. Among its features are cascades, cliffs, and rare plants and animals. An old RR grade has been constructed into an easy 1 mi *Brush Creek Trail* that leads to the Bluestone River. It must be backtracked. Access is to take WV-20 N from Athens 2.5 mi to Speedway and turn L onto Camp Creek Rd (CO-3). After 2.8 mi turn L at a fork onto a dirt road. Go 0.5 mi to Brush Creek and park at the bridge.

Another preserve is Cranesville Swamp, a 318-acre boreal bog complex in Preston County, S of Cranesville. It is managed by both the West Virginia and the Maryland chapters. The swamp supports a relic colony of northern plant and animal life at a southern latitude. It has the southernmost colony of American larch *(Larix laricina)*, the state's only native deciduous cone-bearing tree. Some of the other trees are red spruce, Canada yew, black ash, black cherry, yellow birch, and hemlock. Access from Cranesville is to take the Cranesville Rd (CO-47) S for 2.2 mi to a jct L with Burnside Camp Rd (CO-49) opposite a church. Go 1 mi and turn L on Feather Rd (CO-47/ 1). Go 0.5 mi to a clearing, R, and past the power line to a parking area. Follow the *Cranesville Swamp Trail* through the woods for 0.3 mi to the boardwalk. The boardwalk extends 500 ft into the swamp. An extension is planned. Backtrack.

The other preserves with possible hiking opportunities are Panther Knob, 376 acres in Pendleton County on the top of North Fork Mountain; Yankauer, 107 acres along the Potomac River in Berkeley County; Greenland Gap, 255 acres in Grant County in New Creek Mountain gap; Hungry Beech, 122 acres in Roane County on Paxton Ridge and along Green Creek; and Murphy, 276 acres in Ritchie County, near Pennsboro. As trails are "not a management emphasis at the preserves," the hiker should contact the conservancy at the address below for more information.

• INFORMATION: The Nature Conservancy, West Virginia Field Office, 1100 Quarrier St, Room 215, Charleston, WV 25301, tel: 304-345-4350. The regional and national office addresses are listed in the Appendix.

Sierra Club

The Sierra Club was founded in 1892 by John Muir, naturalist, conservationist, and writer. It has over 60 chapters nationwide whose nonprofit programs involve legislation; litigation; public information; wilderness outings; white water expeditions; mountaineering; educational workshops; conferences; maintenance of trails, huts, and lodges; and publishing. Additionally, the Sierra Club Foundation was established in 1960 for educational, literary, and scientific projects concerning national and international problems of preserving the natural resources. It also has the Sierra Club Legal Defense Fund to assist citizens' groups in protection of the environment. Its purpose is to explore, enjoy, and preserve the nation's forests, waters, wildlife, wilderness, and other natural resources.

The West Virginia chapter of the Sierra Club was officially formed October 1, 1984, with a membership of 650. Its predecessor, the West Virginia Group of the Potomac chapter, was established in 1977. Individual groups have not been established, but one in Morgantown is in the formative stage. The chapter publishes a bimonthly newsletter, the *Mountain State Sierran*.

Chapter activities, past and present, include the evaluation and redrafting of the Monongahela National Forest's 1985 Land and Resources Management Plan; service outings for reconstructing, cleaning, and maintaining USFS trails; lobbying for state and federal environmental issues; organizing and hosting environmental education workshops on preserving the natural environment; and sponsoring campers for attendance at the state's Department of Natural Resources Junior and State Conservation Camps. Led by Mary Wimmer and Paul Turner, the chapter has joined forces with the MNF to repair the trails damaged by the 1985 flood.

• INFORMATION: Conservation Committee, West Virginia Chapter, Sierra Club, PO Box 4142, Morgantown, WV 26504, tel: 304-598-0136 or 304-745-4533.

West Virginia Highlands Conservancy

Established in 1967, the West Virginia Highlands Conservancy advocates the prudent management and conservation of the state's natural resources with a historical emphasis on the 849,783-acre Monongahela National Forest and the surrounding eastern highlands. Traditionally, the conservancy has been active in legislative procedures for wilderness preservation; wilderness designation; protection of public lands and water resources, water and air quality, and river conservation; regulating surface mining; and involvement in other environmental issues that affect the state's quality of life.

As a citizens' group of more than 800 individual members and 26 organizational members, it relies primarily on volunteers to pursue its conservation programs. When necessary, it also retains professional assistance in working with the state legislature and Congress in seminars, reports on technical and public policy issues, litigation, negotiations, formal regulatory proceedings, and public hearings to serve as a citizen's advocate before governmental agencies.

As part of its administrative process, it has two annual conferences with pertinent speakers, workshops, and field trips. Additionally, it sponsors a regular year-round outings program that includes hiking, backpacking, skiing, canoeing, spelunking, and other outdoor activities.

The legacy of the conservancy leadership is remarkably successful. Some of the major examples are: 1965, Spruce Knob/Seneca Rocks Natural Recreation Area; 1973, a federal litigation landmark (National Forest Management Act of 1976) that reformed clear-cutting in national forests nationwide; 1975, Otter Creek (20,000 acres) and Dolly Sods (10,215 acres) Wilderness Areas; 1976, Gauley River Canyon preserved from hydropower dam; 1978, worked with the Izaak Walton League to create the New River Gorge National River Park; 1979, preservation of 35,000-acre Canaan Valley wetlands area; 1983, USFS withdrawal of proposals for threefold increases in timbering, mining, and road construction in the MNF.

The conservancy is a nonprofit, tax-exempt West Virginia corporation and has an inviolate endowment fund whose investment income is applied to conservation work. "The endowment fund is dedicated to working for the conservation and wise management of West Virginia's scenic rivers, natural heritage, historical sites, and environmental quality of public lands," said Larry W. George, conservancy president. In addition to cash gifts and bequests, real estate, mineral rights, and stocks and bonds, and other tangible properties are of benefit to its services. The conservancy has a constant need for volunteers in field trips, attorneys, engineers, researchers, speakers, and writers. The conservancy publishes a monthly newsletter, the *Highland Voice*, and has also published a *Hiking Guide to Monongahela National Forest* with details and maps of the trails.

• INFORMATION: For information on memberships, endowment, gifts, guidebooks, volunteers, and general information, contact West Virginia Highlands Conservancy, Suite 201, 1206 Virginia St E, Charleston, WV 25301, tel: 304-344-8833.

West Virginia Scenic Trails Association

The West Virginia Scenic Trails Association was incorporated August 19, 1974, and work began on its chief commitment, the *Allegheny Trail*, in 1975. "It is still our primary goal," said Bob Tabor, cofounder of both the trail and the association concept. Tabor and Nick Lozano, the other cofounder, first discussed the subject in October 1971, and in November 1972, met with a group of about 40 people at St John's Episcopal Church in Charleston. Lozano was elected president of the

WVSTA, Tabor was vice president, and Bruce Bond was the secretary-treasurer. Tabor had been on the Board of Managers of the Appalachian Trail Conference from 1961 to 1971; his knowledge of government officials and citizen trail supporters led him to model the *Allegheny Trail* and the WVSTA after the *AT* and the ATC. Among the other early leaders and associates were Charley Carlson, Frank Pelurie, Norman Williams, Zip Little, and John Ballantine.

In addition to the goals of completing the 300 mi *Allegheny Trail* from SW Virginia to Pennsylvania, the association plans to have chapters such as the Mary Ingles chapter develop a 500 mi trail from SW Virginia to N Kentucky along the New, Kanawha, and Ohio rivers, and the Northwest Passage chapter extend the *Allegheny Trail* jurisdiction into Pennsylvania for a connection with the *Warrior Trail* and *Laurel Highlands Trail*.

Among the general objectives are to improve and enlarge the state trail system; to communicate with the appropriate local, state, and federal agencies in developing and coordinating the trail establishments; and to create local interest groups to participate in trail development and management. "Our immediate objectives are to attract new members. Whatever we accomplish will be made possible by the enthusiasm of our volunteers," said John Giacalone, 1986 association president. The 180-member association invites individuals and organizations to join, has an annual meeting, conducts weekly outings and trail development projects, and publishes a bimonthly newsletter, *Whoop n' Holler*. It has also published the *Hiking Guide to the Allegheny Trail,* a trail point narrative with detailed maps.

• INFORMATION: For information on membership, goals, and trail conditions, contact WVSTA, PO Box 4042, Charleston, WV 25304, tel: 304-744-6157; for the guidebook: Publications Division, WVSTA, 633 West Virginia Ave, Morgantown, WV 26505, tel: 304-296-5158.

▶ AGENCIES AND OTHER SOURCES OF INFORMATION

There are more than 100 addresses of national, state, and local forests, parks, agencies, and some private organizations listed under *address* or *information* in the narrative. A few other allied government agencies, citizens' groups, and centers whose addresses do not appear elsewhere in the book but are related to West Virginia are listed below.

United States Government Departments

Department of Agriculture
Forest Service
PO Box 2417
Washington, DC 20013
(202-477-3975)

Regional Foresters
Region #9
310 W Wisconsin Ave
Milwaukee, WI 53203
(414-291-3693)

Department of Agriculture
Soil Conservation Service
PO Box 2890
Washington, DC 20013
(202-447-4543)

Regional Biologists
160 E 7th St
Chester, PA 19013

State Biologist
75 High St, Rm 301
Morgantown, WV 26505

Army Corps of Engineers
Office of the Chief
Pulaski Bldg
20 Massachusetts Ave, NW
Washington, DC 20314
(202-272-0001)

Department of the Interior
C St, Interior Bldg
Washington, DC 20240
(202-343-1100)

Bureau of Land
Management
(202-343-1100)

Bureau of Mines
(202-634-1004)

State Directors: Eastern
350 S Pickett St
Alexandria, VA 22304
(703-235-2833)

National Park Service
Interior Bldg
Washington, DC 20240
(202-343-4747)

Regional Directors
North Atlantic
15 State St
Boston MA 02109
(617-223-3769)

US Fish and Wildlife Service
Washington, DC 20240
(202-343-4717)

Regional Office
One Gateway Ctr,
Suite 700
Newton Corner, MA
02158
(617-965-5100)

Advisory Council on Historic
Preservation
1100 Pennsylvania Ave, NW
Washington, DC 20004
(202-786-0503)

Environmental Protection
Agency
401 M St, SW
Washington, DC 20460
(202-755-2673)

Region III
Curtis Bldg
6th and Walnut Sts
Philadelphia, PA 19106
(215-597-9814)

Interstate Commissions

Appalachian Regional
Commission
1666 Connecticut Ave, NW
Washington, DC 20235
(202-673-7835)

Ohio River Valley Water
Sanitation Commission
414 Walnut St.
Cincinnati, OH 45202
(513-421-1151)

*Interstate Organizations
(nongovernment)*

American Camping Assoc,
Inc.
Bradford Woods
Martinsville, IN 46151
(317-342-8456)

American Conservation
Assoc, Inc.
30 Rockefeller Plaza
Rm 5510
New York, NY 10112
(212-247-3700)

American Fisheries Society
5410 Grosvenor Ln
Bethesda, MD 20814
(301-897-8616)

American Forestry
Association
1319 18th St, NW
Washington, DC 20036
(202-467-5810)

American Hiking Society
1701 18th St, NW
Washington, DC 20009
(202-234-4609)

American Nature Study
Society
4881 Cold Brook Rd
Homer, NY 13077
(607-749-3655)

American Rivers
Conservation Council
322 4th St, NE
Washington, DC 20002
(202-547-6900)

American Wilderness
Alliance
4260 E Evans, Suite 3
Denver, CO 80222
(303-758-5018)

Appalachian Mountain Club
5 Joy St
Boston, MA 02108
(617-523-0636)

Brooks Bird Club, Inc.
707 Warwood Ave.
Wheeling, WV 26003

Conservation Foundation
1717 Massachusetts Ave,
NW
Washington, DC 20036
(202-797-4300)

Defenders of Wildlife
1244 19th St, NW
Washington, DC 20036
(202-659-9510)

Friends of the Earth
1045 Sansome St
San Francisco, CA 94111
(415-433-7373)

Izaak Walton League of
America
1701 N Fort Myer Dr
Suite 1100
Arlington, VA 22209
(703-528-1818)

League of Conservation
Voters
310 4th St, NE
Washington, DC 20002
(202-547-7200)

National Audubon Society
950 Third Ave
New York, NY 14221
(212-832-3200)

National Campers and
Hikers Assoc
7172 Transit Rd
Buffalo, NY 14221
(716-634-5433)

National Geographic Society
17 and M Sts, NW
Washington, DC 20036
(202-857-7000)

National Trails Council
Box 493
Brookings, SD 57006

National Wildlife Federation
1412 16th St, NW
Washington, DC 20036
(202-797-6800)

  Region 3, Route 15
  Box 557A
  Lexington, NC 27292
  (704-787-5364)

Nature Conservancy
1800 N Kent St, Suite 800
Arlington, VA 22209
(703-841-5300)

  Eastern Region
  294 Washington St
  Rm 740
  Boston, MA 02108
  (617-542-1908)

Sierra Club
2044 Fillmore St
San Francisco, CA 94115
(415-567-6100)

Student Conservation
Association
Box 550
Charlestown, NH 03603
(603-826-5206)

Wilderness Society
1400 I St, NW, 10th Floor
Washington, DC 20005
(202-828-6600)

West Virginia Government Agencies

Geological and Economic
Survey
Box 879
Morgantown, WV 26507
(304-594-2331)

State Extension Services
Forestry, State 4-H Camp
PO Box 429
Weston, WV 26452
(304-269-6681)

  Forest Management
  315C Percival Hall
  WVU, Morgantown, WV
    26506
  (304-293-3911)

West Virginia Citizens' Groups

Eastern Professional River
Outfitters Assoc
PO Box 119
Oak Hill, WV 25901

Elk River Bicycle Touring
  Center
Slatyfork, WV 26291
(304-572-3771)

Izaak Walton League of
  America
215 Holt Lane
Lewisburg, WV 24901
(304-225-4737)

National Fisheries Center
Route 3, Box 700
Kearneysville, WV 25430
(304-725-8461)

National Speleogical Society
Virginia Region
501 Ridgewood Rd
Huntington, WV 25701
(304-523-2094)

Seneca Rocks Climbing
School
Box 53
Seneca Rocks, WV 26884
(304-567-2600)

Trout Unlimited
West Virginia Council
PO Box 38
Charlton Heights, WV
25040
(304-779-2476)

   Kanawha Valley Chapter
   PO Box 5189
   Charleston, WV 25311
   (304-755-9576)

West Virginia Conservation
Education Council
227 Hale Ave
Princeton, WV 24740
(304-425-0276)

West Virginia Wildlife
Federation, Inc.
Box 275
Paden City, WV 26159
(304-337-9166)

White Grass Ski Touring
Center
Route 1, Box 37
Davis, WV 26260
(304-866-4114)

Wildlife Society
121 Fairland Dr
Nitro, WV 25143
(304-776-2785)

College and University Organizations

Outings Club
Sport Club Federations
44 Stansbury Hall, WVU
Morgantown, WV 26506
(304-293-5221)

Grotto Club
Sport Club Federations
44 Stansbury Hall, WVU
Morgantown, WV 26506
(304-293-5221)

Equestrian Club
Sport Club Federations
44 Stansbury Hall, WVU
Morgantown, WV 26506

Trails and Outing Club
Coed Hall, Box 160
West Virginia Institute of
Technology
Montgomery, WV 25136
(304-442-3930)

Travel and Recreation
Committee
2W38 MSC, Marshall
University
Huntington, WV 25701
(304-696-3170)

Parks and Recreation
Organization
GH 100-D, Marshall
University
Huntington, WV 25701
(304-696-3170)

Outdoor Recreation Club
University of Charleston
2300 MacCorkle Ave, SE
Charleston, WV 25309
(304-357-4800)

Wilderness Co-op
Davis and Elkins College
Elkins, WV 26241
(304-636-1900, Ext 353)

Mountain Travel Club
Mountain State College
Spring at 16th St
Parkersburg, WV 26101
(Tel: 304-485-5487)

Office of Student Affairs
Concord College
Athens, WV 24712
(304-384-3115)

▶ TRAIL SUPPLIES

The following stores have
a partial or complete
range of supplies and
equipment for hiking,
backpacking, and
camping.

Carolina Ace Hardware
Rte 2, Box 217
Beckley, WV 25801

Leggett, Crossroads Mall
Rte 2, Box 1103
Beckley, WV 25801

Wilderness Country Outfit
108 Main St
Beckley, WV 25801

Ace Hardware
414 Main St
Bridgeport, WV 26330

The Bon Ton
Meadowbrook Mall
Bridgeport, WV 26330

Blue Ridge Outfitters
5701 Capt Jones Ct
Charleston, WV 25414

Montgomery Ward
710 E Washington
Charleston, WV 25301

Sportin' Life
3908 MacCorkle Ave, SE
Charleston, WV 25301

Sports Mart
Lewis and Beauregard
Charleston, WV 25301

Sport Mart
1015 Quarrier St
Charleston, WV 25301

Mountain State Outfitters
300 12th St
Dunbar, WV 25064

Wheeler Sports Center
313 3rd St
Elkins, WV 26241

Johns Army and Navy
327 Adams St
Fairmont, WV 26554

Fort Ashby Sports
Main St
Fort Ashby, WV 26719

Radio Shack and Trails End
705 Elk St
Gassaway, WV 26624

Blue Ridge Outfitters
Harpers Ferry, WV 25425

Amsbarry
949 3rd Ave
Huntington, WV 25701

Class VI River Runners
Ames Height Rd
Lansing, WV 25862

Back Country Outfitters
Mill Point, WV 24959

Outdoors Unlimited, Inc.
136 High St
Morgantown, WV 26505

Pathfinders of WV, Ltd.
182 Willey St
Morgantown, WV 26505

Hoffman Grocery
109 S Chester St
New Cumberland, WV
26047

Stone and Thomas
Rock Branch Int Park
Nitro, WV 25141

Acme Market
1314 Main St
Princeton, WV 24740

Coes Sport Shop
19 E Main
Richwood, WV 26261

Gendarme
Route 1 (PO Box 53)
Seneca Rocks, WV 26884

AJ's Military Surplus
524 D St
South Charleston, WV
25303

Mountain Outfitters
Grand Central Mall
Vienna, WV 26105

Pathfinder of WV
1041 Market St
Wheeling, WV 26003

Surplus Value Center
1067 Main St
Wheeling, WV 26003

The following stores stock topographic maps by the US Geological Survey.

Air Photographics, Inc.
Martinsburg Airport
Route 4, PO Box 500
Martinsburg, WV 25401
(304-263-6976)

Allen Blueprint & Supply Co.
811 Virginia St, E
Charleston, WV 25301
(304-344-1176)

Barb's Drug Store
104 Walnut St
Parsons, WV 26287
(304-478-3291

Baughman Home Appliance
Smith's News Stand
1 Main St
Phillip, WV 26416
(304-457-1391)

Bias Blueprint, Inc.
826 6th Ave (PO Box 1058)
Huntington, WV 25701
(304-529-1388)

Bluefield State College
Bookstore
218 Rock St
Bluefield, WV 24701
(304-325-6083)

Bookstore
104 South Jefferson
Lewisburg, WV 24901
(304-645-6910)

Brackenrich & Associates, Inc.
US 219 N (PO Box 207)
Lewisburg, WV 24901
(304-645-6235)

Brackenrich & Skidmore, Inc.
301 Main St (PO Box 686)
Sutton, WV 26601
(304-765-7394)

College Book Store
Concord College
Athens, WV 24712
(304-384-3115)

C & B Blueprint Company
701 Eighth Ave
Huntington, WV 25701
(304-525-2175)

Dietz Shoe Store, Inc.
13 East Main St (PO Box 189)
Richwood, WV 26261
(304-846-6800)

Gates Supply Company
211 Prince St (PO Box AF)
Beckley, WV 25801
(304-255-9254)

The Gendarme
Route 1 (PO Box 53)
Seneca Rocks, WV 26884
(304-567-2600)

The H. T. Hall Company, Inc.
3622 MacCorkle Ave, SE
Charleston, WV 25304
(304-925-1117)

The James & Law Company
217 West Main St
Clarksburg, WV 26301
(304-624-7401)

Keller's Photoprint Service
808 Kanawha Blvd, E
(PO Box 269)
Charleston, WV 25321
(304-343-1063)

Mountaineer Sports, Inc.
1301 Harrison Ave
Elkins, WV 26241
(304-636-7272)

The S. Spencer Moore Company
118 Capitol St
Charleston, WV 25321
(304-342-6185)

Stephens Blueprint and Supply Store
Old St Mary's Pike, Box 522
Parkersburg, WV 26104
(304-485-6561)

West Virginia Geological Survey
Mont Chateau (PO Box 879)
Morgantown, WV 26505
(304-292-6331)

Wheeler's Sport Center, Inc.
311-313 Third St
(PO Box 1003)
Elkins, WV 26241
(304-636-3078)

The Woodshed
Elkins Road (PO Box 728)
Buckhannon, WV 26201
(304-472-5577)

Aarons Army Store
151 Summers St
Charleston, WV 25301

Charleston Dept Store
1661 W. Washington
Charleston, WV 25311

Hoffman's Trading Post
Rte 1, Box 11
Mill Creek, WV 26280

Doug's Sport Shop
410 S. Main St
Moorefield, WV 26836

Mains US Army Store
137 Pleasant St
Morgantown, WV 26505

Trail Index

Parentheses indicate USFS trail numbers.

How to Find Your Way
in the National Forests

A master map of the detailed maps in this book appears on pp.404-405. Red rectangles and map numbers correspond with the map numbers that follow. The master map of the Monongahela National Forest and part of the George Washington National Forest shows the locations of map numbers 1 through 37. Map number 38, the last in the book, is not included on the master map because it is isolated from the other trail areas. It is in the Blacksburg Ranger District of the Jefferson National Forest NE of Pearisburg, Virginia. Official highway maps of West Virginia and Virginia (see page 9) are essential for using the maps in this book; they provide entrance options from the major highways.

The following 38 trail maps illustrate the hiking trails in the Monongahela, George Washington, and Jefferson National Forests. With permission from the West Virginia Department of Highways, the 1987 county maps have been used as a background for the trail overlays. The county maps were chosen because they have detailed road information that will assist you to locate trailheads, campgrounds, park and forest boundaries, and other significant points of interest conveniently and accurately.

The original map design has only been modified to add new or to delete closed forest roads. For example, FR-76 and FR-108, in the Gauley Ranger District, have been deleted because they are now hiking trails in the Cranberry Wilderness Area; new forest roads such as FR-296 and FR-875, in the White Sulphur Ranger District, have been added to assist you in trail access or connections.

Other modifications include boundary lines for the Cranberry, Dolly Sods, Laurel Fork, and Otter Creek wilderness areas, the title and elevation of some mountain peaks, trail shelter locations, closed or new campgrounds, and North directional symbols. No route modification has been made on any of the county, state or federal highways. The county-map legend has not been changed; it precedes the maps.

All trailheads have a red dot, a symbol larger than the red dashes that indicate the trails. Although not drawn to scale, careful effort has been made to show trail-terminus points as accurately as possible. Each trail name and its forest number (if one has been assigned) is marked (in red) near the trail route. Where trails continue at crossings, no trailhead sign is indicated. The maps begin with Number 1, for the Cheat Ranger District of the Monongahela National Forest, and end with Number 38, for the Blacksburg Ranger District of the Jefferson National Forest. On some maps, sections of the *Allegheny Trail* are included because the trail passes through that area. Trails in the Seneca State Forest have also been added on the appropriate maps, for the convenience of the hiker.

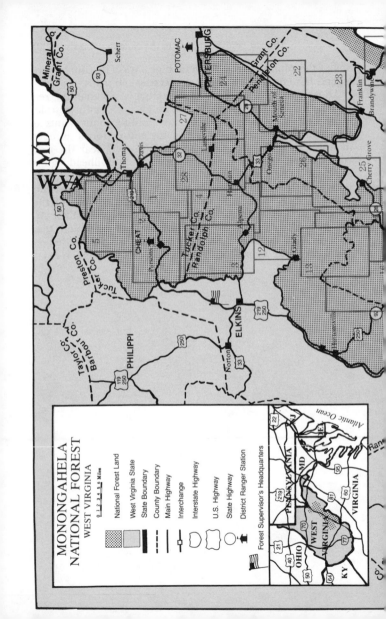

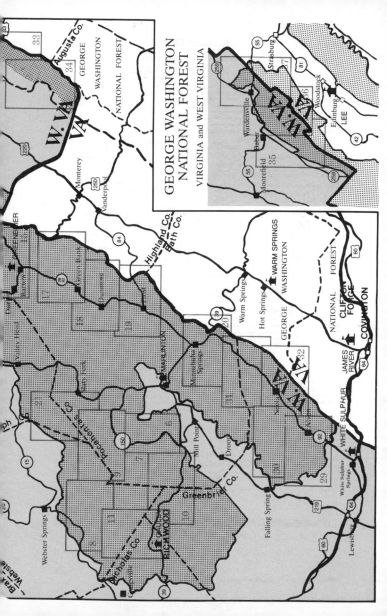

GEORGE WASHINGTON
NATIONAL FOREST
VIRGINIA and WEST VIRGINIA

LEGEND

ROADS AND ROADWAY FEATURES
SURFACE TYPES

TRAIL
IMPASSABLE ROAD
PRIMITIVE ROAD
UNIMPROVED ROAD
GRADED AND DRAINED ROAD
SOIL SURFACED ROAD
GRAVEL OR STONE ROAD
BITUMINOUS ROAD—LOW TYPE
PAVED ROAD
DIVIDED HIGHWAY

HIGHWAY SIGN SYSTEMS

INTERSTATE ROUTE
U.S. NUMBERED HIGHWAY
W. VA. NUMBERED HIGHWAY
W. VA. COUNTY NUMBERED ROUTE
DELTA ROUTE (MAINTENANCE ONLY)

FEDERAL-AID SYSTEMS

FEDERAL AID PRIMARY
FEDERAL AID SECONDARY
END OF FAS ROUTE

FUNCTIONAL SYSTEMS

EXPRESSWAY
TRUNKLINE
FEEDER
STATE LOCAL SERVICE

ROADS NOT ON STATE SYSTEM

PUBLIC ROAD
PRIVATE ROAD
SIDE ROADS AND STREETS IN INSETS AND MUNICIPALITIES
U.S. FOREST SERVICE ROAD
W. VA. DEPT. NAT. RESOURCES ROAD

RAILROADS

RAILROAD (ANY NUMBER OF TRACKS)
NARROW GAGE RAILROAD
RAILROAD STATION
GRADE CROSSING
RAILROAD ABOVE
RAILROAD BELOW
RAILROAD BRIDGE (WIDE STREAM)
RAILROAD TUNNEL

DRAINAGE

NARROW STREAM
WIDE STREAM
MARSH OR SWAMP
DAM, WITHOUT ROAD

STRUCTURES

HIGHWAY BRIDGE (MORE THAN 20' SPAN)
BRIDGE, GENERAL (WIDE STREAM)
SUSPENSION BRIDGE
TRUSS OR GIRDER BRIDGE
CANTILEVER BRIDGE
DAM WITH ROAD
HIGHWAY TUNNEL
FORD
TOLL BRIDGE

CONSERVATION OR RECREATION

PICNIC GROUND
PLAYGROUND, BALLFIELD
BATHING BEACH OR POOL
SCENIC SITE
CAMPING AREA
CAMP OR LODGE
FOREST RANGER STATION
FISH HATCHERY (BASIN) (POND)
ZOO
LOOKOUT TOWER
COUNTRY CLUB
GOLF COURSE
DRIVE-IN THEATER
ATHLETIC FIELD
AMUSEMENT PARK
FAIRGROUND OR RACE TRACK
RIDING ACADEMY
RIFLE CLUB
ROADSIDE PARK

DWELLINGS, FARM UNITS, ETC.

	(IN USE)	(NOT IN USE)
FARM UNIT		
DWELLING (OTHER THAN FARM)		
ROW OF HOUSES (WITH NUMBER OF DWELLINGS)		
TRAILER PARK		
HOUSE AND STORE (JOINT USE)		
SEASONAL DWELLING		
HOTEL		
MOTEL		
HOSPITAL		
REST HOME		
CHURCH		
CEMETERY		
CHURCH WITH CEMETERY		

EDUCATIONAL

PUBLIC SCHOOL
OTHER EDUCATIONAL INSTITUTIONS
COMMUNITY HALL
MUSEUM

BOUNDARIES

STATE LINE
COUNTY LINE
MAGISTERIAL DISTRICT LINE

INCORPORATED TOWN
PARK OR FOREST BOUNDARY

MISCELLANEOUS

MILITARY POST
MINE
GATE
SINK OR DEPRESSION
LATITUDE AND LONGITUDE
HIGHWAY INTERCHANGE

CITY AND VILLAGE CENTERS

STATE CAPITOL
COUNTY SEAT
OTHER CITIES AND VILLAGES

2   1   0   1   2 MILES

1 INCH = 0.64 MILE

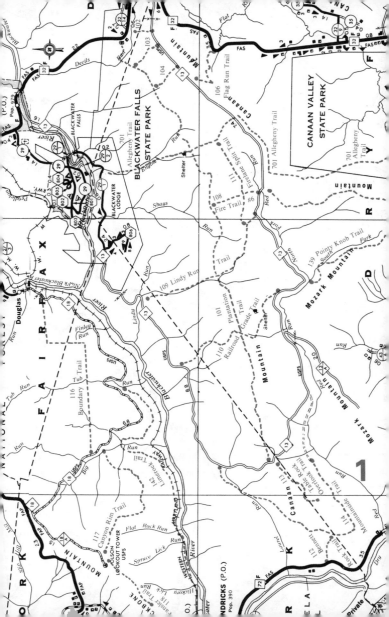

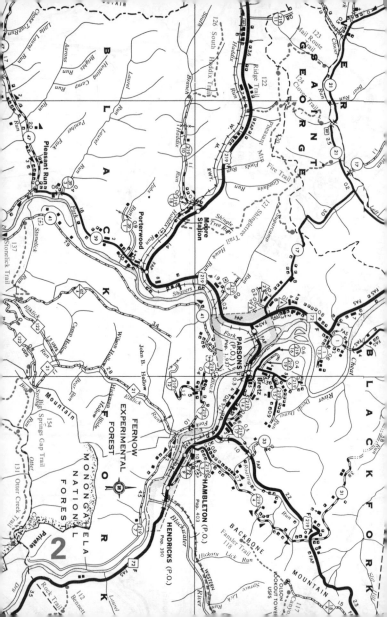

2

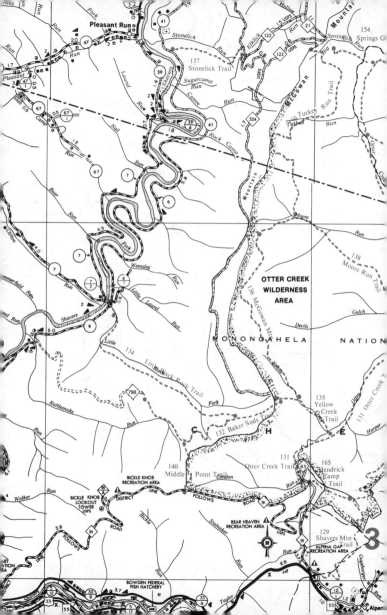

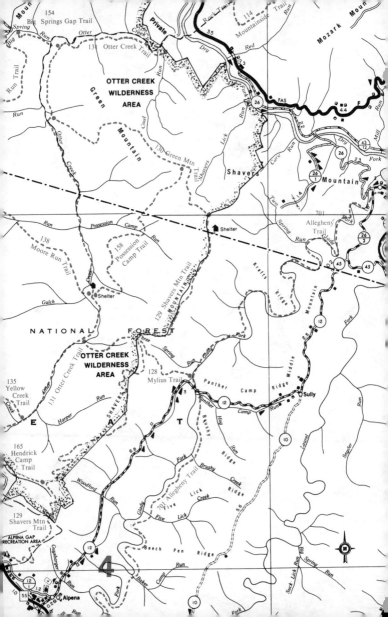

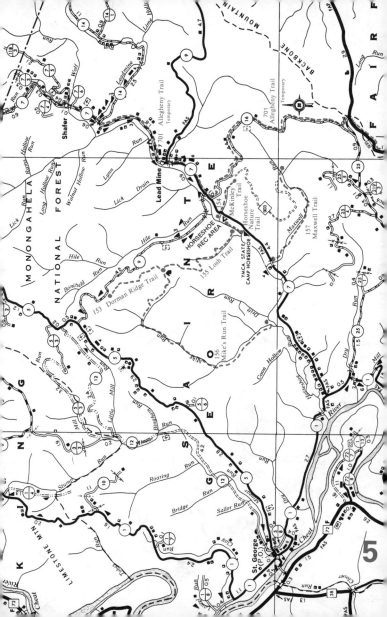

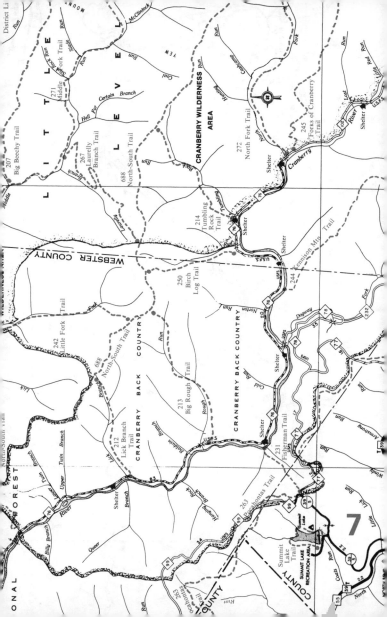

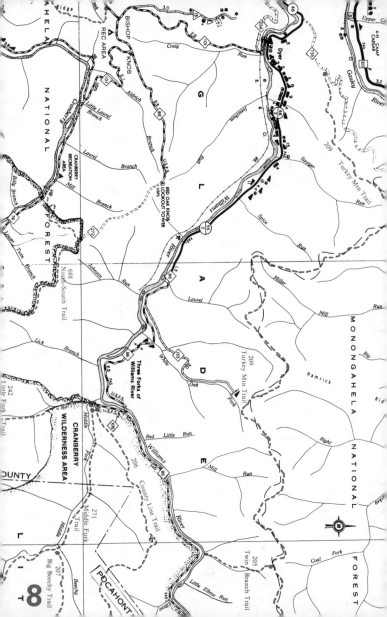

8

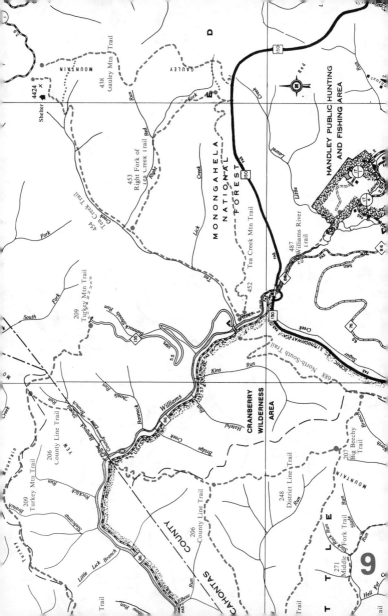

D

MOUNTAIN

GAULEY

438
Gauley Mtn Trail

4424
×

Shelter

Red

150

91

453
Right Fork of
Tea Creek Trail

Run

Red

454
Tea Creek Trail

Fork

MONONGAHELA   NATIONAL   FOREST

30

Creek

Lick

Creek

HANDLEY PUBLIC HUNTING
AND FISHING AREA

Panel

Run

Little   Williams River

487
Williams River
Trail

USFS

66

Tea Creek Mtn Trail

452

Tea

River

25

30

20

845

86

South

Fork

209
Turkey Mtn Trail

Fork

85

Run

Bannock Shoals

Lick

5.5

Run

River

North-South Trail

Creek

Sugar

845

86

SCENIC HIGHWAY

Williams

137

Run

Kins

Run

689

CRANBERRY
WILDERNESS
AREA

Hateful

Run

206
County Line Trail

YEW

Bannock

Branch

Creek

Bridge

Run

207
Big Beechy
Trail

208

Turkey Mtn Trail

Run

Rocklick

Run

Slickamp

County

206
County Line Trail

Creek

248
District Line Trail

Run

MOUNTAIN

Mountain

209
Branch

85

Little Lick Branch

PO
CAHONTAS   COUNTY

Run

Elbow

271
Middle Fork Trail

Run

Fork

Hell

Run

L   E   T

9

Trail

Turkey

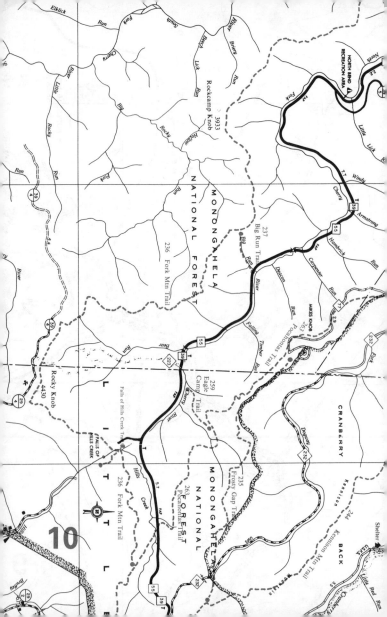

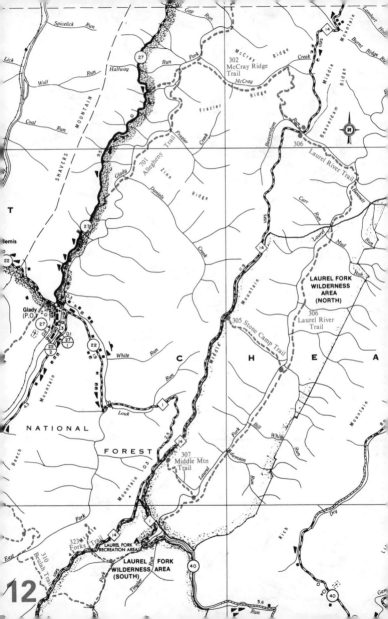

12

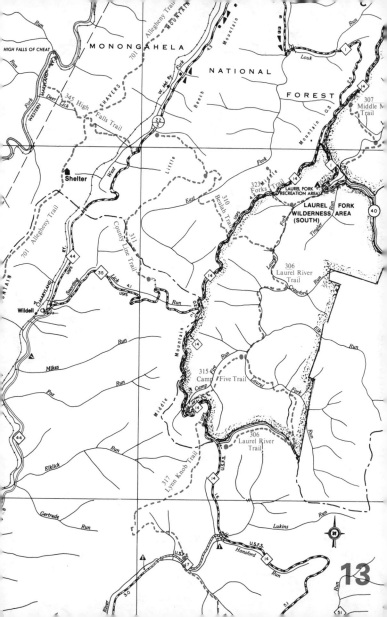

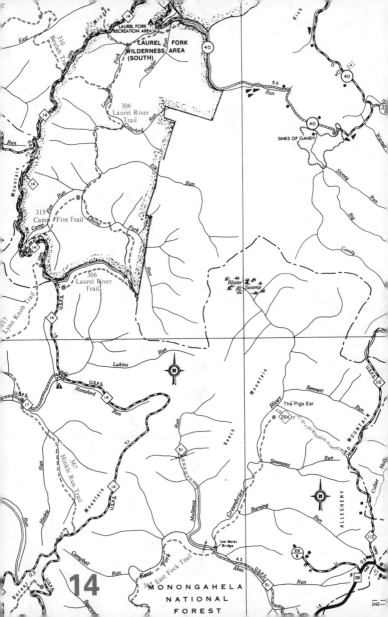

14

M O N O N G A H E L A

N A T I O N A L

F O R E S T

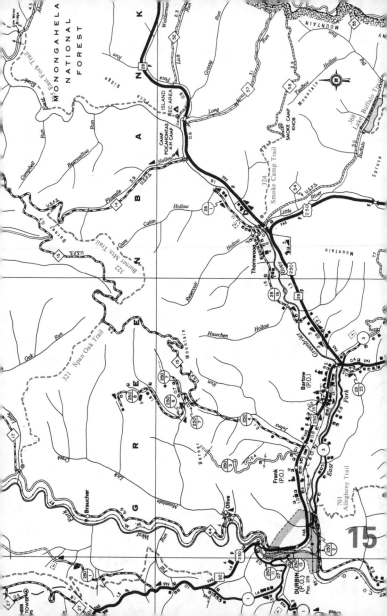

15

16

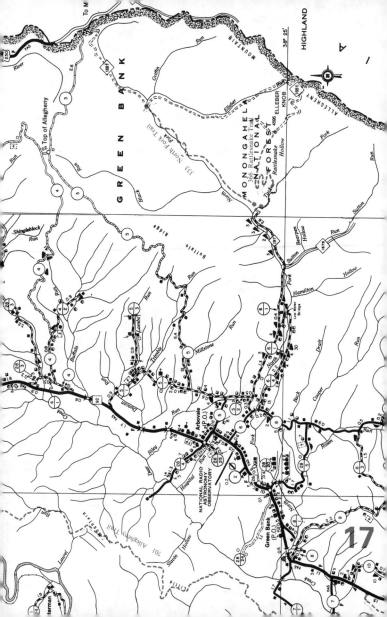

17

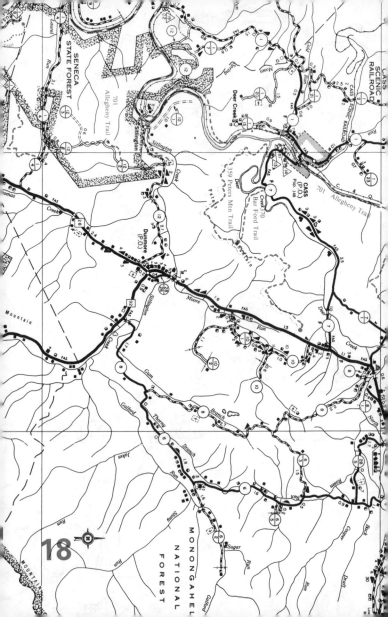

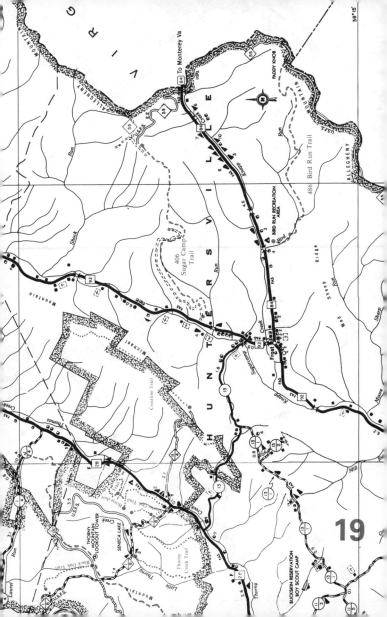

19

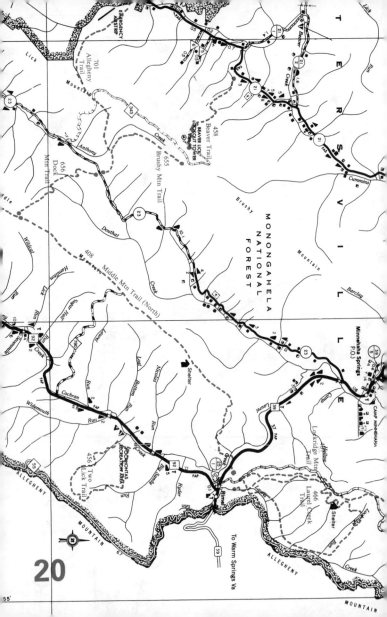

20

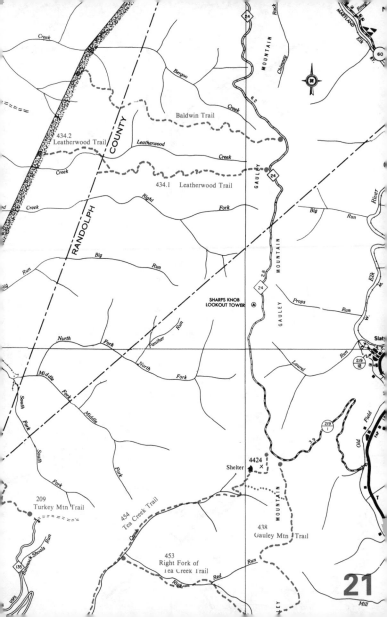

Creek

Bergoo

Baldwin Trail

Creek

434.2
Leatherwood Trail

Leatherwood

COUNTY

Creek

Creek

434.1   Leatherwood Trail

RANDOLPH

Creek

Right

Fork

GAULEY

Big   Run

River

Big   Run

Chimney

MOUNTAIN

60

62

24

24

24

2.8

GAULEY   MOUNTAIN

SHARPS KNOB
LOOKOUT TOWER

Props

Run

Run

Elk

W.

Slat

North   Fork

Panther   Run

North   Fork

Middle

South   Fork

Fork

Middle

Middle

Fork

South

Fork

Laurel

Run

219
12

219
1

3.9

Old   Field

Shelter

4424
×

209
Turkey Mtn Trail

454
Tea Creek Trail

Creek

438
Gauley Mtn Trail

MOUNTAIN

135

Run

453
Right Fork of
Tea Creek Trail

Right

Red

Run

LEY

Mill

21

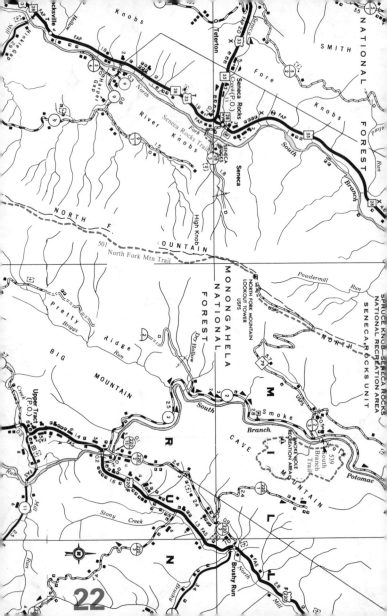

22

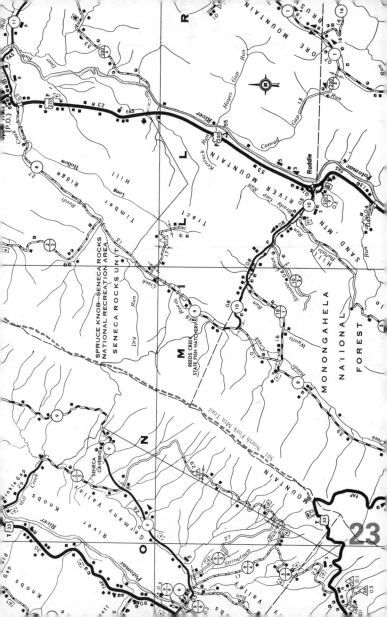

23

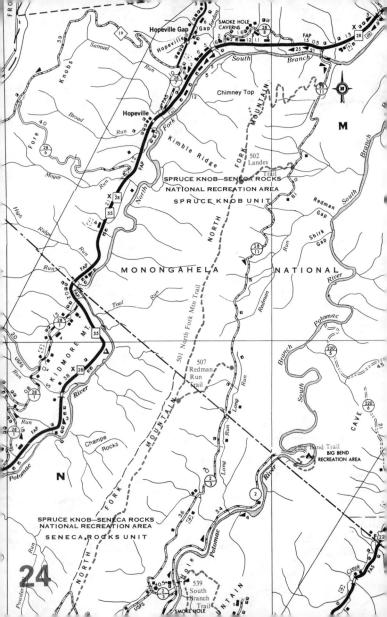

25

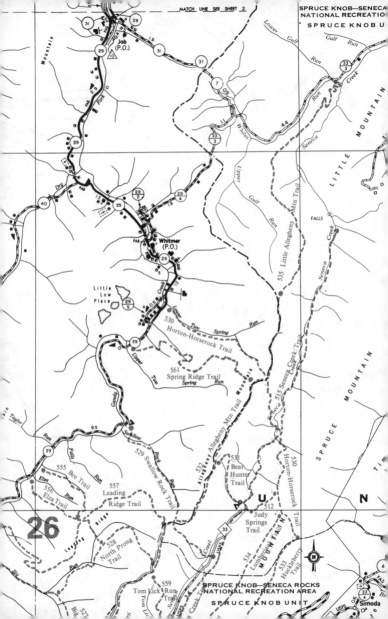

LITTLE MOUNTAIN

Job
(P.O.)

Whitmer
(P.O.)

Little
Low
Place

530
Horton-Horserock Trail

561 Spring Ridge Trail

535 Little Allegheny Mtn Trail

515 Seneca Creek Trail

532 Allegheny Allegheny Mtn Trail Mountain

SPRUCE MOUNTAIN

555 Bee Trail

550 Elza Trail

557 Leading Ridge Trail

529 Swallow Rock Trail

530 Bear Hunter Trail

530 Horton-Horserock Trail

U

N

512 Judy Springs Trail

26

528 North Prong Trail

559 Tom Lick Run Trail

534 Lumberjack Trail N

533 Huckleberry Trail

Simoda

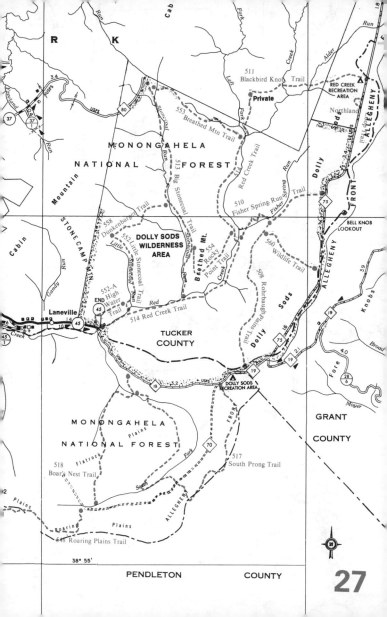

R   K

511
Blackbird Knob Trail

RED CREEK
RECREATION
AREA

Northland

Private

MONONGAHELA

NATIONAL   FOREST

USFS

80

553
Breathed Mtn Trail

Stonecoal Run

Left Fork

Cab

Fork

Creek

Run

Alder Run

ALLEGHENY

Dolly

Sods

37

37

Breezland Run

3 4

Mountain

513
Big Stonecoal Trail

512
Red Creek Trail

510
Fisher Spring Run Trail

Fisher Spring Run

75

BELL KNOB
LOOKOUT

STONE   CAMP   MTN.

558
Duskenbarger Trail

**DOLLY SODS
WILDERNESS
AREA**

552 Little Stonecoal Trail

Little Stonecoal Trail

554
Rocky Point Trail

Breathed Mt.

Stonecoal

560
Wildlife Trail

ALLEGHENY

FRONT

Cabin

Candy Run

552-A
END High Water Trail

45

Red

514 Red Creek Trail

508 Rohrbaughs Plains Trail

Dolly   Sods

Knobs

3 9

Laneville

14
10   45

45

Creek

45
1

TUCKER
COUNTY

19

75

16

19

21

Broad

19

28
6

4 0

Fore

Moyer

19

3 2

USFS

DOLLY SODS
RECREATION AREA

19

FRONT

MONONGAHELA

NATIONAL   FOREST

Plains

Flatrock

Plains

518
Boars Nest Trail

South   Fork

70

517
South Prong Trail

GRANT

COUNTY

ALLEGHENY

2

Plains

Roaring   Plains

548 Roaring Plains Trail

38° 55'

PENDLETON   COUNTY

N

27

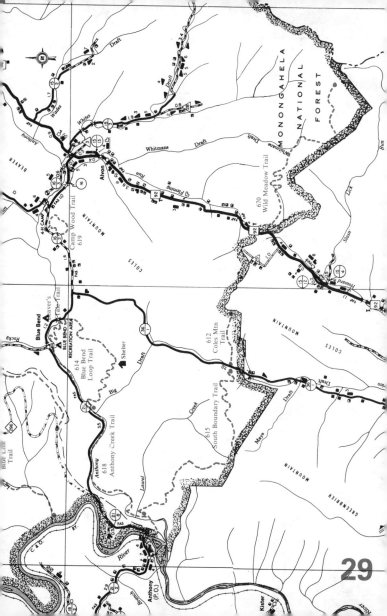

29

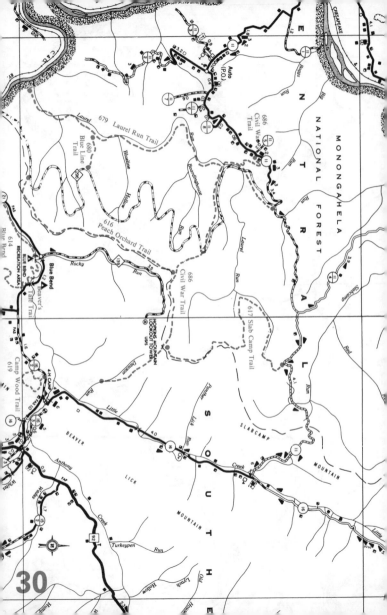

CENTRAL

MONONGAHELA

NATIONAL

FOREST

CHESAPEAKE

Auto
(P.O.)

679 Laurel Run Trail
Laurel

680
Blue Line
Trail

686
Civil War
Trail

Blueline

Boardinghouse

616
Peach Orchard Trail
Run

Laurel

686
Civil War
Trail
Run

617 Slab Camp Trail

Slabcamp

Red

RECREATION
AREA

BLUE BEND

Blue Bend

614
Blue Bend

Rocky
Run

Taft Trail

Beaver's

HORNS MOUNTAIN
LOOKOUT TOWER
USFS

SLAB CAMP

MOUNTAIN

619
Camp Wood Trail

Camp Wood Trail

Dawson
Run

BEAVER

Little

Lick
Run

Run

Panther

Creek

Anthony

Hughes

LICK

MOUNTAIN

Whites

Creek

92

Turkeypen
Run

SOUTHEAST

Blue
Bend

Hughes

Little

30

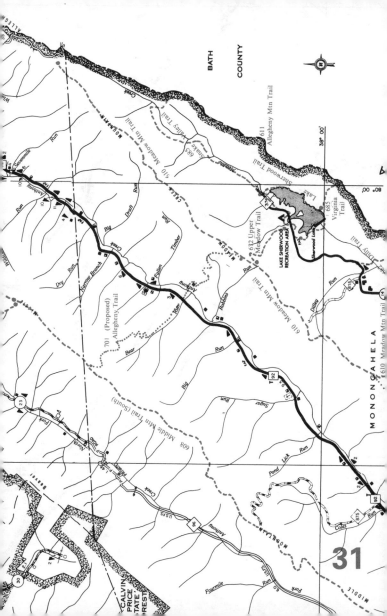

BATH

COUNTY

Allegheny Mtn Trail
611
Sherwood Trail

36° 00'
80° 00'

685 510 Meadow Mtn Trail
685 Shaws Valley Trail

Wild Meadow

N Mtn Trail

Anthony Run

Seneca Run

Mill Run

Dry Run

Big Creek

Back Creek

Draft Run

Thunder Run

Arrow Branch

Fallen Run

672 Upper Meadow Trail

LAKE SHERWOOD
RECREATION AREA

Lake Sherwood

685 Virginia Trail

Laurel Trail

Meadow Run

701 (Proposed) Allegheny Trail

Bear Run

Robins Run

Anthony Run

610 Meadow Mtn Trail

Dilley Run

MONONGAHELA

610 Meadow Mtn Trail

92

92

Big Run

Sugar Run

608 Middle Mtn Trail (South)

North Fork Trail

Pond Lick Run

Coles Run

675

CALVIN
PRICE
STATE
FOREST

BEAVER

North Fork

Laurel Creek

U.S.F.S.

96

96

Anthony Creek

Fourmile Run

MIDDLE MOUNTAIN

510 North Fork

MIDDLE

30

31

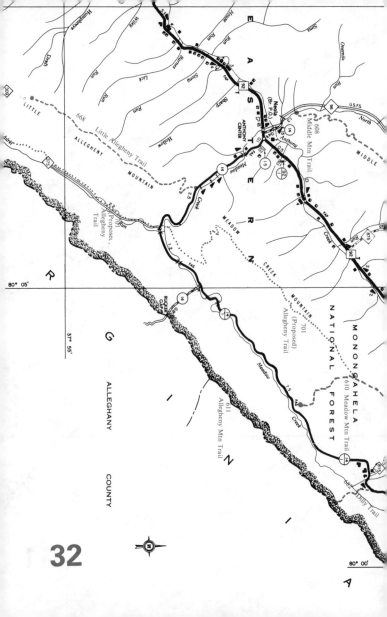

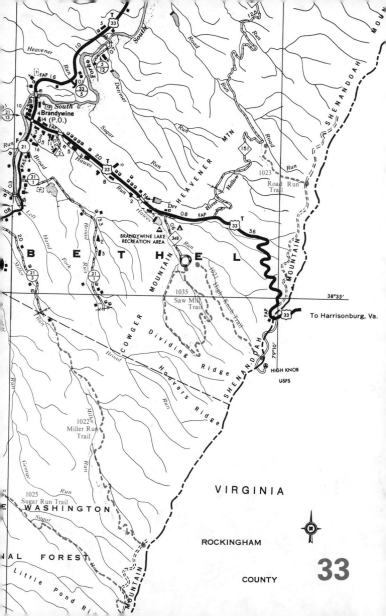

South Brandywine (P.O.)

Heavener Run

South Fork

Detmer Run

FAP 16

South Brandywine (P.O.)

FAP

Sugar Run

Broad

Hawes Run

BETHEL

Left Hand Fork

Broad Fork

Miller Run

Broad Run

Brandywine Lake Recreation Area

348

BRANDYWINE LAKE RECREATION AREA

1035 Saw Mill Trail

COWGER MOUNTAIN

DIVIDING RIDGE

HEAVENER MTN

HIGH KNOB USFS

1421 High Knob Trail

1023 Road Run Trail

Run

River Hollow

Dry Run

FAP

SHENANDOAH MOUNTAIN

SHENANDOAH MOUNTAIN

To Harrisonburg, Va.

38°35'

79°00'

Hoovers Ridge

1022 Miller Run Trail

Miller Run

George Run

1025 Sugar Run Trail

WASHINGTON

Sugar Run

NATIONAL FOREST

Little Pond River

VIRGINIA

ROCKINGHAM

COUNTY

33

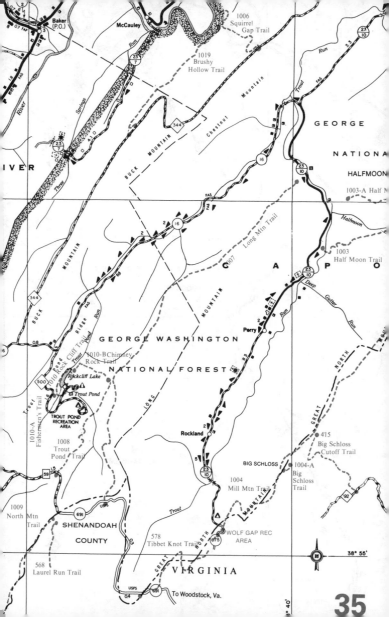

RIVER SINKS

WARDENSVILLE (P.O.)
Pop.241

1006
Squirrel
Gap Trail

1019
Brushy
Hollow Trail

1013.3
County Line Trail
Big Blue Trail

400
Vances Cove
Trail

GEORGE   WASHINGTON

NATIONAL   FOREST

HALFMOON MOUNTAIN

1003-A Half Moon Lookout Trail

WILSON COVE

Long Mtn Trail

1013.2
Pond Run Trail
Big Blue Trail

1003
Half Moon Trail

1002
Peer Trail

Deep

571
Little Stony Creek
Trail

Big Blue Trail

Perry

SHINGTON

SHENANDOAH

COUNTY

FOREST

36

VIRGINIA

Rockland

415
Big Schloss
Cutoff Trail

BIG SCHLOSS

1004-A
Big
Schloss
Trail

1004
Mill Mtn Trail

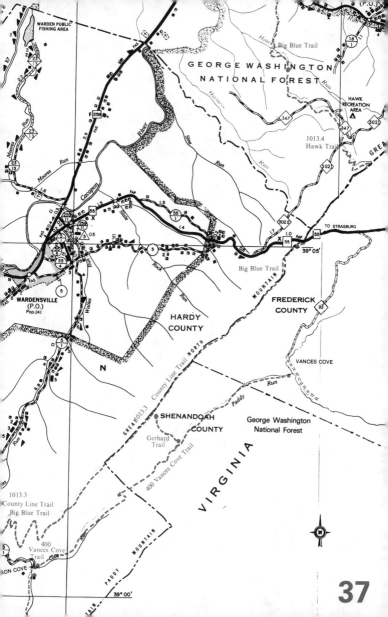

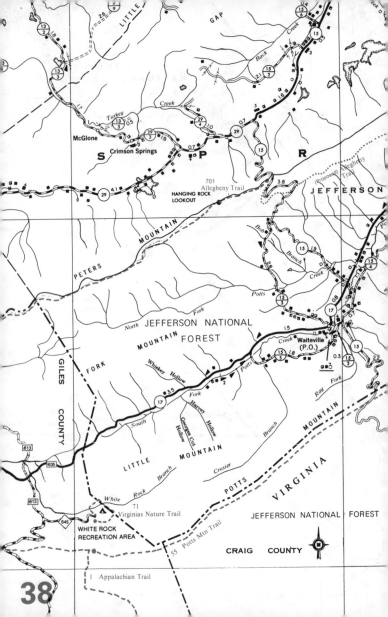

38